Shadow Boxing
Art and Craft in Creative Nonfiction

Kristen Iversen
University of Memphis

PEARSON
Prentice
Hall

Upper Saddle River, New Jersey 07458

Library of Congress Cataloging-in-Publication Data

Iversen, Kristen.
  Shadow boxing : art and craft in creative nonfiction / Kristen
Iversen.
    p. cm.
  Includes index.
  ISBN 0-13-099442-1
  1. College readers.   2. Creative writing—Problems, exercises, etc.
3. Journalism—Authorship—Problems, exercises, etc.   4. English
language—Rhetoric—Problems, exercises, etc.   5. Reportage
literature—Authorship—Problems, exercises, etc.   I. Title.
PE1417 .I94 2004
808' .0427—dc22

                                     2003015975

Editor-in-Chief: Leah Jewell
Senior Acquisitions Editor: Carrie Brandon
Editorial Assistant: Jennifer Migueis
Production Liaison: Joanne Hakim
Senior Marketing Manager: Rachel Falk
Marketing Assistant: Adam Laitman
Permissions Supervisor: Mary Dalton-Hoffman
Manufacturing Buyer: Brian Mackey
Cover Art Director: Jayne Conte

Cover Design: Robert Farrar-Wagner
Cover Illustration/Photo: Sean
  Ellis/Getty Images, Inc.
Cover Image Specialist: Karen Sanatar
**Composition/Full-Service Project
  Management:** Karen Berry/
  Pine Tree Composition
Printer/Binder: Courier Stoughton

Credits and acknowledgments borrowed from other sources and reproduced, with permission, in this textbook appear on appropriate page within text.

Pearson Education LTD., London
Pearson Education Singapore, Pte. Ltd
Pearson Education, Canada, Ltd
Pearson Education–Japan
Pearson Education Australia PTY,
  Limited

Pearson Education North Asia Ltd
Pearson Educación de Mexico,
  S.A. de C.V.
Pearson Education Malaysia, Pte. Ltd
Pearson Education, Upper Saddle River,
  New Jersey

10 9 8 7 6 5 4 3 2 1

ISBN: 0-13-099442-1

Contents

Chapter 3   Literary Journalism   85

Chapter 6   The Nonfiction Novel   **226**

Chapter 7   The Writerly Life   **262**

Appendix   **287**

Preface

Shadow Boxing: Art and Craft in Creative Nonfiction is a book unlike others on the subject and presents a new approach to a relatively new genre. What is creative nonfiction, and why is everyone talking about it? This book will begin to answer that question and pose some interesting new questions about it.

A balance of model readings and practical writing exercises, *Shadow Boxing: Art and Craft in Creative Nonfiction* is primarily designed for students in creative writing workshops at the undergraduate and graduate level, and may also be useful in composition courses. However, writers outside of academia who are interested in creative nonfiction—and there are many of them—will find this book helpful as well.

Just as the term *creative nonfiction* is problematic (how many genres are defined by what they are *not*?), it is almost impossible to draw distinct, irrefutable lines between its various subgenres: memoir, the personal essay, literary journalism, biography/history, and the nonfiction novel. One form merges into the next, and even the line between fiction and nonfiction can be (as any good writer knows) oblique, blurred, or downright invisible. How closely must the creative nonfiction writer adhere to fact? What role does imagination play? One of the goals of this book is to examine the ethics of creative nonfiction and, inevitably, the ethical questions that any writer of prose or poetry faces whenever they put words on a page.

The term *shadow boxing* has a long history. In contemporary sport boxing, it is most often used to describe sparring with an imaginary partner for exercise or training purposes. The writer of creative nonfiction spars with all sorts of shadowy opponents: readers, critics, writers, and peers, who are quick to point out what should and shouldn't be done when one chooses to write in a genre that engages both fact and imagination. Each particular genre also poses its own particular problems: for example, a memoirist may feel the shadow of a parent, living or dead, as a heavy influence on the work. The literary journalist might struggle with the professional standards of conventional journalism and the literary technique that allows the development of character-driven narrative. Ultimately, though, writing—like shadow boxing—is a solitary battle. In Chinese shadow boxing, the boxer struggles with his or her own shadow to attain the highest form and expression of the self. The shadow becomes representative of the ego itself. Thus each of us as writers must struggle with our own shadows, internal and external, to determine our own highest form of meaning and creative expression.

My interest in creative nonfiction arises from years of working as a journalist and editor before deciding to return to graduate school and pursue a Ph.D. in English/Creative Writing. I began to teach fiction and creative nonfiction, and the readings and exercises in this book grew from those years of workshop experiences. This book follows the approach I take in my workshops: a focused discussion of genre and style; an analysis of model readings that represent various approaches to the genre; writing exercises intended to spark and generate new creative work; and, finally, a thorough approach to revision and re-visioning.

I am deeply indebted to the people who helped bring this book to fruition: Julie Lewis, Dan Choi, Shannon Rauwerda, my good friend and colleague Chris Fink, and all the students over the past few years who have graced me with their presence.

I also want to thank the reviewers who helped me to improve this book: David Lenoir, Western Kentucky University; Andrew Furmar, Florida Atlantic University; Howard Kerner, Polk Community College; Glenda Conway, University of Montevallo; Stuart C. Brown, New Mexico State University; and Alex Albright, East Carolina University.

Introduction

When Is Nonfiction Not Creative?

Try this experiment: Walk into a bookstore and ask the clerk where to find the section on "creative nonfiction." Most likely you'll be met with a blank look. "Do you mean memoir?" the salesperson will ask. "Nature writing? Essays? Biography?" Or—as I was asked recently—"True Crime?"

The label "creative nonfiction" is problematic for a number of reasons. For one thing, the distinction between fiction and creative nonfiction is blurred at best. (One student asked if I taught classes in "noncreative fiction." Well—that's the subject of a different textbook!) Writers and readers alike can't seem to agree on exactly what falls into the category of creative nonfiction. Some critics take a rather narrow view and limit the field to the personal essay and some types of literary or "immersion" journalism. Other critics are more liberal and include just about anything that doesn't fall unquestionably into the genres of fiction, poetry, or drama.

There are two essential qualities to creative nonfiction. First—simply stated—creative nonfiction is prose that demonstrates skillful use of literary technique. Voice, mood, tone, symbol, metaphor, dialogue, characterization, plot, epiphany—all the elements used by the fiction writer, or *any* good writer, serve the creative nonfiction writer.

These elements, however, serve a slightly different function for the writer who not only writes imaginatively but also desires to grapple with the "real" world, with real life, real people, real situations. Creative nonfiction is literary writing that is based—perhaps loosely, perhaps rigidly—on real-life situations. Creative nonfiction depends upon factual information in ways that fiction does not. The tools of reality—fact, research, history, investigative reporting, experience, and memory—are essential to the creative nonfiction writer. Like fiction, however, creative nonfiction is based on good storytelling. It's just that the elements of the story come from the "real" world rather than a "purely imagined" one.

But these definitions may not be as hard and fast as we would like. What about that novel, you ask, that was loosely based on the author's experience? Was that a purely imagined text? Is *any* text purely imagined? On the other hand, is any text purely *factual*? Why are so many biographies, for example, written about the same person? Or the same historical event? The 1864 Sand Creek Massacre is today considered a great tragedy in American history. If you read an 1864 newspaper account, however, you get a far different perspective; what is considered a tragedy today was then reported as a triumph in western newspapers.

On a more personal level, recall a memorable family holiday—a day when something unexpected, exciting, or even disastrous happened. How do you tell the story? Now consider how many other people experienced that event with you. How would they tell the story? Reality, to a certain extent, consists of different points of view, of many different truths.

The creative nonfiction writer is faced with difficult choices and ethical dilemmas at every turn. What does it mean to write "literary" prose? What type of prose is not literary? And—far more difficult to pin down—what is fact? What is literal truth? Is there ever a single, undeniable truth, or an all-inclusive truth that is ultimately correct?

I chose the title *Shadow Boxing* for this book because it so aptly describes the process of writing creative nonfiction. When we write, publish, and talk about creative nonfiction, we're facing shadowy opponents within ourselves and in the academic and publishing environments. The creative nonfiction writer bears a commitment to the subject, to the language, and to the reader—but also an allegiance to truth. Part of that commitment means interrogating these terms, of engaging the tension between truth and storytelling, factual truth and emotional truth. What is truth, ultimately, but the essence of what we discover in our hearts to be real? Storytelling is the way in which we recognize and create meaning in our lives, the path we travel to discover that essence. Emily Dickinson wrote, "Tell the truth, but tell it slant."

Creative nonfiction engages the reader just as any good fiction, poetry, or lyrical prose does by allowing the reader to tap into emotions and experiences they may not have felt or understood before. Some types of nonfiction are clearly not creative. Examples of this might include tax booklets, computer manuals, dictionaries, or even phone books. Writing that is purely transactional or informative, presented in a strongly objective tone, is not creative nonfiction. The author is invisible. In this type of writing there is no authorial presence or acknowledgment, and the language is not consciously shaped in any way beyond the structural requirements of the form. Even within this strict definition, however, there are bound to be exceptions. Who put together the dictionary? What cultural or linguistic bias might it represent? Not all computer manuals are dry or without personality.

Creative nonfiction is also distinct in that it allows the author to potentially enter into the text in various ways. In most creative nonfiction, the author is not invisible but present in the writing in an intensely self-reflective manner, or as a voice or character in the story itself. Creative nonfiction often self-consciously reflects on the method that produced it; for example, an essay may be about the process of writing as much as it is about hiking in the woods or exploring a childhood experience. By its emphasis on symbolism, metaphor, voice, and tone, creative nonfiction is artful prose. In this way, creative nonfiction may be closer to poetry than fiction. In poetry, we can often suppose that the "I" or the persona in the poem is the poet. In creative nonfiction, we can generally assume that the "I" is the author. Such an assumption would not necessarily be correct in fiction.

This book divides creative nonfiction into six subgenres: memoir, the personal essay, literary journalism, nature writing, biography/history, and the nonfiction novel. The lines between these subgenres are sometimes blurred; the categories often overlap. These boundaries, however, provide us with a way to begin thinking and talking about creative nonfiction in ways that spark and generate new creative work of our own.

Mark Twain once humorously commented, "Get your facts first, and then you can distort them as much as you please." As you begin to do the exercises in this book, remember that the moment you begin to compose, you are selecting, interpreting, and inventing. This is true whenever you tell a story, or even think to yourself about something that has happened to you. The act of remembering is in itself an act of selection, interpretation, composition, and invention. Everything that evolves from the creative imagination is a combination of dream and reality. As you write, try to keep an open mind about the distinctions between fact and invention, reality and imagination while staying faithful to your own sense of artistic integrity. In the short story "The Things They Carried," a tale the author calls "a true story that never happened," Tim O'Brien writes, "In the end, of course, a true war story is never about war. It's about sunlight. It's about the special way that dawn spreads out on a river when you know you must cross the river and march into the mountains and do things you are afraid to do. It's about love and memory. It's about sorrow."

Think of the difference between a painter and a photographer. If the sky isn't blue, the painter may not care but the photographer does. The artist may set up her easel anyway, reach for a brush, and paint what she sees before her or, conversely, find the right shade of blue on her palette or in her imagination. The photographer may pack up and wait for a clear day. As an artist, as a writer, as a journalist, where should your loyalty lie? To reality or imagination? Who would dare say that the photographer is not an artist, filtering images of reality not only through the eye of the camera but the particular lens of her own creativity and aesthetic sensibility? And is the painter uninterested in real objects, real landscapes, real people? Another way of asking this question is, Is photography purely objective, and painting purely subjective? Both the painter and photographer are impassioned by pursuing a vision that goes beyond their own individual experience and technique, in communicating through image and metaphor a way of making sense of the world.

About the Author

Kristen Iversen is the author of *Molly Brown: Unraveling the Myth*, winner of the Colorado Book Award in Biography, and the forthcoming *Full Body Burden*, based on her experience of growing up near Rocky Flats, a nuclear weaponry facility in Colorado. She has taught in the creative writing programs at Naropa University and San Jose State University, and currently teaches at the University of Memphis.

Chapter 1

Memoir

Introduction

At one point or another, nearly every person on the planet has silently marveled that his or her life would certainly make a good book.

But only a fraction goes on to write it.

Few things in life are as rewarding as writing your life story, and few things in life are as difficult. Writing memoir requires deep and purposeful self-reflection. It requires a willingness to explore difficult truths that may have been hidden for a long time. Memoir asks the writer to give up the mask of the fiction writer and to reveal aspects of the self, intellectually and emotionally, that take courage to reveal.

With a clear and honest approach, a writer of memoir can connect with a reader in ways that are unlike other forms of creative writing. Some authors call this "the appeal of the real": This is my experience. I have lived it. Perhaps it will have meaning for you, too.

Memoir is a collage of memory, reflection, information, dream, and human desire. Memoir is pure enchantment. In no other genre do we so fully enter the life of another human being.

Memoir is not autobiography. Autobiography is the unfiltered storyline of an individual's life, often a famous, influential, or notorious person. Autobiography focuses on topic and subject in a straightforward, historical way. Memoir is a different game altogether in which the purpose of the work is to extend beyond the strict subject of the story and reach toward greater human connection and truth. Through voice, tone, and metaphor, memoir engages readers in an intimate way and takes them on a personal journey.

People write memoirs for all sorts of reasons. Perhaps you want to bring a tale into the world that needs to be told—a story unlike any other. You might want to share your story with others as a way of gaining clarification for yourself, or tell a generational tale so that your children and grandchildren will know the story of your life.

Anyone can write a memoir or life story. Age doesn't matter. Profession doesn't matter. Years of life experience don't matter. You may be a student, a high school teacher, a bartender, an engineer, a waitress, a taxi driver, or a CEO. Perhaps you've done something extraordinary in your life; perhaps not. You don't have to be an adventurer. It takes only two things to write a memoir: the experience of living, and the desire to write about it.

Everyday life, carefully observed, has all the elements of a good story. It is the small details of life that become meaningful, that lead to greater understanding and enlightenment. What you have to say, and how you say it, will have meaning for a reader if you write it well. How have your experiences shaped you into the person you are today? What matters is how you see your life, not what you have done, and how you can bring that experience to the page.

After completing a memoir chart (the exercise in this chapter), one student wrote in her class journal, "Trying to graph the peaks and valleys of my lifetime in my memoir chart was a mortifying experience. My peaks seem trite: falling in love, the births of my children, getting a promotion at work. And there are many valleys I'm still not ready to re-cross." Each of these peaks and valleys represents an experience to be explored on the page. But it takes courage and the willingness to consider and accept the notion that your life is not trite, and that your life experiences contain meaning not only for yourself but for others as well.

How many memoirs can one person write? Just as there are many aspects to each individual's personality, each life history contains stories to be told and retold in countless configurations. Mary Karr, whose work appears in this chapter, has thus far written two memoirs about her life. How many memoirs could you write? Think of all the experiences you've had, of the rich history of your family, of the potential information you could gain by interviewing your parents, grandparents, even great-grandparents. The list is probably endless.

For most writers, an exploration of the self involves writing about painful experiences as well as positive ones. It's not uncommon to feel embarrassed or shameful about things that have happened in our lives, but it's important to remember that no one escapes suffering. Death, divorce, abuse, illness, car accidents—all are common experiences that readers can identify with. Writing about a painful or difficult experience can be a powerful way of healing, of pulling your life back into focus and equilibrium and reconnecting to the larger world. As a writer, you must be willing to explore all aspects of life, experience, and personality—the positive and the negative, the light and the dark—in yourself and in your characters, real or imagined. Our stories validate who we are by conveying what we value and what we believe to be true. The act of writing can be a powerful act of creation, of understanding and of connecting beyond the self.

One student wrote, "I tried writing about the sad stuff, and I thought it sounded victimized and clichéd. I tried writing about the positive stuff, and I thought it sounded saccharine and glossed-over. Then I tried heading straight into the middle of the truth and my voice changed; the tone took a turn I've never heard before."

Don't steer clear of your strength as a writer or as a person. Head straight into the middle of the truth.

There are familiar roadblocks on the way to writing a good memoir. How much should you reveal, about yourself and others, and how much should you conceal? Should you reveal everything? That would be impossible, of course (which doesn't mean you shouldn't do your homework). What details are significant and what details are insignificant? Keep thinking about what moves the story forward and what contributes to the greater theme or intention of the story.

Can you invent details? How much can you invent without "lying"? In many cases, emotional truth is more important than literal truth. If you're writing a scene about the time your brother pulled you out of the lake by your shirt collar, does it matter if you can't remember the color of the shirt? No. Would it help to "imagine" a color? Well, yes. Painting a vivid picture in the mind of the reader is crucial. If you make the shirt yellow when it might have been blue, but capture the story on the page in such a way that it allows the reader to understand the epiphany of the story, you have done your job well. Use your imagination to fill in memory, fact, and experience. Your creative imagination and ethical judgment must always balance one another and ultimately serve the story in the best way possible.

Does a memoir have to follow the narrative structure of an essay, novel, or short story? Just as in other genres, you can get away with just about anything if you do it skillfully. But remember that narrative structure is what provides clarity and coherence—the scaffolding or interpretive framework that allows the reader to understand the deeper themes of your story. Untempered, unfiltered emotional outpourings do not necessarily constitute good writing. The thoughtful choice of words and images and the conscientious construction of paragraphs and scenes are essential to a good memoir. Think about narrative arc: where your story begins and ends, how tension builds to a point of climax or epiphany, and when the dénouement or unraveling of the action or plot occurs.

How will other people feel about what you've written? Writing about your experiences, your childhood, and your personal traumas and triumphs can bring up all sorts of difficult questions. One of the primary concerns in writing memoir, particularly if you are writing about childhood, is the feelings and opinions of other people in your life. How will they feel about what you're writing? Will they feel betrayed or upset? Can you or should you change the names of people in your memoir?

There is no simple answer. Certainly you should feel a responsibility to consider the privacy and feelings of those close to you. On the other hand, you have a right, perhaps even a responsibility, to write about your own experience, and writing often brings about clarity and resolution in unexpected ways. If you explain what you're doing, you may find unexpected support. Or, if people disagree with your version of things, you can remind them that they're perfectly entitled to write their own story. It's okay to change the names of characters and still preserve the integrity of the story. Many writers handle this issue by writing a brief explanatory paragraph at the front of the book or essay. Some writers prefer to write under pseudonyms to prevent embarrassment or avoid legal complications. The biggest roadblocks, however, usually exist in our own minds. Ultimately the only real truth we can hope to convey on the page is our own truth, and for that we must feel obligated and responsible. Like poetry, creative nonfiction is a way of seeing and interpreting the world.

Finally, can you trust your own memory? The sources of memoir are endless. "Hard" research includes photographs, personal objects, interviews, journals, public records, letters, facts, anecdotes, and observation. "Soft" research, on the other hand, involves memory, dream, daydream, and imagination. But nothing is quite so troublesome as memory. Memory is fueled by emotion and clouded by time. Memory is subjective, selective, unreliable, and contradictory. Memory relies on symbol and metaphor. A memory that seems completely inconsequential can be flooded with meaning when you realize its symbolic implications.

Nurture your memories. Interrogate them in a gentle manner. Listening to music from a particular era can help jog memories. Smell works in a similar way. I can recall the rich aroma of cut grass when my father mowed the lawn and my siblings and I would skip along behind him in a corridor of green. It was a feeling of pure happiness, and I felt light as a butterfly. The smell of freshly cut lawns can still restore this sense of lightness and innocence for me. If I begin to write about this experience, I will start to recall the color of the neighbor's fence, the way their dog yapped at our calico cat, and the blue line of the mountains against the pink summer sky. If I keep writing, I can recall the color of my tennis shoes and how my little brother always had a milk mustache.

Give yourself permission to write. Go beyond fact and memory to satisfy your own moral aesthetic and creative imagination. Many a writer and philosopher has said that we live the stories we tell; that what shapes our lives is how we tell our own stories. Tell your story.

Readings with Discussion Questions

Tobias Wolff
This Boy's Life

Tobias Wolff, short story writer, novelist, editor, journalist, and memoirist, was born June 19, 1945 in Birmingham, Alabama. He received the Wallace Stegner fellowship in 1975 and has been a highly acclaimed author since the publication of his first collection of short stories in 1981. Wolff's numerous awards include the PEN/Faulkner Award for fiction in 1985 for The Barracks Thief, *and the Los Angeles Times Book Prize in 1989 as well as the Ambassador Book Award of the English-Speaking Union for* This Boy's Life.*

     This Boy's Life: A Memoir is Wolff's autobiographical account of his teenage years following his parents' divorce, years spent with his mother and distanced from his father and brother. It was made into a film in 1993.

Our car boiled over again just after my mother and I crossed the Continental Divide. While we were waiting for it to cool we heard, from somewhere above us, the bawling of an airhorn. The sound got louder and then a big truck came around the corner and shot past us into the next curve, its trailer shimmying wildly. We stared after it. "Oh, Toby," my mother said, "he's lost his brakes."

The sound of the horn grew distant, then faded in the wind that sighed in the trees all around us.

By the time we got there, quite a few people were standing along the cliff where the truck went over. It had smashed through the guardrails and fallen hundreds of feet through empty space to the river below, where it lay on its back among the boulders. It looked pitifully small. A stream of thick black smoke rose from the cab, feathering out in the wind. My mother asked whether anyone had gone to report the accident. Someone had. We stood with the others at the cliff's edge. Nobody spoke. My mother put her arm around my shoulder.

For the rest of the day she kept looking over at me, touching me, brushing back my hair. I saw that the time was right to make a play for souvenirs. I knew she had no money for them, and I had tried not to ask, but now that her guard was down I couldn't help myself. When we pulled out of Grand Junction I owned a beaded Indian belt, beaded moccasins, and a bronze horse with a removable, tooled-leather saddle.

It was 1955 and we were driving from Florida to Utah, to get away from a man my mother was afraid of and to get rich on uranium. We were going to change our luck.

We'd left Sarasota in the dead of summer, right after my tenth birthday, and headed West under low flickering skies that turned black and exploded and cleared just long enough to leave the air gauzy with steam. We drove through Georgia, Alabama, Tennessee, Kentucky, stopping to cool the engine in towns where people moved with arthritic slowness and spoke in thick, strangled tongues. Idlers with rotten teeth surrounded the car to press peanuts on the pretty Yankee lady and her little boy, arguing among themselves about shortcuts. Women looked up from their flower beds as we drove past, or watched us from their porches, sometimes impassively, sometimes giving us a nod and a flutter of their fans.

Every couple of hours the Nash Rambler boiled over. My mother kept digging into her little grubstake but no mechanic could fix it. All we could do was wait for it to cool, then drive on until it boiled over again. (My mother came to hate this machine so much that not long after we got to Utah she gave it away to a woman she met in a cafeteria.) At night we slept in boggy rooms where headlight beams crawled up and down the walls and mosquitoes sang in our ears, incessant as the tires whining on the highway outside. But none of this bothered me. I was caught up in my mother's freedom, her delight in her freedom, her dream of transformation.

Everything was going to change when we got out West. My mother had been a girl in Beverly Hills, and the life we saw ahead of us was conjured from her memories of California in the days before the Crash. Her father, Daddy as she called him, had been a navy officer and a paper millionaire. They'd lived in a big house with a turret. Just before Daddy lost all his money and all his shanty-Irish relatives' money and got himself transferred overseas, my mother was one of four girls chosen to ride on the Beverly Hills float in the Tournament of Roses. The float's theme was "The End of the Rainbow" and it won that year's prize by acclamation. She met Jackie Coogan. She had her picture taken with Harold Lloyd and Marion Davies, whose movie *The Sailor Man* was filmed on Daddy's ship. When Daddy was at sea she and her mother lived a dream life in which, for days at a time, they played the part of sisters.

And the *cars* my mother told me about as we waited for the Rambler to cool—I should have seen the cars! Daddy drove a Franklin touring car. She'd been courted by a boy who had his own Chrysler convertible with a musical horn. And of course there was the Hernandez family, neighbors who'd moved up from Mexico after finding oil under their cactus ranch. The family was large. When they were expected to appear somewhere together they drove singly in a caravan of identical Pierce-Arrows.

Something like that was supposed to happen to us. People in Utah were getting up poor in the morning and going to bed rich at night. You didn't need to be a mining engineer or a mineralogist. All you needed was a Geiger counter. We were on our way to the uranium fields, where my mother would get a job and keep her eyes open. Once she learned the ropes she'd start prospecting for a claim of her own.

And when she found it she planned to do some serious compensating: for the years of hard work, first as a soda jerk and then as a novice secretary, that had gotten her no farther than flat broke and sometimes not that far. For the breakup of our family five years earlier. For the misery of her long affair with a violent man. She was going to make up for lost time, and I was going to help her.

We got to Utah the day after the truck went down. We were too late—months too late. Moab and the other mining towns had been overrun. All the motels were full. The locals had rented out their bedrooms and living rooms and garages and were now offering trailer space in their front yards for a hundred dollars a week, which was what my mother could make in a month if she had a job. But there were no jobs, and people were getting ornery. There'd been murders. Prostitutes walked the streets in broad daylight, drunk and bellicose. Geiger counters cost a fortune. Everyone told us to keep going.

My mother thought things over. Finally she bought a poor man's Geiger counter, a black light that was supposed to make uranium trace glow, and we started for Salt Lake City. She figured there must be ore somewhere around there. The fact that nobody else had found any meant that we would have the place pretty much to ourselves. To tide us over she planned to take a job with the Kennecott Mining Company, whose personnel officer had responded to a letter of inquiry she'd sent from Florida some time back. He had warned her against coming, said there was no work in Salt Lake and that his own company was about to go out on strike. But his letter was so friendly! My mother just knew she'd get a job out of him. It was as good as guaranteed.

So we drove on through the desert. As we drove, we sang—Irish ballads, folk songs, big-band blues. I was hooked on "Mood Indigo." Again and again I world-wearily crooned "You ain't been blue, no, no, no" while my mother eyed the temperature gauge and babied the engine. Then my throat dried up on me and left me croaking. I was too excited anyway. Our trail was ending. Burma Shave ads and bullet-riddled mileage signs ticked past. As the numbers on those signs grew smaller we began calling them out at the top of our lungs.

Questions for Discussion

1. Why does Tobias Wolff begin his story with the image of a truck going off the road?

2. Immediately after the truck incident, Wolff writes, "For the rest of the day she kept looking at me, touching me, brushing back my hair. I saw that the time was right to make a play for souvenirs." What does this say at the onset about these two characters and their relationship?

3. What are the differences between fiction and creative nonfiction or fiction and memoir? (Be specific!) What are the similarities?

Mary Karr
The Liars' Club

Mary Karr, poet and memoirist, is a Texas native. She is a two-time winner of the Pushcart *Prize in poetry and was awarded the PEN/Martha Albrand Award (1996), the Carr P. Collins Prize from Texas Institute of Letters (1996), and the New York Public Library Award, all for* The Liars' Club.

Karr received critical acclaim for the energy, wit, humor, and precision of language in The Liars' Club *that captured the cadence of East Texas. The sequel,* Cherry, *continues Karr's autobiography with her adolescence in the same Texas setting.*

Chapter 1

My sharpest memory is of a single instant surrounded by dark. I was seven, and our family doctor knelt before me where I sat on a mattress on the bare floor. He wore a yellow golf shirt unbuttoned so that sprouts of hair showed in a V shape on his chest. I had never seen him in anything but a white starched shirt and a gray tie. The change unnerved me. He was pulling at the hem of my favorite nightgown—a pattern of Texas bluebonnets bunched into nosegays tied with ribbon against a field of nappy white cotton. I had tucked my knees under it to make a tent. He could easily have yanked the thing over my head with one motion, but something made him gentle. "Show me the marks," he said. "Come on, now. I won't hurt you." He had watery blue eyes behind thick glasses, and a mustache that looked like a caterpillar. "Please? Just pull this up and show me where it hurts," he said. He held a piece of hem between thumb and forefinger. I wasn't crying and don't remember any pain, but he talked to me in that begging voice he used when he had a long needle hidden behind his back. I liked him but didn't much trust him. The room I shared with my sister was dark, but I didn't fancy hiking my gown up with strangers milling around in the living room.

It took three decades for that instant to unfreeze. Neighbors and family helped me turn that one bright slide into a panorama. The bed frame tilted against the wall behind the doctor had a scary, spidery look in the dark. In one corner, the tallboy was tipped over on its back like a stranded turtle, its drawers flung around. There were heaps of spilled clothes, puzzles, comics, and the Golden Books I could count on my mom to buy in the supermarket line if I'd stayed in the carriage. The doorway framed the enormous backlit form of Sheriff Watson, who held my sister, then nine, with one stout arm. She had her pink pajamas on and her legs wrapped around his waist. She fiddled with his badge with a concentration too intense for the actual interest such a thing might hold for her. Even at that age she was cynical about authority in any form. She was known for mocking nuns in public and sassing teachers. But I could see that she had painted a deferential look on her face. The sheriff's cowboy hat kept the details of his expression in deep shadow, but I made out a sort of soft half-smile I'd never seen on him.

I had a knee-jerk fear of the sheriff based on my father's tendency to get in fights. He'd pull open the back screen with knuckles scraped and bleeding, then squat down to give instructions to me and Lecia (pronounced, she would have me tell you, "Lisa"). "If the sheriff comes by here, you just tell him you ain't seen me in a few days." In fact, the sheriff never came by, so my ability to straight-faced lie to the law was never tested. But just his presence that night flooded me with an odd sense: *I done something wrong and here's the sheriff.* If I had, that night, possessed a voice, or if anyone nearby felt like listening, that's what I might have said. But when you're a kid and something big is going on, you might as well be furniture for all anybody says to you.

It was only over time that the panorama became animate, like a scene in some movie crystal ball that whirls from a foggy blur into focus. People developed little distinct motions; then the whole scene jerked to smooth and sudden life. Sheriff Watson's jaw dipped into the light and returned to shadow with some regularity as he said things that I couldn't hear to my blond, suddenly cherubic-acting sister. Some firemen wearing canary-colored slickers started to move through the next room, and Dr. Boudreaux's thick fingers came again to rub the edge of my speckled nightgown the way old ladies at the five-and-dime tested yard goods. There must have been an ambulance outside, because at intervals big triangles of red light slashed across the room. I could almost feel them moving over my face, and in the window, through a web of honeysuckle, I saw in my own backyard flames like those of a football bonfire.

And the volume on the night began to rise. People with heavy boots stomped through the house. Somebody turned off the ambulance siren. The back screen opened and slammed. My daddy's dog, Nipper, was growling low and making his chain clank in the yard. He was a sullen dog trained to drink beer and bite strangers. He'd been known to leap from a speeding truck's window to chase down and fight any hound he saw. He'd killed one lady's Chihuahua, then just shook it like a rag while Daddy tried to coax him out of her garage and she hollered and cried. When a voice I didn't know told some sonofabitch to get out of the way, I knew it meant Nipper, who disappeared that night into the East Texas bayou—or more likely, my sister later figured out, the gas chamber at the local pound. Anyway, we never saw him again, which was okay by me. That dog had bitten me more than once.

More door slams, the noise of boots, and some radio static from the cruiser in the road. "Come on, baby," Dr. Boudreaux said, "show me the marks. I'm not about to hurt you." I kept waiting to make eye contact with my sister to get some idea of how to handle this, but she was dead set on that badge.

I don't remember talking. I must eventually have told Dr. Boudreaux there weren't any marks on me. There weren't. It took a long time for me to figure that out for certain, even longer to drive my memory from that single place in time out toward the rest of my life.

The next thing I knew, I was being led away by Sheriff Watson. He still held Lecia, who had decided to pretend that she was asleep. My eyes were belt-level with his service revolver and a small leather sap that even then must have been illegal in the state of Texas. It was shaped like an enormous black tear. I resisted the urge to touch it. Lecia kept her face in his neck the whole time, but I knew she was scudging sleep. She slept like a cat, and this was plenty of hoopla to keep her awake. The sheriff held my left hand. With my free one, I reached up and pinched her dirty ankle. Hard. She kicked out at me, then angled her foot up out of reach and snuggled back to her fake sleep on his chest.

The highway patrolmen and firemen stood around with the blank heaviness of uninvited visitors who plan a long stay. Somebody had made a pot of coffee that laid a nutty smell over the faint chemical stink from the gasoline fire in the backyard. The men in the living room gave our party a wide berth and moved toward the kitchen.

I knew that neither of my parents was coming. Daddy was working the graveyard shift, and the sheriff said that his deputy had driven out to the plant to try and track him down. Mother had been taken Away—he further told us—for being Nervous.

I should explain here that in East Texas parlance the term Nervous applied with equal accuracy to anything from chronic nail-biting to full-blown psychosis. Mr. Thibideaux down the street had blown off the heads of his wife and three sons, then set his house on fire before fixing the shotgun barrel under his own jaw and using his big toe on the trigger. I used to spend Saturday nights in that house with his daughter, a junior high twirler of some popularity, and I remember nothing more of Mr. Thibideaux than that he had a crew cut and a stern manner. He was a refinery worker like Daddy, and also a deacon at First Baptist.

I was in my twenties when Mr. Thibideaux killed his family. I liked to call myself a poet and had affected a habit of reading classical texts (in translation, of course—I was a lazy student). I would ride the Greyhound for thirty-six hours down from the Midwest to Leechfield, then spend days dressed in black in the scalding heat of my mother's front porch reading Homer (or Ovid or Virgil) and waiting for someone to ask me what I was reading. No one ever did. People asked me what I was drinking, how much I weighed, where I was living, and if I had married yet, but no one gave me a chance to deliver my lecture on Great Literature. It was during one of these visits that I found the Thibideauxs' burned-out house, and also stumbled on the Greek term *ate*. In ancient epics, when somebody boffs a girl or slays somebody or just generally gets heated up, he can usually blame *ate*, a kind of raging passion, pseudo-demonic, that banishes reason. So Agamemnon, having robbed Achilles of his girlfriend, said, "I was blinded by *ate* and Zeus took away my understanding." Wine can invoke *ate*, but only if it's ensorcered in some way. Because the *ate* is supernatural, it releases the person possessed of it from any guilt for her actions. When neighbors tried to explain the whole murder-suicide of the Thibideaux clan after thirty years of grass-cutting and garbage-taking-out and dutiful church-service attendance, they did so with one adjective, which I have since traced to the Homeric idea of *ate:* Mr. Thibideaux was Nervous. No amount of prodding on my part produced a more elaborate explanation.

On the night the sheriff came to our house and Mother was adjudged more or less permanently Nervous, I didn't yet understand the word. I had only a vague tight panic in the pit of my stomach, the one you get when your parents are nowhere in sight and probably don't even know who has a hold of you or where you'll wind up spending the night.

I could hear the low hum of neighbor women talking as we got near the front door. They had gathered on the far side of the ditch that ran before our house, where they stood in their nightclothes like some off-duty SWAT team waiting for orders. The sheriff let go of my hand once we were outside. From inside the tall shadow of his hat, with my sister still wrapped around him in bogus slumber, he told me to wait on the top step while he talked to the ladies. Then he went up to the women, setting in motion a series of robe-tightenings and sweater-buttonings.

The concrete was cold on my bottom through the thin nightgown. I plucked two june bugs off the screen and tried to line them up to race down a brick, but one flew off, and the other just flipped over and waggled its legs in the air.

At some point it dawned on me that my fate for the night was being decided by Sheriff Watson and the neighbor ladies. It was my habit at that time to bargain with God, so I imagine that I started some haggling prayer about who might take us home. *Don't let it be the Smothergills*, I probably prayed. They had six kids already and famously strict rules about who ate what and when. The one time we'd spent the night there, Lecia and I wound up in the bathroom eating toothpaste past midnight. We'd eaten a whole tube, for which we had been switch-whipped in the morning by a gray-faced Mr. Smothergill. He was undergoing weekly chemotherapy treatments for mouth cancer at the time, and every kid in the neighborhood had an opinion about when he would die. Cancer and death were synonymous. His sandpaper voice and bleak disposition scared us more than any whipping. His kids called him Cheerful Chuck behind his back. The oldest Smothergill daughter had been permitted to visit my house only once. (Our house was perceived as Dangerous, a consequence of Mother's being Nervous.) She was so tickled by the idea that we could open the refrigerator at will that she melted down a whole stick of butter in a skillet and drank it from a coffee mug. *Lord, I would rather eat a bug than sleep on that hard pallet at the Smothergills'. Plus in the morning the boys get up and stand around the TV in their underpants doing armpit farts. Let it be the Dillards', and I'll lead a holy life forever from this day. I will not spit or scratch or pinch or try to get Babby Carter to eat doo-doo.* Mrs. Dillard stood with the other ladies in her pale blue zip-front duster, her arms folded across her chest. She made Pillsbury cinnamon rolls in the morning and let me squiggle on the icing. Plus her boys had to wear pajama pants when we were there. But the Dillards had space for only one of us, and that on the scratchy living room sofa. *Maybe Lecia could go to the Smothergills',* I proposed to whatever God I worshiped, *and I could take the Dillards.* I wished Lecia no particular harm, but if there was only one banana left in the bowl, I would not hesitate to grab it and leave her to do without. I decided that if the june bug could be herded the length of a brick before I could count five I'd get what I wanted. But the june bug kept flipping and waggling before it had even gone an inch, and Mrs. Dillard went out of her way, it seemed, not to look at me.

I don't remember who we got farmed out to or for how long. I was later told that we'd stayed for a time with a childless couple who bred birds. Some memory endures of a screened-in breezeway with green slatted blinds all around. The light was lemon-colored and dusty, the air filled with blue-and-green parakeets, whose crazy orbits put me in mind of that Alfred Hitchcock movie where birds go nuts and start pecking out people's eye-balls. But the faces of my hosts in that place—no matter how hard I squint—refuse to be conjured.

Because it took so long for me to paste together what happened, I will leave that part of the story missing for a while. It went long unformed for me, and I want to keep it that way here. I don't mean to be coy. When the truth would be unbearable the mind often just blanks it out. But some ghost of an event may stay in your head. Then, like the smudge of a bad word quickly wiped off a school blackboard, this ghost can call undue attention to itself by its very vagueness. You keep studying the dim shape of it, as if the original form will magically emerge. This blank spot in my past, then, spoke most loudly to me by being blank. It was a hole in my life that I both feared and kept coming back to because I couldn't quite fill it in.

Questions for Discussion

1. Mary Karr is a poet as well as a memoirist. What do you notice stylistically about the following sentence? "The bed frame tilted against the wall behind the doctor had a scary, spidery look in the dark. In one corner, the tallboy was tipped over on its back like a stranded turtle, its drawers flung around."

2. How does Karr manage to capture the voice and feelings of a young child? Does it feel authentic to you?

3. Several times in this passage, Karr capitalizes the word Nervous. Why does she do this? How does it affect the tone and voice?

Judith Ortiz Cofer
Silent Dancing

Born in 1952 in Hormigueros, Puerto Rico, Judith Ortiz Cofer immigrated with her parents in 1956 to the United States, where she was raised and educated. Her poems, memoirs, novels, and short stories reflect the contradictions inherent in a Puerto Rican-American identity. Cofer received the Pushcart *Prize for Nonfiction in 1990, the O. Henry Prize for short story in 1994, and a Pulitzer Prize nomination in 1989 for her novel,* The Line of the Sun.

Cofer's memoir, Silent Dancing: A Partial Remembrance of a Puerto Rican Childhood, *takes its name from a home movie of Cofer's parents, two revelers in a conga line, a metaphor for the family's cross-cultural "dance."*

Casa

At three or four o'clock in the afternoon, the hour of *café con leche,* the women of my family gathered in Mamá's living room to speak of important things and to tell stories for the hundredth time, as if to each other, meant to be overheard by us young girls, their daughters. In Mamá's house (everyone called my grandmother Mamá) was a large parlor built by my grandfather to his wife's exact specifications so that it was always cool, facing away from the sun. The doorway was on the side of the house so no one could walk directly into her living room. First they had to take a little stroll through and around her beautiful garden where prize-winning orchids grew in the trunk of an ancient tree she had hollowed out for that purpose. This room was furnished with several mahogany rocking chairs, acquired at the births of her children, and one intricately carved rocker that had passed down to Mamá at the death of her own mother. It was on these rockers that my mother, her sisters and my grandmother sat on these afternoons of my childhood to tell their stories, teaching each other and my cousin and me what it was like to be a woman, more specifically, a Puerto Rican woman. They talked about life on the island, and life in *Los Nueva Yores,* their way of referring to the U.S., from New York City to California: the other place, not home, all the same. They told real-life stories, though as I later learned, always embellishing them with a little or a lot of dramatic detail, and they told *cuentos,* the morality and cautionary tales told by the women in our

"Casa" by Judith Ortiz Cofer is reprinted with permission from the publisher of *Silent Dancing: A Partial Remembrance of a Puerto Rican Childhood* (Houston: Arte Publico Press—University of Houston, 1990).

family for generations: stories that became a part of my subconscious as I grew up in two worlds, the tropical island and the cold city, and which would later surface in my dreams and in my poetry.

One of these tales was about the woman who was left at the altar. Mamá liked to tell that one with histrionic intensity. I remember the rise and fall of her voice, the sighs, and her constantly gesturing hands, like two birds swooping through her words. This particular story would usually come up in a conversation as a result of someone mentioning a forthcoming engagement or wedding. The first time I remember hearing it, I was sitting on the floor at Mamá's feet, pretending to read a comic book. I may have been eleven or twelve years old: at that difficult age when a girl is no longer a child who can be ordered to leave the room if the women wanted freedom to take their talk into forbidden zones, or really old enough to be considered a part of their conclave. I could only sit quietly, pretending to be in another world, while absorbing it all in a sort of unspoken agreement of my status as silent auditor. On this day, Mamá had taken my long, tangled mane of hair into her ever busy hands. Without looking down at me or interrupting her flow of words, she began braiding my hair, working at it with the quickness and determination which characterized all her actions. My mother was watching us impassively from her rocker across the room. On her lips played a little ironic smile. I would never sit still for *her* ministrations, but even then, I instinctively knew that she did not possess Mamá's matriarchal power to command and keep everyone's attention. This was particularly evident in the spell she cast when telling a story.

"It is not like it used to be when I was a girl." Mamá announced, "Then, a man could leave a girl standing at the church altar with a bouquet of fresh flowers in her hands and disappear off the face of the earth. No way to track him down if he was from another town. He could be a married man, with maybe even two or three families all over the island. There was no way to know. And there were men who did this. Hombres with the devil in their flesh who would come to a pueblo, like this one, take a job at one of the haciendas, never meaning to stay, only to have a good time and to seduce the women."

The whole time she was speaking, Mamá was weaving my hair into a flat plait which required pulling apart the two sections of hair with little jerks that made my eyes water; but knowing how grandmother detested whining and *boba* (sissy) tears, as she called them, I just sat up as straight and stiff as I did at La Escuela San José, where the nuns enforced good posture with a flexible plastic ruler they bounced off slumped shoulders and heads. As Mamá's story progressed, I noticed how my young aunt Laura had lowered her eyes, refusing to meet Mamá's meaningful gaze. Laura was seventeen, in her last year of high school, and already engaged to a boy from another town who had staked his claim with a tiny diamond ring, then left for Los Nueva Yores to make his fortune. They were planning to get married in a year; but Mamá had expressed serious doubts that the wedding would ever take place. In Mamá's eyes, a man set free without a legal contract was a man lost. She believed that marriage was not something men desired, but simply the price they had to pay for the privilege of children, and of course, for what no decent (synonymous with "smart") woman would give away for free.

"María la Loca was only seventeen when *it* happened to her." I listened closely at the mention of this name. María was a town "character," a fat middle-aged woman who lived with her old mother on the outskirts of town. She was to be seen around the pueblo delivering the meat pies the two women made for a living. The most peculiar thing about María, in my eyes, was that she walked and moved like a little girl, though she had the thick body and wrinkled face of an old woman. She would swing her hips in an exaggerated, clownish way, and sometimes even hop and skip up to someone's house. She spoke to no one. Even if you asked her a question, she would just look at you and smile, showing her yellow teeth. But I had heard that if you got close enough, you could hear her humming a tune without words. The kids yelled out nasty things at her, calling her *la Loca,* and the men who hung out at the bodega playing dominoes sometimes whistled mockingly as she passed by with her funny, outlandish walk. But María seemed impervious to it all, carrying her basket of *pasteles* like a grotesque Little Red Riding Hood through the forest.

María la Loca interested me, as did all the eccentrics and "crazies" of our pueblo. Their weirdness was a measuring stick I used in my serious quest for a definition of "normal." As a Navy brat, shuttling between New Jersey and the pueblo, I was constantly made to feel like an oddball by my peers, who made fun of my two-way accent: a Spanish accent when I spoke English; and, when I spoke Spanish, I was told that I sounded like a "Gringa." Being the outsiders had already turned my brother and me into cultural chameleons, developing early the ability to blend into a crowd, to sit and read quietly in a fifth story apartment building for days and days when it was too bitterly cold to play outside; or, set free, to run wild in Mamá's realm, where she took charge of our lives, releasing mother for a while from the intense fear for our safety that our father's absences instilled in her. In order to keep us from harm when father was away, mother kept us under strict surveillance. She even walked us to and from Public School No. 11, which we attended during the months we lived in Paterson, New Jersey, our home base in the States. Mamá freed the three of us like pigeons from a cage. I saw her as my liberator and my model. Her stories were parables from which to glean the *Truth.*

"María la Loca was once a beautiful girl. Everyone thought she would marry the Méndez boy." As everyone knew, Rogelio Méndez was no other than the richest man in town. "But," Mamá continued, knitting my hair with the same intensity she was putting into her story, "this *macho* made a fool out of her and ruined her life." She paused for the effect of her use of the word "macho," which at that time had not yet become a popular epithet for an unliberated man. This word had for us the crude and comical connotation of "male of the species," stud; a *macho* was what you put in a pen to increase your stock.

I peeked over my comic book at my mother. She too was under Mamá's spell, smiling conspiratorially at this little swipe at men. She was safe from Mamá's contempt in this area. Married at an early age, an unspotted lamb, she had been accepted by a good family of strict Spaniards whose name was old and respected, though their fortune had been lost long before my birth. In a rocker Papá had painted sky blue sat Mamá's oldest child, Aunt Nena. Mother of three children, stepmother of two more, she was a quiet woman who liked books but had married an ignorant and abusive widower whose main interest in life was accumulating wealth. He too was in the mainland working on his dream of returning home rich and triumphant to buy the *finca* of his dreams. She was waiting for him to send for her. She would leave her children with Mamá for several years while the two of them slaved away in factories. He would one day be a rich man, and she a sadder woman. Even now her life-light was dimming. She spoke little, an aberration in Mamá's house, and she read avidly, as if storing up spiritual food for the long winters that awaited her in Los Nueva Yores without her family. But even Aunt Nena came alive to Mamá's words, rocking gently, her hands over a thick book in her lap. Her daughter, my cousin Sara, played jacks by herself on the tile porch outside the room where we sat. She was a year older than I. We shared a bed and all our family's secrets. Collaborators in search of answers, Sara and I discussed everything we heard the women say, trying to fit it all together like a puzzle that once assembled would reveal life's mysteries to us. Though she and I still enjoyed taking part in boy's games—chase, volleyball and even *vaqueros,* the island version of cowboys and Indians involving cap-gun battles and violent shootouts under the mango tree in Mamá's backyard—we loved best the quiet hours in the afternoon when the men were still at work and the boys had gone to play serious baseball at the park. Then Mamá's house belonged only to us women. The aroma of coffee perking in the kitchen, the mesmerizing creaks and groans of the rockers, and the women telling their lives in *cuentos* are forever woven into the fabric of my imagination, braided like my hair that day I felt my grandmother's hands teaching me about strength, her voice convincing me of the power of story-telling.

That day Mamá told of how the beautiful María had fallen prey to a man whose name was never the same in subsequent versions of the story; it was Juan one time, José, Rafael, Diego, another. We understood that the name, and really any of the facts, were not important, only that a woman had allowed love to defeat her. Mamá put each of us in María's place by describing her wedding dress in loving detail: how she looked like a princess in her lace as she waited at the altar. Then, as Mamá approached the tragic denouement of her story, I was distracted by the sound of my Aunt Laura's violent rocking. She seemed on the verge of tears. She knew the fable was intended for her. That week she was going to have her wedding gown fitted, though no firm date had been set for the marriage. Mamá ignored

Laura's obvious discomfort, digging out a ribbon from the sewing basket she kept by her rocker while describing María's long illness, "a fever that would not break for days." She spoke of a mother's despair: "that woman climbed the church steps on her knees every morning, wore only black as a *promesa* to the Holy Virgin in exchange for her daughter's health." By the time María returned from her honeymoon with death, she was ravished, no longer young or sane. "As you can see she is almost as old as her mother already," Mamá lamented while tying the ribbon to the ends of my hair, pulling it back with such force that I just knew that I would never be able to close my eyes completely again.

"That María is getting crazier every day." Mamá's voice would take a lighter tone now, expressing satisfaction, either for the perfection of my braid, or for a story well-told; it was hard to tell. "You know that tune she is always humming?" Carried away by her enthusiasm, I tried to nod, but Mamá would still have me pinned between her knees.

"Well, that's the wedding march." Surprising us all, Mamá sang out, "*Da, da, dará . . . da, da, dará.*" Then lifting me off the floor by my skinny shoulders, she led me around the room in an impromptu waltz—another session ending with the laughter of women, all of us caught up in the infectious joke of our lives.

Questions for Discussion

1. Cofer occasionally mixes Spanish with English in her text. What is the effect of this overall? Is it necessary to translate the Spanish words into English, as she occasionally does?
2. How is the narrator caught between cultures? Find three specific passages that show this conflict.
3. Describe the mother-daughter relationship in this piece. What lessons does the daughter learn from the mother? What is the meaning of the last line?

Jeanette Winterson
Mother from Heaven

Jeanette Winterson, a writer of unique talent and range, was born in Manchester, England and educated at St. Catherine's College, Oxford. Her awards include the Publishing for People Award and the Whitbread Award for best first novel for Oranges Are Not the Only Fruit *(1985). Written on the Body, Winterson's 1994 novel, was awarded the Lambda Literary Award for Lesbian Fiction.*

"Mother from Heaven" appeared in The New Yorker.

My mother was a reincarnation of the Virgin Mary. An angel came to her and told her that she would have a child, but as she wasn't prepared to do this by any ordinary method, she took a trip to the orphanage and got me.

My new parents were working-class, suspicious of education, and deeply religious. The book I was given to read was the Bible. Everything else had to be vetted by my mother, whose argument against books ran something like "The trouble with a book is that you never know what's in it until it's too late."

A pamphleteer by temperament, my mother knew that sedition and controversy are fired by printed matter. It was because she knew the power of books that she avoided them, countering any chance influence with exhortations of her own, pasted about the house.

The strange thing is that although there were only six books in our house, including "Cruden's Complete Concordance to the Old & New Testaments," we lived in a world of print. There were colored cards stuck behind the lights and pinned under the coat hooks. My hook said, "Think of God Not the Dog." In the kitchen, on a loaf wrapper, my mother had written, "Man Shall Not Live by Bread Alone." In the outside toilet, those who stood up read, "Linger Not at the Lord's Business." Those who sat down read, "He Shall Melt Thy Bowels Like Wax." (It was not as bad as it sounds; my mother was having trouble with her movements, which I suspect was connected to the loaf of white sliced we couldn't live without.) It was quite normal for me to find a little sermon written over my packed lunch, or a few Bible verses, with commentary, stuffed inside my hockey cleats. Fed words, and shod with them, I began to see them as clues. I hunted them down, knowing they would tell me something about which I knew very little—myself.

I began to smuggle books into the house. Anyone who has a single bed, standard size, and a collection of paperbacks, standard size, will discover that seventy-seven can be accommodated, per layer, under the mattress. I began to worry that my mother might realize that her daughter's bed was rising visibly. She suspected me of harboring print. Library books that had been vetted and returned never bothered her. Close association was what she feared: a book might fall into my hands and stay there. It never occurred to her that I fell into the books—that I put myself inside them for safekeeping.

One night, when I was sleeping closer to the ceiling than to the floor, my mother realized the awful truth and, dragging out a corner of D. H. Lawrence, collapsed my wordy tower and threw the books out of the window and into the back yard. Then she went outside and burned them.

Not all of them. I had started to shift some of my hoard to a friend's house, and I still have a few of those first books, carefully bound in plastic, none of their spines broken.

The battle between my mother and me was really a battle between happiness and unhappiness. She was an unhappy woman, difficult and intense. I was a happy child, difficult and intense. She wanted to keep me, Rapunzel-like, in her own gray tower, surrounded by thorns. I wanted to escape. I wasn't looking out for the prince. I had guessed early that I would be doing most of the prince-work myself.

Some time later, when I told her about my girlfriend, she said, "I think my varicose veins are going to burst." When the bloody pressure-spout hit the ceiling, she looked up and said, "If you loved me, you would have told me before I finished decorating."

How could I say that no one could tell her anything while she was decorating? When she was asked if she wanted to come and eat supper, she replied, "I'll have a sandwich up the ladder."

How could I say that no one had ever been able to tell her anything, whether or not she was decorating? Her latter-day role as the Virgin Mary went no further than Immaculate Conception. It would have been unwise to ask her to intercede with God. She *was* God. She didn't know this because she was born before feminism.

Irascible, impossible, unknowable, unmovable, She Is That She Is, and dead but not forgotten. "The Devil guided me to the wrong crib," she said whenever I made her angry, which was often. Well, the Devil must have a sense of humor, or perhaps he just likes books. When I no longer had any books left to read, I began to write one of my own. My mother never forgave me for that, but it didn't matter, because I forgave her. It's all you can do.

Questions for Discussion

1. How does the setting in this essay—the house and everything in it—reflect the lives and personalities of the author and her mother?

2. Define the word *irony*. How is the tone in this essay ironic?

3. Compare the mother-daughter relationship in this piece to the earlier piece by Judith Ortiz Cofer. How are the voices similar? Dissimilar?

Student Writing

Tone

Each of these essays by students deals with childhood experiences and memories of parents and siblings. The voice and tone in each essay, however, is quite distinct to the author. The tone of one essay is light and humorous; another is quite dark. Of these three essays, which tone do you find the most compelling?

Sherry Ann Jackson
Dancing Girls

Sherry Ann Jackson is a fiction writer and MFA Creative Writing candidate. She is currently working on a collection of short stories about her rural-minded relatives. Her work appears in Poetry Flash, Riverwind, *and* ZYZZYVA.

Me and mama are dancing to Hank Williams. She's reeled me in after spinning me out and around. The camera caught us at this moment: Mama hugs me close from behind, my arms are crossed against my chest, our hands are clasped. In this one-beat pause, she nips her bottom lip; there is music all over her face. Smiling over my shoulder, our eyes are locked. It is my favorite snapshot.

When I can't fall asleep, I reach for the snapshot and study it by the green glow of the clock radio. Beyond our moment frozen, I hear Hank Williams play on.

This picture was taken years ago, when I was in high school and before Mama was confined to a wheel chair. Mama loved to dance and Daddy was no kind of dancer. She compensated with four dancing daughters. Not that she ever taught us to dance, we just did; she transferred its appeal to us.

When we were little kids, Saturday was Country Music Night on TV. Mama'd adjust the foil-draped rabbit ears of the black and white, then push the unit flush against the wall. We got The Buck Owens Music Hour, The Bill Anderson Show, and Ernest Tubb Tonight, back to back, 8 o'clock, Channel 10. And we danced. Living room furniture shoved up against the walls, rug rolled back, floors sprinkled in baby powder, we danced. We paused only on Mama's occasional directive when Smiley, Bill Anderson's steel guitar player, took a solo. His name wasn't really Smiley, but that was what Mama called him.

"Looky girls, Smiley." Me and the sisters would have to pause midstep, mute the snap of our fingers, and look at a grainy close-up of the grinning guitarist. "Sits there so calm-like and smiles up at the camera. Sucker just a'playin away at that steel. Would never know by just lookin." And then she'd peel her attention away from the screen, roll her eyes up to the music in her head, and dig in on flexed elbows. We'd all start up to dancing again.

At the end of the night we debriefed after the shows. Mama'd ask, "Who was your favorite tonight?" Diane, the youngest, bottled, diapered, and shirtless, remained anchored to the coffee table, having spent Country Music Night on bouncing knees. In a wide-eyed stare, exaggerated by the sudden void of music, Mama answered for her: "Baby Girl liked Smiley."

Diane flexed on her dimpled knees and bounced on an empty beat. It was all the confirmation we needed.

"Mine's Buck," Virginia would pipe in, and commence to sing: I got a tiger by the tail, it's plain to see. One by one, through the process of elimination, each girl would stake her claim to a favorite. There were no wrong choices.

Family wedding dances occurred at the VFW or West Fraternal Hall in Leroy, Texas, cotton and corn country where Mama grew up. Mama called the wedding-going farmers and cattlemen "My Folk": mostly relatives, although I could never quite figure out how I was kin. Worse was when Mama tried to explain. "That there's Henry Willemburg, Jr. Rubilee's nephew's, you know, Big Chuck's wife's brother." She'd wave her arms across the hall at a round bellied, red-faced man, guffawing in a huddle of people, fisting a plastic cup of beer. "Hey, Henry! Get over here! Are you gettin' more goodlookin' or is my eyesight gettin' bad?" That was my clue to run off across the hall, find the other kids, and avoid a possible introduction.

While the country band kicked in and all the Henrys, Rubilees, and Big Chucks danced, if you were a kid, you kicked off your shoes and joined the Saw Dust Slide. This involved winding into a long run to slide across the saw dust floor at the back of the hall, over and over again. Early in the night you started out on your feet, but then it progressed into butt slides and finally full-on belly slides until someone got hurt. Grown-ups directed loud, good-natured complaints to us in suspiciously close earshot of one another. "Girl, you'd think I raised you in a barn. Can't take you nowhere." That would prompt a reprimand from another parent. "Quit running around like a wild hoodlum! And where's your shoes? Looks like we can cha'k those socks up for ruin." Off we'd run, all a'slide and skid, as the music whang-whanged and started up again. The adults claimed dance partners with the circling of a waist and an arm draped across a shoulder and commenced to two-step in a counter clockwise shuffle-and-glide.

Mama was well liked, and as I grew older, I was popular through proximity and never lacked for a dance partner. She was easy to locate across the great sea of partying people. This is what I looked for: the most prominent huddle of folk, leaned in together over abandoned beer cups pooled on a banquet table. A circle of convening heads, like a school of feeding fish, with faces baited in widening grins. And when the circle broke, the heads thrown back in explosive laughter, there'd be Mama, buoyed in the middle of all that attention. One helluva storyteller. A real hoot, they called her.

Making my way to the table to get a quarter from Mama for something other than the free music, food, and drink, I'd be met by some old guy, red in the face from laughter, peeling himself away from Mama's fan club. "Jeanette, I'm dancing with your girl!" On a dying chuckle, over the rising music he'd say, "What a cut-up your mama is!" As he shook his head as if to by-golly off the last of Mama's lingering funny, I completed his thought, "Yeah, a real hoot."

Mama's Folk were there to dance. Generally these aged dancers didn't give much to personal attention. Their minds seemed to be in two places: inward on the music and outward on other dancers. They were eager to acknowledge long unseen friends and family, and I'd be shuffled backwards into the throng. "If I could ter-ust my eyesight, I'd might could say you're gettin' better lookin'!" The recipient of the compliment would be spun out of earshot by a boozed and twirling partner.

Smelling of Old Spice and oiled up in Bryl Creme, my dance partners were long-time country dwellers, none too tall, all heavy bellied and spindly of leg. Their builds reminded me of Sir Froggy in my old kindergartner reader: inflated tummy with knees bowing outward in step, buckling under his girth. Like Sir Froggy, their jaunty strut and outgoing nature cut them a wide berth in the community as cheerful, pragmatic characters. On occasion I might dance with a retired deputy or constable-of-sorts who retained some remote clout in the county; the type of guy that had some half-assed badge somewhere in a bottom drawer.

Such were the men who two-stepped me through my adolescence until I cut a path in the sawdust into my own dance haunts, away from Mama and her Folk. I went off to college. Mama, in her late 50's, had her first back surgery, which compromised her dancing. Yet she danced vicariously through me with a barrage of questions during my occasional weekends home. She wanted to know where I danced, the bands I saw, the songs they played. What girlfriends came along and what men did I dance with?

A lot of our catching-up took place in the car. She didn't like to drive much after her surgery and her walker had become a common sight. I drove her to the grocery store, to the doctor, to the hairdresser, to church. When I had sufficiently answered her initial deluge of questions and temporarily satiated her pumping for particulars, she'd grow quiet at a stop light. She'd look over each corner of the intersection as if piecing my stories together into a comprehensive whole. "All's I can say," she'd say, breaking from thought with the changing of the light, "is girl, have fun while your body still can."

Texas is a refrigerated state, and even in the height of a heat wave, the frozen food section of the Piggly Wiggly raises goose bumps. You can chill the back of your neck just bending into a freezer. We shopped a lot in frozen foods, as Mama found it hard to stand at the stove too long. After yet another surgery, I was gently guiding Mama on her walker down the freezer aisle lined in glass doors. The tiled floors were buffed to a high, icy shine. I tried not to look at the scar at the base of her neck, inching above her loose and scoop-necked housedress. It hurt to look; it made me ache for her. I forced my attention instead on the florescent-bright aisle before me. But the stark chrome trim of the frosted freezer doors cold-bladed my back. I hurt for Mama more, and loved her more than I ever had.

Though Mama and I were a generation apart, I see now that I'd never moved that far from her traditional country and western music and dance. In college you wouldn't have caught me at any place as old fogy as a VFW. I took what felt like a sharp detour into more progressive country, country folk, and Texas blues. In the 1970's, Willie Nelson started growing pigtails and having campout concerts. Willie's 4th of July Picnics were latter-day Woodstocks that smacked a strong regionalism—more bandana, less tie-dye. More boot, less moccasin. The Red-Headed Stranger billed the likes of Jerry Jeff Walker, Ray Wylie Hubbard, and Gary P. Nunn at his summer extravaganzas. But it was the same as Mama's music, I suppose, except the musicians were younger, longhaired, hip. They smoked dope and sang about it. They were outlaws. They had three names.

Willie grew up in Abbot, Texas, just up the road from Leroy, Mama's hometown. They were peers; to hear Mama tell it, they were friends. Mama's brother, my Uncle Junior, cut his teeth learning fiddle with Willie and the boys. Way before Willie's braids—an ass kicking for sure. Way before anyone would pay to see a high school barn band: one lousy on the fiddle, another that couldn't sing, neither good looking. Mama was there. She mentioned more than once that she was known to fill in on the tambourine if the boys were ever in a pinch.

So we maintained plenty to exchange about music, even though I was hip and she was not. She could connect just about any of my outlaw musicians to someone she was well familiar with in her hey-day. If she couldn't claim an immediate familiarity, she'd relentlessly enquire about all the band members and eventually trace his lineage, many times removed, sometimes through marriage, to someone who knew Junior and therefore knew her, too. She'd conclude the matter: "When you see him play next time, tell him you're George Uptmor Jr.'s niece." She'd pause to emphasize the importance of its accuracy. "Don't just say Junior. Say you're Jeanette Uptmor's daughter." She'd look dead at me and fall silent, as if a little time was needed for the strict particulars to embed themselves in my long-term memory. "And tell him I said hi."

I said I would. And then I'd look away, knowing there was no way in hell that Mama, Junior, or Leroy, Texas was an identity I wanted to tout. In college I strove to bandy myself about with a more "Austin" repute. More rolling hill country, less farm. More wildflower, less corn. More outlaw, less in-law.

In my youth I considered aging a matter of choice. Not so much in physique or form—I'd seen tires wear out, tractors give out, and old things rust—but in spirit. I thought a person chose to relinquish her enthusiasm, her fervor for experience and movement. If life was infinite in allure, any person not acting on its appeal was doing so consciously and by choice. This is how one chose to be old. But form does somehow dictate function; I didn't know that then. Nor did I acknowledge that Mama's searing passion was alive and burning in a body that was wearing out, giving out, rusting.

Meanwhile, young and oiled, I danced on.

True to my image, my college friends and I frequented the popular Texas music establishments of the renegade hill country: Big Annie's, The Devil's Backbone Tavern, and Cheatham Street Warehouse. We called them clubs; they were cool, they were timeless, they didn't have the manicured hokiness of a VFW that underwent timely upkeep and modernization. These places were contemporary in all their antiquity. And unlike the fraternal halls of home, my haunts had crude board walls rather than paneling. Old farming implements rusted on display, rather than decomposing in a junk pile out back. The air was stirred on elliptical creaking ceiling fans instead of a window Refridgidaire. And rather than the Illumi-Lite plastic Coors clock ticking above a vinyl trimmed bar, my places were alight in the vigor and buzz of neon red and blue.

Our most frequent hangout was Cheatham Street Warehouse, a defunct warehouse turned music hall. Shabby and peeling of paint, it was backed against the Katy Line above the banks of the San Marcos River. Inside, the band played against a wide-open wall and the doors of the warehouse rolled open to the black and cricketed night. Between sets me and the girlfriends would hop across stage through the freight doors and, if we were lucky, get high with the band. The night air cooled the sweat on my body to a fine mist as I threw my head back, blowing the sweet smoke into the stars. Me and the girls would then have a scurried and stony go-down below the tracks, a quick strip-and-slip into the river. The night waters of the San Marcos closed over me dark and seamless, teleporting me into an underworld away from the press of hot bodies and smoky air of Cheatham. When we heard the thomping bass of the band, we skirted back up the banks. Often we'd lost our seats but we had our reserved box seating, as we called it: a broken butcher's case. It's common for Texas folk to have an extra radiator lying around a yard or a hot water heater on the front porch. Cheatham had a defunct refrigerator case along a side wall. Before long it was up and down the chrome monstrosity to dance, get beers, go to the bathroom. Or catch the band on another break. When the crowd pounded their boots on the wooden floor, we stood on the meat case and stomped along. Music rose from the wooden floors, vibrated through the metal case, pounded low in my diaphragm, and rose pulsating in my chest. I have never felt more alive. Music, which I'd followed for so long, turned and met me, homed itself in me, penetrated my inners, all while I was stomping atop a broken sausage case.

But things get more complicated with age. I've lost the desire to climb up and down broken appliances. I don't go dancing much any more, but I am nostalgic for it. I live on the West Coast now and none of the men here can dance. I can't find my music; my bearded and braided outlaws have been replaced with tam-bearing ska musicians and World Beat. Nor do I have a pack of dancing girls to run with. Besides, it seems less flattering in my forties to run all over town chasing music than it did in my twenties. I'm not sure I would hoist my ass on top of a meat case even if I could.

But I feel music alive and coiled in me, ready to spring forth like new upholstery in an aging car. Maybe I should dance more, while the body's still holding up. It might not be hard to find Willie playing somewhere on this Pacific coast. I'd dance, even if it meant dancing alone. Maybe I'd walk up to him between sets, lean in and say, "I'm George Uptmor Jr.'s niece. Jeanette's daughter."

And when the music started up again, I'd kick off my shoes and look for someone to shuffle me out onto the dance floor. And just cha'k my socks up for ruin.

Eran Williams
Lost at a Love-In

Eran Williams has published fiction and nonfiction in The Monserrat Review, *the* Santa Monica Review, *and the* Crab Orchard Review. *He is the recent recipient of an Associated Writing Programs (AWP) Intro Journal Award and a Steinbeck Fellowship.*

"What happened that year you brought me to New York?" I asked the question casually, as though the details had slipped my mind. Actually, in the 36 years since, I had never asked directly about my infancy. What I knew about the drugs and rehab, the affairs and divorce I put together from shards with the patience of an archeologist. But as a new father, I had to know, "What happened when I was one?"

The birth of my son was a warrant and this meeting with my mother was the first hard knock on the door of my childhood. Did she even know she was a suspect? We sat in the early summer evening at an outdoor café behind the Natural History Museum in New York.

My mom began, "This friend of ours, Chris, was driving out to New York and I was heading to Europe, or I thought I was, so I got a ride with him. He was doing a lot of speed so I started to do speed."

"So we just took off one day with another man? What did dad think about your going?" I asked after a drink of red.

"Oh, I think he probably missed you a lot but that was the way things were. He was busy with his own plans, trying to finish school . . ." My mom could see my displeasure at the thought of not being a part of my father's own plans. "Those were the sixties. Everyone was falling in love with everyone. We believed we could love the whole world at once. We were reinventing the wheel, trying not to make the mistakes our parents made. So we thought we could love more than one person and we thought we should live out our love."

"But you weren't in love with Chris."

"Not at first, that came later. By the time we got to New York I had forgotten about Europe. I just wanted to live with Chris. We found a place in the lower East Side. It was all Puerto Ricans and us. Twenty-five dollars a month or something ridiculous but it was a pit."

"So what did you do with your time? What did you do for a year?"

"We didn't work. Chris was dealing small time. The cops somehow got the idea he was a bigger deal than he was. I did a little art, probably, I don't really remember. We made a little money here and there and we lived cheap. We found a lot of what we needed in trash cans. The trash cans in New York are amazing, just as good as the stores in California. We begged some, too."

"What about me?"

"You were there. You were always with us. People loved you wherever you went, your blond, curly hair. You got a lot of attention. You had a good time."

I pictured the junkies playing with me. "And you were shooting speed?"

"Yeah, but never enough to be dangerous. I always made sure you were safe."

A belly ache like hunger grew as my mom described that year in New York and the fallout. Running from the police for half a year, they finally chased us all the way back to California where Chris and the cops ran off into La Jolla canyon, right out of our lives. The ache wasn't so much from the stories of that time, but from the confident air of the recounting. My mother didn't admit that she was incompetent as a mother, or even dangerous. I didn't want to accuse her of it. I wanted what every child wants, for their parents to be good. But my own parenthood was forcing me to judge my own parents in order to decide how I was going to raise a kid. Throughout the questioning of that afternoon with my mother, the alibi she resorted to again and again was "I loved you." Was that enough? Was that all a parent could do?

By the time my long-term memory began recording, life had calmed down considerably. My parents were separated but in the same town, my mother was doing drugs but not speed, we didn't own a kitchen table but we did have a set of folding individual TV tables that we could use to put dinner plates on, if anyone wanted to. And we lived in a small town in California which served as a haven for children of the 60s so my patched, embroidered clothes didn't stand out.

Pot permeated the air like . . . air. The smell of a burning joint was as common to me as the scent of the ocean in the winter fog. Today, a whiff of a doubie at a concert or a campground takes me back, as no other smell can, to my childhood home. A two-story white Victorian with roses and camellias slowly overgrowing the cement walkway, that house held the same aroma as a surf film at the Civic Center. My mom used the top of my Monopoly box to clean her stash. The sound of the hard green seeds tumbling down the inclined lid is still intimate. Gently, repeatedly, the flap of the rolling paper package would scoop up the dried, twisted leaves like a rake moving grass up a slope. The seeds would end up at the bottom, eventually to be used in brownies.

My mother would smoke to do her art. She saw getting high as a part of the creative process. Like dancing, it loosened her up. She said everyone had their drug, and it didn't seem to bother her or anyone else around that hers were illegal. Usually I came home from school to find her in her studio, dancing to the Rolling Stones at full volume, in the middle of a joint that lay in a roach clip at the edge of her drawing table. Or she'd be working on a color pencil drawing of one of her twelve cats. "Hi, Eran, how was school?" she asked, the final "l" lost in an exhalation of smoke.

I remember playing at getting stoned. I passed a redwood cone around to a group of kids whose parents were getting high for real in the house. We held tightly, between the thumb and forefinger, the dry brown stem of a redwood cone and sucked air between our pursed lips. I fell backwards after my hit. "Wow, man, that's good shit," I coughed out until all of us were laughing uncontrollably. At the time I had the theory that the stuff smoked was inconsequential, it was the breathing technique that made adults silly, something about holding the breath.

But I never smoked. When whatever company we were entertaining passed the joint to me I always said politely, "No thank you," and passed it to the next person in line. I knew from my summers with grandparents, and from school and TV, that it was not right for adults to be passing drugs to minors, even related minors. While my parents had been arrested a few times, put on academic probation, or suspended, I couldn't have been more law abiding. I couldn't even cut across lawns. While other kids sneaked out of the house at midnight to go participate in *Rocky Horror,* my dad invited me to go with him. Even if I wanted to be bad, my parents beat me to it.

When my mom sat me down to have that special talk about sex and drugs she strayed from the script: "Eran, if you are ever interested in trying cocaine or other hard drugs, please get them from me," she lectured. "On the street drugs are often cut with speed or worse. You never know what you are getting. With me, you know what you are getting and you won't have to worry about the police or the price." The sex portion of the talk consisted of a handful of condoms to let me know they supported my newfound desires. "You don't have to hide in the park or the backs of cars, your date is welcome to spend the night here." Making love, she explained, was one of life's great pleasures. What a burden it was to be given such liberty, to have a mother who spoke of the carnal without blushing. I rebelled: I didn't do drugs and the handful of condoms, well, they lasted well into my sophomore year in college.

Not that I didn't benefit from my mother's permissiveness. There was the time I ran into a drug deal in junior high. During fourth period I asked for a hall pass to use the toilet. I never went to the bathrooms during recess. Too dangerous. More dangerous, even, than the locker room, the milk line, and the row of trees at the end of the field. Opening the bathroom door I discovered one boy passing another boy a sandwich bag of pot. Both boys turned their heads to look at me. The pot froze between them.

"You smoke dope?" the dealer, an eighth grader, asked. He wanted to know if I was cool.

"No . . ." I couldn't lie when I was that age. The truth forced itself out of my throat as though I were the second coming of St. Augustine. And I wasn't even Catholic. My mother was Jewish and my father believed in UFOs, but I couldn't lie. Still, in the bathroom, I knew "No" was the wrong answer, the answer that would hurt me, so I searched for a mitigating truth. Something to keep my head out of the toilet.

"No, I don't smoke," I said, and added with a smile of hope, "but my mother does."

This seemed to satisfy the interrogator, for the bag of pot moved one way and the money the other. Who would nark with jailable parents? I went into a stall and found I couldn't pee, walked back to the class where we were writing pretend checks to prepare for real life, and handed back my hall pass. Once again my parents had made up for my own lack of cool.

My mother's bohemian lifestyle was particularly impressive to my repressed schoolmates. In junior high my mom decided to get involved in my education. She decided to teach art to my class. I was in a special program called Student Centered Curriculum (SCC) which allowed us to make up our own study projects and just take two or three regular classes. Most of the kids in this alternative program weren't doing so well in the regular system but I was there because my parents were big fans of alternatives. They had been founding members in the Santa Cruz Free School and then, with help from the grandparents, enrolled me in Montessori, but that only went through fifth grade, so they were pleased to find an innovative program at the local junior high.

For a year of Thursdays the whole of SCC would come over to my house, get stoned and draw perfectly tubular waves. Not that my mom was getting these kids stoned. She was just around while they were getting stoned and she was stoned too. I'm trying to remember if students were required to bring their own stuff. I can't remember. This is a legal move on the part of my memory.

At that time I was small, with a high-pitched voice and an overbite. My voice was so high that when my school did a production of Fiddler on the Roof, my role was to stand backstage and sing with the girls. That is no crime except in junior high where some kids were already mature. These kids knew they were as big as they were ever going to be and they knew that the rest of us would grow up, too, so they beat us up while they had the chance. I would have been dead meat if not for the solidarity of my fellow SCC outcasts, and they only loved me, I was convinced, due to my relation to a cool mom. I might never have gained the respect of my peers without a mother who got high.

Art class at my house was where I first had *The Dark Side of the Moon* explained. Kevin, a big kid who could play the guitar and had counted his girlfriends on both hands, put the record on and described how each song was part of a space odyssey. We debated which was better, Kiss or the Beatles. It was at this art class where mature eighth-grade girls first sat on my bed, taking little breakout sessions from the art to discuss seriously any relationships amongst us. And there they would be, three real women, 8th graders, sitting in a row on *my* bed. Once, after class, one of them kissed me goodbye.

But I was terrified by our old Victorian full of stoned thirteen-year-olds and only one stoned adult—my mom. I could see the bust go down and with it our little alternative corner of Branciforte Junior High, and then, probably the junior high itself would be burned in a kind of purification rite. What would Mr. Ouse say when he found out the paintings he proudly displayed on the classroom walls were created under the influence of pot? What was the likelihood of such a triumph—the triumph of finally getting credit for doing wrong—not spreading around the school? Some algebra teacher would get wind of this. One of the SCC bunch would come into class reeking and he would ask the student where they had been the period before. "I was in class at Eran's house." I wouldn't be arrested. I rehearsed my speech to the police constantly, the one that would show just enough loyalty to family but then cave in to my total loyalty to law.

But none of my worries came true. More forgiving times, I guess. Scandal wasn't what it is today. My mom was never nervous; the whole thing was her idea. It was why I had to worry so much as a kid—no one else was doing it.

It wasn't until I moved away to college that I stopped fretting. There, I told tales of my colorful past to amuse people at parties. What I knew was that my parents loved me. I had survived my childhood so I didn't complain. I seemed to have none of the parent-child hang-ups of my friends. But then, at 35 I became a father and the pretty diorama of my childhood began to look different.

Having a baby wasn't what I thought it would be. I planned for it, bought clothes and party favors as though birth were a wedding or a birthday, just another section in the greeting card section of Safeway. Having a baby is not a birthday, though. It's more like a conversion, the kind where you fall off your horse in spasms. When you get up your horse is gone and nothing in the world looks as it did before. I was converted and I didn't even want to be.

I thought I was having a baby so he could meet my parents, my wonderful family and friends. It didn't work out that way. All my relationships have changed since the birth: My wife is now a mother; my friends are turning into strangers; instead of my kid meeting my parents, *I* am meeting my parents for the first time.

From my parental perspective, what had been a road trip begins to look like abandonment. When I was three months old, my mother drove from Santa Barbara to New York, leaving me with my dad for a few months. She went with a guy not my dad who she had fallen in love with on acid. This fact never struck me until I had a baby. I didn't know what three months old meant until I held it in my arms. My own three months in my own arms.

I ask my mom for confirmation, "You left me for three months to go to New York?"

"It was a different time," my mother says. "It was the sixties. Everyone was in love with everyone. We were exploring all the possibilities. You were with your dad and your grandma; you were fine."

To a new father the story my mother tells about our day in the park begins to look like negligence. "I lost you at a love-in at Golden Gate Park," my mother remembers. "A lot of bands were playing. I can't remember who but the vibes were great. I was tripping and dancing with you—you were a great dancer when you were three—and then I turned around and you weren't there. I wasn't worried, though, after all, it was a love-in. Everyone there was so positive and they were really into you. You were so beautiful with your curly blond hair. And sure enough, a while later you appeared with your bottle and blanket. You were fine," my mother tells me, as if it was her confidence that protected me.

I have never been able to suggest to my parents that their own behavior during my first years was less than splendid. Instead I have responded through parenting. I am trying to avoid the mistakes of my parents' generation. This is my revolution of the wheel.

I have bought into all the safety precautions: The latches on the doors and toilet bowl, the gates at the stairs, the inflatable cushion to pad the bathtub spigot. I never let my son out of my sight. The hot water heater in the house is turned down so he doesn't get scalded. I have pulled up all the poison oak in our part of the forest. I avoid being apart from my son. I work part time so I can be with him as much as possible. My wife and I have never used day-care or a babysitter. Our baby sleeps in our bed and disturbs our sleep as he pleases. We hold food up to his lips even when he might not be hungry. I do what he asks of me, whether it is to move away or pick him up. And when his grandmother tells him that there are no worries, that there is no reason to cry, I tell him to whine, to complain, to let his feelings be known. I never want him to have to be fine the way I had to be.

Cathy Patterson
Chester

Cathy Patterson writes creative nonfiction for her own growth and healing. This is her first published work.

When he first came to live with me, he had a vest with shamrocks on it. I don't know what happened to the vest; I have no memory of it. Mattel Toy Company called him Chester O'Chimp and he spoke with an Irish brogue. That was all lost on me. I called him Chester and I loved him.

The imaginary monkeys had always been with me. I blamed all of my naughtiness on them. Somewhat of a monkey myself, I began climbing out of my cage at an early age and my mother would lock me in at night.

Santa brought me Chester. There was a moment when suddenly Chester was in my life. I was awestruck that he existed. Santa gifts were never wrapped in my house and he had been removed from the box. He was sitting there on the green wool carpet next to the stocking. My beaming face had no eyes for anything but Chester. He became the most important thing in my life. I never sucked my thumb or had a blanket, but now I had a chimp. I had been asking for a real monkey but Chester would do.

The gifts that Chester possessed were amazing. The outer plastic of his eyes popped off. I had to be careful not to lose his pupils, so naturally I couldn't trust anyone else to perform that magical feat. They could, however, pull his string. Most incredible of all, he talked! He said things like, "Let's go to the zoo and see the wild children," and "Don't feed me bananas. I like people food, too." I ignored this last bit of advice. I knew that bananas were his favorite food. His felt pink tongue, inside his protruding rubber lips, always smelled faintly of bananas.

Chester's coarse black fur and hard body (I suppose he had a voice machine inside of him) made cuddling difficult, but that didn't stop me. His hands were covered with orange velour, but the interior structure was wire. He could hang on around my neck by grasping his paws together, and he hung there often.

Hiding in dark places was my constant pastime. I avoided my mother's unpredictable anger this way, and with solitude came safety. Chester and terror were my constant companions. I worried that my mother could read my mind. If she knew how much I hated her, she would probably kill me.

A more real fear was fire. We lived in a split-level house and my bedroom was upstairs. We saw those safety films at school and they said that you should sleep with your bedroom doors closed. My mother thought that idea was silly. I wanted one of those ladders you could let down in case of a fire. Another silly idea. She explained the procedure I was to use: open my window, knock out the screen, hang by my hands, and drop to the pavement. "You might break both of your legs but at least you won't burn to death," she said. That was enough comfort to keep me from sleeping soundly for two years. I tried to stay awake in an effort to detect the fire early enough to get out the front door. We never had a fire.

Grumpy and a slow starter, mornings were never good for me. My sister might have slept through our childhood, but she was out of bed at the crack of dawn. When school started in the fall, I was a bear in the morning. I would fall back asleep sitting on the edge of the bed. Captain Crunch helped me become a little more sociable, but not much. My family avoided me in the mornings but I had a job to do in the afternoon.

I was responsible for the universe. My sister was three years older than I, but I was smarter and therefore responsible for making sure that she could read and get her homework done. I worried about her constantly. If she didn't pass, it was my fault. There wasn't much that wasn't my fault. My mother had wanted to adopt four kids. It was only my sister and me. "You were so difficult that I couldn't handle the idea of adopting any more that might be like you," she said. I was even responsible for the size of our family. Consequently, I was a very responsible kid. I got things done. Always. Unless it was beyond my control.

On our final morning, Chester and I got up as usual. I ate Captain Crunch cereal for breakfast and got dressed. When I left for school, I thought I left Chester lying on the bed. Some mornings I was rushed from having dawdled too long, and he got left in a heap on the floor or around the house with some of my other stuffed animals.

It was the spring of my first grade year. I liked school but I was often bored. I had Miss Ross, and I knew that I was the best reader in the class. My sister was two grades ahead and she had the witch, Miss Peaster. She was really old and we were afraid of her. Her hands were like claws and she would shake you if you weren't looking. I was really angry the day she shook my sister because she didn't know her multiplication tables.

Getting held back in school was always a reality for my sister. I don't know if she worried about it. It was clear to me that I would be held responsible if it happened. We practiced reading every night and drilled on those multiplication facts. She never seemed to remember them. I knew them all, but she got angry if I gave her the answer without looking on the back of the flashcard. When I was in third grade, I pretended to have trouble with them, too.

The phone call came at lunch time. I was probably throwing away my bologna and peanut butter sandwich at the time. It was my father's favorite combination, and I was my father's girl, therefore I must like it. I also threw away the orange (I'm allergic to citrus) and the peanut butter cookies. The twinkie was good.

While I was waiting to be dismissed from the cafeteria, Mrs. Peaster phoned my mother to explain why my sister needed to repeat third grade.

I walked home from school by myself. Five blocks must have been about three miles back then. The major intersection had a four-way stop sign, and no crossing guard. The section of sidewalk in front of the orchard was black asphalt. I loved turning the corner and seeing our house. The apprehension about coming home hadn't set in yet. I thought we had the most beautiful home. From a long distance, I could see our silver dollar eucalyptus trees swaying in the breeze. The large split-level stood in the most expensive part of town, and I knew we had the best house of all my friends.

Smoke curled out of our fireplace. It seemed out of place on a warm spring day. I went up the stairs and through the double doors. I dumped all of my papers on the green wool carpeted stairs. I was still on the marble landing, putting my things down, when my mother came out of the kitchen door. She was filled with anger. I started apologizing before she even opened her mouth, but she interrupted me. "You should have worked harder," she said. "You should have done better. You never do anything right."

I stood aghast for a moment. "I don't know why I keep you around here," she said. "I can't stand having you in my sight."

"I'm sorry," I said. "I'm sorry." But I didn't know what to be sorry for. I tried to scoot around her and up the stairs to my room.

"Where do you think you're going?" she asked. "You stand right there while I'm talking to you. Look at the shame you have brought onto our family."

So that was it. Somehow, I didn't teach my sister well enough. Now I really am sorry. I offer to go and talk to Mrs. Peaster, even though she terrifies me.

"Stupid ideas are all you have," my mother says. "You shouldn't be allowed to breathe." Suddenly I was gasping for air.

"I'll show you!" she exclaimed. Storming into the living room, she grabbed an armful of my stuffed animals from a chair and headed for the brick fireplace. She dropped a few as she bent to pull open the screen. I darted forward and scooped them up. I watched, horrified, as she shoved the rest into the flames.

Instantly the room was filled with the smell of melting nylon and plastic. My eyes started to burn, and now I really couldn't breathe. I was crying and begging as she hauled the next load toward their doom. Then I saw him. Chester. I dropped the rest and snatched him up and ran with him into the hall. I should have kept going and never stopped.

The smell was unbearable. As soon as the entire pile was smoldering, she turned to me with a triumphant look. And then she saw him. Before I knew what was happening, she had hold of one of his legs. I wouldn't let go. "Please let me keep him," I screamed. "I'll be good. Please don't burn him." My knees were bleeding on the carpet. She wrenched him from my grasp. I collapsed face down on the floor, sobbing. I couldn't watch him melt. He was dead. I couldn't save him. She poked at him with the fireplace tool and then closed the wire screen.

"Stop crying," she said. She went into the kitchen to finish dinner. So, I did. And I never cried again.

■ **Writing Exercise** ■

The first step in thinking about writing a memoir is to create a memoir chart. On the left side of the chart, list emotions from "positive" to "negative" in whatever order you wish. Try not to put value judgments on these emotions but list them according to intensity. Across the bottom axis, chart the years of your life in two-, five-, or ten-year increments. Now plot specific points on your chart according to significant events in your life.

When you've completed your chart, go back and briefly freewrite on each of the points. Give yourself at least five minutes for each event. Try to recall as much detail as possible about the event: what things looked like, felt like, smelled like. How did you feel at the time? How did this particular event affect you?

It's useful to do a memoir chart more than once, or do a completely new one every once in a while. Your thoughts, memories, and perceptions change over time, and your perspective shifts. Try doing a memoir chart for one year of your life, breaking the points down into months.

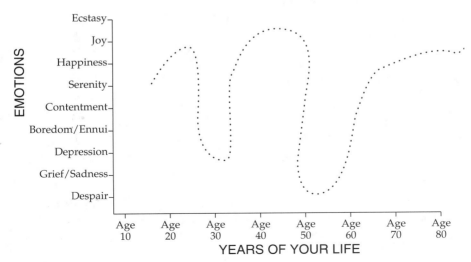

Memoir Chart
Chart the major events of your life according to emotional intensity

Assignment

Choose a point on your memoir chart that represents a time in your childhood or early adolescence when something happened that really changed your view of the world (or your view of yourself in relation to the world). Using the first-person point of view, write an essay that uses description, detail, and at least one scene of dialogue.

If you find it hard to get started, try sitting quietly with your eyes closed and imagining or reimagining the experience you wish to recall. Think about the people, the setting, and the physical objects that are present in the scene. Use your senses to recall specific details. What did things look like, smell like, feel like? What feelings did you hold or experience in your body? Concentrating on the senses will help bring back the details of the experience.

Freewrite until you have exhausted all that you can remember. Then try another point on your memoir chart. It may take several attempts before you find the experience you really want and need to write about at length.

As you develop your essay and polish your prose, keep in mind that your own aesthetic sensibility and voice should be evident in the tone, structure, and style of the essay.

The Writing Workshop

The Workshop Environment

A writing workshop is a unique and often unforgettable experience. The workshop environment is a place where you should feel free to express your creativity and expand your writing skills. You will find support, encouragement, and enthusiasm for your work. For many people, their first experience in a workshop or any type of writing group can be both exhilarating and terrifying. It may be the first time you've received acknowledgment and praise for what you do well in your writing, and conversely, the first time you've heard solid suggestions and constructive criticism for areas you need to improve. Both can be tough on the ego!

Writing is a solitary business, and you might find that one of the greatest joys of being in a workshop is just getting to know other writers. Many groups continue after the formal workshop has ended. Nevertheless, a writing workshop is not merely a "mutual admiration society," and good writing is much more than just a matter of taste. You will receive suggestions on everything from the psychology of characters to narrative structure to the finer details of style and grammar. Some workshop members will likely respond to your work more enthusiastically than others. This is true for everyone. It's important to keep the overall workshop environment upbeat, energetic, and engaged.

Effective participation in a writing workshop is a difficult skill to master and involves two things: (1) learning to effectively critique the work of other students, and (2) learning how to take comments and criticism from other workshop members about your own work. As your group progresses from week to week, evaluate yourself and consider how you are engaging in the workshop or group process and what you might do to improve your workshop skills. It's a good idea to bring this question up in the group from time to time and let people air their views on how well the workshop is or isn't working, and discuss strategies to keep everyone equally involved and the spirit positive and enthusiastic.

Workshops often work best if the author remains silent while his or her work is being discussed and sits outside of the circle taking notes. Workshop members should avoid addressing the author directly and instead direct their energies to analyzing the work. Agree upon how much time should be spent discussing each piece, and set a timer to stay on task. Each workshop member should have read the work thoroughly prior to class and be prepared to discuss the work and also provide the author with written commentary.

You will be pushing yourself as a writer and as a reader. Writing workshops are an enormous amount of work. But they're also a lot of fun.

Revision Tips and Strategies

Sentiment versus Sentimentality

Attempting to write about your own life in a way that impacts the reader emotionally and intellectually can lead to overdramatization that may, in fact, detract from the quality of the work. The emotions that we all experience—joy, despair, grief, longing, lust—can easily become abstractions on the page. As a writer, you may feel overwhelmed by trying to re-create these emotions. The result can be a string of clichés or flat stereotypes that allow the reader to skate off the surface of your prose without really experiencing what it is you want to express.

Sentiment in literature strives for the delicate and authentic expression of feelings and emotions in such a way that it moves the reader to a new or fuller understanding of an emotion or experience—of what it is to be human. Sentimentality, on the other hand, is extravagant, excessive, and affected. Sentimentality is predictable and contrived.

(continued)

Revision Tips and Strategies *(continued)*

Think about the difference between drama and melodrama. Good drama strives to tell a serious story, to show a dramatic presentation of characters and events that leads to a particular emotional effect that feels authentic to the reader. Good drama is about creativity, individuality, a way of seeing and understanding the world in a new way. Melodrama, on the other hand, is marked by simple and exaggerated emotions and stereotypical characters. The emotion is predictable and histrionic, calculated in its effect.

How do writers avoid sentimentality? First of all, do your homework. Through research, interviews, freewriting, dream work, or simple reflection, investigate the feelings and experiences you are writing about. Then reveal and illuminate these experiences through detail and description rather than labels. Instead of writing, "Mary felt sad," show Mary's experience through all the details, obvious and subtle, that make the way she looks, the way she feels, the way she talks expressive and unique. Let the reader come to the conclusion that Mary is sad. And remember that writing is often most powerful when emotions are implied or understated rather than laid out plainly.

Past or Present Tense?

Should you write the events of your life as if they happened in the past, or as if they are happening in the present? Using the present tense lends a sense of immediacy to your writing and can allow your reader to enter more fully into the story and experience the thoughts and feelings of the character. Using the past tense, however, can create a more adult perspective on the events you describe and contribute to the reflective or contemplative aspect of your voice and style. Writing in the past tense may seem easier, but the pitfall is that you can inadvertently create a large gap between the reader and the story. Readers may feel as if they're viewing the story through a long telescope. The danger of using the present tense, however, is that the voice may seem too innocent or childish, or the perspective of the character too narrow and confined.

Experiment with both past and present tense to discover which one intuitively feels most comfortable and accurate for your story. Keep the tense consistent, unless you have a good reason for switching and you provide the reader with adequate transitions. Unintentionally slipping between past and present tense can be more than confusing to the reader; it can feel like being a backseat passenger in a car that is thrust back and forth into forward and reverse.

The Naked Truth about Commas

Did you ever hear the rule that you should use a comma whenever you pause to take a breath? Forget that rule. Commas aren't nearly that mysterious. There are very specific rules regarding when to put a comma in and when to take a comma out. The same holds true for colons, semicolons, dashes, periods, and ellipses. And what about dangling modifiers and coordinating conjunctions? Do you have to know about those, too?

Learning about punctuation and grammar as a writer is like learning traffic signs before getting behind the wheel of a car. There's very little mystery to a stop sign or a semicolon. But a good driver knows much more than what a stop sign means; she can negotiate the curves of a steep hillside road with grace and style and make driving an art. Good style—creative style—begins with an understanding of how language works on the most intimate level. You may have been an avid reader since the age of five but don't rely on guessing or intuition. Take a grammar class. Get a good stylebook (and sleep with it under your pillow). Browse through a copy of Fowler's *Modern English Usage*. Do your editing at the library and dip into the *Oxford English Dictionary* for inspiration on a word or phrase. Always have a good thesaurus on hand (and don't rely strictly on your computer's thesaurus).

You're an artist. Understand your tools. Remember the old advice about knowing the rules before you can break them? It's true.

Chapter 2
The Personal Essay

Introduction

Writing is always a journey, for the writer and the reader, and no other literary form is quite so rewarding in this respect as the personal essay. This form of creative nonfiction offers the reader a virtual window into the heart, mind, and soul of the writer. Conversational and relatively informal in tone, the personal essay establishes a connection and intimacy that takes the reader into the inner life and psyche of the writer. The structure of this type of essay usually follows the path of the author's thoughts, feelings, and considerations, culminating in a moment of epiphany (or at least a hint of one). The writer is acutely conscious of the reader and of having an audience that is an active part of the intellectual and emotional process. Throughout the essay, the writer is deliberately and artfully engaging in a dialogue with the reader and with the self. As such, the personal essay can be one of the most intellectually and emotionally rigorous forms of writing.

As with the field of creative nonfiction itself, the personal essay is not a new form. The essays of Michel Montaigne, Ralph Waldo Emerson, Henry David Thoreau, and Virginia Woolf—just to name a few—have all had a significant impact on the literary landscape. But the way in which writers and readers think about the personal essay is always in flux. Today, essays are experimental in structure and speculative, personal, and even dramatic in tone. Like stories, essays can follow a narrative arc involving tension, climax, and denouement, or they can take a more leisurely excursion toward a revelation that only becomes clear near the end of the essay. An essay might include anecdotes or digressions that lead eventually to the heart or kernel of the piece but don't necessarily follow a linear, chronological, or logical narrative line. The voice of the author and tone of the piece overall act as a lens, reflecting the broader world into the writer's inner life, and as readers we learn to see and understand the world in a different way as a result of the process.

Part of the reason we think differently about the personal essay today is that it has become a significant part of our culture and media in ways that could not have been anticipated by writers like Thoreau or Emerson. Andy Rooney's short pieces on the television show *60 Minutes* led to the development of similar programs on National Public Radio and many of the major television networks. Magazines and literary journals began to publish essays in greater quantity, with publications such as *The New Yorker, Harper's,* and the *Atlantic Monthly* regularly publishing high-quality personal essays to an enthusiastic readership. Online journals such as *Salon* and *Slate* provided a new and exciting format for the personal essay that often involved live commentary from readers. (Check the end of the book for a full list of magazines and journals). The subject of the personal essay broadened and moved beyond the more formal and conventional political or philosophical arena to embrace a wide variety of subjects and incorporate a more flexible structure and personal tone. The advent of bare-your-soul talk shows and "reality" television removed many of the conventional social and cultural taboos about what subjects we can or should speak about in public. The personal essay has become an important barometer of how our personal lives reflect greater political and cultural issues.

The downside of this may be what some critics call the "confessional" aspect of personal essays. The word *confessional* carries many different connotations, some of them pejorative. Just like other types of creative nonfiction, an essay may err on the side of sentimentality or melodrama. The author may, wittingly or unwittingly, reveal aspects of himself or herself that can appear narcissistic, egotistical, or even self-pitying. But this is not good writing, in this genre or any other genre. A good essayist takes the reader on a journey, defining and commenting upon a real-life experience or observation in a detailed and insightful manner that leads to a broader understanding of life and a greater sense of meaning or self-fulfillment. The responsibility of the writer lies in showing a connection or intersection of personal experience with the larger world. This is accomplished through careful detail, sensory description, and reflection. As a writer, it's important to give yourself permission to write about aspects of your life that seem deeply personal and be willing to engage social and cultural issues that may—in the moment, anyway—seem too big to take on. Your perceptions and opinions matter. Do people want to read what you have to say? Yes. But you bear a responsibility to write well and clearly, to do your research (both "internal"—in your own heart and mind—and "external," through investigative research), and to maintain an honest and ethical approach.

Choosing a subject for your personal essay can be daunting. "The challenge of this assignment," one student writes, "is to pick the right subject or event. Something that makes me turn inward and makes me think about who I am as a person. I have to find something that is significant to me, but something I can write about in detail." Think about your life experiences and what events have been turning points for you. You don't necessarily have to go beyond the ordinary, the everyday. Often the best subject matter is in your own back yard.

Writing a personal essay requires experience, observation, insight, intuition, and deep reflection. It requires a willingness to fully drop the mask or veil that often exists in other forms of literature (such as poetry or fiction) between the reader and writer, and present yourself on the page in an honest and forthright manner. It requires you to think about your life and your experiences, and consider who you are as a writer and as a person. What do you have to say that might have relevance or meaning for other people? Lucid thinking translates into lucid prose; a fresh, honest tone will connect you to your reader through a bond of intimacy and trust. You don't have to be anyone other than yourself. You don't have to be fancy. Remember that beauty in language often comes through clarity and simplicity.

Readings with Discussion Questions

Naomi Shihab Nye
Thank You in Arabic

Born in St. Louis, Missouri to a Palestinian father and an American mother of German and Swiss descent, Naomi Shihab Nye incorporates mixed cultural elements into her work. In addition to a childhood spent in St. Louis, Nye spent a year in Jerusalem, where she attended a year of high school before her family returned to the United States to settle in San Antonio, Texas. Among her awards are the Voertman Poetry Prize in 1980 for Different Ways to Pray *and in 1982 for* Hugging the Jukebox, *the Jane Addams Children's Book Award in 1994 for* Habibi, *and numerous American Library Association notable book citations. Her most recent book of poetry is* 19 Varieties of Gazelle: Poems of the Middle East.

Shortly after my mother discovered my brother had been pitching his Vitamin C tablets behind the stove for years, we left the country. Her sharp alert, "Now the truth be known!" startled us at the breakfast table as she poked into the dim crevice with the nozzle of her vacuum. We could hear the pills go click, click, up the long tube.

My brother, an obedient child, a bright-eyed, dark-skinned charmer who scored high on all his tests and trilled a boy's sweet soprano, stared down at his oatmeal. Four years younger than I, he was also the youngest and smallest in his class. Somehow he maintained an intelligence and dignity more notable than that of his older, larger companions, and the pills episode, really, was a pleasant surprise to me.

Naomi Shihab Nye, "Thank You in Arabic" from *Never in a Hurry: Essays on People and Places*. University of South Carolina Press, 1996, pp. 32–47. Reprinted by permission.

Companions in mischief are not to be underestimated, especially when everything else in your life is about to change.

We sold everything we had and left the country. The move had been brewing for months. We took a few suitcases each. My mother cried when the piano went. I wished we could have saved it. My brother and I had sung so many classics over its keyboard— "Look for the Silver Lining" and "Angels We Have Heard on High"— that it would have been nice to return to a year later, when we came straggling back. I sold my life-size doll and my toy sewing machine. I begged my mother to save her red stove for me, so I could have it when I grew up—no one else we knew had a red stove. So my mother asked some friends to save it for me in their barn.

Our parents had closed their imported-gifts stores, and our father had dropped out of ministerial school. He had attended the Unity School of Christianity for a few years, but decided not to become a minister after all. We were relieved, having felt like impostors the whole time he was enrolled. He wasn't even a Christian, to begin with, but a gently non-practicing Muslim. He didn't do anything like fasting or getting down on his knees five times a day. Our mother had given up the stern glare of her Lutheran ancestors, raising my brother and me in the Vedanta Society of St. Louis. When anyone asked what we were, I said, "Hindu." We had a Swami, and sandalwood incense. It was over our heads, but we liked it and didn't feel very attracted to the idea of churches and collection baskets and chatty parish good-will.

Now and then, just to keep things balanced, we attended the Unity Sunday School. My teacher said I was lucky my father came from the same place Jesus came from. It was a passport to notoriety. She invited me to bring artifacts for Show and Tell. I wrapped a red and white *keffiyah* around my friend Jimmy's curly blond head while the girls in lacy socks giggled behind their hands. I told about my father coming to America from Palestine on the boat and throwing his old country clothes overboard before docking at Ellis Island. I felt relieved he'd kept a few things, like the *keffiyah* and its black braided band. Secretly it made me mad to have lost the blue pants from Jericho with the wide cuffs he told us about.

I enjoyed standing in front of the group talking about my father's homeland. Stories felt like elastic bands that could stretch and stretch. Big fans purred inside their metal shells. I held up a string of olive wood camels. I didn't tell our teacher about the Vedanta Society. We were growing up ecumenical, though I wouldn't know that word till a long time later in college. One night I heard my father say to my mother in the next room, "Do you think they'll be confused when they grow up?" and knew he was talking about us. My mother, bless her, knew we wouldn't be. She said, "At least we're giving them a choice." I didn't know then that more clearly than all the stories of Jesus, I'd remember the way our Hindu swami said a single word three times, "Shanti, shanti, shanti"—peace, peace, peace.

Our father was an excellent speaker—he stood behind pulpits and podiums easily, delivering gracious lectures on "The Holy Land" and "The

Palestinian Question." He was much in demand during the Christmas season. I think that's how he had fallen into the ministerial swoon. While he spoke, my brother and I hovered toward the backs of the auditoriums, eyeing the tables of canapés and tiny tarts, slipping a few into our mouths or pockets.

What next? Our lives were entering a new chapter, but I didn't know its title yet.

We had never met our Palestinian grandmother, Sitti Khadra, or seen Jerusalem, where our father had grown up, or followed the rocky, narrow alleyways of the Via Dolorosa, or eaten an olive in its own neighborhood. Our mother hadn't either. The Arabic customs we knew had been filtered through the fine net of folktales. We did not speak Arabic, though the lilt of the language was familiar to us—our father's endearments, his musical blessings before meals—but that language had never lived in our mouths.

And that's where we were going, to Jerusalem. We shipped our car, a wide golden Impala the exact color of a cigarette filter, over on a boat. We would meet up with it later.

The first plane flight of my whole life was the night flight out of New York City across the ocean. I was fourteen years old. Every glittering light in every skyscraper looked like a period at the end of the sentence. Good-bye, our lives.

We stopped in Portugal for a few weeks. We were making a gradual transition. We stopped in Spain and Italy and Egypt, where the pyramids shocked me by sitting right on the edge of the giant city of Cairo, not way out in the desert as I had imagined them. While we waited for our baggage to clear customs, I stared at six tall African men in brilliantly patterned dashikis negotiating with an Egyptian customs agent and realized I did not even know how to say "Thank you" in Arabic. How was this possible? The most elemental and important of human phrases in my father's own tongue had evaded me till now. I tugged on his sleeve, but he was busy with visas and passports. "Daddy," I said. "Daddy, I have to know. Daddy, tell me. Daddy, why didn't we ever *learn?*" An African man adjusted his turban. Always thereafter, the word *shookrun*, so simple, with a little roll in the middle, would conjure up the vast African baggage, the brown boxes looped and looped in African twine.

We stayed one or two nights at the old Shepherd's Hotel downtown, but couldn't sleep because of the heat and honking traffic beneath our windows. So our father moved us to the famous Mena House Hotel next to the pyramids. We rode camels for the first time, and our mother received a dozen blood-red roses at her hotel room from a rug vendor who apparently liked her pale brown ponytail. The belly dancer at the hotel restaurant twined a gauzy pink scarf around my brother's astonished ten-year-old head as he tapped his knee in time to her music. She bobbled her giant cleavage under his nose, huge bosoms prickled by sequins and sweat.

Back in our rooms, we laughed until we fell asleep. Later that night, my brother and I both awakened burning with fever and deeply nauseated, though nobody ever threw up. We were so sick that a doctor hung a Quarantine sign in Arabic and English on our hotel room door the next day. Did he know something we didn't know? I kept waiting to hear that we had malaria or typhoid, but no dramatic disease was ever mentioned. We lay in bed for a week. The aged doctor tripped over my suitcase every time he entered to take our temperatures. We smothered our laughter. "Shookrun," I would say. But as soon as he left, to my brother, "I feel bad. How do you feel?"

"I feel really, really bad."

"I think I'm dying."

"I think I'm already dead."

At night we heard the sound and lights show from the pyramids drifting across the desert air to our windows. We felt our lives stretching out across thousands of miles. The Pharaohs stomped noisily through my head and churning belly. We had eaten spaghetti in the restaurant. I would not be able to eat spaghetti again for years.

Finally, finally, we appeared in the restaurant again, thin and weakly smiling, and ordered the famous Mena House *shorraba*, lentil soup, as my brother nervously scanned the room for the belly dancer. Maybe she wouldn't recognize him now.

In those days Jerusalem, which was then a divided city, had an operating airport on the Jordanian side. My brother and I remember flying in upside down, or in a plane dramatically tipped, but it may have been the effect of our medicine. The land reminded us of a dropped canvas, graceful brown hillocks and green patches. Small and provincial, the airport had just two runways, and the first thing I observed as we climbed down slowly from the stuffy plane was all my underwear strewn across one of them. There were my flowered cotton briefs and my pink panties and my slightly embarrassing raggedy ones and my extra training bra, alive and visible in the breeze. Somehow my suitcase had popped open in the hold and dropped its contents the minute the men pried open the cargo door. So the first thing I did on the home soil of my father was recollect my underwear, down on my knees, the posture of prayer over that ancient holy land.

Our relatives came to see us at a hotel. Our grandmother was very short. She wore a long, thickly embroidered Palestinian dress, had a musical, high-pitched voice and a low, guttural laugh. She kept touching our heads and faces as if she couldn't believe we were there. I had not yet fallen in love with her. Sometimes you don't fall in love with people immediately, even if they're your own grandmother. Everyone seemed to think we were all too thin.

We moved into a second-story flat in a stone house eight miles north of the city, among fields and white stones and wandering sheep. My brother was enrolled in the Friends Girls School and I was enrolled in the Friends Boys School in the town of Ramallah a few miles farther north—it seemed a little confused. But the Girls School offered grades one through eight in English and high school continued at the Boys School. Most local girls went to Arabic-speaking schools after eighth grade.

I was a freshman, one of seven girl students among two hundred boys, which would cause me problems later. I was called in from the schoolyard at lunchtime, to the office of our counselor who wore shoes so pointed and tight her feet bulged out pinkly on top.

"You will not be talking to them anymore," she said. She rapped on the desk with a pencil for emphasis.

"To whom?"

"All the boy students at this institution. It is inappropriate behavior. From now on, you will only speak with the girls."

"But there are only six other girls! And I only like one of them!" My friend was Anna, from Italy, whose father ran a small factory that made matches. I'd visited it once with her. It felt risky to walk the aisles among a million filled matchboxes. Later we visited the factory that made olive oil soaps and stacked them in giant pyramids to dry.

"No, thank you," I said. "It's ridiculous to say that girls should only talk to girls. Did I say anything bad to a boy? Did anyone say anything bad to me? They're my friends. They're like my brothers. I won't do it, that's all."

The counselor conferred with the headmaster and they called a taxi. I was sent home with a note requesting that I transfer to a different school. The charge: insolence. My mother, startled to see me home early and on my own, stared out the window when I told her.

My brother came home from his school as usual, full of whistling and notebooks. "Did anyone tell you not to talk to girls?" I asked him. He looked at me as if I'd gone goofy. He was too young to know the troubles of the world. He couldn't even imagine them.

"You know what I've been thinking about?" he said. "A piece of cake. That puffy white layered cake with icing like they have at birthday parties in the United States. Wouldn't that taste good right now?" Our mother said she was thinking about mayonnaise. You couldn't get it in Jerusalem. She'd tried to make it and it didn't work. I felt too gloomy to talk about food.

My brother said, "Let's go let Abu Miriam's chickens out." That's what we always did when we felt sad. We let our fussy landlord's red and white chickens loose to flap around the yard happily, puffing their wings. Even when Abu Miriam shouted and waggled his cane and his wife waved a dishtowel, we knew the chickens were thanking us.

My father went with me to the St. Tarkmanchatz Armenian School, a solemnly ancient stone school tucked deep into the Armenian Quarter of the Old City of Jerusalem. It was another world in there. He had already called them on the telephone and tried to enroll me, though they didn't want to. Their school was for Armenian students only, kindergarten through twelfth grade. Classes were taught in three languages, Armenian, Arabic and English, which was why I needed to go there. Although most Arab students at other schools were learning English, I needed a school where classes were actually taught in English—otherwise I would have been staring out the windows triple the usual amount.

The head priest wore a long robe and a tall cone-shaped hat. He said, "Excuse me, please, but your daughter, she is not an Armenian, even a small amount?"

"Not at all," said my father. "But in case you didn't know, there is a stipulation in the educational code books of this city that says no student may be rejected solely on the basis of ethnic background, and if you don't accept her, we will alert the proper authorities."

They took me. But the principal wasn't happy about it. The students, however, seemed glad to have a new face to look at. Everyone's name ended in *-ian*, the beautiful, musical Armenian ending—Boghossian, Minassian, Kevorkian, Rostomian. My new classmates started calling me Shihabian. We wore uniforms, navy blue pleated skirts for the girls, white shirts, and navy sweaters. I waited during the lessons for the English to come around, as if it were a channel on television. While my friends were on the other channels, I scribbled poems in the margins of my pages, read library books, and wrote a lot of letters filled with exclamation points. All the other students knew three languages with three entirely different alphabets. How could they carry so much in their heads? I felt humbled by my ignorance. Again and again and again. One day I felt so frustrated in our physics class—still another language—that I pitched my book out the open window. The professor made me go collect it. All the pages had let loose at the seams and were flapping into the gutters along with the white wrappers of sandwiches.

Every week the girls had a hands-and-fingernails check. We had to keep our nails clean and trim, and couldn't wear any rings. Some of my new friends would invite me home for lunch with them, since we had an hour-and-a-half break and I lived too far to go to my own house.

Their houses were a thousand years old, clustered beehive fashion behind ancient walls, stacked and curled and tilting and dark, filled with pictures of unsmiling relatives and small white cloths dangling crocheted edges. We ate spinach pies and white cheese. We dipped our bread in olive oil, as the Arabs did. We ate small sesame cakes, our mouths full of crumbles. They taught me to say, "I love you" in Armenian, which sounded like *yes-kay-see-goo-see-rem*. I felt I had left my old life entirely.

Every afternoon I went down to the basement of the school where the kindergarten class was having an Arabic lesson. Their desks were pint-sized, their full white smocks tied around their necks. I stuffed my fourteen-year-old self in beside them. They had rosy cheeks and shy smiles. They must have thought I was a very slow learner.

More than any of the lessons, I remember the way the teacher rapped the backs of their hands with his ruler when they made a mistake. Their little faces puffed up with quiet tears. This pained me so terribly I forgot all my words. When it was my turn to go to the blackboard and write in Arabic, my hand shook. The kindergarten students whispered hints to me from the front row, but I couldn't understand them. We learned horribly useless phrases: "Please hand me the bellows for my fire." I wanted words simple as tools, simple as *food* and *yesterday* and *dreams*. The teacher never rapped my hand, especially after I wrote a letter to the city newspaper, which my father edited, protesting such harsh treatment of young learners. I wished I had known how to talk to those little ones, but they were just beginning their English studies and didn't speak much yet. They were at the same place in their English that I was in my Arabic.

From the high windows of St. Tarkmanchatz, we could look out over the Old City, the roofs and flapping laundry and television antennas, the pilgrims and churches and mosques, the olive-wood prayer beads and fragrant *falafel* lunch stands, the intricate interweaving of cultures and prayers and songs and holidays. We saw the barbed wire separating Jordan from Israel then, the bleak, uninhabited strip of no-man's land reminding me how little education saved us after all. People who had differing ideas still came to blows, imagining fighting could solve things. Staring out over the quiet roofs of afternoon, it seemed so foolish to me. I asked my friends what they thought about it and they shrugged.

"It doesn't matter what we think about it. It just keeps happening. It happened in Armenia too, you know. Really, really bad in Armenia. And who talks about it in the world news now? It happens everywhere. It happens in *your* country one by one, yes? Murders and guns. What can we do?"

Sometimes after school, my brother and I walked up the road that led past the crowded refugee camp of Palestinians who owned even less than our modest relatives did in the village. The kids were stacking stones in empty tin cans and shaking them. We waved our hands and they covered their mouths and laughed. We wore our beat-up American tennis shoes and our old sweatshirts and talked about everything we wanted to do and everywhere else we wished we could go.

"I want to go back to Egypt," my brother said. "I sort of feel like I missed it. Spending all that time in bed instead of exploring—what a waste."

"I want to go to Greece," I said. "I want to play a violin in a symphony orchestra in Austria." We made up things. I wanted to go back to the United States most of all. Suddenly I felt like a patriotic citizen. One of my friends, Sylvie Markarian, had just been shipped off to Damascus, Syria, to marry a man who was fifty years old, a widower. Sylvie was exactly my age—we had turned fifteen two days apart. She had never met her future husband before. "Tell your parents no thank you," I urged her. I thought this was the most revolting thing I had ever heard of. "Tell them you *refuse*."

Sylvie's eyes were liquid, swirling brown. I could not see clear to the bottom of them.

"You don't understand," she told me. "In United States you say no. We don't say no. We have to follow someone's wishes. This is the wish of my father. Me, I am scared. I never slept away from my mother before. But I have no choice. I am going because they tell me to go." She was sobbing, sobbing on my shoulder. And I was stroking her long, soft hair. After that, I carried two fists inside, one for Sylvie and one for me.

Most weekends my family went to the village to sit with the relatives. We sat and sat and sat. We sat in big rooms and little rooms, in circles, on chairs or on woven mats or brightly-covered mattresses piled on the floor. People came in and out to greet my family. Sometimes even donkeys and chickens came in and out. We were like movie stars or dignitaries. They never seemed to get tired of us.

My father translated the more interesting tidbits of conversation, the funny stories my grandmother told. She talked about angels and food and money and people and politics and gossip and old memories from my father's childhood, before he emigrated away from her. She wanted to make sure we were going to stick around forever, which made me feel very nervous. We ate from mountains of rice and eggplant on large silver trays—they gave us plates of our own since it was not our custom to eat from the same plate as other people. We ripped the giant wheels of bread into triangles. Shepherds passed through town with their flocks of sheep and goats, their long canes and cloaks, straight out of the Bible. My brother and I trailed them to the edge of the village, past the lentil fields to the green meadows studded with stones, while the shepherds pretended we weren't there. I think they liked to be alone, unnoticed. The sheep had differently colored dyed bottoms, so shepherds could tell their flocks apart.

During these long, slow, smoke-stained weekends—the men still smoked cigarettes a lot in those days, and the old *taboon*, my family's mounded bread-oven, puffed billowy clouds outside the door—my crying jags began. I cried without any warning, even in the middle of a meal. My crying was usually noiseless but dramatically wet—streams of tears pouring down my cheeks, onto my collar or the back of my hand.

Everything grew quiet.

Someone always asked in Arabic, "What is wrong? Are you sick? Do you wish to lie down?"

My father made valiant excuses in the beginning. "She's overtired," he said. "She has a headache. She is missing her friend who moved to Syria. She is feeling homesick."

My brother stared at me as if I had just landed from Planet X.

Worst was our drive to school every morning, when our car came over the rise in the highway and all Jerusalem lay sprawled before us in its golden, stony splendor pockmarked with olive trees and automobiles. Even the air above the city had a thick, religious texture, as if it were a shining brocade filled with broody incense. I cried hardest then. All those hours tied up in school lay just ahead. My father pulled over and talked to me. He sighed. He kept his hands on the steering wheel even when the car was stopped and said, "Someday, I promise you, you will look back on this period in your life and have no idea what made you so unhappy here."

"I want to go home." It became my anthem. "This place depresses me. It weighs too much. I hate all these old stones that everybody keeps kissing. I'm sick of pilgrims. They act so pious and pure. And I hate the way people stare at me here." Already I'd been involved in two street skirmishes with boys who stared too hard and long, clucking with their tongues. I'd socked one in the jaw and he socked me back. I hit the other one straight in the face with my purse.

"You could be happy here if you tried harder," my father said. "Don't compare it to the United States all the time. Don't pretend the United States is perfect. And look at your brother—he's not having any problems!"

"My brother is eleven years old."

I had crossed the boundary from uncomplicated childhood where happiness was a good ball and a horde of candy-coated Jordan almonds.

One problem was that I had fallen in love with four different boys who all played in the same band. Two of them were even twins. I never quite described it to my parents, but I wrote reams and reams of notes about it on loose-leaf paper that I kept under my sweaters in my closet.

Such new energy made me feel reckless. I gave things away. I gave away my necklace and a whole box of shortbread cookies that my mother had been saving. I gave my extra shoes away to the gypsies. One night when the gypsies camped in a field down the road from our house, I thought about their mounds of white goat cheese lined up on skins in front of their tents, and the wild *oud* music they played deep into the black belly of the night, and I wanted to go sit around their fire. Maybe they could use some shoes.

I packed a sack of old loafers that I rarely wore and walked with my family down the road. The gypsy mothers stared into my shoes curiously. They took them into their tents. Maybe they would use them as vases or drawers. We sat with small glasses of hot, sweet tea until a girl bellowed from deep in her throat, threw back her head, and began dancing. A long bow thrummed across the strings. The girl circled the fire, tapping and clicking, trilling a long musical wail from deep in her throat. My brother looked nervous. He was remembering the belly dancer in Egypt, and her scarf. I felt invisible. I was pretending to be a gypsy. My father stared at me. Didn't I recognize the exquisite oddity of my own life when I sat right in the middle of it? Didn't I feel lucky to be here? Well, yes I did. But sometimes it was hard to be lucky.

When we left Jerusalem, we left quickly. Left our beds in our rooms and our car in the driveway. Left in a plane, not sure where we were going. The rumbles of fighting with Israel had been growing louder and louder. In the barbed-wire no-man's land visible from the windows of our house, guns cracked loudly in the middle of the night. We lived right near the edge. My father heard disturbing rumors at the newspaper that would soon grow into the infamous Six-Day War of 1967. We were in England by then, drinking tea from thin china cups and scanning the newspapers. Bombs were blowing up in Jerusalem. We worried about the village. We worried about my grandmother's dreams, which had been getting worse and worse, she'd told us. We worried about the house we'd left, and the chickens, and the children at the refugee camp. But there was nothing we could do except keep talking about it all.

My parents didn't want to go back to Missouri because they'd already said good-bye to everyone there. They thought we might try a different part of the country. They weighed the virtues of various states. Texas was big and warm. After a chilly year crowded around the small gas heaters we used in Jerusalem, a warm place sounded appealing. In roomy Texas, my parents bought the first house they looked at. My father walked into the city newspaper and said, "Any jobs open around here?"

I burst out crying when I entered a grocery store—so many different kinds of bread.

A letter on thin blue airmail paper reached me months later, written by my classmate, the bass player in my favorite Jerusalem band. "Since you left," he said, "your empty desk reminds me of a snake ready to strike. I am afraid to look at it. I hope you are having a better time than we are."

Of course I was, and I wasn't. *Home* had grown different forever. *Home* had doubled. Back *home* again in my own country, it seemed impossible to forget the place we had just left: the piercing call of the *muezzin* from the mosque at prayer time, the dusky green tint of the olive groves, the sharp, cold air that smelled as deep and old as my grandmother's white sheets flapping from the line on her roof. What story hadn't she finished?

Our father used to tell us that when he was little, the sky over Jerusalem crackled with meteors and shooting stars almost every night. They streaked and flashed, igniting the dark. Some had long golden tails. For a few seconds, you could see their whole swooping trails lit up. Our father and his brothers slept on the roof to watch the sky. "There were so many of them, we didn't even call out every time we saw one."

During our year in Jerusalem, my brother and I kept our eyes cast upwards whenever we were outside at night, but the stars were different since our father was a boy. Now the sky seemed too orderly, stuck in place. The stars had learned where they belonged. Only people on the ground kept changing.

Questions for Discussion

1. Nye writes of her grandmother: "I had not yet fallen in love with her. Sometimes you don't fall in love with people immediately, even if they're your own grandmother." What does this reveal about the narrator of the story? About the situation in which she finds herself?

2. Choosing an appropriate, provocative title for an essay—one that hints at the heart of the essay without giving too much away—is often difficult. What is the significance of the title of this essay?

3. Naomi Shihab Nye writes poetry in addition to prose. What are some of the more lyrical aspects of her prose? Identify key metaphorical images.

Molly Ivins
Texas Women: True Grit and All the Rest

Columnist and Texas liberal Molly Ivins is known for her sharp wit and insight as a political commentator. She has worked as a reporter for the Chronicle, Houston, Texas; *the* Star Tribune, Minneapolis, Minnesota; *and the* Texas Observer, Austin; *and was the Rocky Mountain bureau chief in Denver, Colorado from 1977 to 1980. Since 1980, Ivins has been a columnist for the* Dallas Times Herald *and a regular magazine contributor. Her brand of commentary reached an even larger audience when she published her first book, a collection of essays and articles called* Molly Ivins Can't Say That, Can She? *in 1991.*

They used to say that Texas was hell on women and horses—I don't know why they stopped. Surely not because much of the citizenry has had its consciousness raised, as they say in the jargon of the women's movement, on the issue of sexism. Just a few months ago one of our state representatives felt moved to compare women and horses—it was the similarity he wanted to emphasize. Of course some Texas legislator can be found to say any fool thing, but this guy's comments met with general agreement from his colleagues. One can always dismiss the entire Legislature as a particularly deplorable set of Texans, but as Sen. Carl Parker observes, if you took all the fools out of the Lege, it wouldn't be a representative body anymore.

I should confess that I've always been more of an observer than a participant in Texas Womanhood: the spirit was willing but I was declared ineligible on grounds of size early. You can't be six feet tall and cute, both. I think I was first named captain of the basketball team when I was four and that's what I've been ever since. I spent my girlhood as a Clydesdale among thoroughbreds. I clopped along amongst them cheerfully, admiring their grace, but the strange training rituals they went through left me secretly relieved that no one would ever expect me to step on a racetrack. I think it is quite possible to grow up in Texas as an utter failure in flirting, gentility, cheerleading, sexpottery, and manipulation and still be without any permanent scars. Except one. We'd all rather be blonde.

Please understand I'm not whining when I point out that Texas sexism is of an especially rank and noxious variety—this is more a Texas brag. It is my belief that it is virulence of Texas sexism that accounts for the strength of Texas women. It's what we have to overcome that makes us formidable survivors, say I with some complacency.

As has been noted elsewhere, there are several strains of Texan culture: They are all rotten for women. There is the Southern belle nonsense of our Confederate heritage, that little-woman-on-a-pedestal, flirtatious, "you're so cute when you're mad," Scarlett O'Hara myth that leads, quite naturally, to the equally pernicious legend of the Iron Magnolia. Then there's the machismo of our Latin heritage, which affects not only our Chicana sisters, but has been integrated into Texas culture quite as thoroughly as barbecue, rodeo, and Tex-Mex food.

Next up is the pervasive good-ol'-boyism of the *Redneckus texensis*, that remarkable tribe that has made the pickup truck with the gun rack across the back window and the beer cans flying out the window a synonym for Texans worldwide. Country music is a good place to investigate and find reflected the attitudes of kickers toward women (never ask what a kicker kicks). It's your basic, familiar virgin/whore dichotomy—either your "Good-Hearted Woman" or "Your Cheatin' Heart," with the emphasis on the honky-tonk angels. Nor is the jock idolatry that permeates the state helpful to our gender: Football is not a game here, it's a matter of blood and death. Woman's role in the state's national game is limited, significantly, to cheerleading. In this regard, I can say with great confidence that Texas changeth not—the hopelessly intense, heartbreaking longing with which most Texas girls still want to be cheerleader can be observed at every high school, every September.*

Last but not least in the litany of cultures that help make the lives of Texas women so challenging is the legacy of the frontier—not the frontier that Texas women lived on, but the one John Wayne lived on. Anyone who knows the real history of the frontier knows it is a saga of the strength of women. They worked as hard as men, they fought as hard as men, they suffered as much as men. But in the cowboy movies that most contemporary

---

*In February 1991, a woman in Channelview, Texas, was indicted for plotting the murder of the mother of her own daughter's chief rival for the cheerleading squad.

Texans grew up on, the big, strong man always protects "the little lady" or "the gals" from whatever peril threatens. Such nonsense. Mary Ann Goodnight was often left alone at the JA Ranch near the Palo Duro Canyon. One day in 1877, a cowboy rode into her camp with three chickens in a sack as a present for her. He naturally expected her to cook and eat the fowl, but Goodnight kept them as pets. She wrote in her diary, "No one can ever know how much company they were." Life for farm and ranch wives didn't improve much over the next 100 years. Ruth White raised nine children on a farm near High, Texas, in the 1920s and thirties. She used to say, "Everything on this farm is either hungry or heavy."

All of these strains lead to a form of sexism so deeply ingrained in the culture that it's often difficult to distinguish the disgusting from the outrageous or the offensive from the amusing. One not infrequently sees cars or trucks sporting the bumper sticker HAVE FUN—BEAT THE HELL OUT OF SOMEONE YOU LOVE. Another is: IF YOU LOVE SOMETHING, SET IT FREE. IF IT DOESN'T COME BACK, TRACK IT DOWN AND KILL IT. I once heard a legislator order a lobbyist, "Get me two sweathogs for tonight." At a benefit "roast" for the battered women's shelter in El Paso early in 1985, a couple of the male politicians told rape jokes to amuse the crowd. Most Texas sexism is not intended to be offensive—it's entirely unconscious. A colleague of mine was touring the new death chamber in Huntsville last year with a group of other reporters. Their guide called to warn those inside they were coming through, saying, "I'm coming over with eight reporters and one woman." Stuff like that happens to you four or five times a day for long enough, it will wear you down some.

Other forms of the phenomenon are, of course, less delightsome. Women everywhere are victims of violence with depressing regularity. Texas is a more violent place than most of the rest of America, for reasons having to do with guns, machismo, frontier traditions, and the heterogeneous population. While the law theoretically applies to male and female alike, by unspoken convention, a man who offs his wife or girlfriend is seldom charged with murder one: we wind up filed under the misnomer manslaughter.

That's the bad news for Texas women—the good news is that all this adversity has certainly made us a bodacious bunch of overcomers. And rather pleasant as a group, I always think, since having a sense of humor about men is not a luxury here; it's a necessity. The feminists often carry on about the importance of role models and how little girls need positive role models. When I was a kid, my choice of Texas role models went from Ma Ferguson to the Kilgore Rangerettes. Of course I wanted to be a Rangerette: Ever seen a picture of Ma? Not that we haven't got real women heroes, of course, just that we were never taught anything about them. You used to have to take Texas history two or three times in order to get a high school diploma in this state: The Yellow Rose of Texas and Belle Starr were the only women in our history books. Kaye Northcott notes that all the big cities in the state have men's last names—Houston, Austin, Dallas. All women got was some small towns called after their front names: Alice, Electra, Marfa. This is probably because, as Eleanor Brackenridge of San Antonio (1837–1924) so elegantly put it, "Foolish modesty lags behind while brazen impudence goes forth and eats the pudding." Brackenridge did her part to correct the lag by founding the Texas Woman Suffrage Association in 1913.

It is astonishing how recently Texas women have achieved equal legal rights. I guess you could say we made steady progress even before we could vote—the state did raise the age of consent for a woman from 7 to 10 in 1890—but it went a little smoother after we got some say in it. Until June 26, 1918, all Texans could vote except "idiots, imbeciles, aliens, the insane and women." The battle over woman's suffrage in Texas was long and fierce. Contempt and ridicule were the favored weapons against women. Women earned the right to vote through years of struggle; the precious victory was not something handed to us by generous men. From that struggle emerged a generation of Texas women whose political skills and leadership abilities have affected Texas politics for decades. Even so, Texas women were not permitted to serve on juries until 1954. As late as 1969, married women did not have full property rights. And until 1972, under Article 1220 of the Texas Penal Code, a man could murder his wife and her lover if he found them "in a compromising position" and get away with it as "justifiable homicide." Women, you understand, did not have equal shooting rights. Although Texas was one of the first states to ratify the Equal Rights Amendment, which has been part of the Texas Constitution since 1972, we continue to work for fairer laws concerning problems such as divorce, rape, child custody, and access to credit.

Texas women are just as divided by race, class, age, and educational level as are other varieties of human beings. There's a pat description of "what every Texas woman wants" that varies a bit from city to city, but the formula that Dallas females have been labeled with goes something like this: "Be a Pi Phi at Texas or SMU, marry a man who'll buy you a house in Highland Park, hold the wedding at Highland Park Methodist (flowers by Kendall Bailey), join the Junior League, send the kids to St. Mark's and Hockaday in the winter and Camps Longhorn and Waldemar in the summer, plus cotillion lessons at the Dallas Country Club, have an unlimited charge account at Neiman's as a birthright but buy almost all your clothes at Highland Park Village from Harold's or the Polo Shop, get your hair done at Paul Neinast's or Lou's and drive a Jeep Wagoneer for carpooling and a Mercedes for fun." There is a kicker equivalent of this scenario that starts, "Every Texas girl's dream is a double-wide in a Lubbock trailer park. . . ." But I personally believe it is unwise ever to be funny at the expense of kicker women. I once met a kicker lady who was wearing a blouse of such a vivid pink you could close your eyes and still see the color; this confection was perked up with some big rhinestone buttons and a lot of ruffles across an impressive bosom. "My," said I, "where did you get that blouse?" She gave me a level look and drawled. "Honey, it come from mah coutouri-ay, Jay Cee Penn-ay." And if that ain't class, you *can* kiss my grits.

To my partisan eye, it seems that Texas women are more animated and friendly than those from, say, Nebraska. I suspect this comes from early training: Girls in Texas high schools are expected to walk through the halls smiling and saying "Hi" to everyone they meet. Being enthusiastic is bred into us, as is a certain amount of obligatory social hypocrisy stemming from the Southern tradition of manners, which does rather tend to emphasize pleasantness more than honesty in social situations. Many Texas women have an odd greeting call—when they haven't seen a good friend for a long time, the first glimpse will provoke the cry, "Oooooooo—honey, how good to see yew again!" It sounds sort of like the "Soooooey, pig" call.

Mostly Texas women are tough in some very fundamental ways. Not unfeminine, nor necessarily unladylike, just tough. It may be possible for a little girl to grow to womanhood in this state entirely sheltered from the rampant sexism all around her—but it's damned difficult. The result is that Texas women tend to know how to cope. We can cope with put-downs and come-ons, with preachers and hustlers, with drunks and cowboys. And when it's all over, if we stick together and work, we'll come out better than the sister who's buried in a grave near Marble Falls under a stone that says, "Rudolph Richter, 1822–1915, and Wife."

Questions for Discussion

1. How would you describe Ivins's style and voice? Copy a page, line by line, in your journal (by hand or on computer). Now try imitating her style.
2. How is this essay structured? Does it move logically from point to point? Would you consider this a persuasive essay?
3. Ivins writes that "having a sense of humor about men is not a luxury here; it's a necessity." That line could likely be extended to her view on life in general. How does humor help Molly Ivins get her point across?

Barry Lopez
The Stone Horse

Barry Holstun Lopez was born in Port Chester, New York but spent most of his first ten years in southern California, where he developed his long-standing affinity for the west coast. His work on subjects of natural history and the environment have taken him to the arctic, the Galapagos Islands, Kenya, Australia, Antarctica, and other remote locales. Lopez has contributed to numerous periodicals, such as Harper's *and*

National Geographic, *as well as authored several books, both fiction and nonfiction, including* Desert Notes: Reflections in the Eye of a Raven *(1976),* Of Wolves and Men *(1978), and* Arctic Dreams: Imagination and Desire in a Northern Landscape. *His many awards include the John Burroughs Medal for distinguished natural history writing in 1979, and an Award in Literature from the American Academy and Institute of Arts and Letters in 1986 for his body of work.*

I

The deserts of southern California, the high, relatively cooler and wetter Mojave and the hotter, dryer Sonoran to the south of it, carry the signatures of many cultures. Prehistoric rock drawings in the Mojave's Coso Range, probably the greatest concentration of petroglyphs in North America, are at least three thousand years old. Big-game-hunting cultures that flourished six or seven thousand years before that are known from broken spear tips, choppers, and burins left scattered along the shores of great Pleistocene lakes, long since evaporated. Weapons and tools discovered at China Lake may be thirty thousand years old; and worked stone from a quarry in the Calico Mountains is, some argue, evidence that human beings were here more than 200,000 years ago.

Because of the long-term stability of such arid environments, much of this prehistoric stone evidence still lies exposed on the ground, accessible to anyone who passes by—the studious, the acquisitive, the indifferent, the merely curious. Archaeologists do not agree on the sequence of cultural history beyond about twelve thousand years ago, but it is clear that these broken bits of chalcedony, chert, and obsidian, like the animal drawings and geometric designs etched on walls of basalt throughout the desert, anchor the earliest threads of human history, the first record of human endeavor here.

Western man did not enter the California desert until the end of the eighteenth century, 250 years after Coronado brought his soldiers into the Zuni pueblos in a bewildered search for the cities of Cibola. The earliest appraisals of the land were cursory, hurried. People traveled *through* it, en route to Santa Fe or the California coastal settlements. Only miners tarried. In 1823 what had been Spain's became Mexico's, and in 1848 what had been Mexico's became America's; but the bare, jagged mountains and dry lake beds, the vast and uniform plains of creosote bush and yucca plants, remained as obscure as the northern Sudan until the end of the nineteenth century.

Before 1940 the tangible evidence of twentieth-century man's passage here consisted of very little—the hard tracery of travel corridors; the widely scattered, relatively insignificant evidence of mining operations; and the fair expanse of irrigated fields at the desert's periphery. In the space of a hundred years or so the wagon roads were paved, railroads were laid down, and canals and high-tension lines were built to bring water and electricity across the desert to Los Angeles from the Colorado River. The dark mouths of gold, talc, and tin mines yawned from the bony flanks of desert ranges. Dust-encrusted chemical plants stood at work on the lonely edges of dry lake beds. And crops of grapes, lettuce, dates, alfalfa, and cotton covered the Coachella and Imperial valleys, north and south of the Salton Sea, and the Palo Verde Valley along the Colorado.

These developments proceeded with little or no awareness of earlier human occupations by cultures that preceded those of the historic Indians—the Mojave, the Chemehuevi, the Quechan. (Extensive irrigation began actually to change the climate of the Sonoran Desert, and human settlements, the railroads, and farming introduced many new, successful plants into the region.)

During World War II, the American military moved into the desert in great force, to train troops and to test equipment. They found the clear weather conducive to year-round flying, the dry air and isolation very attractive. After the war, a complex of training grounds, storage facilities, and gunnery and test ranges was permanently settled on more than three million acres of military reservations. Few perceived the extent or significance of the destruction of the aboriginal sites that took place during tank maneuvers and bombing runs or in the laying out of highways, railroads, mining districts, and irrigated fields. The few who intuited that something like an American Dordogne Valley lay exposed here were (only) amateur archaeologists; even they reasoned that the desert was too vast for any of this to matter.

After World War II, people began moving out of the crowded Los Angeles basin into homes in Lucerne, Apple, and Antelope valleys in the western Mojave. They emigrated as well to a stretch of resort land at the foot of the San Jacinto Mountains that included Palm Springs, and farther out to old railroad and military towns like Twentynine Palms and Barstow. People also began exploring the desert, at first in military-surplus jeeps and then with a variety of all-terrain and off-road vehicles that became available in the 1960s. By the mid-1970s, the number of people using such vehicles for desert recreation had increased exponentially. Most came and went in innocent curiosity; the few who didn't wreaked a havoc all out of proportion to their numbers. The disturbance of previously isolated archaeological sites increased by an order of magnitude. Many sites were vandalized before archaeologists, themselves late to the desert, had any firm grasp of the bounds of human history in the desert. It was as though in the same moment an Aztec library had been discovered intact various lacunae had begun to appear.

The vandalism was of three sorts: the general disturbance usually caused by souvenir hunters and by the curious and the oblivious; the wholesale stripping of a place by professional thieves for black-market sale and trade; and outright destruction, in which vehicles were actually used to ram and trench an area. By 1980, the Bureau of Land Management estimated that probably 35 percent of the archaeological sites in the desert had been vandalized. The destruction at some places by rifles and shotguns, or by power winches mounted on vehicles, was, if one cared for history, demoralizing to behold.

In spite of public education, land closures, and stricter law enforcement in recent years, the BLM estimates that, annually, about 1 percent of the archaeological record in the desert continues to be destroyed or stolen.

II

A BLM archaeologist told me, with understandable reluctance, where to find the intaglio. I spread my Automobile Club of Southern California map of Imperial County out on his desk, and he traced the route with a pink felt-tip pen. The line crossed Interstate 8 and then turned west along the Mexican border.

"You can't drive any farther than about here," he said, marking a small X. "There's boulders in the wash. You walk up past them."

On a separate piece of paper he drew a route in a smaller scale that would take me up the arroyo to a certain point where I was to cross back east, to another arroyo. At its head, on higher ground just to the north, I would find the horse.

"It's tough to spot unless you know it's there. Once you pick it up . . ." He shook his head slowly, in a gesture of wonder at its existence.

I waited until I held his eye. I assured him I would not tell anyone else how to get there. He looked at me with stoical despair, like a man who had been robbed twice, whose belief in human beings was offered without conviction.

I did not go until the following day because I wanted to see it at dawn. I ate breakfast at four A.M. in El Centro and then drove south. The route was easy to follow, though the last section of road proved difficult, broken and drifted over with sand in some spots. I came to the barricade of boulders and parked. It was light enough by then to find my way over the ground with little trouble. The contours of the landscape were stark, without any masking vegetation. I worried only about rattlesnakes.

I traversed the stone plain as directed, but, in spite of the frankness of the land, I came on the horse unawares. In the first moment of recognition I was without feeling. I recalled later being startled, and that I held my breath. It was laid out on the ground with its head to the east, three times life size. As I took in its outline I felt a growing concentration of all my senses, as though my attentiveness to the pale rose color of the morning sky and other peripheral images had now ceased to be important. I was aware that I was straining for sound in the windless air, and I felt the uneven pressure of the earth hard against my feet. The horse, outlined in a standing profile on the dark ground, was as vivid before me as a bed of tulips.

I've come upon animals suddenly before, and felt a similar tension, a precipitate heightening of the senses. And I have felt the inexplicable but sharply boosted intensity of a wild moment in the bush, where it is not until some minutes later that you discover the source of electricity—the warm remains of a grizzly bear kill, or the still moist tracks of a wolverine.

But this was slightly different. I felt I had stepped into an unoccupied corridor. I had no familiar sense of history, the temporal structure in which to think: this horse was made by Quechan people three hundred years ago. I felt instead a headlong rush of images: people hunting wild horses with spears on the Pleistocene veld of southern California; Cortés riding across the causeway into Montezuma's Tenochtitlán; a short-legged Comanche, astride his horse like some sort of ferret, slashing through cavalry lines of young men who rode like farmers; a hoof exploding past my face one morning in a corral in Wyoming. These images had the weight and silence of stone.

When I released my breath, the images softened. My initial feeling, of facing a wild animal in a remote region, was replaced with a calm sense of antiquity. It was then that I became conscious, like an ordinary tourist, of what was before me, and thought: this horse was probably laid out by Quechan people. But when? I wondered. The first horses they saw, I knew, might have been those that came north from Mexico in 1692 with Father Eusebio Kino. But Cocopa people, I recalled, also came this far north on occasion, to fight with their neighbors, the Quechan. And *they* could have seen horses with Melchior Díaz, at the mouth of the Colorado River in the fall of 1540. So, it could be four hundred years old. (No one in fact knows.)

I still had not moved. I took my eyes off the horse for a moment to look south over the desert plain into Mexico, to look east past its head at the brightening sunrise, to situate myself. Then, finally, I brought my trailing foot slowly forward and stood erect. Sunlight was running like a thin sheet of water over the stony ground and it threw the horse into relief. It looked as though no hand had ever disturbed the stones that gave it its form.

The horse had been brought to life on ground called desert pavement, a tight, flat matrix of small cobbles blasted smooth by sand-laden winds. The uniform, monochromatic blackness of the stones, a patina of iron and magnesium oxides called desert varnish, is caused by long-term exposure to the sun. To make this type of low-relief ground glyph, or intaglio, the artist either selectively turns individual stones over to their lighter side or removes areas of stone to expose the lighter soil underneath, creating a negative image. This horse, about eighteen feet from brow to rump and eight feet from withers to hoof, had been made in the latter way, and its outline was bermed at certain points with low ridges of stone a few inches high to enhance its three-dimensional qualities. (The left side of the horse was in full profile; each leg was extended at 90 degrees to the body and fully visible, as though seen in three-quarter profile.)

I was not eager to move. The moment I did I would be back in the flow of time, the horse no longer quivering in the same way before me. I did not want to feel again the sequence of quotidian events—to be drawn off into deliberation and analysis. A human being, a four-footed animal, the open land. That was all that was present—and a "thoughtless" understanding of the very old desires bearing on this particular animal: to hunt it, to render it, to fathom it, to subjugate it, to honor it, to take it as a companion.

What finally made me move was the light. The sun now filled the shallow basin of the horse's body. The weighted line of the stone berm created the illusion of a mane and the distinctive roundness of an equine belly. The change in definition impelled me. I moved to the left, circling past its rump, to see how the light might flesh the horse out from various points of view. I circled it completely before squatting on my haunches. Ten or fifteen minutes later I chose another view. The third time I moved, to a point near the rear hooves, I spotted a stone tool at my feet. I stared at it a long while, more in awe than disbelief, before reaching out to pick it up. I turned it over in my left palm and took it between my fingers to feel its cutting edge. It is always difficult, especially with something so portable, to rechannel the desire to steal.

I spent several hours with the horse. As I changed positions and as the angle of the light continued to change I noticed a number of things. The angle at which the pastern carried the hoof away from the ankle was perfect. Also, stones had been placed within the image to suggest at precisely the right spot the left shoulder above the foreleg. The line that joined thigh and hock was similarly accurate. The muzzle alone seemed distorted—but perhaps these stones had been moved by a later hand. It was an admirably accurate representation, but not what a breeder would call perfect conformation. There was the suggestion of a bowed neck and an undershot jaw, and the tail, as full as a winter coyote's, did not appear to be precisely to scale.

The more I thought about it, the more I felt I was looking at an individual horse, a unique combination of generic and specific detail. It was easy to imagine one of Kino's horses as a model, or a horse that ran off from one of Coronado's columns. What kind of horses would these have been? I wondered. In the sixteenth century the most sought-after horses in Europe were Spanish, the offspring of Arabian stock and Barbary horses that the Moors brought to Iberia and bred to the older, eastern European strains brought in by the Romans. The model for this horse, I speculated, could easily have been a palomino, or a descendant of horses trained for lion hunting in North Africa.

A few generations ago, cowboys, cavalry quartermasters, and draymen would have taken this horse before me under consideration and not let up their scrutiny until they had its heritage fixed to their satisfaction. Today, the distinction between draft and harness horses is arcane knowledge, and no image may come to mind for a blue roan or a claybank horse. The loss of such refinement in everyday conversation leaves me unsettled. People praise the Eskimo's ability to distinguish among forty types of snow but forget the skill of others who routinely differentiate between overo and to-biano pintos. Such distinctions are made for the same reason. You have to do it to be able to talk clearly about the world.

For parts of two years I worked as a horse wrangler and packer in Wyoming. It is dim knowledge now; I would have to think to remember if a buckskin was a kind of dun horse. And I couldn't throw a double-diamond hitch over a set of panniers—the packer's basic tie-down—without guid-ance. As I squatted there in the desert, however, these more personal memo-ries seemed tenuous in comparison with the sweep of this animal in human time. My memories had no depth. I thought of the Hittite cavalry riding against the Syrians 3,500 years ago. And the first of the Chinese emperors, Ch'in Shih Huang, buried in Shensi Province in 210 B.C. with thousands of life-size horses and soldiers, a terra-cotta guardian army. What could I know of what was in the mind of whoever made this horse? Was there some racial memory of it as an animal that had once fed the artist's ancestors and then disappeared from North America? And then returned in this strange al-liance with another race of men?

Certainly, whoever it was, the artist had observed the animal very closely. Certainly the animal's speed had impressed him. Among the first things the Quechan would have learned from an encounter with Kino's horses was that their own long-distance runners—men who could run down mule deer—were no match for this animal.

From where I squatted I could look far out over the Mexican plain. Juan Bautista de Anza passed this way in 1774, extending El Camino Real into Alta California from Sinaloa. He was followed by others, all of them astride the magical horse: *gente de razón*, the people of reason, coming into the country of *los primitivos*. The horse, like the stone animals of Egypt, urged these memories upon me. And as I drew them up from some forgot-ten corner of my mind—huge horses carved in the white chalk downs of southern England by an Iron Age people; Spanish horses rearing and wheel-ing in fear before alligators in Florida—the images seemed tethered before me. With this sense of proportion, a memory of my own—the morning I al-most lost my face to a horse's hoof—now had somewhere to fit.

I rose up and began to walk slowly around the horse again. I had taken the first long measure of it and was now looking for a way to depart, a new angle of light, a fading of the image itself before the rising sun, that would break its hold on me. As I circled, feeling both heady and serene at the encounter, I realized again how strangely vivid it was. It had been cre-ated on a barren bajada between two arroyos, as nondescript a place as one could imagine. The only plant life here was a few wands of ocotillo cactus. The ground beneath my shoes was so hard it wouldn't take the print of a heavy animal even after a rain. The only sounds I heard here were the voices of quail.

The archaeologist had been correct. For all its forcefulness, the horse is inconspicuous. If you don't care to see it you can walk right past it. That pleases him, I think. Unmarked on this bleak shoulder of the plain, the site signals to no one; so he wants no protective fences here, no informative plaque, to act as beacons. He would rather take a chance that no motorcyclist, no aimless wanderer with a flair for violence and a depth of ignorance, will ever find his way here.

The archaeologist had given me something before I left his office that now seemed peculiar—an aerial photograph of the horse. It is widely believed that an aerial view of an intaglio provides a fair and accurate depiction. It does not. In the photograph the horse looks somewhat crudely constructed; from the ground it appears far more deftly rendered. The photograph is of a single moment, and in that split second the horse seems vaguely impotent. I watched light pool in the intaglio at dawn; I imagine you could watch it withdraw at dusk and sense the same animation I did. In those prolonged moments its shape and so, too, its general character changed—noticeably. The living quality of the image, its immediacy to the eye, was brought out by the light-in-time, not, at least here, in the camera's frozen instant.

Intaglios, I thought, were never meant to be seen by gods in the sky above. They were meant to be seen by people on the ground, over a long period of shifting light. This could even be true of the huge figures on the Plain of Nazca in Peru, where people could walk for the length of a day beside them. It is our own impatience that leads us to think otherwise.

This process of abstraction, almost unintentional, drew me gradually away from the horse. I came to a position of attention at the edge of the sphere of its influence. With a slight bow I paid my respects to the horse, its maker, and the history of us all, and departed.

III

A short distance away I stopped the car in the middle of the road to make a few notes. I could not write down what I was thinking when I was with the horse. It would have seemed disrespectful, and it would have required another kind of attention. So now I patiently drained my memory of the details it had fastened itself upon. The road I'd stopped on was adjacent to the All American Canal, the major source of water for the Imperial and Coachella valleys. The water flowed west placidly. A disjointed flock of coots, small, dark birds with white bills, was paddling against the current, foraging in the rushes.

I was peripherally aware of the birds as I wrote, the only movement in the desert, and of a series of sounds from a village a half-mile away. The first sounds from this collection of ramshackle houses in a grove of cottonwoods were the distracted dawn voices of dogs. I heard them intermingled with the cries of a rooster. Later, the high-pitched voices of children calling out to each other came disembodied through the dry desert air. Now, a little after seven, I could hear someone practicing on the trumpet, the same rough phrases played over and over. I suddenly remembered how as children we had tried to get the rhythm of a galloping horse with hands against our things, or by fluttering our tongues against the roofs of our mouths.

After the trumpet, the impatient calls of adults summoning children. Sunday morning. Wood smoke hung like a lens in the trees. The first car starts—a cold eight-cylinder engine, of Chrysler extraction perhaps, goosed to life, then throttled back to murmur through dual mufflers, the obbligato music of a shade-tree mechanic. The rote bark of mongrel dogs at dawn, the jagged outcries of men and women, an engine coming to life. Like a thousand villages from West Virginia to Guadalajara.

I finished my notes—where was I going to find a description of the horses that came north with the conquistadors? Did their manes come forward prominently over the brow, like this one's, like the forelocks of Blackfeet and Assiniboin men in nineteenth-century paintings? I set the notes on the seat beside me.

The road followed the canal for a while and then arced north, toward Interstate 8. It was slow driving and I fell to thinking how the desert had changed since Anza had come through. New plants and animals—the MacDougall cottonwood, the English house sparrow, the chukar from India—have about them now the air of the native-born. Of the native species, some—no one knows how many—are extinct. The populations of many others, especially the animals, have been sharply reduced. The idea of a desert impoverished by agricultural poisons and varmint hunters, by off-road vehicles and military operations, did not seem as disturbing to me, however, as this other horror, now that I had been those hours with the horse. The vandals, the few who crowbar rock art off the desert's walls, who dig up graves, who punish the ground that holds intaglios, are people who devour history. Their self-centered scorn, their disrespect for ideas and images beyond their ken, create the awful atmosphere of loose ends in which totalitarianism thrives, in which the past is merely curious or wrong.

I thought about the horse sitting out there on the unprotected plain. I enumerated its qualities in my mind until a sense of its vulnerability receded and it became an anchor for something else. I remembered that history, a history like this one, which ran deeper than Mexico, deeper than the Spanish, was a kind of medicine. It permitted the great breadth of human expression to reverberate, and it did not urge you to locate its apotheosis in the present.

Each of us, individuals and civilizations, has been held upside down like Achilles in the River Styx. The artist mixing his colors in the dim light of Altamira; an Egyptian ruler lying still now, wrapped in his byssus,* stored against time in a pyramid; the faded Dorset culture of the Arctic; the Hmong and Samburu and Walbiri of historic time; the modern nations. This great, imperfect stretch of human expression is the clarification and encouragement, the urging and the reminder, we call history. And it is inscribed

---

*byssus: Ancient cloth.

everywhere in the face of the land, from the mountain passes of the Himalayas to a nameless bajada in the California desert.

Small birds rose up in the road ahead, startled, and flew off. I prayed no infidel would ever find that horse.

Questions for Discussion

1. Consider the amount of detail Lopez uses to describe the landscape and the horse, and the variety of technical terms he uses. How would you describe his style? How does his use of diction serve his style?

2. What happens with Lopez's sense of time and history when he encounters the stone horse? How does this moment serve as a turning point for the essay?

3. Why is this essay divided into three parts? How does the essay progress from one part to the next? What is the significance of the last line of the essay?

Student Writing

Identity and Point of View

Each of these student essays is written from a first-person point of view. As you read, think about how each author presents herself on the page. How does the author enter into the text? Is it obvious or subtle? Do you have a mental picture of the author or speaker as a character in the story? One of the most important things to keep in mind in the personal essay is how the author establishes himself or herself as a believable and compelling narrative voice and presence.

Joan Barnett
Coming to Shelter

Joan McMillan Barnett's work has appeared in Poetry, Reed, Quarry West, Onthebus, *and* Paterson Literary Review. *She is the mother of four children and is currently working on a memoir of her Italian-American childhood.*

I am part of a sorority which nobody dreams they will join at the hopeful beginning of a marriage. The members are former residents of Mariposa House, a battered women's shelter in Santa Cruz County. I can't tell you what Mariposa House looks like on the outside. I can't tell you if it stands on a residential street in Watsonville, innocuous in its resemblance to other houses. For all anyone knows, it's near Harvey West Park, with a view of Costco and the pioneer cemetery. Before anyone checks into Mariposa House, they take an oath of secrecy as to the shelter's location. *It might endanger other women*, I was told. *Someone could find out, we had a guy try to break in once.* I took the oath willingly; I was familiar with concealment.

I don't have to keep the shelter's interior a secret, though I try to forget it. My life contains so much good now: nobody hits me if I do something wrong. Still, the memory hovers at the edge of this goodness. No metaphors apply to it; it's not like a storm cloud or a ghost. It just appears. The memory returned recently when I sat on the edge of an examination table in the Santa Cruz Women's Health Center. I wore one of those voluminous paper gowns, tied shut with a plastic strip. Posters covered the walls: a pink rose, unfurled, with a fuzzy black bee at the center. A photograph of a mountain drenched in wildflowers. An Astrobright Green flyer advertising an eight-week class in tribal belly dance. Underneath the window, a large poster with a gray background: four women in a circle, their hands holding up a small blue-and-tan Earth. Beneath the women, in white block letters, the slogan *Imagine a Violence-Free World*.

The last time I saw that poster, I stood at a deep sink filled with thick white suds. Next to me, stacks of plain china plates, no pattern, silverware, cups, a few plastic baby bottles. Every woman in the shelter had a daily task. Mine was kitchen duty: wash dishes, sponge off the speckled Formica counters, water the one straggly spider plant on the chipped gray windowsill. Windex the front of the two steel refrigerators, vacuum the red braided rug. I sprayed Lemon Pledge on the round oak table, buffed the dark wood to a mirror shine, swept beneath the table with a worn straw broom, replaced the assortment of chairs.

Back at the sink, I filled cups with hot water, scoured them with a green plastic scrubber. Tacked to the wall in front of me, a poster: women holding up a basketball-sized world. There might have been other posters with edifying slogans in the shelter, but I don't remember them. Perhaps they weren't as common eight years ago. They're all over the place now. The other day, I saw a Santa Cruz bus with the sentence *Warning: Domestic Violence May Be Hazardous To Your Health* emblazoned on the side in crimson. On the other side of the bus, an ad for George Roper's Bail Bonds. Both signs had numbers to call, 24 hours, day or night.

You'd think the hallways of a battered women's shelter would be filled with screams or sobs, but there was almost no sound. We could have all been in a chapel, the silence was that deep and reverent. It was the silence of people who have learned how shutting up might save your life. Nobody paced the long hall which ran the length of the shelter and opened onto the kitchen. In the daytime, skylights flooded the hall with dusty brightness. At night, the front door security alarm glowed like a car's instrument panel.

No light shone beneath the closed doors of the rooms lining the hall. Like children, we had to be in bed by ten.

I'm going to call my husband "Tom" for this narrative, because the description of Tom Buchanan in *The Great Gatsby* fits him so well: *He was a sturdy, straw haired man of about thirty, with a rather hard mouth.* What landed me in the sorority house for battered women was a threat which emerged from that hard mouth, during an argument over Tom's American Express bill. I didn't even have a credit card of my own and found the bill by accident, casually tossed on a pile of homework. To this day, I don't know what Tom purchased to make the balance skyrocket to nine hundred dollars.

When I confronted Tom about the American Express bill, saying it would be hard to make the house payment that month, he flew into a rage, opening cabinets, flinging dishes and food to the floor. He finally stopped to say, "I'm taking a little drive now, and when I come back, I'm going to kill you." Tom's eyes, always a polar blue, were so arctic and hard that I knew he meant it. When our van roared out of the driveway, I dialed the local domestic violence hotline, a tsunami of fear making my arms and legs shake uncontrollably. Then I called a neighbor, who came over immediately and took us to a coffeeshop in Santa Cruz, where a shelter worker met us.

During my life with Tom, I tried to pretend everything was fine, that we were a "good-enough" family. I held onto small hopes like consolation prizes. If a few months went by without Tom hitting me, I thought the violence was over forever. Every spring, I planted sunflowers in the front yard of our house, choosing the ones with the most fanciful names: Sunrich, Autumn Splendor, Russian Mammoth. All summer they blazed; by October, their heads drooped, heavy with small black seeds. I wanted to be a woman with a nice garden, like the other mothers on my street, the ones who invited me to get-togethers.

I never fit in at these gatherings, which were elaborations on Tupperware parties, with "country theme" items for sale. For one thing, I didn't have cash to spend on a fifty-dollar maple sewing basket from Vermont, or candlesticks shaped like artichokes. I envied the women's problems, too: my neighbor Annie described how her husband didn't buy her a single present she liked on her birthday. My other neighbor, Ruth, paraded her two children in front of us, making them smile to show their braces; she complained at length about the cost. Occasionally, I felt like saying something outrageous in its truth, such as *my husband beat the shit out of me once when I caught him reading my journal*, but I never did. Later, when I became a single parent, my neighbors went out of their way to help me. Annie gave me rides to town whenever my car was in the shop. One winter, I had no extra money to buy wood for the woodstove, the sole source of heat in my house. A red pickup truck pulled up one day in my driveway and two men unloaded a cord of oak and madrone, courtesy of Ruth and her family.

I tried to leave Tom many times, the longest for a month, just before our son Christopher's second birthday. Whatever we fought about that night is not memorable: probably money, or not doing the laundry. The fight ended in its predictable manner: Tom administered what he later referred to as "teeny little slaps" to the side of my face. These "teeny slaps" felt like being smacked with a rock. I told him to leave; after four weeks, I asked him to come back. I had an array of excuses, fanned out like a poker hand. There was a recession. I couldn't find work right away and when I did, the child-care for Chris ate up all the money, and besides, Tom came by with small gifts for our son, and sometimes for me. He promised to change; I believed him. We repeated this pattern for the next ten years, on and off, in the midst of adding three more children to our household.

Why I stayed in this kind of relationship feels incomprehensible to me now at forty-two. Understanding it involves returning to my beliefs as a twenty-three-year-old, a very young mother with children she did not want to grow up without a father. That younger edition of myself sat in a therapy session once with a counselor named Dora. I liked Dora; she told me things I knew were real: that my parents didn't just have a "drinking problem," they were drunks. She said it was okay to tell my mother not to call me at 3 a.m. Dora was the first person I told about Tom. For some reason, I remember how nice Dora's hair looked that day, pure white and freshly styled in a short cut. Dora asked me about the best aspects of my relationship with Tom; I mentioned the plays we saw together, his sense of humor. When she asked for the worst part, I said casually, as if reciting my grocery list for the week, "Well, he hits me, you know. But I deserve it." Dora stared at me for several minutes after that sentence came tumbling out of my mouth. I thought she would respond with, "What do you do to make him hit you?" Instead, she finally said, "Joan, you don't deserve to be hit." When I protested and began my litany of serious personal failings, she repeated, "You don't deserve it."

Which leads, of course, to why I thought I deserved it. Perhaps the roots of my belief stretch back to my earliest memory of my parents. In 1985, I wrote about it in a journal: *I stand screaming in front of the wooden door to their bedroom. I'm four years old, maybe five. The door has a brass lock, the old-fashioned kind for a skeleton key. Tears are running down my face and I am screaming because my mother, on the other side of the door, is also screaming. I know my dad is hitting her; I can hear him telling her to shut up, to stop crying.*

Earlier that day, I helped my father wash the car. He showed me how to wipe a sudsy rag over the fender of our blue-and-white Chevrolet station wagon, then dry it with a clean cloth. His ever-present yellow can of Coors stood on the blacktop. Dad smelled of Coors, Old Spice, and Salem cigarettes; he kept a pack rolled up in his T-shirt sleeve. By the time I entered first grade, I had it figured out: there was a "daytime" daddy and a "nighttime" daddy, like a child's version of Jekyll and Hyde. Soon after I started school, my mother began drinking in the afternoons, so eventually I believed that about her, too.

Within my years of marriage, I began to write poems, stealthily and steadily. I secreted each one away, along with my journals, beneath a box of old baby clothes in the laundry room. When I began to publish, I took the acceptance letters to Tom, like a child with a straight-A report card. At first, he expressed genuine delight and even bought me an electronic typewriter and a roll of postage stamps. As time went on and my work began to appear in better-known magazines, Tom grew sour and surly. Finally, after hearing him say, "Who gives a fuck?" too many times, I stopped telling him about the acceptances.

After that, poetry became a lifeline for me, like sending coded messages to the outside world. I began to write about my mother; one poem, "Bird of Paradise," described her as being like a sleepwalker. The poem says, "All night my father / prowled our rooms, / flung words like objects / for piercing, cutting." I then described how my mother neglected her garden, except for one bird-of-paradise, its orange and violet spikes like a suddenly uplifted weapon. I recited this poem at readings, wondering if anyone in the audience guessed it was actually about me.

I came to the shelter with a pillowcase full of clothes, diapers for three-year-old Matthew, and five dollars in my wallet. Christopher, age twelve, put his baseball cards in the pillowcase, too. My daughters, Stephanie and Emily, spent most of their shelter days in the playroom which opened off the kitchen. It stood at the very end of the house, next to a living room decorated in 1950s decor, down to a lamp with a beige ruffled shade and a cabinet-style television. Like the other children in the shelter, mine acted subdued. All the children eventually became friends; they "visited" by going down the hall to each other's rooms.

Our bedroom had an industrial gray carpet, flat and rough, a bunkbed, a rollaway futon, a twin bed, one small wooden dresser, and a shuttered window. Each bed had a thick white comforter, worn to threadbare smoothness. I stayed awake long after lights-out, staring into the dark. Mostly I fixated on whether the cat was being fed, or if Tom was neglecting her. I felt sure he was still at the house. When I first entered the shelter, I filed a restraining order and injunction for him to move, but I thought Tom would simply ignore it. After years of vigilance, I believed I could second-guess everything he did, my instincts like trip wires, taut and invisible.

One shelter rule involved "establishing a normal routine for you and your family." This meant, on our first morning, cooking breakfast for the kids. I scrambled eggs and made toast; it was the first time we'd eaten a breakfast like that in four years. We stopped eating eggs when Tom threw open the front door one day, brandishing a copy of John Robbins' *Diet for a New America* with a red, white, and blue cover. *Diet for a New America* depicted the environmental ravages of eating meat. Tom adored the environment and our household supplies reflected this. I used Ivory Flakes instead of laundry detergent, even though it gave our clothes a slightly gummy texture. Baking soda instead of Comet for scrubbing, Dr. Bronner's Peppermint Soap for washing floors. I liked the fragrance of the mint soap, despite the label printed with Dr. Bronner's obsessive and somewhat loony "Essene Wisdom."

Now Tom had a new cause to singlehandedly save the environment: complete vegetarianism. Tom's unique concept of the vegan diet included small amounts of tofu, soy cheese, soy milk, and tempeh, occasional portions of rice and vegetables, sometimes fruit. Since Tom bought all the groceries by that time, I felt obliged to comply. Tom allowed the children to eat the hot meals in the free lunch program at school. I told them it was okay to have the meat in those lunches. I began to lose too much weight and had recurring dreams about cafeterias with trays full of every conceivable meat dish, served by elderly women in hairnets and pink uniforms who urged me to eat. That year, when our neighbors held their annual pre-Thanksgiving party, Tom kept an eagle eye on me as I put only squash, salad, cranberry sauce, and potatoes on my plate. Later that night, Tom sat down next to me, his own dish heaped with ham and turkey. *I just couldn't resist,* he whispered, *but don't let me see you sneaking any.*

Fear of not being able to make it financially also kept me in the marriage, even though I had income from a teaching job. I dutifully deposited my checks in a joint account and accepted an allowance from Tom for classroom supplies. Tom did all the bookkeeping; I told him I wasn't good at such things. My responsibilities seemed at times like burdens to me and I relinquished them willingly, piece by piece. When Tom asked, I signed over the title of my van to him, since he paid the registration and insurance anyway. I didn't believe then that Tom was trying to take control of anything; I told myself he wanted our marriage to proceed in an orderly fashion. Besides, he read to the children every night; they always had expensive pairs of shoes and new clothes. At the time, I thought this made up for the violence they witnessed.

Recently, my eldest daughter told me her most indelible memory about her father, when he punched me full-force in the back because I withdrew forty dollars from our savings account. We had a shutoff notice for the water bill; I forgot to tell him. I forgot to tell him a lot of things. Now both my children and I have memories of our mothers being hit. These memories are like a string of shadowy pearls passed through generations, something nobody wants to inherit.

There were three other women in the shelter: Teresa, Jean, and Julie. Teresa and I occasionally spoke in hushed tones about our husband's violence. Teresa said, "I always knew when he was going to go after me. He closed all the doors and windows so nobody would hear." Teresa's face looked swollen on the left side. She said it was much worse a week ago. Jean was young, not even twenty, and seemed happy. Her room's cheerful clutter included clothes, toys for her daughter, makeup and bottles of nail polish. Julie and I talked privately only once, after Beth, a social worker, breezed into the shelter one day with a copy of the Santa Cruz Sentinel. "Time to look for jobs, ladies!" she chirped. Beth dressed in flowing purple tops and matching pants; her hair hung in a long gray braid down her back. She always referred to us as "ladies," as if we wore tea gloves and wide-brimmed pastel hats.

Julie and I took the classified ads to the kitchen table. My teaching job would start again in a month, but circling ads seemed like the right thing to do anyway. Julie told me she lived with a woman for five years, helped raise her children. "But then it got really bad," she said softly, "The crisis workers in San Diego sent me up to Northern California to hide." Then she asked me, "Do you really think I can make it here, in this town?" It was a question I'd asked of myself since the day I came here. I replied, "Yes, I really think you can," though I wasn't sure about any of us.

After four days in the shelter, my mind began to lose some of the numbness into which it had tunneled for years, like a mole. I worried about what was happening at my house, and when the social worker took all the children to a park in the afternoon, I telephoned my neighbor Annie.

She told me she hadn't seen any cars parked in our driveway for a day or two. "I think he's gone," she said, her voice falling to a whisper, almost as if Tom lurked nearby. "But you should wait a couple more days. Call me and I'll come get you. Stay at my house for awhile, if you feel safer." She also promised to look after the cat. I thanked her and hung up. Questions flashed though my mind, like images in a too-fast slide show: *I need to change the deadbolts on the front door right away. I have to get my own checking account. What will our lives be like after we leave here?*

On my last night at Mariposa House, the other women and I decided to make dinner together. The idea began when Julie opened the refrigerator and noticed a bag of ten Van De Kamp's Fish Fillets, almost at the expiration date. She arranged them in rows on a baking sheet, slid them into the oven. I made white rice in a steel pot with a mismatched green lid. Julie and Teresa chopped vegetables for salad into tiny squares, including the lettuce. I'd never seen salad made that way; it looked like salsa. Jean set the table, gave the children a few chores: my girls folded yellow paper napkins, my eldest son set up high chairs for the younger kids.

Jean chatted about getting emergency welfare payments, a voucher for housing. Teresa said she had two interviews tomorrow, office jobs, ten dollars an hour. Julie mentioned the Santa Cruz Medical Clinic; she thought it might be a good place to put in an application. We could have been women who lived on the same block, sitting down at a table together, pouring juice into cups for our children. The difference was that nobody knew where we were, each one of us vanished like a mirage from our regular lives. Somewhere outside the locked door of this place, the people we escaped prowled the streets. They called friends and relatives on the phone: *Is she there? Do you know where she's staying?* I knew they'd never stop looking.

I could wrap things up neatly if this were a movie, the phrase "Eight Years Later" appearing on a black screen. But there are no tidy endings to this kind of story. Everything I feared about leaving my marriage came true:

no child support from Tom, nearly losing my home, not having enough money, no car for almost eleven months. Nothing was worse than Tom's fist slamming into me for some transgression, imagined or real.

If I could find one image to represent the past eight years, I would say they resemble a mosaic stepping stone. They're popular these days; the neighbor women recently invited me to a party where we constructed them. We shattered old china plates and tumblers with a hammer, pressed the pieces into rounds of wet concrete. I made a bird-of-paradise, composed from fragments of colored glass. There was a time when I read a poem about a bird-of-paradise to an audience of strangers, hoping someone would recognize what I was saying and rescue me. By entering Mariposa House, I answered my own cry for help. It was the first step in making a different life for myself, like the mosaic stone I put in my garden, bright shards repieced to create something entirely new and whole.

Julie Lewis
Fifteen Minutes

Julie Lewis is a poet and the mother of three children. She has won Phelan Literary Awards for her poetry, fiction, and satire. Her poetry appears in Reed *magazine and* The Formalist. *Julie is completing a book of poetry entitled* Exile by Design.

The training materials for Program Tutorial Reading show that fifteen minutes of reading a day is the optimal allotment of intensive one-on-one reading instruction for elementary school students. Any more time, and boredom or frustration sets in and the time spent becomes counterproductive. So each of my students gets fifteen minutes a day. It doesn't sound like much, but fifteen minutes of, "Let's try it again," or "Point to the word in the box" seems like an hour sometimes. And fifteen minutes of relentlessly positive reinforcement can sometimes feel disingenuous. But the program works: kids who didn't read before read now and, more importantly to the school district, the positive results are reflected in an improvement in the standardized test scores for the state.

Berryessa Union School District nestles against San Jose's east hills at the edge of Silicon Valley's early 1970's suburban sprawl. An almost affordable pocket of housing in this obscenely expensive area of California, the neighborhoods draw a mix of immigrant high tech workers, first time homeowners, and a few longtime families with roots deep in the soil of the Santa Clara Valley. Like the more affluent districts on the west side, Berryessa faces the daunting task of providing an education to a vastly diverse population of children. The demographic of the school where I teach is sixty percent Asian—a catch-all term for dozens of language groups; twenty percent Hispanic; ten percent White; two percent Black; and eight percent Other—another catch-all including American Indians and Pacific Islanders among others.

It becomes necessary to give some of these children individual attention or they are lost in a system they cannot understand. And, of course, the sooner we can address their needs, the more successful they are at school. A win-win situation. For my small part, I teach reading to twelve students a day. With three other tutors, I work in a converted supply closet off the multi-purpose room. In this cramped space, each of us has a double student desk, a set of materials, and a different student every fifteen minutes.

Not all children transform. The program was not designed to teach English to a fourth grader who never learned to read even in her native Vietnamese. It was not designed to mitigate the learning disabilities of fetal alcohol syndrome. It was not designed to cure the complex social ills brought on by poverty and discrimination. Some of the students are already hard and worldly. Third-grade girls, at the grand old age of eight, scrape their hair back into buns in imitation of the tough girls in middle school. Little boys with their gang colors and their baggy pants are already more interested in perfecting their swagger than their lessons.

For some, fifteen minutes a day is not enough.

But I am not their mother or their grandmother or their aunt. I do not take them home with me and give them a snack and supervise their homework. I do not give them a bath and read them a bedtime story and tuck them between clean sheets in a bed of their own. I do not buy them bikes or take them on vacations or plan their birthday parties. I do not give them clothes and combs and toothbrushes. They must look to other sources or, as often as not, do without.

I give them books and smiles and hugs. I give them fifteen minutes.

That is what Jenny Alvarez got. Jenny was a little first-grade beauty with obsidian eyes and shoulder-length brown hair. She dressed in out-of-date My Little Pony pants and Power Ranger T-shirts straight from the crisis closet at St. Victor's. Jenny's smile was contagious and so was her recurring case of head lice. She came back to school after her third infestation with her hair cropped above her ears. Her grandmother was tired of battling the bugs that passed from sister to sister to sister and had simplified the nit-combing process by cutting off all of their beautiful braids. Jenny's grandmother had her hands full.

With her father in prison and her mother in a drug rehabilitation halfway house, Jenny pined for her parents with all the heart-wrenching devotion a six-year-old can muster. Time after time, her mother would promise a visit on a weekend release and then never show up.

"Guess what, Mrs. Lewis," Jenny would burst out in the middle of a lesson. "I'm going to have a picnic with my mommy tomorrow!" We sat side by side at the little desk, my left arm draped around the back of her chair, my right arm curved over the book, guiding her reading with the eraser end of my pencil. We would pause then, and quietly, trying not to disturb the other sets of tutors and readers, we talked.

After the first couple of times, though, I learned to make my response low key. "That's neat, Jenny. You can tell me about it on Monday. Point to the upper case K."

Many a Monday rolled around when we didn't accomplish much. I would just read to her. Maybe her mom broke some rule and lost her weekend out of the house. Or maybe something came up. Jenny was left dejected. Eventually, the court appointed Jenny an advocate to help her deal with the disappointment that was her life.

I have never been particularly demonstrative, and I am as squeamish about head lice as the next person, but Jenny just required hugs. Every day she came to me with her heart in her big black eyes, and I gave her a hug. She needed them and I gave them. It was simple.

Not everything was simple though. She wasn't easy to teach at first. She didn't know her letters. She had never owned a book. No one had ever spent any time with her and she had no base to start from. So we started with a pre-primer and fifteen minutes.

> *Point to the letter that stands for the beginning sound in the word bat.*
> *Listen again, Jenny. Point to the letter that stands for the beginning sound in the word bat.*
> *What did I ask you to do?*
> *Good! Now do what I asked you to do . . .*
> *Watch while I point to the letter that stands for the beginning sound in the word bat.*
> *Now you do it.*
> *Great, Jenny!*

She progressed slowly at first, but she progressed. Jenny learned the alphabet, but she was still behind her grade level at the end of the year.

When Jenny entered second grade, her mother moved back home. I gave Jenny crayons and a pad of paper to celebrate and she brought me pictures of flowers and hearts and rainbows that I hung on the sheetrock around the desk where we worked. Jenny skipped and danced and grinned. And she learned.

> *Who will help me bake the bread?*
> *"Not I," said the cat.*
> *"Not I," said the pig.*
> *"Then I will bake it myself," said the hen.*
> *Perfect, Jenny! Go on.*

But raising a house full of girls without a dad and without enough money is hard. Jenny's mother violated probation and went back to jail. Jenny was tougher this time. She was more philosophical than a seven-year-old should ever need to be. This time she didn't wear her heart on her sleeve or her disappointment in her eyes. She didn't mention her mother anymore and I didn't pry. She stopped bringing pictures.

When her natural resiliency took over, she started smiling again. She worked hard and things started to click.

> *When two vowels go awalkin', the first one does the talkin'.*
> *Drop the final e before adding -ing.*
> *Way to go, Jenny!*

At the end of her second grade year, Jenny graduated from the program; she had achieved grade level reading scores. The girl who came to me with so little left with so much. I like to think that I triumphed with Jenny, but I know that really isn't true. Jenny triumphed with me. We celebrated with cupcakes and punch. I gave her a bookmark that said *Keep On Reading!* and a brand new copy of *Charlotte's Web* for third grade.

I wanted to give her the world, and in a way, maybe I did. But it wasn't enough. Reading is great, but it isn't everything. Reading is not clean clothes and warm meals and a mother's love.

I still see some of my former students, but I don't see Jenny anymore. Every school year I place twelve more students into my program, twelve more Antonios and Tiffanys, Akashes, Chai-Wens and Hoangs. Some of them learn to read. Many of them, like Jenny, find a permanent place in my heart. Wherever she is, I hope she is growing her braids back. I hope someone has fifteen minutes for Jenny.

Kate Evans
The Waiting Is the Hardest Part:
A Meditation of Writing and Mortality

Kate Evans's poetry and fiction have appeared in Elixir, PMS: poemmemoirstory, Wavelength, *and* Happy. *Her nonfiction book,* Negotiating the Self, *was published in 2002 by Routledge. She lives in Santa Cruz, California. This essay first appeared in* Under the Sun.

The first thing always is to lie back. Sterile paper crinkles, and my breasts fall to my sides as if resigned. My doctor's fingertips probe my right breast, circle and press, circle and press. Guilt floods me; I'm always too frightened to attempt such thoroughness each month in the shower. I can't, with such deliberateness, search for something I don't want to find.

I watch my doctor's eyes, try to read them. I've always wondered how her face might change if she found something. Today, I see. Her eyes sweep up to the fluorescent light as though to avoid the spot on my breast where her fingers have stopped.

"Hm," she says.

I want to leap out of my body—this body of breasts and bones and brains—and float out of the high window into the heaven of my bed with its homemade quilt and my lover warming me.

"Here, feel this," she says, lifting my hand to the spot I least want to touch on my whole body. I imagine this probing might jar errant cells, which break loose and run scattershot through my body.

I pretend to feel the lump. I can't feel anything right now. Only fear. In a hopeful, yet skewed attempt, my thoughts surface the names of my friends who paved the way: Susannah, Marie, Melinda, Joan, Catherine. All alive and well. And two who aren't: Jan. Aunt Edrie.

"This may be just a premenstrual breast, but I need to be sure," she says. A piece of her brown hair, woven with gray strands, has escaped her ponytail and is grazing her cheek. Dr. McFinney always looks a bit disheveled, as though she wears her hectic life-with-two-year-old-twins-and-a-medical-practice on her wrinkled sleeve.

She tells me I need to come back in ten days. If the lump has disappeared or changed, it's benign.

At home I kneel on the bedroom floor and bury my face in my cat's gray fur. Her pleasure purrs up. She is always so present, responding so immediately to everything: my touch, a patch of sun on the carpet, a sparrow jumping on the other side of the window. Compared to a human life, hers is on the fast track. Does she see everything differently from the dimension of human years? Are her perceptions as different from mine, as mine are from a redwood tree, whose lingering years swirl slowly inside?

An echo of my doctor's touch rushes back. My right breast burns, the bright spot on a mammography, the embers of a campfire. I envy solid redwood existence and my cat's nine lives. Everything is a likely poison. My three daily cups of coffee. The pipes in our 100-year-old house. The fruit I didn't wash. My mother's genes. The four times I dropped acid. And all those hangovers and second-hand smoke. Months of living mainly on Top Ramen and Doritos. Ten years on the pill. Even an old chestnut: An underwater kick to my budding breast at age eleven in the public pool. Why did I think I'd somehow escape? No one does. Life is a summer swimming pool where you're kicked by a rowdy kid, then you get cancer, then you die.

Ten days, I tell Annie, my lover, that night in bed. She's lightly touching my bare back and reading a book, coincidentally, by Rachel Carson. Carson's evocations on the poisoned earth are fitting, but they seem too large right now for my little life. I'm trying to be like my cat, purring to Annie's touch, being here in this bed as though I have, in fact, flown from the exam room and landed in my life's homemade quilt.

But I can't sustain a sense of being present. A loop tape of the doctor giving me two different versions of the news plays over and over. My heart beats like an old film reel flapping around and around after the film has ended but no one is there to turn off the projector.

Dr. McFinney has two different looks in each version in my mind's eye. In the first version, her tall body slopes into the room, with knotted hair and wrinkled white coat. Coffee on her breath and eyes averted, she tells me I have cancer and that furthermore I'm pre-menopausal so I should take every precaution, including a mastectomy, radiation, and chemo and that furthermore with a maternal aunt who died of breast cancer I shouldn't hold out much hope. I feel this scene in my body—my legs, arms, and head tingle so insistently that something in me separates, as though half of me has walked out into the hallway leaving the other half behind.

When the tape loops to the next version, Dr. McFinney is very rested. Her twin two-year-olds slept through the night, so her white coat is crisp and properly buttoned. Her stethoscope hangs authoritatively from her willowy neck, and her brown hair sways at her shoulders, gray threads combing through like tinsel on a Christmas tree. Her gift to me unwraps in her smile and settled eyes: "Just as I thought, a mere premenstrual breast."

At the Santa Cruz Beach Boardwalk, the amusement park on the beach a few blocks from our house, a saltwater taffy machine's movements pull a wad of rubbery candy out to its stretching point then back again. Its beginnings and endings intersect, a Moebius strip in sticky motion. Like that taffy, I am repeatedly pulled apart and put back together, in the milliseconds it takes the mind to fool the body into believing it has experienced the future over and over again.

A few days into the wait, my heart occasionally races and I'm vaguely nauseous off and on, as though I have a teenage crush. I can't concentrate for long—can't write, can't read much of anything except junk mail fliers. One afternoon I see auras around the juicer, the rose bush, and even my neighbor who, in her raggedy orange bathrobe, picks up the newspaper off the walk at 2 p.m.

Annie has great news: our friends can't go to the Indigo Girls concert so are giving us their tickets. These are coveted tickets, for the Indigos hold court as an immensely popular duo, who happen to be lesbians, playing in a small, sold-out venue in our very lesbian town. I have a feeling that somehow Annie finagled these tickets to distract and entertain me, but I don't ask. I know she's worried and that my nervous energy and talk of seeing auras around the rose bush is driving her nuts.

Dressing for the concert, I quickly put on my bra, avoiding contact with "the spot." My breasts are rather large, a 38C on my 5'8 frame. Usually they are like breathing: I don't much notice them unless I'm physically exerting myself. For running I wear two jog bras to avoid what I only half-jokingly call "boob sprain." Once I ran a couple of blocks with a regular bra on, and my right breast ached for a week. Another candidate to add to the "potential causes" list.

When I was 18, my boyfriend John told me that the thing he loved about my breasts is that they stand up in a perky way, even without a bra. Other breasts, like those of his former 33-year-old girlfriend, did not have the shape of mine, he reported. Sometimes when I see my breasts drooping, feel their rounded undersides graze my ribs, I wonder if John ever realized that gravity had not yet taken hold of my young breasts, unlike those of his older ex-girlfriend. Whatever his knowledge of the physics of breasts, John loved bodies. He loved to look good and have his girlfriend look good: the latest fashions (like wrap-around pants), the latest hairstyles (like feathered, hair-sprayed wings), the latest toys (like Pong or an ATM card).

It's curious how John has remained part of my awareness of my physical body, in more ways than one. He thought I was beautiful when he first met me, followed by a year of trying to improve me. We remained friends after a series of breakups involving a girl named Candy. I wonder what he would think of me now with my unshaved armpits and my thick, relaxed breasts. At age 28, John fell off a ladder while painting a house. He died soon after. Sometimes I feel like he's right here, telling me that the body is to be enjoyed, not fretted over, and that I'm lucky to be freer while still alive.

Women and a few men swarm around, drinks in hand, while Annie and I sit at the bar, waiting for the concert to start. I catch snippets of conversation: one woman hopes that the Indigo Girls will play her favorite song, another complains about her high school students' inability to spell, and a third waxes philosophical about the effects of a hungry, stray dog appearing on her front lawn. I am struck by the minutiae of life, how its electricity continually buzzes. I could be sitting here with cancer in my breast, and the most familiar cliché rings true: life goes on. I wonder what hidden pain, disease, and fears the other women around me harbor. I suddenly feel a surprising affection for life's details, as though they are excited little children whose exuberance forces us to live in the naive moment.

"Oh, look who's here," Annie says, and I peer over the rim of my wine glass mid-sip. A brown-haired woman stands before us, broadly smiling, displaying what looks like a bit of cream cheese lodged between her two front teeth. For a fleeting second I can't place her. Then a shock of white coat flashes in my mind's eye, replacing her turtleneck sweater. Dr. McFinney. It's as though my hidden thoughts have uncannily materialized.

"What a coincidence," Annie says. They ensue on a point/counter-point about the Indigo Girls' lyrics and intricate harmonies. Irrational thoughts seize me: What right does she have to hang out enjoying live music when she holds my fate in her hands? How can it be that she doesn't notice the cream cheese in her teeth?

I have been a teacher for many years, and when my students run into me at the grocery store, I can tell they marvel at the fact that the woman who conducts their classes actually buys bananas and bread. That means their teacher is a person and has a body that engages in bodily functions. They blink at me like they've just exited a dark theater.

Why do we deny authorities their bodies? The body is vulnerable, subject to embarrassing noises and messy disease. The body is a personal space, and "professional" is supposed to be the opposite of "personal." So separating the professionals from bodies imbues them with power. And a false immunity is also lent through the trappings of their professional authority: the black board, the white coat. The figure of the professional provides us with some relief from ubiquitous mortality. The professional somehow seems to have transcended death.

As Dr. McFinney animatedly chats with Annie, I ache with the recognition of her humanness, her vulnerability. Someone who blindly smiles with cream cheese in her teeth—and who attends pop concerts—wilts my shred of confidence. Forget human. I want a superhero for a doctor.

So many of my women friends and family members have located breast lumps that have turned out to be "nothing." This thought provides me with sporadic comfort in the days until my doctor's appointment. Breasts, apparently, are lumpy, and the quality of that lumpiness changes throughout the month. Sometimes they are like cottage cheese, other times like gravel. Lumpiness is normal, even though "lump" is so often conflated with "cancer." I can't fully convince myself, however, that the equation of lump = cancer is faulty since for several women in my life the equation was accurate, including my best friend, Marie, her daughter Melinda, and her sister Jan.

Two years ago, Marie, who is 56, hit her five-year-with-no-recurrence mark, which means she is ostensibly cured. The next year, her 48-year-old sister died after battling the disease for three years. Soon after, her 37-year-old daughter called her from overseas, where she was studying, to tell her she'd found some blood in her bra.

"I've never heard of bleeding through the nipple as a sign of breast cancer, have you?" Marie had asked me on the phone one spring morning. Her voice ached for me to share her perception.

"No," I said, trying to veer my friend's life away from tragedy. I had a vague sense that I had once heard that such bleeding was a sign of cancer, but what I said at that moment would not alter her daughter's diagnosis. If there was any truth to the saying that thoughts are things, I wanted my thoughts to be cures.

After their agonizing equivalent of my current ten-day wait, Marie called to ask if I would take her to the airport. Her daughter's doctor was pressing for a mastectomy, and Marie wanted to be there. Every day I checked my email for ongoing letters from Marie, who detailed the events with the clarity of a journalist. The email subject headings piled up like headlines: Melinda and I Search for More Information, Doctor Recommends Implant Over Reconstruction, A Needed Night of Belgian Beer, Melinda Set for Surgery. There was something terrifying and reassuring in these missives, like wires from the front line. But the combatants were not faceless soldiers; they were my best friend and her daughter. The final email I received from Marie before she returned home buoyed me with its irreverent pugnaciousness: Melinda Fortified with Bionic Tit.

At the Pride Parade in San Francisco a few years back, a topless woman wove among thousands of people colorfully displaying their banners and bodies. One breast hung long and thin; the other was non-existent. In its place, ribs protruded, the ribs a woman usually doesn't reveal. Inlaid in the skin covering the ribs was a long, clean scar like the line of foam a wave leaves behind.

I imagine my breasts erased from my chest. My inner arms would cleanly rise from my sides, rather than grazing these knolls of flesh. Could I run without jog bras, or would my phantom breasts heave? Can we really leave the body, or parts of it, behind?

I haven't been running for nine days, as though I'm avoiding my body. Perhaps I'm also avoiding the ocean, the vast sheet of saltwater that won't let me pretend that I'm indispensable.

It's an incredible day, one of those days where you can't feel your skin the air is so light. Our cat sits on the warm concrete porch, watching Annie water the hydrangeas. No matter what Dr. McFinney tells me tomorrow, a path is spread out before me. An earthquake seems to happen suddenly, but the shifting of the ground has subtly preceded it for years, counting its own geologic time. Stasis is an illusion, and one day my molecules will mix with the dirt. That's not exactly a reassuring thought. It's just the truth, the only one I can count on.

Nestled in my perfectly fitting running shoes and favorite blue jogging shorts, I take off slowly. My breasts, bound in two black jogging bras, span my chest—a ledge of flesh. My breath takes a few minutes to settle in. I reach the end of our street and turn to run along West Cliff Drive, overlooking the blue-gray expanse of sea, which flashes its expansiveness. A V of pelicans swoops near me, and for a minute I can pretend I am flying with them. In unison, they dive down, the tips of their wings gracing the water. I am suddenly so light, as though I am already my ashes, thrown out by someone's hand, released from the weight of the body.

I can't end this piece with transcendence. One day I can embrace the thought of being ashes, while the next I hold tight to this earth. Once again I am on my back as Dr. McFinney feels my breast. My body thumps like a huge heart, and a tear of sweat slides from my armpit down my rib. I begin to feel like the waiting has been the worst part. Whatever it is, I will deal with it. I will grieve, go into shock, get my own bionic tit—live until I die. I just need a label: benign or malignant.

Dr. McFinney gropes a bit more, her eyes revealing nothing. Finally she says, "Yep, it's gone. You're fine."

A flush of freedom washes over me. I know at another point in my life I'll likely have another ten-day wait. Perhaps I'll find a lump myself when I'm ineffectively patting my breasts in the shower. But just for a moment I want to savor the tall tale of immortality.

■ Writing Exercise ■

Begin by making a list of ten specific experiences you have had as an adult that reveal something about who you are. These could be sports or adventure experiences, such as hiking in the Alps, learning to guide a canoe, or even bungee jumping. Or you might list cooking your favorite dish, browsing in a bookstore, or Christmas shopping with a grandchild. The first time you read a particular author. How you dealt with the death of a friend or relative. Buying a gift for a lover. Dealing with an unexpected medical problem. The potential subjects are endless. Remember, though, that what you want for this assignment is a specific event or circumstance that caused you to turn within, to reflect upon who you are, to examine yourself in a different way.

As you edit your final piece, take the gloves off. Shock us, entertain us, make us learn something. Experiment with style and voice. Shake things up. Make us pay attention to what you have to say. And have a reason to say what you do.

The Writing Workshop

Evaluating the Work of Other Students

You may find it helpful to take a somewhat methodical approach to reading the creative work of your peers. Here are some suggestions.

Read the manuscript through once without making any critical commentary. For the first time, read for enjoyment and also to gain some understanding of the work as a whole.

Next, read through the manuscript a second time with a pen in hand. What aspects of the writing work best? Put plus marks or small notations next to what strikes you as most compelling or effective: image, detail, dialogue, description, a distinctive voice or tone. Be as specific as possible. Mark paragraphs, lines, or individual words whenever possible.

Finally, go through the work a third time and look for areas that could be changed, expanded, developed, or even excluded. Again, make notations. Consider using different-colored pens to make these steps distinct. What does the reader need to know to more fully understand the piece? Are there any areas that are unnecessarily vague or obscure?

Stay focused as much as possible on craft and technique. Also try to understand what the writer is ultimately attempting to achieve with the work rather than whether or not you agree with what's being expressed. In creative nonfiction, it's easy—almost irresistible—to argue about what aspects of the work seem most "real." This is a valid discussion, to a point. But move beyond this and ask, does the work stand alone as a creative, literary work? How can you help the writer revise and revision the work—that is, look at it from a different and more illuminating perspective?

The last step is to mark problems with grammar, spelling, punctuation, and style. Is this step important? Very. Is it the most important? No.

Revision Tips and Strategies

Writer's Block Is a Myth

Writer's block is the apparent inability to begin or move forward on a writing project. It can leave a writer feeling stuck, frozen, frustrated, and even terrified. Sometimes it doesn't take much to bring it on. A looming deadline, a sense of not knowing what to do next on a project, or sometimes simply having the desire to write is enough to summon all the symptoms.

Often we feel blocked because our lives are hectic and we don't allow ourselves the time and energy to be creative or to store creative energy. Most people don't give themselves much opportunity to be reflective or contemplative. Sometimes a project is difficult to begin just because it hasn't had adequate time to simmer in your mind. Day dreams and night dreams are a useful and necessary source of writing ideas. Nurture your inner life and pay it heed.

Put a pen and notebook next to your bed each night and say a little mantra: I will remember my dreams. Begin to write as soon as you wake up in the morning—before your coffee, before your shower, before your mind has a chance to fully leave the reality of dream. Don't read what you've written right away. Tell yourself each night that you'll remember a bit more this time. Your mind will embrace the habit.

Carry a small notebook and pen in your purse or your pocket. Write down the details of your life. Describe the people and things around you. Jot down bits of conversation you overhear on the bus, in the subway, in a restaurant. (Don't have a pad of paper? A cocktail napkin will do.) Carry a dictaphone or tape recorder in your car on long drives and talk out your story. Even if you never use the conversation you caught in the elevator or the description of the baby in the park swing, it might jog your creative energies or illuminate some aspect of the piece you're trying to start.

The biggest reason why we don't write, however, is fear. It's the tiny voice in the back of your mind that tells you you're no good. Why should anyone read what you write? What do you have to say about anything? This voice is very different from the voice of the Editor, a useful tool you'll need later when you're ready to revise and edit. No, this is the voice of the Destroyer. The Destroyer is nondiscriminatory and plagues experienced and beginner writers alike.

But it's easy to trick the Destroyer. Put a note next to your writing table or computer that reads: I give myself full permission to write badly every day. The next time you're feeling frozen in front of your computer, reach over and switch off the screen. Then write. The words will begin to flow and you can't go back and "fix" them (at least not yet). Turn off the phone, send the kids next door, and set your kitchen timer for ten minutes. For that ten minutes, write madly—without thought to subject, style, or structure. Just keep your pen moving. Stop when the timer goes off. Do it again the next day. And again.

The most important writing advice is the simplest: keep your butt in the chair.

Writer's block is a myth. But don't tell anyone.

Show, Don't Tell

This is the oldest writing advice in the world. But what does it mean?

One way to think about this is to refrain from telling the reader how to feel. Tell your story forthrightly, avoiding adjectives, adverbs, and outright summary, and let the reader decide in her own heart and mind how to feel about what's going on. Rarely does "telling" invoke an emotional response in the reader because the experience is already interpreted. Instead of writing "John was angry at how he had been treated," write "John stomped into the room, threw his books on the table, and jerked out the chair from behind the desk." The reader will get the point.

(continued)

Revision Tips and Strategies *(continued)*

Try this exercise. Rent your favorite movie and focus on a particular scene. First, write what happens in the scene. Summarize the action. This is "telling." Now, write the scene again but this time focus on the details. Describe the color of the sky, the way a character walks across a room, the scent of lilacs in the air, how the rumble of the train feels as it roars across the tracks. Let us live the scene with you and see it in our mind's eye. Paint a mind picture for the reader. This is "showing." Showing is like watching a close-up in a film instead of reading a film review.

Good writing is a blend of showing and telling, close-ups and long shots. Sometimes you have to summarize briefly or at length to cover periods of time or awkward transitions. But use summary very sparingly. Keep your language conscious and alive; bring the reader into every moment, every movement, every detail.

Why You Should Feel Edgy about Adjectives

Imagine the slender hand of a young woman resting on a lace tablecloth. Now imagine each finger of that hand weighed down with large, garish rings of rhinestone and cubic zirconium.

Adjectives can burden your writing style and make it feel cluttered and overwrought. This seems ironic, doesn't it? You want to develop and "flesh out" your descriptions and add flavor to your story. Putting in a few more adjectives ought to do the trick. But adjectives are cagey. Rarely will they perform as you hope they will. Try eliminating your adjectives completely and making your sentences as clear and concise as possible. Allow action and concrete details—details that invoke all the senses—to create the mood and feel of the piece. Just as in poetry and fiction, you have to make every word count.

While you're at it, try killing a few pronouns along the way as well. He, she, it, they—try to substitute names or concrete nouns instead. (Just like adjectives, you can always add a few back in if you like!) Clarity is everything. Let your prose shimmer.

Chapter 3

Literary Journalism

Introduction

Compared to the personal essay, writing literary journalism is like stepping from the privacy of your writing office or space into a crowded bar or airport. People mill around, jostling one another, talking, arguing, flirting, and debating the topics of the day. The conversation level is so high you can hardly hear yourself think. Indeed, you have to step back to take it all in. How do you fit into this chaotic puzzle of humanity?

As a writer of literary journalism, you essentially enter into a conversation, dialogue, or debate with all those around you. Depending upon your topic, this involves not only your anticipated readers but other writers or journalists, politicians, travelers, medical professionals, economists, lawyers, students, teachers, bus drivers, or plumbers. The list is endless. In the personal essay, you reveal the self. The personal essay is essentially a journey *within*—a soul-searching, intimate, revelatory journey that is undertaken with the reader at your shoulder. Conversely, in literary journalism you reveal the self in relation to the world. Literary journalism is a journey *outside* the self and involves active engagement with significant social, cultural, political, or philosophical themes. The purpose of literary journalism is to respond to public life in a personal and reflective manner, and to examine how the different spheres of the personal and the public intersect or even clash.

An author begins writing literary journalism by fully researching a person, place, event, issue, or idea. This might include doing research in the library, looking into newspaper archives, conducting interviews, and observing or participating in a particular event. This information is then filtered through the writer's perception, understanding, and creative imagination, and presented in a thoughtful, meaningful manner. The tone of a literary journalism piece can be serious, funny, straightforward, or ironic. The author may choose to use a very personal, first-person point of view or a more objective, third-person perspective. As in the personal essay, the writer's tone and approach is often the most compelling aspect of the piece.

Students, readers, and even writers sometimes feel confused about the difference between journalism and literary journalism. Is there a real difference? Can it be defined? One student writes, "I just don't understand the idea of literary journalism. A journalist—that is, someone who writes for a newspaper, magazine, or wire service—is interested in fact. Newspapers supply facts, and they must be reliable. But how does this mesh with creative writing? Do the literary parts of the story need to be as 'true' as the facts?"

In journalism or straight reportage, the writer is bound by professional and ethical standards to report on actual people and events in as objective a manner as possible. The author usually remains invisible and has no presence in the text. A journalist is primarily concerned with the "five W's": who, what, when, where, and—occasionally, but not always—why. These standards vary, depending upon the publication, the market, the readership, the editorial standards of specific publishers, and even the taste and style of particular editors. A newspaper editor is generally not interested in the attitudes or feelings a reporter may have about a particular event. Judgments, feelings, and opinions are usually limited to the op-ed page. Occasionally a magazine editor may ask a writer or reporter to take a slightly more subjective view. Nevertheless, the focus is on fact. Straight journalism does not generally employ literary tropes such as metaphor, simile, or irony. The writing does not depend upon prose rhythms and literary style. Many publications have strict standards of form and style in which the writer is allowed very little latitude.

Literary journalism, on the other hand, is more self-conscious about language and style and involves literary technique that might include description, scene composition, character development, and metaphor. Sentence variety, rhythm, and diction are important as well. Like other forms of creative nonfiction, literary journalism can at times be ironic and deeply self-referential, examining the role of the writer and the writing process itself while engaging and pursuing the stated topic of the piece.

Travel writing often falls into the category of literary journalism, and there is usually a clear distinction between travel writing that is literary journalism and travel writing that is not. In a "straight" travel piece on Rome, for example, the writer might concentrate primarily on describing the best hotels, recommending a few restaurants, and suggesting one- or two-day tours. In a literary journalism piece, the author might begin her essay by describing how she felt the first time she walked into the extraordinary arena of the ruins of the Coliseum and how she felt drawn into a sense of history. Her feelings and perceptions are relevant to the essay; in a "straight" travel piece, she would keep these thoughts and considerations to herself.

However, literary journalism brings up more than a baker's dozen of ethical questions. How do you write a piece that is based on fact but still engages the creative imagination? Where do fact and fiction intersect—if at all? How does the writer's complex web of personal bias alter an event? Can a writer develop scenes, create dialogue, restructure or revise events, or make up composite characters and still write a "true" story?

Occasionally journalists have lost their jobs or their reputations have suffered as a result of embellished or fabricated details and the use of composite characters. In 1981, a reporter who had been awarded the Pulitzer Prize for a story about an eight-year-old heroin addict lost her award when it was revealed that the story was substantially fictionalized. Some critics, writers, and readers take umbrage at what they feel is an author's attempt to compromise truth. The issue of ethics in journalism and the media is an important one and necessitates serious consideration at every stage of the writing process.

However, the issue is a little more complicated than it might appear at first. Does "nonfiction" always mean "true"? Consider something as simple and straightforward as a fender-bender on a busy street corner. Let's say a young woman, late for work, rear-ends a grandmother driving to the grocery store during morning rush hour. Two people witness the event as it happens: a woman standing at an apartment window looking directly down at the scene, and a man facing the cars from the opposite direction, waiting at the light.

A police officer arrives and records the following information. According to the woman at the high-rise window, the second car plowed into the first without warning. According to the man in the third car, everything was fine until the grandmother's car suddenly shot out into the intersection. He can't say whether this was a result of the car being hit from behind or an errant foot on the gas pedal. The grandmother says she was hit from behind without warning. The young woman says that the grandmother's car moved forward with the green light and then stopped suddenly, and the brake lights weren't working. The reporter who arrives on the scene twenty minutes after the event can find only one person still on the scene to interview: a man selling newspapers on the opposite side of the street. "All I know is that there was an ambulance here," he states, "and a whole group of cars over there holding things up." The reporter calls his editor to report an injury incident involving at least two cars, probably more, and heads off to his office to try to uncover more details.

This is a relatively simple example. Context and point of view must always be taken into consideration. Whether we like it or not, reality—to a certain extent—consists of different points of view.

This is not to say that fact does not exist. Some facts are irrefutable and it would be unethical to change them. You could state with certainty that the accident mentioned above happened on a Tuesday at 8:42 A.M. The grandmother was driving a two-door sedan and the young woman was driving a sports utility vehicle. No one appeared to be injured. The damage was estimated at $500.

Unless you are writing fiction and the incident is merely research or background for a story that you will essentially fabricate, it's important to let hard facts stand as hard facts. However, of all the information you uncover during your research, irrefutable fact will likely constitute only a small part. Every writer or journalist is faced with problems of selection, of deciding what to leave in and what to leave out, what perspective to take, where to develop or dramatize the story, and where to let the facts stand alone.

Remember that even newspapers cannot be entirely objective. It's common for many cities to have more than one local newspaper, one that generally takes a politically conservative stance and one that tends to be more liberal. Notice how the same story is written up in different newspapers. An astute reader is always aware of context and perspective.

A writer's work is based on observation. You have an ethical responsibility to observe things as carefully as possible, to research your subjects as fully and objectively as you can, and to write prose that reflects an intelligent and balanced approach. At the same time, you have to keep your reader engaged—substantiate your points, create a clear and effective voice, and tell a good story at the same time.

So how should you deal with these issues in your own writing? Much of it rests on the contract or agreement you make with the reader, implicitly or explicitly, in the first few paragraphs of your essay. Let the reader know—tactfully and artfully—the name of the game. Are you sticking strictly to fact? Do you feel certain about the facts you present? Are you *questioning* the facts? How clear is your line between fact and imagination? Generally speaking, don't create composite characters unless you make it clear to the reader that you are doing so. If you write scenes involving dialogue, do so as accurately as possible and let the reader know—in the essay or in footnotes or citations—that you are relying upon specific sources such as interviews, tapes, or written conversations. If you are creating conversations based upon your research—or, conversely, based strictly upon your imagination—subtly but clearly let the reader know what you're up to.

Names can sometimes present a problem. If you are using people's real names in your essay, you might want to ask them to sign an approval form. Understand, of course, that this does not guarantee smooth sailing—and you might feel extraordinarily self-censored or pressured to present a particular person or event in a more positive light than it deserves. You can change names, of course, as long as the reader is aware that you are doing so. These orchestrations can be accomplished smoothly with lines like "A 42-year-old machinist from Seattle, whom I will call George . . ." or something similar.

Begin your own literary journalism piece by thinking about the social and cultural issues that you deeply care about. How have such issues affected your life personally? (Remember the oft-quoted line, "The personal is the political.") Get out into the community, onto the street, into the library. Research, research, research! How can you involve yourself, as a person and as a writer, in the process? One student decided to ride on a city ambulance for an entire night, and then combined that experience with thorough research into the city's statistics of violent crime and domestic abuse. The result was a very moving and thought-provoking essay.

Once you have completed your research, outline your materials and then brainstorm and freewrite on how to develop them. Use vivid detail, characterization, tension, and plot to bring your essay to life. How has this issue affected your life personally, and further, how does it affect the lives of others? What do you have to say about this issue or experience that will make a difference in the world?

After a lively class discussion on literary journalism, one student wrote, "Now I feel that every time I use the words 'fact' or 'truth', I have to put quotation marks around them." Keep questioning. Keep pushing. Use your intellectual acumen and creative ability to move the reader, to present an issue or situation in a new light.

Like the personal essay, literary journalism is a journey into the heart and mind of the writer. However, it takes this process one step further by taking us out into the world and engaging significant cultural and political issues, by engaging the reader in the complex intertwinings of our public and personal lives.

Readings with Discussion Questions

Hunter S. Thompson
Fear and Loathing in Las Vegas

Hunter S. Thompson began his career as a sports writer in Florida. He went on to make his mark as a "Gonzo Journalist," a phrase he coined to describe the type of new journalism that reflected the disillusionment and volatility of the 1960s. Thompson has been a contributor to or a correspondent for numerous publications including Time, National Observer, *and* Rolling Stone.

Thompson's work includes Hell's Angels: A Strange and Terrible Saga *(1966),* Fear and Loathing in Las Vegas: A Savage Journey to the Heart of the American Dream *(1972), and* Fear and Loathing on the Campaign Trail '72 *(1973). His most recent work is* Kingdom of Fear: Loathsome Secrets of a Star-Crossed Child in the Final Days of the American Century *(2003).*

We were somewhere around Barstow on the edge of the desert when the drugs began to take hold. I remember saying something like "I feel a bit lightheaded; maybe you should drive. . . ." And suddenly there was a terrible roar all around us and the sky was full of what looked like huge bats, all swooping and screeching and diving around the car, which was going about a hundred miles an hour with the top down to Las Vegas. And a voice was screaming: "Holy Jesus! What are these goddamn animals?"

Then it was quiet again. My attorney had taken his shirt off and was pouring beer on his chest, to facilitate the tanning process. "What the hell are you yelling about?" he muttered, staring up at the sun with his eyes closed and covered with wraparound Spanish sunglasses. "Never mind," I said. "It's your turn to drive." I hit the brakes and aimed the Great Red Shark toward the shoulder of the highway. No point mentioning those bats, I thought. The poor bastard will see them soon enough.

It was almost noon, and we still had more than a hundred miles to go. They would be tough miles. Very soon, I knew, we would both be completely twisted. But there was no going back, and no time to rest. We would have to ride it out. Press registration for the fabulous Mint 400 was already underway, and we had to get there by four to claim our sound-proof suite. A fashionable sporting magazine in New York had taken care of the reservations, along with this huge red Chevy convertible we'd just rented off a lot on the Sunset Strip . . . and I was, after all, a professional journalist; so I had an obligation to *cover the story,* for good or ill.

The sporting editors had also given me $300 in cash, most of which was already spent on extremely dangerous drugs. The trunk of the car looked like a mobile police narcotics lab. We had two bags of grass, seventy-five pellets of mescaline, five sheets of high-powered blotter acid, a salt shaker half full of cocaine, and a whole galaxy of multi-colored uppers, downers, screamers, laughers . . . and also a quart of tequila, a quart of rum, a case of Budweiser, a pint of raw ether and two dozen amyls.

All this had been rounded up the night before, in a frenzy of high-speed driving all over Los Angeles County—from Topanga to Watts, we picked up everything we could get our hands on. Not that we *needed* all that for the trip, but once you get locked into a serious drug collection, the tendency is to push it as far as you can.

The only thing that really worried me was the ether. There is nothing in the world more helpless and irresponsible and depraved than a man in the depths of an ether binge. And I knew we'd get into that rotten stuff pretty soon. Probably at the next gas station. We had sampled almost everything else, and now—yes, it was time for a long snort of ether. And then do the next hundred miles in a horrible, slobbering sort of spastic stupor. The only way to keep alert on ether is to do up a lot of amyls—not all at once, but steadily, just enough to maintain the focus at ninety miles an hour through Barstow.

"Man, this is the way to travel," said my attorney. He leaned over to turn the volume up on the radio, humming along with the rhythm section and kind of moaning the words: "One toke over the line, Sweet Jesus . . . One toke over the line . . ."

One toke? You poor fool! Wait till you see those goddamn bats. I could barely hear the radio . . . slumped over on the far side of the seat, grappling with a tape recorder turned all the way up on "Sympathy for the Devil." That was the only tape we had, so we played it constantly, over and over, as a kind of demented counterpoint to the radio. And also to maintain our rhythm on the road. A constant speed is good for gas mileage—and for some reason that seemed important at the time. Indeed. On a trip like this one *must* be careful about gas consumption. Avoid those quick bursts of acceleration that drag blood to the back of the brain.

My attorney saw the hitchhiker long before I did. "Let's give this boy a lift," he said, and before I could mount any argument he was stopped and this poor Okie kid was running up to the car with a big grin on his face, saying, "Hot damn! I never rode in a convertible before!"

"Is that right?" I said. "Well, I guess you're about ready, eh?"

The kid nodded eagerly as we roared off.

"We're your friends," said my attorney. "We're not like the others."

O Christ, I thought, he's gone around the bend. "No more of that talk," I said sharply. "Or I'll put the leeches on you." He grinned, seeming to understand. Luckily, the noise in the car was so awful—between the wind and the radio and the tape machine—that the kid in the back seat couldn't hear a word we were saying. Or could he?

How long can we *maintain?* I wondered. How long before one of us starts raving and jabbering at this boy? What will he think then? This same lonely desert was the last known home of the Manson family. Will he make that grim connection when my attorney starts screaming about bats and huge manta rays coming down on the car? If so—well, we'll just have to cut his head off and bury him somewhere. Because it goes without saying that we can't turn him loose. He'll report us at once to some kind of outback nazi law enforcement agency, and they'll run us down like dogs.

Jesus! Did I *say* that? Or just think it? Was I talking? Did they hear me? I glanced over at my attorney, but he seemed oblivious—watching the road, driving our Great Red Shark along at a hundred and ten or so. There was no sound from the back seat.

Maybe I'd better have a chat with this boy, I thought. Perhaps if I *explain* things, he'll rest easy.

Of course. I leaned around in the seat and gave him a fine big smile . . . admiring the shape of his skull.

"By the way," I said. "There's one thing you should probably understand."

He stared at me, not blinking. Was he gritting his teeth?

"Can you *hear* me?" I yelled.

He nodded.

"That's good," I said. "Because I want you to know that we're on our way to Las Vegas to find the American Dream." I smiled. "That's why we rented this car. It was the only way to do it. Can you grasp that?"

He nodded again, but his eyes were nervous.

"I want you to have all the background," I said. "Because this is a very ominous assignment—with overtones of extreme personal danger. . . . Hell, I forgot all about this beer; you want one?"

He shook his head.

"How about some ether?" I said.

"What?"

"Never mind. Let's get right to the heart of this thing. You see, about twenty-four hours ago we were sitting in the Polo Lounge of the Beverly Hills Hotel—in the patio section, of course—and we were just sitting there under a palm tree when this uniformed dwarf came up to me with a pink telephone and said, 'This must be the call you've been waiting for all this time, sir.' "

I laughed and ripped open a beer can that foamed all over the back seat while I kept talking. "And you know? He was right! I'd been *expecting* that call, but I didn't know who it would come from. Do you follow me?"

The boy's face was a mask of pure fear and bewilderment.

I blundered on: "I want you to understand that this man at the wheel is my *attorney!* He's not just some dingbat I found on the Strip. Shit, *look* at him! He doesn't look like you or me, right? That's because he's a foreigner. I think he's probably Samoan. But it doesn't matter, does it? Are you prejudiced?"

"Oh, hell *no!*" he blurted.

"I didn't think so," I said. "Because in spite of his race, this man is extremely valuable to me." I glanced over at my attorney, but his mind was somewhere else.

I whacked the back of the driver's seat with my fist. "This is *important,* goddamnit! This is a *true story!*" The car swerved sickeningly, then straightened out. "Keep your hands off my fucking neck!" my attorney screamed. The kid in the back looked like he was ready to jump right out of the car and take his chances.

Our vibrations were getting nasty—but why? I was puzzled, frustrated. Was there no communication in this car? Had we deteriorated to the level of *dumb beasts?*

Because my story *was* true. I was certain of that. And it was extremely important, I felt, for the *meaning* of our journey to be made absolutely clear. We had actually been sitting there in the Polo Lounge—for many hours— drinking Singapore Slings with mescal on the side and beer chasers. And when the call came, I was ready.

The Dwarf approached our table cautiously, as I recall, and when he handed me the pink telephone I said nothing, merely listened. And then I hung up, turning to face my attorney. "That was headquarters," I said. "They want me to go to Las Vegas at once, and make contact with a Portuguese photographer named Lacerda. He'll have the details. All I have to do is check into my suite and he'll seek me out."

My attorney said nothing for a moment, then he suddenly came alive in his chair. "God *hell!*" he exclaimed. "I think I see the *pattern.* This one sounds like real trouble!" He tucked his khaki undershirt into his white rayon bellbottoms and called for more drink. "You're going to need plenty of legal advice before this thing is over," he said. "And my first advice is that you should rent a very fast car with no top and get the hell out of L.A. for at least forty-eight hours." He shook his head sadly. "This blows my weekend, because naturally I'll have to go with you—and we'll have to arm ourselves."

"Why not?" I said. "If a thing like this is worth doing at all, it's worth doing right. We'll need some decent equipment and plenty of cash on the line—if only for drugs and a super-sensitive tape recorder, for the sake of a permanent record."

"What kind of a story is this?" he asked.

"The Mint 400," I said. "It's the richest off-the-road race for motorcycles and dune-buggies in the history of organized sport—a fantastic spectacle in honor of some fatback *grossero* named Del Webb, who owns the luxurious Mint Hotel in the heart of downtown Las Vegas . . . at least that's what the press release says; my man in New York just read it to me."

"Well," he said, "as your attorney I advise you to buy a motorcycle. How else can you cover a thing like this righteously?"

"No way," I said. "Where can we get hold of a Vincent Black Shadow?"

"What's that?"

"A fantastic bike," I said. "The new model is something like two thousand cubic inches, developing two hundred brake-horsepower at four thousand revolutions per minute on a magnesium frame with two styrofoam seats and a total curb weight of exactly two hundred pounds."

"That sounds about right for this gig," he said.

"It is," I assured him. "The fucker's not much for turning, but it's pure hell on the straightaway. It'll outrun the F-111 until takeoff."

"Takeoff?" he said. "Can we handle that much torque?"

"Absolutely," I said. "I'll call New York for some cash."

Questions for Discussion

1. Describe the tone and style of this piece. Is the narrator reliable or unreliable?

2. What is Thompson saying about the American Dream? What does he imply about American culture? Would you classify his work as literary journalism?

3. Do you find Thompson's style compelling? Copy a page or two into your journal. Take one of your own experiences and see if you can imitate Thompson's style and pace.

Simon Winchester
The Professor and the Madman

Simon Winchester is a prolific author and travel writer, penning such well-known books as Krakatoa: The Day the World Exploded: August 27, 1883; The Professor and the Madman; The Map That Changed the World; *and* The Fracture Zone, *among others. Born in England, Winchester studied geology at Oxford and went on to write for publications including* Conde Nast Traveler, Smithsonian, *and* National Geographic. *His work has also appeared in* Harper's, Granta, The New York Times, *and* The Atlantic Monthly. *Winchester has lived all over the world but currently divides his time between Massachusetts and the Western Isles of Scotland.*

The Professor and the Madman is an extraordinary chronicle of the making of the Oxford English Dictionary and the story of two men involved in its creation: Professor James Murray, who led the committee involved in compiling the dictionary, and Dr. W. C. Minor, an American civil war veteran who contributed more than 10,000 definitions to the dictionary. When the committee sought to honor Dr. Minor, it was discovered that he was an inmate at an asylum for the criminally insane.

Preface

Mysterious (mistī·riəs), *a.* [f. L. *mysterium* Mystery[1] + ous. Cf. F. *mystérieux*.]
    1. Full of or fraught with mystery; wrapt in mystery; hidden from human knowledge or understanding; impossible or difficult to explain, solve, or discover; of obscure origin, nature, or purpose.

Popular myth has it that one of the most remarkable conversations in modern literary history took place on a cool and misty late autumn afternoon in 1896, in the small village of Crowthorne in the county of Berkshire.

One of the parties to the colloquy was the formidable Dr. James Murray, the editor of the *Oxford English Dictionary.* On the day in question he had traveled fifty miles by train from Oxford to meet an enigmatic figure named Dr. W. C. Minor, who was among the most prolific of the thousands of volunteer contributors whose labors lay at the core of the dictionary's creation.

For very nearly twenty years beforehand these two men had corresponded regularly about the finer points of English lexicography, but they had never met. Dr. Minor seemed never willing or able to leave his home at Crowthorne, never willing to come to Oxford. He was unable to offer any kind of explanation, or to do more than offer his regrets.

Dr. Murray, who himself was rarely free from the burdens of his work at his dictionary headquarters, the famous Scriptorium in Oxford, had nonetheless long dearly wished to see and thank his mysterious and intriguing helper. And particularly so by the late 1890s, with the dictionary well on its way to being half completed: Official honors were being showered upon all its creators, and Murray wanted to make sure that all those involved—even men so apparently bashful as Dr. Minor—were recognized for the valuable work they had done. He decided he would pay a visit.

Once he had made up his mind to go, he telegraphed his intentions, adding that he would find it most convenient to take a train that arrived at Crowthorne Station—then actually known as Wellington College Station, since it served the famous boys' school situated in the village—just after two on a certain Wednesday in November. Dr. Minor sent a wire by return to say that he was indeed expected and would be made most welcome. On the journey from Oxford the weather was fine; the trains were on time; the auguries, in short, were good.

At the railway station a polished landau and a liveried coachman were waiting, and with James Murray aboard they clip-clopped back through the lanes of rural Berkshire. After twenty minutes or so the carriage turned up a long drive lined with tall poplars, drawing up eventually outside a huge and rather forbidding red-brick mansion. A solemn servant showed the lexicographer upstairs, and into a book-lined study, where behind an immense mahogany desk stood a man of undoubted importance. Dr. Murray bowed gravely, and launched into the brief speech of greeting that he had so long rehearsed:

"A very good afternoon to you, sir. I am Dr. James Murray of the London Philological Society, and Editor of the *Oxford English Dictionary*. It is indeed an honour and a pleasure to at long last make your acquaintance—for you must be, kind sir, my most assiduous helpmeet, Dr. W. C. Minor?"

There was a brief pause, a momentary air of mutual embarrassment. A clock ticked loudly. There were muffled footsteps in the hall. A distant clank of keys. And then the man behind the desk cleared his throat, and he spoke:

"I regret, kind sir, that I am not. It is not at all as you suppose. I am in fact the Governor of the Broadmoor Criminal Lunatic Asylum. Dr. Minor is most certainly here. But he is an inmate. He has been a patient here for more than twenty years. He is our longest-staying resident."

Although the official government files relating to this case are secret, and have been locked away for more than a century, I have recently been allowed to see them. What follows is the strange, tragic, yet spiritually uplifting story they reveal.

1   The Dead of Night in Lambeth Marsh

Murder (mɐ·ɹdəɹ), *sb.* Forms: a. 1 morþor, -ur, 3–4 morþre, 3–4, 6 murthre, 4 myrþer, 4–6 murthir, morther, 5 *Sc.* murthour, murthyr, 5–6 murthur, 6 mwrther, *Sc.* morthour, 4–9 (now *dial.* and *Hist.* or *arch.*) murther; β. 3–5 murdre, 4–5 moerdre, 4–6 mordre, 5 moordre, 6 murdur, mourdre, 6– murder. [OE. *mor* or neut. (with pl. of masc. form *mor ras*) = Goth. *maur r* neut.:–OTeut. *murþro*ᵐ:–pre-Teut. *mrtro-m*, f. root *mer-: mor-: mr-* to die, whence L. morī to die, *mors* (*morti-*) death, Gr. μορτός, βροτός mortal, Skr. *mr* to die, *mará* masc., *mrti* fem., death, *márta* mortal, OSl. *mĭrĕti*, Lith. *mirti* to die, Welsh *marw*, Irish *mar* dead.

The word has not been found in any Teut. lang. but Eng. and Gothic, but that it existed in continental WGer. is evident, as it is the source of OF. *murdre, murtre* (mod. F. *meurtre*) and of med. L. *mordrum, murdrum,* and OHG. had the derivative *murdren* MURDER *v.* All the Teut. langs. exc. Gothic possessed a synonymous word from the same root with different suffix: OE. *mor* neut., masc. (MURTH[1]), OS. *mor* neut., OFris. *morth, mord* neut., MDu. *mort, mord* neut. (Du. *moord*), OHG. *mord* (MHG. *mort,* mod. G. *mord*), ON. *mor* neut.:–OTeut. **mur o-:*–pre-Teut. **mrto-.*

The change of original into *d* (contrary to the general tendency to change *d* into before syllabic *r*) was prob. due to the influence of the AF. *murdre, moerdre* and the Law Latin *murdrum.*]

1. The most heinous kind of criminal homicide; also, an instance of this. In *English* (also *Sc.* and *U.S.*) *Law,* defined as the unlawful killing of a human being with malice aforethought; often more explicitly *wilful murder.*

In OE. the word could be applied to any homicide that was strongly reprobated (it had also the senses 'great wickedness', 'deadly injury', 'torment'). More strictly, however, it denoted *secret* murder, which in Germanic antiquity was alone regarded as (in the modern sense) a crime, open homicide being considered a private wrong calling for blood-revenge or compensation. Even under Edward I, Britton explains the AF. *murdre* only as felonious homicide of which both the perpetrator and the victim are unidentified. The 'malice aforethought' which enters into the legal definition of murder, does not (as now interpreted) admit of any summary definition. A person may even be guilty of 'wilful murder' without intending the death of the victim, as when death results from an unlawful act which the doer knew to be likely to cause the death of some one, or from injuries inflicted to facilitate the commission of certain offences. It is essential to 'murder' that the perpetrator be of sound mind, and (in England, though not in Scotland) that death should ensue within a year and a day after the act presumed to have caused it. In British law no degrees of guilt are recognized in murder; in the U.S. the law distinguishes 'murder in the first degree' (where there are no mitigating circumstances) and 'murder in the second degree'.

In Victorian London, even in a place as louche and notoriously crime-ridden as Lambeth Marsh, the sound of gunshots was a rare event indeed. The marsh was a sinister place, a jumble of slums and sin that crouched, dark and ogrelike, on the bank of the Thames just across from Westminster; few respectable Londoners would ever admit to venturing there. It was a robustly violent part of town as well—the footpad lurked in Lambeth, there had once been an outbreak of garroting, and in every crowded alley were the roughest kinds of pickpocket. Fagin, Bill Sikes, and Oliver Twist would have all seemed quite at home in Victorian Lambeth: This was Dickensian London writ large.

But it was not a place for men with guns. The armed criminal was a phenomenon little known in the Lambeth of Prime Minister Gladstone's day, and even less known in the entire metropolitan vastness of London. Guns were costly, cumbersome, difficult to use, hard to conceal. Then, as still today, the use of a firearm in the commission of a crime was thought of as somehow a very un-British act—and as something to be written about and recorded as a rarity. "Happily," proclaimed a smug editorial in Lambeth's weekly newspaper, "we in this country have no experience of the crime of 'shooting down,' so common in the United States."

So when a brief fusillade of three revolver shots rang out shortly after two o'clock on the moonlit Saturday morning of February 17, 1872, the sound was unimagined, unprecedented, and shocking. The three cracks—perhaps there were four—were loud, very loud, and they echoed through the cold and smokily damp night air. They were heard—and, considering their rarity, just by chance instantly recognized—by a keen young police constable named Henry Tarrant, then attached to the Southwark Constabulary's L Division.

The clocks had only recently struck two, his notes said later; he was performing with routine languor the duties of the graveyard shift, walking slowly beneath the viaduct arches beside Waterloo Railway Station, rattling the locks of the shops and cursing the bone-numbing chill.

When he heard the shots, Tarrant blew his whistle to alert any colleagues who (he hoped) might be on patrol nearby, and he began to run. Within seconds he had raced through the warren of mean and slippery lanes that made up what in those days was still called a village, and had emerged into the wide riverside swath of Belvedere Road, from whence he was certain the sounds had come.

Another policeman, Henry Burton, who had heard the piercing whistle, as had a third, William Ward, rushed to the scene. According to Burton's notes, he dashed toward the echoing sound and came across his colleague Tarrant, who was by then holding a man, as if arresting him. "Quick!" cried Tarrant. "Go to the road—a man has been shot!" Burton and Ward raced toward Belvedere Road and within seconds found the unmoving body of a dying man. They fell to their knees, and onlookers noted they had cast off their helmets and gloves and were hunched over the victim.

There was blood gushing onto the pavement—blood staining a spot that would for many months afterward be described in London's more dramatically minded papers as the location of A HEINOUS CRIME, A TERRIBLE EVENT, AN ATROCIOUS OCCURRENCE, A VILE MURDER.

The Lambeth Tragedy, the papers eventually settled upon calling it—as if the simple existence of Lambeth itself were not something of a tragedy. Yet this was a most unusual event, even by the diminished standards of the marsh dwellers. For though the place where the killing occurred had over the years been witness to many strange events, the kind eagerly chronicled in the penny dreadfuls, this particular drama was to trigger a chain of consequences that was quite without precedent. And while some aspects of this crime and its aftermath would turn out to be sad and barely believable, not all of them, as this account will show, were to be wholly tragic. Far from it, indeed.

Even today Lambeth is a singularly unlovely part of the British capital, jammed anonymously between the great fan of roads and railway lines that take commuters in and out of the city center from the southern counties. These days the Royal Festival Hall and the South Bank Centre stand there, built on the site of the 1951 fairgrounds where an entertainment was staged to help cheer up the rationed and threadbare Londoners. Otherwise it is an unlovely, characterless sort of place—rows of prisonlike buildings that house lesser government ministries, the headquarters of an oil company around which winter winds whip bitterly, a few unmemorable pubs and newspaper shops, and the lowering presence of Waterloo Station—lately expanded with the terminal for the Channel Tunnel express trains—which exerts its dull magnetic pull over the neighborhood.

The railway chiefs of old never bothered to build a grand station hotel at Waterloo—though they did build monster structures of great luxury at the other London stations, like Victoria and Paddington, and even St. Pancras and King's Cross. Lambeth has long been one of the nastier parts of London; until very recently, with the further development of the Festival Hall site, no one of any style and consequence has ever wanted to linger there, neither a passenger back in the days of the Victorian boat trains, nor anyone for any reason at all today. It is slowly improving; but its reputation dogs it.

A hundred years ago it was positively vile. It was still then low, marshy, and undrained, a swampy gyre of pathways where a sad little stream called the Neckinger seeped into the Thames. The land was jointly owned by the archbishop of Canterbury and the duke of Cornwall, landlords who, rich enough in their own right, never bothered to develop it in the manner of the great lords of London—Grosvenor, Bedford, Devonshire—who created the squares, mansions, and terraces on the far side of the river.

So it was instead a place of warehouses, tenant shacks, and miserable rows of ill-built houses. There were blacking factories (shoe polish makers, like the one in which the young Charles Dickens worked) and soap boilers, small firms of dyers and lime burners, and tanning yards where the leatherworkers used a substance for darkening skins that was known as "pure" and that was gathered from the streets each night by the filthiest of the local indigents—"pure" being a Victorian term for dog turds.

A sickly smell of yeast and hops lay over the town, wafting from the chimneys of the great Red Lion Brewery, which stood on Belvedere Road, just north of the Hungerford Bridge. And this bridge was symbolic of what encompassed the entire marsh—the railways, hefted high over the swamps, on viaducts on which the trains (including those of the London Necropolis Railway, built to take corpses to the cemeteries in the suburb of Woking) chuffed and snorted, and across which miles of wagons lurched and banged. Lambeth was widely regarded as one of the noisiest and most sulfurous parts of a capital that had already a grim reputation for din and dirt.

Lambeth Marsh was also, as it happened, just beyond the legal jurisdiction of both the Cities of London and Westminster. It belonged administratively—at least until 1888—to the County of Surrey—meaning that the relatively strict laws that applied to the capital's citizens did not apply to anyone who ventured, via one of the new bridges, like Waterloo, Blackfriars, Westminster, or Hungerford, into the wen of Lambeth. The village thus fast became known as a site of revelry and abandon—a place where public houses, brothels, and lewd theaters abounded, and where a man could find entertainment of all kinds—and disease of all varieties—for no more than a handful of pennies.

To see a play that would not pass muster with the London censors, to be able to drink absinthe into the small hours of the morning, to buy the choicest pornography newly smuggled from Paris, or to have a girl of any age and not be concerned that a Bow Street runner (as London's early police were known), or her parents, might chase after you—you "went Surreyside," as they said, to Lambeth.

But, as with most slums, its cheapness attracted respectable men to live and work in Lambeth too, and by all accounts George Merrett was one of them. He was a stoker at the Red Lion Brewery; he had been there for the previous eight years, employed all the time as one of the gang who kept the fires burning through the day and night, keeping the vats bubbling and the barley malting. He was thirty-four years old and he lived locally, at 24 Cornwall Cottages, on the Cornwall Road.

George Merrett was, like so many younger workers in Victorian London, an immigrant from the countryside, and so was his wife, Eliza. He came from a village in Wiltshire, she from Gloucestershire. They had both been farm laborers and—with no protection by unions, no solidarity with their fellows—had been paid trifling sums to perform humiliating tasks for pitiless masters. They had met at a farm show in the Cotswolds and had vowed to leave together for the immeasurable possibilities offered by London, only two hours away on the new express train from Swindon. They moved first to north London, where their first daughter, Clare, was born in 1860; then they shifted into the city center; and finally in 1867, the family having become too large and costly and manual work too scarce, they found themselves near the brewery site in the bustling sty of Lambeth.

The young couple's surroundings and lodgings were exactly as the illustrator Gustave Doré had drawn on one of his horrified expeditions from Paris: a dim world of bricks and soot and screeching iron, of huddled tenements, of tiny backyards, each with a privy and clothes boiler and washing line, and everywhere an air of damp and sulfurous stench, and even a rough-hewn, rollicking, hugger-mugger, devil-may-care, peculiarly London type of good cheer. Whether the Merretts missed the fields and the cider and the skylarks, or whether they imagined that that ideal had ever truly been the world they had left, we shall never know.

By the winter of 1871 George and Eliza had, as was typical of the inhabitants of the dingier quarters of Victorian London, a very substantial family: six children, ranging from Clare at nearly thirteen to Freddy at twelve months. Mrs. Merrett was about to be confined with her seventh pregnancy. They were a poor family, as were most in Lambeth: George Merrett brought home twenty-four shillings a week, a miserable sum even then. With rent payable to the archbishop, and with food needed for the eight ever-open mouths, theirs were straitened circumstances indeed.

On the Saturday morning, just before 2 A.M., Merrett was awakened by a neighbor tapping on his window, as prearranged. He rose from bed, and readied himself for the dawn shift. It was a bitter morning, and he dressed as warmly as he could afford: a threadbare greatcoat over the kind of smock-jacket that Victorians called a slop, a tattered gray shirt, corduroy trousers tied at the ankle with twine, heavy socks, and black boots. The clothes were none too clean, but he was to heave coal for the next eight hours, and could not be too bothered with appearance.

His wife recalled him striking a light before leaving home: Her last sight of him was under one of the bright gas-lamps with which Lambeth's streets had recently been equipped. His breath was visible in the cold night air—or maybe he was just puffing on his pipe—and he walked purposefully down to the end of Cornwall Road before turning into Belvedere Road. The night was clear and starlit and, once his footsteps had faded, soundless except for the clanking and puffing of the ever-present railway engines.

Mrs. Merrett had no reason to be concerned: She assumed, as she had for each of the twenty previous nights on which her husband had worked the dawn shift, that all would be well. George was simply making his way as usual toward the high walls and ornate gates of the great brewery where he worked, shoveling coal beneath the shadow of the great red lion that was one of London's better-known landmarks. There may have been little money in the job; but working at so famous an institution as the Red Lion Brewery, well, that was some reason for pride.

But that night George Merrett never reached his destination. As he passed the entrance to Tennison Street, between where the south side of the Lambeth Lead Works abutted onto the north wall of the brewery, there came a sudden cry. A man shouted at him, appeared to be chasing him, was yelling furiously. Merrett was frightened: This was something more than a mere footpad—that silent and menacing figure who lurked in the dark carrying a lead-tipped cosh and wearing a mask; this was something quite out of the ordinary, and Merrett began to run in terror, slipping and sliding on the frost-slick cobbles. He looked back: The man was still there, still chasing after him, still shouting angrily. Then, quite incredibly, he stopped and raised a gun, took aim, and fired.

The shot missed, whistling past him and striking the brewery wall. George Merrett tried to run faster. He cried out for help. There was another shot. Perhaps another. And then a final shot that struck the unfortunate Merrett in the neck. He fell heavily onto the cobbled pavement, his face down, a pool of blood spreading around him.

Moments later came the running footfalls of Constable Burton, who found the man, lifted him, and attempted to comfort him. The other policeman, William Ward, summoned a passing hansom cab from the still-busy thoroughfare of Waterloo Road. They gently picked the wounded man up from the ground, hoisted him into the vehicle, and ordered the driver to take them as fast as possible to St. Thomas's Hospital, five hundred yards farther south on Belvedere Road, across from the archbishop's London palace. The horses did their best, their hooves striking sparks from the cobbles as they rushed the victim to the emergency entrance.

It was a futile journey. Doctors examined George Merrett and attempted to close the gaping wound in his neck. But his carotid artery had been severed, his spine snapped by two large-caliber bullets.

The man who had perpetrated this unprecedented crime was, within moments of committing it, in the firm custody of Constable Tarrant. He was a tall, well-dressed man of what the policeman described as "military appearance," with an erect bearing and a haughty air. He held a still-smoking revolver in his right hand. He made no attempt to run but stood silently as the policeman approached.

"Who is it that has fired?" asked the constable.

"I did," said the man, holding up the gun. Tarrant snatched it from him.

"Whom did you fire at?" he asked.

The man pointed down Belvedere Road, to the figure lying motionless beneath a street lamp just outside the brewery store. He made the only droll remark that history records him as having made—but a remark that, as it happens, betrayed one of the driving weaknesses of his life.

"It was a man," he said, with a tone of disdain. "You do not suppose I would be so cowardly as to shoot a *woman*!"

By now two other policemen had arrived on the scene, as had inquisitive locals—among them the Hungerford Bridge toll collector, who at first had not dared go out "for fear I would take a bullet," and a woman undressing in her room on Tennison Street—a street in which it was apparently far from uncommon for women to be undressing at all hours. Constable Tarrant, pointing toward the victim and ordering his two colleagues to see what they could do for him and to prevent a crowd from gathering, escorted the supposed—and unprotesting—murderer to the Tower Street police station.

On the way his prisoner became rather more voluble, though Tarrant described him as cool, collected, and clearly not affected by drink. It had all been a terrible accident; he had shot the wrong man, he insisted. He was after someone else, someone quite different. Someone had broken into his room; he was simply chasing him away, defending himself as anyone surely had a perfect right to do.

"Don't handle me!" he said, when Tarrant put a hand on his shoulder. But then, rather more gently, he said to the policeman: "You have not searched me, you know."

"I'll do that at the station," replied the constable.

"How do you know I haven't got another gun, and might shoot you?"

The policeman, plodding and imperturbable, replied that if he did have another gun, perhaps he would be so kind as to keep it in his pocket for the time being.

"But I do have a knife," replied the prisoner.

"Keep that in your pocket also," said the stolid constable.

There turned out to be no other gun, but a search did turn up a long hunting knife in a leather sheath, strapped to the man's belt behind his back.

"A surgical instrument," it was explained. "I don't always carry it with me."

Tarrant, once he had completed the search, explained to the desk sergeant what had happened on Belvedere Road a few moments before. The pair then set about formally interviewing the arrested man.

His name was William Chester Minor. He was thirty-seven years old, and, as the policemen suspected from his bearing, a former army officer. He was also a qualified surgeon. He had lived in London for less than a year and had taken rooms locally, living alone in a simple furnished upstairs room nearby at 41 Tennison Street. He evidently had no financial need to live so economically, for he was in fact a man of very considerable means. He hinted that he had come to this lubricious quarter of town for reasons other than the simply monetary, though what those reasons might be did not emerge in the early interrogations. By dawn he was taken off to the Horse-monger Lane jail, charged with murder.

But there was one additional complication. William Minor, it turned out, came from New Haven, Connecticut. He had a commission in the U.S. Army. He was an American.

This put a wholly new complexion on the case. The American legation had now to be told: And so in midmorning, despite its being a Saturday, the Foreign Office formally notified the U.S. minister in London that one of their army surgeons had been arrested and was being held on a charge of murder. The shooting on Belvedere Road, Lambeth—already because of its rarity a cause célèbre—had now become an international incident.

The British papers, always eager to vent editorial spleen on their transatlantic rivals, made hay with this particular aspect of the story.

"The light estimation in which human life is held by Americans," sniffed the *South London Press,* may be noted as one of the most significant points of difference between them and Englishmen, and this is a most shocking example of it brought to our own doors. The victim of a cruel mistake has left a wife near confinement, and seven children, the eldest only thirteen, to the mercy of the world. It is gratifying to be able to record that the benevolent are coming forward with alacrity to the succour of the widow and the fatherless, and it is most sincerely to be hoped that all who can spare even a trifle will do their best to help the victims of this dreadful tragedy. The American Vice-Consul General has, in the most thoughtful manner, opened a subscription list, and issued an appeal to Americans now in London to do what they can to alleviate the misery which an act of their countryman's has entailed.

Scotland Yard detectives were soon put onto the case, so important had it suddenly become that justice was seen to be done on both sides of the Atlantic. Since Minor, silent in his prison cell, was offering no help except to say that he did not know the victim and had shot him in error, they began to investigate any possible motive. In doing so they uncovered the beginnings of the trail of a remarkable and tragic life.

Questions for Discussion

1. Winchester begins each chapter in this book with a definition of a word, as demonstrated in this excerpt. How does this help establish the structure and tone of each chapter?
2. How does this author balance description and plot? What parts of the story constitute "telling" versus "showing"?
3. Note this author's range of vocabulary and the varying length and structure of his sentences. How would you describe his style? Is this a typical style for a writer of history?

Susan Sontag
On AIDS

Susan Sontag has written novels, short stories, plays, screenplays, and essays as well as the nonfiction critiques for which she is best known. Her work insists on a distinction between morality and art with style, not content, as the defining element of art. Sontag's critical writings on everything from film and art to history and photography continuously challenge conventional notions of language and meaning. Sontag received her BA from the University of Chicago, and an MA in English and an MA in philosophy from Harvard. Her many awards include a National Book Award nomination (1966) for Against Interpretation, and Other Essays; *National Book Critics*

Circle for Criticism (1978) for On Photography; *and a National Book Award (2000) for* In America.

Sontag survived a near fatal case of cancer in the 1970s, during which time she wrote Illness as Metaphor. *In this piece, she examines further how the way in which we describe and articulate a particular disease may immensely impact our treatment of the people who suffer from that disease.*

"Plague" is the principal metaphor by which the AIDS epidemic is understood. And because of AIDS, the popular misidentification of cancer as an epidemic, even a plague, seems to be receding: AIDS has banalized cancer.

Plague, from the Latin *plaga* (stroke, wound), has long been used metaphorically as the highest standard of collective calamity, evil, scourge—Procopius, in his masterpiece of calumny, *The Secret History*, called the Emperor Justinian worse than the plague ("fewer escaped")—as well as being a general name for many frightening diseases. Although the disease to which the word is permanently affixed produced the most lethal of recorded epidemics, being experienced as a pitiless slayer is not necessary for a disease to be regarded as plague-like. Leprosy, very rarely fatal now, was not much more so when at its greatest epidemic strength, between about 1050 and 1350. And syphilis has been regarded as a plague—Blake speaks of "the youthful Harlot's curse" that "blights with plagues the Marriage hearse"—not because it killed often, but because it was disgracing, disempowering, disgusting.

It is usually epidemics that are thought of as plagues. And these mass incidences of illness are understood as inflicted, not just endured. Considering illness as a punishment is the oldest idea of what causes illness, and an idea opposed by all attention to the ill that deserves the noble name of medicine. Hippocrates, who wrote several treatises on epidemics, specifically ruled out "the wrath of God" as a cause of bubonic plague. But the illnesses interpreted in antiquity as punishments, like the plague in *Oedipus*, were not thought to be shameful, as leprosy and subsequently syphilis were to be. Diseases, insofar as they acquired meaning, were collective calamities, and judgments on a community. Only injuries and disabilities, not diseases, were thought of as individually merited. For an analogy in the literature of antiquity to the modern sense of a shaming, isolating disease, one would have to turn to Philoctetes and his stinking wound.

The most feared diseases, those that are not simply fatal but transform the body into something alienating, like leprosy and syphilis and cholera and (in the imagination of many) cancer, are the ones that seem particularly susceptible to promotion to "plague." Leprosy and syphilis were the first illnesses to be consistently described as repulsive. It was syphilis that, in the earliest descriptions by doctors at the end of the fifteenth century, generated a version of the metaphors that flourish around AIDS: of a disease that was not only repulsive and retributive but collectively invasive. Although Erasmus, the most influential European pedagogue of the early sixteenth century, described syphilis as "nothing but a kind of leprosy" (by 1529 he called it "something worse than leprosy"), it had already been understood as something different, because sexually transmitted. Paracelsus speaks (in Donne's paraphrase) of "that foule contagious disease which then had invaded mankind in a few places, and since overflowes in all, that for punishment of generall licentiousnes God first inflicted that disease." Thinking of syphilis as a punishment for an individual's transgression was for a long time, virtually until the disease became easily curable, not really distinct from regarding it as retribution for the licentiousness of a community—as with AIDS now, in the rich industrial countries. In contrast to cancer, understood in a modern way as a disease incurred by (and revealing of) individuals, AIDS is understood in a premodern way, as a disease incurred by people both as individuals and as members of a "risk group"—that neutral-sounding, bureaucratic category which also revives the archaic idea of a tainted community that illness has judged.

Not every account of plague or plague-like diseases, of course, is a vehicle for lurid stereotypes about illness and the ill. The effort to think critically, historically, about illness (about disaster generally) was attempted throughout the eighteenth century: say, from Defoe's *A Journal of the Plague Year* (1722) to Alessandro Manzoni's *The Betrothed* (1827). Defoe's historical fiction, purporting to be an eyewitness account of bubonic plague in London in 1665, does not further any understanding of the plague as punishment or, a later part of the script, as a transforming experience. And Manzoni, in his lengthy account of the passage of plague through the duchy of Milan in 1630, is avowedly committed to presenting a more accurate, less reductive view than his historical sources. But even these two complex narratives reinforce some of the perennial, simplifying ideas about plague.

One feature of the usual script for plague: the disease invariably comes from somewhere else. The names for syphilis, when it began its epidemic sweep through Europe in the last decade of the fifteenth century, are an exemplary illustration of the need to make a dreaded disease foreign. It was the "French pox" to the English, *morbus Germanicus* to the Parisians, the Naples sickness to the Florentines, the Chinese disease to the Japanese. But what may seem like a joke about the inevitability of chauvinism reveals a more important truth: that there is a link between imagining disease and imagining foreignness. It lies perhaps in the very concept of wrong, which is archaically identical with the non-us, the alien. A polluting person is always wrong, as Mary Douglas has observed. The inverse is also true: a person judged to be wrong is regarded as, at least potentially, a source of pollution.

The foreign place of origin of important illnesses, as of drastic changes in the weather, may be no more remote than a neighboring country. Illness is a species of invasion, and indeed is often carried by soldiers. Manzoni's account of the plague of 1630 begins:

> The plague which the Tribunal of Health had feared might enter the Milanese provinces with the German troops had in fact entered, as is well known; and it is also well known that it did not stop there, but went on to invade and depopulate a large part of Italy.

Defoe's chronicle of the plague of 1665 begins similarly, with a flurry of ostentatiously scrupulous speculation about its foreign origin:

> It was about the beginning of September, 1664, that I, among the rest of my neighbours, heard in ordinary discourse that the plague was returned again in Holland; for it had been very violent there, and particularly at Amsterdam and Rotterdam, in the year 1663, whither, they say, it was brought, some said from Italy, others from the Levant, among some goods which were brought home by their Turkey fleet; others said it was brought from Candia; others from Cyprus. It mattered not from whence it came; but all agreed it was come into Holland again.

The bubonic plague that reappeared in London in the 1720s had arrived from Marseilles, which was where plague in the eighteenth century was usually thought to enter Western Europe: brought by seamen, then transported by soldiers and merchants. By the nineteenth century the foreign origin was usually more exotic, the means of transport less specifically imagined, and the illness itself had become phantasmagorical, symbolic.

At the end of *Crime and Punishment* Raskolnikov dreams of plague: "He dreamt that the whole world was condemned to a terrible new strange plague that had come to Europe from the depths of Asia." At the beginning of the sentence it is "the whole world," which turns out by the end of the sentence to be "Europe," afflicted by a lethal visitation from Asia. Dostoevsky's model is undoubtedly cholera, called Asiatic cholera, long endemic in Bengal, which had rapidly become and remained through most of the nineteenth century a worldwide epidemic disease. Part of the centuries-old conception of Europe as a privileged cultural entity is that it is a place which is colonized by lethal diseases coming from elsewhere. Europe is assumed to be by rights free of disease. (And Europeans have been astoundingly callous about the far more devastating extent to which they—as invaders, as colonists—have introduced *their* lethal diseases to the exotic, "primitive" world: think of the ravages of smallpox, influenza, and cholera on the aboriginal populations of the Americas and Australia.) The tenacity of the connection of exotic origin with dreaded disease is one reason why cholera, of which there were four great outbreaks in Europe in the nineteenth century, each with a lower death toll than the preceding one, has continued to be more memorable than smallpox, whose ravages increased as the century went on (half a million died in the European smallpox pandemic of the early 1870s) but which could not be construed as, plague-like, a disease with a non-European origin.

Plagues are no longer "sent," as in Biblical and Greek antiquity, for the question of agency has blurred. Instead, peoples are "visited" by plagues. And the visitations recur, as is taken for granted in the subtitle of Defoe's narrative, which explains that it is about that "which happened in London during the Last Great Visitation in 1665." Even for non-Europeans, lethal disease may be called a visitation. But a visitation on "them" is invariably described as different from one on "us." "I believe that about one half of the whole people was carried off by this visitation," wrote the English traveler Alexander Kinglake, reaching Cairo at a time of the bubonic plague (sometimes called "oriental plague"). "The Orientals, however, have more quiet fortitude than Europeans under afflictions of this sort." Kinglake's influential book *Eothen* (1844)—suggestively subtitled "Traces of Travel Brought Home from the East"—illustrates many of the enduring Eurocentric presumptions about others, starting from the fantasy that peoples with little reason to expect exemption from misfortune have a lessened capacity to *feel* misfortune. Thus it is believed that Asians (or the poor, or blacks, or Africans, or Muslims) don't suffer or don't grieve as Europeans (or whites) do. The fact that illness is associated with the poor—who are, from the perspective of the privileged, aliens in one's midst—reinforces the association of illness with the foreign: with an exotic, often primitive place.

Thus, illustrating the classic script for plague, AIDS is thought to have started in the "dark continent," then spread to Haiti, then to the United States and to Europe, then. . . . It is understood as a tropical disease: another infestation from the so-called Third World, which is after all where most people in the world live, as well as a scourge of the *tristes tropiques*. Africans who detect racist stereotypes in much of the speculation about the geographical origin of AIDS are not wrong. (Nor are they wrong in thinking that depictions of Africa as the cradle of AIDS must feed anti-African prejudices in Europe and Asia.) The subliminal connection made to notions about a primitive past and the many hypotheses that have been fielded about possible transmission from animals (a disease of green monkeys? African swine fever?) cannot help but activate a familiar set of stereotypes about animality, sexual license, and blacks. In Zaire and other countries in Central Africa where AIDS is killing tens of thousands, the counterreaction has begun. Many doctors, academics, journalists, government officials, and other educated people believe that the virus was sent to Africa from the United States, an act of bacteriological warfare (whose aim was to decrease the African birth rate) which got out of hand and has returned to afflict its perpetrators. A common African version of this belief about the disease's provenance has the virus fabricated in a CIA–Army laboratory in Maryland, sent from there to Africa, and brought back to its country of origin by American homosexual missionaries returning from Africa to Maryland.

At first it was assumed that AIDS must become widespread elsewhere in the same catastrophic form in which it has emerged in Africa, and those who still think this will eventually happen invariably invoke the Black Death. The plague metaphor is an essential vehicle of the most pessimistic reading of the epidemiological prospects. From classic fiction to the latest journalism, the standard plague story is of inexorability, inescapability. The unprepared are taken by surprise; those observing the recommended precautions are struck down as well. *All* succumb when the story is told by an omniscient narrator, as in Poe's parable "The Masque of the Red Death" (1842), inspired by an account of a ball held in Paris during the cholera epidemic of 1832. Almost all—if the story is told from the point of view of a traumatized witness, who will be a benumbed survivor, as in Jean Giono's Stendhalian novel *Horseman on the Roof* (1951), in which a young Italian nobleman in exile wanders through cholera-stricken southern France in the 1830s.

Plagues are invariably regarded as judgments on society, and the metaphoric inflation of AIDS into such a judgment also accustoms people to the inevitability of global spread. This is a traditional use of sexually transmitted diseases: to be described as punishments not just of individuals but of a group ("generall licentiousnes"). Not only venereal diseases have been used in this way, to identify transgressing or vicious populations. Interpreting any catastrophic epidemic as a sign of moral laxity or political decline was as common until the later part of the last century as associating dreaded diseases with foreignness. (Or with despised and feared minorities.) And the assignment of fault is not contradicted by cases that do not fit. The Methodist preachers in England who connected the cholera epidemic of 1832 with drunkenness (the temperance movement was just starting) were not understood to be claiming that *everybody* who got cholera was a drunkard: there is always room for "innocent victims" (children, young women). Tuberculosis, in its identity as a disease of the poor (rather than of the "sensitive"), was also linked by late-nineteenth-century reformers to alcoholism. Responses to illnesses associated with sinners and the poor invariably recommended the adoption of middle-class values: the regular habits, productivity, and emotional self-control to which drunkenness was thought the chief impediment. Health itself was eventually identified with these values, which were religious as well as mercantile, health being evidence of virtue as disease was of depravity. The dictum that cleanliness is next to godliness is to be taken quite literally. The succession of cholera epidemics in the nineteenth century shows a steady waning of religious interpretations of the disease; more precisely, these increasingly coexisted with other explanations. Although, by the time of the epidemic of 1866, cholera was commonly understood not simply as a divine punishment but as the consequence of remediable defects of sanitation, it was still regarded as the scourge of the sinful. A writer in *The New York Times* declared (April 22, 1866): "Cholera is especially the punishment of neglect of sanitary laws; it is the curse of the dirty, the intemperate, and the degraded."

That it now seems unimaginable for cholera or a similar disease to be regarded in this way signifies not a lessened capacity to moralize about diseases but only a change in the kind of illnesses that are used didactically. Cholera was perhaps the last major epidemic disease fully qualifying for plague status for almost a century. (I mean cholera as a European and American, therefore a nineteenth-century, disease; until 1817 there had never been a cholera epidemic outside the Far East.) Influenza, which would seem more plague-like than any other epidemic in this century if loss of life were the main criterion, and which struck as suddenly as cholera and killed as quickly, usually in a few days, was never viewed metaphorically as a plague. Nor was a more recent epidemic, polio. One reason why plague notions were not invoked is that these epidemics did not have enough of the attributes perennially ascribed to plagues. (For instance, polio was construed as typically a disease of children—of the innocent.) The more important reason is that there has been a shift in the focus of the moralistic exploitation of illness. This shift, to diseases that can be interpreted as judgments on the individual, makes it harder to use epidemic disease as such. For a long time cancer was the illness that best fitted this secular culture's need to blame and punish and censor through the imagery of disease. Cancer was a disease of an individual, and understood as the result not of an action but rather of a failure to act (to be prudent, to exert proper self-control, or to be properly expressive). In the twentieth century it has become almost impossible to moralize about epidemics—except those which are transmitted sexually.

The persistence of the belief that illness reveals, and is a punishment for, moral laxity or turpitude can be seen in another way, by noting the persistence of descriptions of disorder or corruption as a disease. So indispensable has been the plague metaphor in bringing summary judgments about social crisis that its use hardly abated during the era when collective diseases were no longer treated so moralistically—the time between the influenza and encephalitis pandemics of the early and mid-1920s and the acknowledgment of a new, mysterious epidemic illness in the early 1980s— and when great infectious epidemics were so often and confidently proclaimed a thing of the past. The plague metaphor was common in the 1930s as a synonym for social and psychic catastrophe. Evocations of plague of this type usually go with rant, with antiliberal attitudes: think of Artaud on theatre and plague, of Wilhelm Reich on "emotional plague." And such a generic "diagnosis" necessarily promotes antihistorical thinking. A theodicy as well as a demonology, it not only stipulates something emblematic of evil but makes this the bearer of a rough, terrible justice. In Karel Čapek's *The White Plague* (1937), the loathsome pestilence that has appeared in a state where fascism has come to power afflicts only those over the age of forty, those who could be held morally responsible.

Written on the eve of the Nazi takeover of Czechoslovakia, Čapek's allegorical play is something of an anomaly—the use of the plague metaphor to convey the menace of what is defined as barbaric by a mainstream

European liberal. The play's mysterious, grisly malady is something like leprosy, a rapid, invariably fatal leprosy that is supposed to have come, of course, from Asia. But Čapek is not interested in identifying political evil with the incursion of the foreign. He scores his didactic points by focusing not on the disease itself but on the management of information about it by scientists, journalists, and politicians. The most famous specialist in the disease harangues a reporter ("The disease of the hour, you might say. A good five million have died of it to date, twenty million have it and at least three times as many are going about their business, blithely unaware of the marble-like, marble-sized spots on their bodies"); chides a fellow doctor for using the popular terms, "the white plague" and "Peking leprosy," instead of the scientific name, "the Cheng Syndrome"; fantasizes about how his clinic's work on identifying the new virus and finding a cure ("every clinic in the world has an intensive research program") will add to the prestige of science and win a Nobel Prize for its discoverer; revels in hyperbole when it is thought a cure has been found ("it was the most dangerous disease in all history, worse than the bubonic plague"); and outlines plans for sending those with symptoms to well-guarded detention camps ("Given that every carrier of the disease is a potential spreader of the disease, we *must* protect the uncontaminated from the contaminated. All sentimentality in this regard is fatal and therefore criminal"). However cartoonish Čapek's ironies may seem, they are a not improbable sketch of catastrophe (medical, ecological) as a managed public event in modern mass society. And however conventionally he deploys the plague metaphor, as an agency of retribution (in the end the plague strikes down the dictator himself), Čapek's feel for public relations leads him to make explicit in the play the understanding of disease *as* a metaphor. The eminent doctor declares the accomplishments of science to be as nothing compared with the merits of the dictator, about to launch a war, "who has averted a far worse scourge: the scourge of anarchy, the leprosy of corruption, the epidemic of barbaric liberty, the plague of social disintegration fatally sapping the organism of our nation."

Camus's *The Plague,* which appeared a decade later, is a far less literal use of plague by another great European liberal, as subtle as Čapek's *The White Plague* is schematic. Camus's novel is not, as is sometimes said, a political allegory in which the outbreak of bubonic plague in a Mediterranean port city represents the Nazi occupation. This plague is not retributive. Camus is not protesting anything, not corruption or tyranny, not even mortality. The plague is no more or less than an exemplary event, the irruption of death that gives life its seriousness. His use of plague, more epitome than metaphor, is detached, stoic, aware—it is not about bringing judgment. But, as in Čapek's play, characters in Camus's novel declare how unthinkable it is to have a plague in the twentieth century . . . as if the belief that such a calamity could not happen, could not happen *anymore,* means that it must.

Questions for Discussion

1. Sontag traces the lineage of words and how word meanings affect our cultural interpretation of a disease. Choose one example from the essay and discuss its connotations, and how those connotations have affected our historical understanding of the disease.
2. This essay was originally published in 1989. Has our understanding of AIDS changed with time? What connotations does the term have today?
3. Sontag is interested in how specific diseases act as metaphors for evil, danger, or punishment, both historically and in the present day. What disease or news topic operates metaphorically today? What does this say about contemporary American culture?

John McPhee
Coming into the Country

John McPhee was born in Princeton, New Jersey in 1931. A career writer, he has been a playwright for the "Robert Montgomery Presents" television show (1955–1957), associate editor for Time *magazine (1957–1964), and is currently a staff writer for* The New Yorker. *McPhee's nonfiction incorporates a combination of extensive research and literary style that makes his work appealing to both lay and scientific readers. Among his most notable works are* Coming into the Country *(1977), a portrayal of the author's experiences in Alaska, and* Annal of the Former World, *a literary treatment of the geological history of the planet, for which he won the Pulitzer Prize in 1999. McPhee has received over a dozen awards and fellowships, including the Award in Literature from the American Academy and Institute of Arts and Letters, the John Wesley Powell Award granted by the United States Geological Society, and, most recently, the Pulitzer Prize.*

For all its miners and trappers and conjugal units on the river, the country seems to have an even higher proportion of people who prefer to be surrounded by but not actually to be in the wilderness. To describe Eagle, for example, the last word that I would once have imagined ever coming to mind is the one that comes to mind now: Eagle, in its way, is suburban. This remote cluster on the Yukon, two hundred air miles from Fairbanks, is as good a place as any to avoid being too much on your own if you wish at the same time to draw a circle around yourself a very great distance from the rest of your life. In all directions from Eagle are tens of thousands of square miles of deep and total wild, into which a large part of the town's population—living in dependence on supplies from cities—rarely sets foot.

Jack Boone came into the country in 1973. "Basically, I'm a square," he says, and in Eagle he has built an octagonal cabin. He makes no effort to conceal his justifiable pride in his work. The cabin is a log structure of clean lines and apt proportions—as apparently durable as it is imaginative. "I have the ability to earn my living completely with my brain, but I don't want to," Boone remarks, making an instant friend of the visiting writer.

He sits at dinner, three children around him—Margaret, Cindy, and Daniel Boone. His wife, Jean, is in Anchorage, five hundred miles away, with a fourth child, who was in need of medical attention. Lacking money to pay for the journey, Boone went down by the river to the cabin of Jim Scott, explained the situation, and sold Scott two cords of firewood as yet uncut. "I don't believe in welfare, in assistance of any kind," Boone says. "There have been times when economic circumstances have forced me to take a small amount of it. Some people here make it a way of life. The poverty level for a family of six is eight grand. I made four grand last year. I do not constitute the way I am living as poor."

He is a big man, whose woolly beard and woolly crewcut surround pale-blue penetrating eyes. There is often a bemused smile. His voice is smoothly rolling and timpanic. He seems to drive it, like a custom-built car, to play it like a slow roll of drums. "You may have noticed my speech is not perfect," he says. "That is deliberate. My language was once a distinct liability. I have had to alter it over the years to get along with the people I have worked with."

I remark that in his conversation there is an indelible aura of culture and education, whether he likes it to be there or not.

"I am putting that on for you," says Boone, opening a quart of homemade beer. "Fifteen years ago, I spoke perfect English. I deliberately destroyed that capability. Every beer drinker in this town has drank this product, admired it, tried to duplicate it, and failed. I can still write perfectly, with no difficulty."

"Why have you come here?"

"The advantages of modern civilization do not impress me."

He grew up in Oroville, in northern California, and for a time studied electronics at Caltech, but had no desire to join the surrounding society. "I do not like the forcing of the individual toward a high-expense manner of living," he explains. "I do not like restrictions placed on one's life just because of close proximity to several million people." He is a direct descendant of Daniel Boone, on what he refers to as "the squaw side." First, he migrated to Juneau, and set up a marine-electronics business, but, as small as Juneau is, even Juneau was too restricting for him. So he chose a town on the Alaskan Yukon, where there was more elbowroom than he would ever care to explore, and not a great deal of employment opportunity. "Those who are trying to live an independent life style in the country are paying a very high price for it," he says. "Unless one's name is John Borg, it is difficult to find much of a job—indeed, any job—in Eagle." Boone eventually found one—as a seasonal laborer with the local road crew. And so did his neighbor Jack Greene. Working together all day, the two scarcely speak. It is a feud of buried origins, apparently deep, a feud not dissimilar from all the countless crosshatching cabin-fever feuds of Eagle, in some measure having to do with the general fierceness of competition for the few available jobs, in some measure with rivalry over the building of their cabins, but mainly as a casualty of place—a community deeply compressed in its own isolation, where a cup of borrowed sugar can go off like a grenade. The Boones and the Greenes live on Ninth Avenue, a euphemism for a pass a bulldozer once made through woods at the uphill end of town, about half a mile from the Yukon. Outside Boone's cabin is a sign that reads "Welcome to Those Who Wish Us Well, and the Rest of You Can Go to Hell." Boone means what it says. "Anyone who walks past that sign is probably broadminded enough that I can get along with them," he explains. "Diana Greene will not walk past that sign."

Diana Greene is a doctor of philosophy in classical literature, her husband an electronics engineer. Their awareness of Boone's sign is in the subbasements of subliminal. They came into the country in 1974—on a ten-thousand-mile journey in search of a place to build—to create a life exotic to the ones they had known before, and a cabin to contain it. He was from Greene, New York, she from Long Island. They had met in Boulder, where she was in graduate school and he with the National Bureau of Standards. He was her first husband, she his second wife. In the course of their quest, Eagle seemed the only choice. ("Everywhere else we went in Alaska, people were really rowdy—no couth.") By mail from Colorado, they later bought a building lot at auction, and, starting with a big wood-sided flatbed Chevrolet truck, began assembling things for Alaska. They bought a two years' supply of food—fifty pounds of rice, fifty pounds of rye, two hundred pounds of wheat, a hundred pounds of salt, and so on to twelve pounds of almonds and twenty-five pounds of black-eyed peas. They packed up their cellar of homemade wines. He built five cabin windows. Each was three panes thick, all quarter-inch glass, heavy as a desk top, set in a redwood frame. The first and third panes were sealed with synthetic rubber, while the inner one gapped an eighth of an inch from the bottom, so air could circulate to either side. This would be a tight cabin. They also piled onto the truck a double bed, a couch, chairs, a rolltop desk, two stoves, chain saws, a generator, a washing machine, a Louis Quatorze boudoir dresser with a mirror that might once have framed Marie Antoinette. With this altitudinous load, they backfired downhill into Eagle one spring day, and braked to a halt at the roadhouse. "I'm embarrassed to say this," said Greene to Ralph Helmer, "but I've come here to build a cabin and I don't know where my land is." Helmer pointed back up the hill.

Greene is as good with his hands as Boone. Their cabins were begun at about the same time, with exchanges of beer and wine. There was a tacit race—to the ridgepole, to completion. The Greenes won, three months to seven. Between them, the two families cut upward of three hundred logs, finding them dead on an old burn forty miles down the road, where the Bureau of Land Management would permit the cutting. The Greenes' cabin is eighteen by twenty-four, with attached foyer, long-lash eaves, and big overhangs at either end supported by a ridgepole thirty-eight feet long. Greene's brother-in-law was with him at the time, and the two of them twitched the big logs out of the forest with rope and brute effort. Boone concluded that he could not do that. He decided that logs twelve feet long were all his daughters could manage. Therefore, he would build an octagonal cabin.

For ceiling poles, the two families cut and peeled an aggregate of five hundred three-to-four-inch green spruce. Each of them also set ten fifty-five-gallon drums, filled with gravel and punctured at the bottom, gingerly into the ground—twenty separate excavations, dug carefully so as not to melt or break away the permafrost. Building his floor, Greene used the shiplapped boards from his truck body—and two kinds of insulation. Boone chinked his walls and insulated his floor and ceiling with moss collected by his children, planning to supplement it with cement and lime, while the Greenes used fibre glass between their logs. With their heating stove and cooking stove, the Greenes had powerful defenses against the coming cold, almost enough to drive them out into the snow, because if their cabin was handsome, it was ten times as sung. A lighted match could make it warm. The Greenes burn wood at the rate of four cords a winter. The Boones, with their larger cabin, use fifteen.

Jack Greene has built an efficient cistern, with an adroit plumbing system that services a kitchen sink and a solar-heated shower. His cabin's interior, while not as soaringly airy as Boone's, is spacious and, like the Greenes themselves, is amply touched with elegance. He is blond, with a strong and handsome face that would not be out of place on an old coin, she light and slim, with brown, quick, smiling eyes. Around their table pass sparkling cherry wine, additional wines from varietal grapes, wines they have made from berries in Eagle, wild-cranberry ketchup, baked salmon, mincemeat made from moose. From under the gable at one end of the cabin protrudes a pair of moose antlers fifty-six inches tip to tip, truly a mighty rack. Greene was humming along in his orange Volkswagen bug one day when the moose stuck its nose out over the road. He has shot spruce grouse from the VW, opening the door and firing a .22. In like manner, with a .30–'06, he dropped the big moose.

"They will not live long here," Boone says of the Greenes. "You have been there. How would you describe their cabin?"

"Very nice."

"It is very fancy, I would say. They serve gourmet meals. No one in Eagle will ever appreciate that. None of us slobs will notice. She's a Ph.D. Between her and this town there's a sociocultural gulf."

Boone rolls himself a smoke while I make a trip to his outhouse. On its interior walls are a set of rules for displaying the flag of the United States.

Boone's octagonal cabin, from the outside, has enough grace of line to be saved from resembling a military blockhouse. He is building an identical structure close by, as a garage and shop. The ceiling of the main cabin is eighteen feet high, and there are two balconies, with two children bunked on each balcony. A footbridge runs between. From window to window, the logs of the walls are horizontal, while above and below the windows the logs are vertical, creating an unusual and effective symmetry. "I'm kind of anti-money," Boone says. "I don't hardly believe in the stuff, but in Auke Bay, near Juneau, I built a place for two thousand dollars that was appraised when I left at forty-three. I'm an accomplished scrounger." He and his tall, sharply intelligent wife are also accomplished teachers. Their children are educated at home, and in national testing place as high as five years ahead of their ages.

He opens another quart of beer. It is brewed in a plastic garbage can, in which the Boones mix twelve gallons of water, ten pounds of sugar, a table-spoon of yeast, and forty-eight ounces of hop-flavored extra-pale malted barley syrup, yielding the equivalent of a six-pack a day, or a little over five cases every three weeks, saving themselves approximately two thousand dollars a year against the twenty-four dollars a case charged by Eagle boot-leggers. Moreover, it is fine beer. One would have to bypass Milwaukee and St. Louis and scour Europe to find its peer. It may be getting to me. Boone says not to worry: "I have drank it for years and never had a hangover." Close by him is a gun rack with three rifles. He sees me looking at them and says they are loaded. "Hunting season comes in the fall, and the fall is the busiest time of year for anyone who is trying to live any kind of subsistence life style," he says, apropos of nothing much, since the season just now is spring.

"Do you hunt a lot?" I ask him.

"No. I cannot say I am a hunter. I have not hunted anything in the three years since we came to Eagle. The purpose of the rifles is protection."

"Do you fish?"

"We buy our salmon."

"Do you use the river?"

"We have a small boat and a kicker but have not yet been out on the Yukon. We have not had time."

"Have you travelled some on foot in the country?"

"Since I've been here, I've done very little that did not have a purpose. I'm not really sure that I could enjoy trekking ten miles without a goal. I don't think I would defend that position. It's probably wrong. It's how I am. I know I'm a freak. That's why I moved to Eagle." He rolls another cigarette. He lights it thoughtfully. He spreads a screen of smoke through the octagon. "If you live in this country awhile," he says at last, "you really get to appreciate a stove and four walls."

Questions for Discussion

1. John McPhee is known for his ability to bring characters to life on the page. How does he describe his characters? Look closely at the style. Does he intersperse dialogue with description?

2. In what way is McPhee writing ironically? Describe his tone.

3. How present is McPhee in the text as author? Are you aware of him as a character in the story, or does he assume an omniscient or omnipotent point of view?

Student Writing

Choosing a Subject

Note the variety of subjects addressed in these student essays. One essay carries a strong personal and political message; the other two address lighter topics. Does literary journalism have to be "serious"? How does the author's voice and style convey the subject matter?

Anne Jennings
All That Stands between Me and Heaven
Is My Husband's Fork

Originally from Gainesville, Florida, Anne Jennings lives and writes in San Jose, California. A high-tech dropout, she is now pursuing her MFA in Creative Writing. Anne is a recipient of an Academy of American Poets prize, the Bonita M. Cox Award for nonfiction, and the Anne Lillis Award for creative writing. Her work has appeared in ZYZZYVA *and* On the Page *magazine.*

The author writes, "Literary journalism calls for a fine balance between entertainment and accuracy. In writing this article, I spent many hours conducting and transcribing phone interviews with the chefs who prepared these gastronomic miracles. Their enthusiasm for the subject was a real thrill to me. Because all of the details relating to the restaurants, dishes, chefs, and producers in the article were researched and reported scrupulously, I felt freer to loosen up with the portions of the article that dealt with the two main 'characters' of the story—my husband and me. To heighten the entertainment value of the article, I put a lot of work into constructing the 'on-screen' relationship between the two of us, using it as a frame to present the works of art I wanted to showcase."

As the lights of San Francisco disappeared behind us, Marc rested his hand gently on my thigh. It was the eve of our one-year wedding anniversary, and I was already thinking about another man: Brian Witner, executive chef at Carneros in Sonoma. I was dreaming about his seared foie gras with roasted pear, blackberry zinfandel gastrique, and warm brioche. I knew Marc would not be able to resist ordering that dish at dinner the following night, and when he did, I'd be ready.

How far we'd come since the night I'd first tasted that sweet, meaty morsel, that delicate sliver of . . . "What are you thinking about?" Marc interrupted.

"Just remembering our first time," I said. He looked over at me and smiled.

My obsession with foie gras had begun nearly two years earlier, when Marc and I were dating. To celebrate my birthday, he had reserved a table at A. P. Stump's in San Jose. Sitting there in our cherry-wood booth, music from the jazz combo filtering over from the bar, Marc had only one thing on his mind: a gleaming, quivering mound of exquisitely pan-seared duck liver.

"You have to at least try it," he said, when the appetizer arrived.

"I've never been a big fan of liver," I replied, eyeing the fleshy pink portion he had allotted just for me. I hurriedly stuffed it in my mouth.

The foie gras enveloped my tongue, a smoky essence of duck infusing its creamy texture, the tart deglacee sauces and fruits that accompanied it on the plate providing the perfect foil. I stared at Marc in amazement, my fork already poised for another strike. Poor Marc—I could see he was torn: how could he refuse me on my birthday? And yet, hadn't he dreamed of this foie gras for weeks now? His fist tightened around his own fork, raised now to defend what had suddenly become disputed territory.

A. P. Stump's chef de cuisine Vito Serpa serves his pan-seared foie gras with sugar roasted figs and a salad of watercress, pomegranate seeds, and Belgian endive atop a toasted brioche, drizzled with a port reduction sauce.

When I called Serpa to talk about his foie gras, he said, "I want to hit a combination of flavor notes and sensations on your tongue: the lusciousness of the foie gras is cut by the brioche, complemented by the sweetness and acidity of the fruit, and accentuated by the bitter taste of the greens."

That first night, I had barely finished Marc's foie gras before I was thinking about when I could get my next fix. I had to wait nearly a month. To celebrate our new engagement, Marc whisked us off to the plush, red dining room of Postrio—Wolfgang Puck's San Francisco–style restaurant at the Venetian Hotel in Las Vegas—where Executive Chef John Lagrone has devised not one, not even two, but three ingenious ways to serve the foie gras.

Lagrone begins with a foie gras mousse, prepared by folding the duck liver into a cream that has been reduced and whipped with a touch of cinnamon and nutmeg. He serves the mousse chilled and stuffed inside a fresh fig. For the second preparation, Lagrone makes a tureen using Wolfgang Puck's own four-day process, wherein the foie gras marinates for one full day in milk and ice to leach any impurities, then one full day in brandy and white port. Lagrone layers the marinated foie gras in the tureen, then bakes at low heat until the inside temperature reaches 120 degrees. After 24 hours of chilling, the tureen is ready to be sliced and served on toasted brioche with pear butter. The third and final preparation, the seared foie gras, comes with a blackberry reduction sauce and small salad of micro-mâche—a spicy green lettuce. All this on one, glorious plate for only $18!

Once again, all that stood between me and heaven was my husband's fork, strategically placed to guard his prize. I diverted his attention by groping his knee under the table. This gave me just enough time to wrest the fork from his fingers and launch a full frontal assault on the Foie Gras Three Ways. Let me just say this about that night: if foie gras one way is good, three ways is better.

Long before I stumbled onto foie gras in the eateries of the Bay area, *foie gras d'oie*, the traditional fattened liver of geese, graced the tables of pharaohs and kings. Ancient Egyptian reliefs dating as far back as 2390 B.C. depict the early technique for fattening geese: moisten grain pellets and force-feed them to the birds by hand. Though most foie gras produced and eaten today comes from ducks, not geese, the force-feeding technique, known today as gavage, has remained virtually unchanged throughout recorded history.

Foie gras spread from Egypt to Greece to the tables of ancient Rome, before settling in Europe, where it found a spiritual home in the haute cuisine of France. Here in the Colonies, only a few German farmers enjoyed its pleasures, until the 1939 World's Fair, which brought French chefs to New York, who, in turn, brought preserved pâté de foie gras. Alas, U.S. law forbade the importation of raw poultry from France for fear of a disease called "Exotic Newcastle." Some renegade chefs smuggled fresh livers into the United States inside cases of fish, but for the most part, the French chefs who stayed behind after the fair had to make do with canned, already-cooked foie gras. It wasn't until the early 1980s, when two foie gras production farms sprang up stateside, that fresh foie gras spread across America, first in French restaurants, and then beyond.

"Because of its versatility, foie gras is no longer just a French restaurant menu item," says Guillermo Gonzalez, owner of Sonoma Foie Gras, one of the pioneering farms. A native of El Salvador, Gonzalez and his wife Junny, along with their two daughters, learned the foie gras trade in Perigord, France, in 1983. "We lived for an entire year with a family who owned a goose foie gras business," said Gonzalez. "We transformed our lives."

Gonzalez attributes the popularity of foie gras in the Bay Area to the nature of its residents. "Foie gras is an acquired taste; Bay Area residents are daring enough to try new and exotic ingredients. And once you try foie gras, if it has been well prepared, you have to like it."

Vito Serpa swears by Gonzalez' Sonoma Foie Gras. He's been using the product exclusively at A. P. Stump's, ever since the company introduced its Mulard Foie Gras in mid-2000. The mulard, a hybrid of Pekin and Muscovy ducks, is bred through artificial insemination. (If the substantially larger Muscovy male attempts to mount the diminutive Pekin female, he falls off; the female then rejects all other suitors and lays infertile eggs.)

"The cellular structure of the Muscovy foie gras is more fragile and will not withstand the same cooking techniques as the mulard," says Gonzalez. While Sonoma Foie Gras still raises a small number of Muscovies for the die-hard fans—including Gonzalez himself, who prefers the silkier texture—the company has adjusted to the market preference for mulard.

Whether they serve it one way, two ways, or even three, most chefs who serve foie gras these days include a "seared" preparation. Hot cooking allows the center of the liver to liquefy, while the outside takes on the smoky flavors of the grill. But there are variations.

Let us examine, for a moment, the question of fruit: most foie gras recipes contain at least one variety to cut and complement the richness of the liver. I personally have had apples, strawberries, cherries, figs, a plum, and even a pear with my foie gras.

A particularly fruity foie gras came my way, quite by chance, on a visit last summer to the Napa Valley. We'd selected Brix, in the town of Yountville, on the reputation of executive chef John Wabeck's tuna sashimi appetizer—fresh ahi, dusted with nori furkake, then seared and served with soy wasabe, pickled cucumber, and ginger. The tuna did not disappoint, but when the waiter brought Marc's appetizer of seared foie gras on a thick slice of Fuji apple with a teriyaki reduction sauce, well, I simply had to think fast.

"Can you believe they've let us go this long without refilling the water glasses?" I said. "After all that wine tasting I'm feeling a bit dizzy!"

"I'll see what I can do, honey," Marc replied, hurrying off in the direction of the nearest busboy. I quickly excised a portion of his foie gras, along with a hearty chunk of Fuji apple, then artfully arranged the garnish of jullienned fruit and *fines herbs* on top of the remainder. "What he doesn't know won't hurt him," I mumbled to myself, stuffing the tangy fusion-*foie* into my mouth, just as Marc returned with the apologetic busboy.

Why, you might ask, do I never order a foie gras of my own? If we set aside for a moment the documented fact that food stolen from someone else's plate always tastes better, thus adding yet another layer of flavor enhancement to the foie gras experience, then we are left with the indisputable obstacle of the price.

Restaurants buy this pink gold for upwards of $75 per liver. By the time it gets to your table, your own little snippet will run you anywhere from $15 to $25, depending on the neighborhood. Even at that price, restaurants don't make much on foie gras. These chefs are on a mission. "I think everyone should eat foie gras!" gushes Serpa, who charges only $15 for A. P. Stump's Foie Gras Two Ways.

But even at those reasonable prices, I have always felt it unwise to order two foie gras appetizers at one sitting. Gluttony and wastefulness—mightn't the gates of Hell open up and swallow us whole for such excess? It has seemed too risky to try, and knowing that my husband would not—nay, could not—resist those two little words, it has always seemed safer to let him order the foie gras, while I make do with a warm goat cheese salad. All will come to rights once the food is on the table.

As our car raced north toward the ripening vineyards of Sonoma, I looked over at Marc and felt a familiar pang. Was it the love of a good man or the anticipation of a good liver that had me so warmhearted? I couldn't say. But I can tell you this: In the nearly two years since that first night, Marc has gotten used to sharing a lot of things—closet space, his shaving cream, the last bagel—but if you asked him whether, deep in his heart, he has ever gotten used to sharing his foie gras, he might just growl, his fork poised to strike.

Shannon Rauwerda
Are You My Mother?

At the age of eight, when she made a room of her own out of a bedroom closet so she could write, Shannon Rauwerda knew someday she would be a writer, and currently she is a graduate student in creative writing. After she graduates, she plans to teach, which she feels is a true calling for her. She notes, "I get such a kick out of seeing when the light goes on in a student's eyes."

Three years ago a simple job search gave birth to a new meaning of family for me. At twenty-eight, it was my first semester as a junior at the local university, and my wallet was filled with lint and unpaid bills. I began scanning the want ads for part-time jobs to supplement my education. The job market was as unappetizing as my lunch—a bologna sandwich and generic potato chips. Near the end of the columns, I spotted something unusual. DONORS WANTED. The words seemed out of place in the classified section of the student newspaper. The Tower Bell began to chime. I stuffed the paper and half eaten lunch into my backpack. The job search would have to wait. Homer and Dante were calling me to class.

Weeks later, I discovered the crumpled classified section at the bottom of my backpack amidst old papers and my oil-stained lunch bag. EGG DONORS. FEMALES AGES 21–30. I had heard about sperm donors—a fifty dollar handshake that had been around for years. But an egg donor? Curious, I called the number, and left my name and address for an information packet. It couldn't hurt. After, I returned to the levels of Dante's hell.

Two days later an 8-by-11 envelope arrived in the mail. The packet contained instructions from Between Women Donor Agency. A general application with the usual statistics: name, address, telephone number. A ten page medical questionnaire. A request for a biography about yourself. A few pictures.

I quickly filled out the application and medical history. The biography about myself didn't take much longer. Dear Expectant Parents, I wrote. Not only am I intelligent and very sociable but I am also damn good looking. I smiled. Now for the photographs. One picture gave a story, but a series of pictures showed a lifetime, and this was the other gift I wanted to give these parents.

From beneath the bed, I slid out the long boxes filled with loose photographs: black and whites, polaroid, and colored; three by five, four by six, and eight by ten. The pictures took the remainder of the evening. Each celluloid contained a story. My puckered lips pouting at months, pushing a grin into two pockets of chubby cheeks. Three years old, sitting in the sandbox shoving sand into my mouth for an afternoon treat. Five years, standing poised on the steps of the house, dressed in pink lace clutching my wicker purse next to my little sister who lifted her dress above her head. Memories flooded. My sister and I, dressed in one-piece wool pj's, heavy lidded and waiting for our mother to come and tuck us in. Although a single mother of three and a working student with books and papers waiting, every night my mother fulfilled her girls' nightly wish—a book before bed. "What will it be tonight?" she'd ask, eyes cupped by dark circles. From inside the faded pink Barbie sleeping bag, my hand emerged with the worn tattered edges of an over-used book. We had already buried our favorite, Green Eggs and Ham, and replaced it with the newest Dr. Seuss book: a tale about a baby bird as he searches from animal to animal to find his mother. After the story, my mother slowly rose to turn off the lights. A small voice called out in the dark, "Mommy, are you my mother?"

"Always." And the sleep came.

Within a week, the agency called me in for an interview. The office was located in a mini-mall outside of town. The inside decorated from the pages of House and Garden. A squat, mousy-haired woman greeted me with a smile so big that it buried her grey eyes in crinkles. "Hi there. I'm Maralee. Come. Come." She waved me into her office with her pudgy hand.

Still smiling, she gestured for me to sit in a next to a small round table. Without missing a beat she began the interview, "So Shannon, tell me why you want to be a donor."

"Well." I stared at her white caps and sinking eyes. "I ain't going to lie to you. The money will really help me out with school. But there is another reason. I can't imagine how much emptiness a woman must be going through because she can't have a baby, and if I can help, well—"

"Yes, yes," she actually giggled, still smiling. "The procedure is difficult, and you will be going through many changes. Everyone here respects your confidentiality and understands your needs of privacy. Do you plan to tell anyone?"

I glanced at the wall across from me covered with different sized photos of infants, all under the age of three months; over a hundred photos covered the wall. Slowly I turned my gaze back to Maralee's squinting eyes. "I plan to tell everyone. It's not like it's some dirty secret."

I looked back to the wall of those babies and thought of their families. Whose child is it? After all, what constitutes motherhood—the law or two breasts, two ovaries, a uterus and the ability to bear fruit? If one answers the law, what guidelines do these lawmakers follow? If one answers biology, is one undermining the identity a child forms from her adopted family, stepfamily, or extended family? Society has determined to define family standards in a set format: biological father, biological mother, two biological offspring, and Spot the dog.

After the personal interview, Maralee administered a five-hundred question personality test. One question it continually asked in differing formats was, "Are there voices talking in your head?" I knew the anticipated response, but the writer in me fought this answer. After all, every time I sit down to write, a continuous debate of words and sentences and questions, discussions and arguments between my characters and between my memories plague my mind. Those little voices continuously battle with each other. But naturally I lied, and wrote what was expected.

Next step, a visit to Dr. Feelgood. The agency required each donor to pass a psychological evaluation. She walked into the waiting room barely reaching five feet tall in her three-inch ivory designer pumps, which matched her ivory pants suit and silk ivory blouse. With a flick of her French manicured nails, she gestured me into her office. She had a Martha Stewart office—pastel curtains that matched the pastel furniture colors with matching pastel pillows that matched the muted colors of the pastel floral prints that were giving me a major pastel migraine.

"So, Shannon," she began, glancing down at her file. "How will you feel about your eggs once they are retrieved?" I stared at her small head hiding underneath the layers of frosted blond hair and the large rimmed brown glasses. My expression remained blank. Lack of coffee, early morning hours, the tingling sensations growing from my toes up my legs, and the same questions asked over and over from different people had triggered a touch of irritation.

"Can I ask you a question?" I didn't wait for her response. "Are men subjected to this series of tests and probes? After all, they only have to show up, look at a few skin magazines, and introduce themselves to Rosy Palm."

A thin grin cracked from beneath her frozen expression. "The medical community has been debating this issue for some time. Some of us feel that stronger policies should be enacted for male donors."

"It's not that I'm taking this decision lightly," I said. "I've thought about it. It's just that men are once again given different standards than women. I don't have the same or different feelings about my eggs than men have about their sperm." I paused, wondering if there was a woman behind that cool exterior as upset as I was over this inequality. But she never cracked, which only made me go on. "People don't ask men if they have paternal feelings over their sperm. I don't have any maternal feelings over my eggs. In fact, once a month they really annoy me. It's simply that society has dictated a different sentimentality for me. Here I am jumping through all these hoops in order to do the same thing that men have been doing for years."

Expressionless, she motioned me to the door. I guess I had passed.

Three weeks later the drugs arrived via Federal Express. Now I was really committed.

The first step was a nasal inhaler, Synarel, a potent inhibitor of gonadotroprin secretion which basically stopped me from menstruating—no more cramps striking in the middle of the night, no more swelling of hands and feet into ballpark-sized sausages, no more swinging moods causing grown men to shake with fear, no more period!

The second step was a bit more involved. Pergonal, the drug that stimulated the follicles to produce a large number of eggs within the ovaries, needed to be injected into a fatty area of the body. After carefully filling the syringe with the liquid, I grabbed a chunk of tummy, and with a deep breath plunged in the medication. A little prick. Not too bad. Nine more of these. I could do this.

Three days after these self-injections, I visited the doctor for an update on my progress. Laying back on the pillow in the OB medical bed, my feet strapped above me in the brackets, I peered over to the ultrasound monitor. On the screen I saw two floating sacks floating filled with tiny, black masses dotted like speckled Easter eggs.

"Are you planning to have children?" the young doctor asked, a startled expression on her face.

My mouth became dry and for a moment I couldn't breath. I hadn't thought of children, but I also hadn't thought of not having them either. "Why?" I choked out.

"Because you won't have any problem. Most donors produce on average 20 eggs. After three days of medication, you have 14 on your right ovary and 10 on your left. Quite remarkable."

After a week on the Pergonal, I could feel the growth. When I walked, I waddled. One morning I caught my reflection in the mirror: my hand rested to support under the protruding, firm roundness in my lower belly, and my clear face glowed. A panic attack started. Sweat beads formed rivulets on my forehead. My breath grew rapid. My body was preparing for something I was not psychologically ready for—reproduction.

Others around me began to respond to these changes. Even though I was not pregnant, my body expanded: my gut, my feet, and my hands all swelled. I felt fat. Men began to take notice. At work, customers asked me out. At school, male classmates became more flirtatious. While out with friends at restaurants or hangouts, I came home with stacks of business cards and heard too many come-on lines. I even got a marriage proposal in the supermarket. At a time in my life when I felt vulnerable and unattractive, men desired me. My rapidly churning hormones were culpable.

The third step before the egg extraction was an intramuscular shot of HCG, a pregnancy hormone that releases the eggs for the retrieval. The timing for this shot was very important. It had to be administered 36 hours before the surgery or else the doctors would not be able to retrieve the eggs. The drug released the eggs, so when I underwent the outpatient procedure, the long needle inserted intravaginally could successfully remove the eggs from the ovaries.

Thirty-six hours later I was lying on the out-patient surgery table. The table was similar to an OB examining bed. My legs straddled on hanging support straps; my feet were strapped in brackets. The doctors administered the anesthesia. It took them forty-five minutes to finish the procedure. As I laid in the recovery room, my eyes groggily focused in on a nurse hovering over my IV, a syringe in her hand. She tapped the syringe filled with pain medication and injected it into the IV. Smiling, she leaned closer, strands of silver hair poking out from her surgical cap. Her cold, leathered hand patted the top of mine. "I hear you're the hero around here," she said. The soothing warmth of the pain medication pulsed through my arm, and as I slowly drifted back into a comfortable rest the last words I heard were, "Forty-seven eggs. Quite an accomplishment."

Two years later, I finished sealing the envelope on my last graduation invitation. I gathered them up and ran outside just as the mailman arrived. We exchanged bundles. Discarding the usual bills on the foyer table, I opened an 8-by-11 envelope with the familiar letterhead from Between Women Donor Agency. I hardly ever thought anymore of my time on the surgery table; it had become a distant memory between final exams and school papers. Inside the envelope, I found a smaller envelope with my name carefully scripted in blue ink. As I opened the card, a photograph slipped onto the floor. While reading the card, I bent over to retrieve the picture.

Shannon—

> *We would like to share with you our most sincere and loving thanks for helping us have our dreams come true. Because of your gift we have a beautiful baby boy who is truly a miracle. Please know how special you will always be to us.*

> *Much love,*
> *A very happy family*

In the photograph, a chubby bundle lay cradled in a blue blanket, his puckered lips in a pout, pushing into two pockets of chubby cheeks. Frozen,

I stared blankly at the card in one hand and the picture in the other. I tried to figure out how I felt. I decided to call a friend but only got her voicemail and stumbled over my words, uncertain what to say. It's a boy!

The silence in the house became overwhelming, so I decided to treat myself to a trip to Barnes and Noble. A good book to clear the mind. As I wandered down the aisles, I hoped to find a cover jacket or a display that would pique my interest. I continued down the rows to the children's section. Small plastic chairs in red, green, and blue were scattered in front of smaller bookshelves. On a round carpet rug, the letters of the alphabet were shaped like animated figures dancing the Hokie Pokie. In the corner, a large cat under a red and white hat stared at me. On the stand next to him, I recognized the familiar image of a little brown bird perched on the head of a brown dog. As I leafed through the pages, smiling at the remembered tale, I felt someone standing close by me.

"My mom used to read me these books all the time," a young woman whispered as she took another copy of my book from the shelf. "This was my favorite."

"Mine too."

"I'm buying a copy for my stepson." She motioned to a freckled-face redhead running from chair to chair, pulling books from the shelf. "Are you buying one for your child?"

"Nope," I said. "For myself." I clutched the book to my chest. And I smiled.

Ian Caton
Escape from Italy, or No Fear and Loathing in the Rome of the North

After failing as a rock and roll drummer, Ian Caton went back to school to pursue a degree in English at San Jose State University. He is now enrolled in the Single-Subject, Secondary Education Credential program and hopes to teach fulltime by the fall of 2003—interrupted only by future travels and his newborn son.

I'm not sure if I had five minutes or an hour of sleep, or if I had even slept at all, but when I opened my eyes and looked down below it was a welcome sight to see those gray overcast skies above the vast, green plains surrounded by walls of tall, slender, perfectly-vertical trees, standing in rigid obedience to the cold vigor of Frankfurt.

"Jonathan, look. Frankfurt," I said.

Jonathan Reagan, my attorney, sat with his chin tucked into his chest, his eyes peacefully closed, hands in his lap and clasped, holding onto his wire-frame spectacles. He was wearing dark blue corduroy slacks, a huge Versace necktie and three days worth of beard on his chin. Caked into the corner of his lip was a white spot of dried saliva. It was just after ten in the A.M. He looked like he could use a drink.

"Huh?" he said, his eyes still closed.

I, on the other hand, never drank in such situations. What we needed was a plan. We were now in Frankfurt after having narrowly escaped with our lives from the thugs and the secret police of Rome. They had chased us from our hotel, waving cleavers and clutching at carbon papers of unpaid bills, with the proprietor's daughter dressed in bare feet and a torn night-gown, crying, pointing at us, screaming something unintelligible in Italian, her long dark hair upturned.

We jumped into the nearest Metro station, EUR Fermi, losing the hired help in the insane crowds that fought to get into this already-packed under-ground tram. We really had no idea where we were going. It took us south, just to the next stop, Laurentina, and then we hopped back onto the next northbound tram—just to throw them off our trail.

And it worked. For a while.

We rode up to Roma Termi. We had to get the hell out of Dodge, and fast. I had no idea what they were angry about—something my attorney must have done. My lawyer was always feeding women with lies, and they usually worked. This time it got us a master suite in the Oikos Grandé—it wasn't my fault all the credit cards I had given them had been declined. If I hadn't had all of my cash stolen in their establishment in the first place, then we'd never have had to go down the unrecompensed liability route at all. (At least that's what it translated to in my pocket Italian-Made-Easy dictio-nary.) My lawyer had assured them all that I was in good standing. And they had all taken his word. Even her.

"Look Jonathan, Frankfurt." And there it was, right out our window: Germany. Safety. And he didn't seem to give a damn.

From Roma Termi we took the first express train available to Pisa where we had booked a flight out of that Mediterranean hellhole. I was smoking a Corona and hiding behind an Italian copy of *FHM*, my lawyer a copy of *GQ*—although neither of us could read Italian. The articles weren't too difficult to follow. Agents in mirrored aviator glasses stalked the terminal, communicat-ing with hidden microphones and tiny earplugs, and it wasn't until the last possible minute—after the conductor cried, "*Andiamo!*"—that we jumped un-noticed onto our car. At my lawyer's insistence we had booked coach so as not to look too obvious.

But once we had arrived at Pisa Centrale it was close to 12:30 at night and no taxi could be found anywhere. What we needed was a place to sleep, and the airport was supposed to be that, so we hoofed it the two and a half miles to Pisa International—which happened to be closed for the night.

"Oh shit, Jonathan. You never told me this might happen. I want new counsel!" I demanded. I had never heard of an international airport closing at night—and obviously, neither had he.

The automatic doors were all bolted shut and from inside a sawing, scraping, high-pitched whirring sound could be heard. The night custodians were busy inside buffing the marble floors. There was no way we could get in. And even if we could have, there was no way we were getting any sleep in there with all that racket going on. I knew as well as he that a law suit in this violate, lawless country would only prove futile—this was, after all, where all the great Spaghetti Westerns were filmed. Here, only the strong survived. The weak were stepped on and starved. Or froze. At this time it was approaching 1:30 and we had no accommodations for the night.

"As your attorney, I advise you to use your bag as a pillow," Jonathan said, taking command of this situation. "Make yourself as comfortable as possible on a bench for the night. There, over there," he pointed. "There's two green benches. Those should be acceptable for the next couple of hours. At least until 5:30 or so. Hell, it's not even that cold." Then he added, "Plus it'll make for some good reading for your travel writing."

"Right. Travel writing," I agreed. "This should be perfect." We grabbed our bags and headed over to the benches, not yet freezing in this Mediterranean night air. "'The worst trips make the best reading'," I said, quoting Paul Theroux. "This should make one helluva story."

Theroux says that good travel writing takes health, strength and confidence. Well, I had plenty of health, and my strength was still holding up—after my lawyer had advised that we stuff our faces with McDonald's hamburgers back at Rome Termi before hopping the train—but my confidence at this time was waning. This wasn't what I had bargained for at all. But Theroux also says that "half of travel was delay or nuisance." Well this must've been exactly what he was talking about. Here we were, Jonathan Reagan and I, hiding out from the mob, trying to lie down on these flimsy green metal benches and catch a few hours of sleep before checking in for our flight. Sleep was just what my attorney had ordered, so we could deal with the next 24 hours in relative sanity. I set my alarm clock for 5:30, placed it in my jacket pocket, clutched my bag-like-pillow, shut my eyes and tried my best to overcome the discomfort of that metal bench . . . and sleep. At least for a little while.

But the bench wasn't big enough for me. Or I was too big for it. I tried my side. I tried my back. I even tried my other side, but this bench wasn't going to work. I tried the ground, but after a short while the pavement began to feel like a meat locker. Then I tried to just sit on the beach and lean against my bag . . . but the night quickly got much colder.

Italy is like an island, out in the middle of the Mediterranean, and those sea breezes began to cut through all my layers of clothing. I was shivering, chattering my teeth.

"Jonathan. Are you asleep?" I asked.

"No."

"What the hell?" I didn't know what kind of response I would get from that profound remark. But after a bit he replied:

"As your attorney I advise you to get some sleep."

"I think I'm going to be looking for some new counsel pretty soon." He knew I was just bluffing. I didn't need another lawyer. What I needed was some hot chicken soup, a warm bath and a soft bed. I got out my travel journal and started writing.

In the Eighteenth Century, when exploration was still possible, Edward Gibbon wrote that a travel writer ought to be "endowed with an active, indefatigable vigor of mind and body, which can . . . support, with a careless smile, every hardship of the road, the weather, or the inn." I guess that would include Ryanair, where we got our tickets out of Pisa. Even getting to Pisa, using Ryanair, we had to use an airport named London Stansted that is so far from London it should be renamed simply Stansted. It took us an hour and a half to get to London Stansted, on a coach, from Leicester Square, at 2:05 in the morning. With zero traffic. We didn't arrive until after 3:30 in the morning. But once there, we at least got to sleep in the airport for a few hours, with a good number of other early morning travelers.

It's like saying it's Los Angeles Airport but flying out from Anaheim. Or San Diego. It's that far. So finding the Pisa International Airport closed at night shouldn't have been that big of a surprise to us. But in my life I've never heard of an international airport closing at night. It was like a big joke to me—or on me—and the punch line being, "Yeah, I was flying Ryanair."

Browsing through my travel journal for a good quote or a tid-bit of information that would brighten my spirits I came across another quote by Theroux: "The truth of travel was unexpected and off-key, and few people ever wrote about it. . . . Travel had to do with movement and truth, with trying everything, offering yourself to experience and then reporting it."

There's a lot invested there, in the Truth. Truth with a capital T. And where was I in all that Truth? What was my part in that Truth?

And then it all came back to me: Why I was here, what we were doing, where we were going, what our plan had been all along. Truth is we were flying into Frankfurt Hahn to catch a train to Bremen so that we could visit with my old friend Holger Klein. I had been on assignment from San Jose State's *Reed* Magazine, the oldest literary magazine west of the Mississippi, with my attorney, so that I could cover the Easter holiday in Rome—but something had gone terribly wrong. The local mob in Rome weren't going to rest until they saw us dead—or worse. So we were headed up to Bremen, the Rome of the North.

No, that's not right either. Truth is, Jonathan wasn't exactly my lawyer. He and I were both SJSU students, on an exchange program with CAPA, living in England for a semester, and traveling through Europe for the Spring Break. What with all my travel reading for class, our substantial lack of sleep from staying at the hostel in Rome, and a healthy influence of Hunter S. Thompson, we were both feeling a little screwy. But he could very well have been my lawyer. And one day when he graduates, he just might be my lawyer. Time will tell.

Still though, Truth is (with a capital T), that that night in Pisa we had about 90 minutes of sleep back at the train station waiting area, where we had walked back after finding Pisa International closed for the night . . . after freezing on a park bench for two hours in front of the airport. At least the train station waiting area was indoors. They had no heat, but there was no wind either. And around two in the morning, with the wind coming right off the Mediterranean and putting the Chill (with a capital C) into the both of us, Jonathan Reagan and I, two university students, traveling around Europe together on Spring Break, by train, coach, boat, bicycle, car, foot, subway—and of course, Ryanair, where every trip is an adventure— had decided to adventure our collective asses back to the train station for an hour or two of shut eye.

The truth is that we were now finally coming into Germany after having had maybe just two hours of sleep for the night. And we were coming from Rome, where in approximately 72 hours we had combed the entire city, had seen virtually everything, staying at our cute little hostel, the Oikos Grandé, and slept as little as possible. Now finally in Germany, we were both completely exhausted. But it felt good getting into Germany.

"Jonathan, look. Frankfurt."

Still no reply.

"Sir, you're going to have to fasten your seat belt," said the stewardess to Jonathan. "We're coming in for a landing."

"Oh, yeah. Thanks," he said.

In this age of Post-Tourism that Paul Fussell writes about, I was set to prove, or at least to find out, that by using trains and small-market airlines, genuine travel was still possible. And with Ryanair, exploration and adventure are just a flight away. Frankfurt Hahn was another of those Ryanair-trick airports. It took us another coach to get into Frankfurt proper where we were to catch our train, at the Hauptbahnhof. And it cost eleven Euros.

Eleven Euros! I was enraged.

Jonathan got in ahead of me.

"Eleven Euros?" I asked the driver.

"Yes."

I gave him a few colorful notes of different sizes and then sat down next to Jonathan. "Shit, this better be a long ride." I'd better be careful what I wish for, I thought.

The coach eventually got us to the Hauptbahnhof, past Frankfurt-am-Main, which was where we were actually supposed to catch our train. We found this out from a kind, English-speaking German who worked behind the Information desk at the Frankfurt Hauptbahnhof. (There seemed to be many kind, English-speaking Germans.) He told us, in very good English, that all we had to do was catch the next train to Frankfurt-am-Main where we would then transfer and catch the following train up into Bremen. We would only be an hour behind our original schedule.

But still, we had thirty minutes to kill and there was another McDonald's to try, so we both had Royals with Cheese, à la *Pulp Fiction,* with plenty of mayonnaise. The Germans love their mayonnaise.

Feeling unfulfilled, I then purchased my first real German bratwurst. It was a Kodak moment.

The train ride to Bremen was a long, luxurious trip that took just over five hours. It made a sweeping arc along the map, east and then up north, following the massive Rhein, past Mainz, and up to Koblenz, and then to Bonn, on the other side of the river, and up into Köln, where they did their farming on sheer vertical slopes of the mountain, sectioning off giant areas of the black cliffs, and then veering back over to Düsseldorf, and into Duisburg, moving north-westerly now, away from the river, up to Essen and Bochum and Dortmund, and then north up into Münster, picking up speed here as the stops got farther away from each other, and up into Osnabrück, and finally Bremen.

I was able to compare the luxurious German trains to the old spaghetti-western trains throughout Italy. In Italy, you have to be sure to sit in one of the front cars, as the back cars have a tendency to unfasten and be taxied away by another engine—to where, and for what reason, I know not. Only that the kind attendant told us in his best broken English, when we left for Pisa, that we had to move up to the first or second cars. The others, he said, were going. "Gone," he said. "Soon. You. Move. Up to front. One or two. Others gone." This was all new information for me. Nobody had ever written about that, as far as I knew. And in fact, another friend of mine, who had traveled extensively throughout Italy during his Spring Break, had had the experience of winding up in Venice when he was originally headed for Florence. His car had simply detached while he slept, and when he woke up, there was water everywhere!

But besides being more comfortable, and having better cafés, and having the first class sections marked clearly and separate from the coach seating, the trains in Germany were also faster. Traveling to Rome we had accidentally sat in the wrong section and were forced to pay fourteen Euros extra, or else be shipped back to America . . . or worse, Canada. But the differences between the seats were very minimal. In fact, I would have rather been in coach the entire time, because there you get your own individual cabin with windows and curtains. In Germany, though, first class seating was like the difference between riding in a Mercedes Benz or in a Volkswagen Bus. An air cooled Volkswagen Bus.

Once in Bremen, I began to wonder how we would find my friend Holger. Previously, I had sent him some e-mails, letting him know I had been in England and was looking forward to visiting him in Germany, and the first few messages he had responded to. But the last one I had sent, that said when we were coming, and for how long, he never replied to.

The Bremen Hauptbahnhof is a large building with almost a shopping mall-like atmosphere. We had found out which side of the station to exit from by walking out of the wrong side. We left from the back where a giant Easter carnival, called the Osterwiese, was set up. They had roller coasters and fun houses and games and food courts and biergartens everywhere. The bright lights of the Ferris wheel and merry-go-rounds and the thumping Bavarian music, the sounds of screams from the people on the whirligigs were all inviting, but our first priority was getting to Holger's flat.

I had a map from the internet, and another, more detailed one that I bought in the Frankfurt Hauptbahnhof, but I wasn't entirely sure if my friend would be home. The last time I had seen him was about a year earlier when he had stopped by my house in San Jose, unannounced, on his way to Hawaii to go wind surfing—but first he had had a couple of days to kill in San Jose. I had some time off myself, so we drove over to Santa Cruz to check out the ocean, then drove north on Highway 1, looking for unpopulated beaches to explore. That was when he had told me to come to Bremen anytime—they saw very few Americans there.

So Jonathan and I started for Holger's place, which I figured was about a mile and a half from the Hauptbahnhof, on Osterdeich, right next to the Weser River. My maps proved to be impeccable and my sense of direction faultless, this time, and very shortly we were standing in front of his flat. Well this is it, I thought. If he's not here we can always stay in a hostel.

I opened the front door to see a line of doorbells, one of them with the name "Holger Klein" neatly typed next to it. I rang it. I looked at Jonathan and smiled. He looked to me very tired. His blonde hair, normally parted sharply, was ragged at best. He had dark bags under his eyes. And he definitely needed a shave. Shit, I could use a shave. And a shower. I hope he's here.

I rang the bell a second time.

"Hallo?" came a voice from the speaker.

"Hello? Holger? It's me, Ian!"

"Oh. Just a minute," came his sleepy response, and then a BUZZ! as the door was unlocked. We opened it and climbed the long spiral staircase toward the very top.

"God damn, Holger. You live in the penthouse!" I exclaimed when I reached him.

"Yeah, I guess so."

I gave him a hug.

"This is my friend Jonathan. Jonathan, Holger."

They shook hands and then he welcomed us in.

"I was going to send you an e-mail and ask when you were going to come," said Holger.

"Didn't you get my last e-mail?" I asked stupidly. Of course not. Then he would have responded. "Well, umm, is it all right if we stay here for a while?"

"Oh yeah, I just have to check with my roommates. They're downstairs right now. Can I get you something to drink? Beer? Water?"

"Yeah, I'll take a water. You want something Jonathan?"

"Yeah, water's good."

When Holger left for beverages, Jonathan turned to me, suddenly awake now, his eyes fierce and bright, and said, "You mean!—he didn't know!—we were coming here?!"

What could I say? I shrugged. "Well he knew we were coming. I sent him an e-mail. I guess he just didn't know when."

Holger came back with a pitcher of water and three glasses and we were set, comfortably finally, sitting on his little white sofa and listening to some music, talking about our trip, shoes off.

That night, Jonathan and I both slept for a complete 12 hours, right around the clock, dreaming about chocolate and girls in lederhosen and what exactly we would do now that we were in Germany.

■ Writing Exercise ■

Write an essay from the first-person point of view that investigates and reveals a significant moral or cultural issue of our time. Your approach, intention, and style should show your own engagement—as a writer, as a person, as a thinking soul—with the larger world. (The tone can be serious, ironic, humorous—experiment!) The essay must involve reporting or journalistic skill and technique, and be based on a real experience you undertake for this assignment. Your own aesthetic sensibility and voice should be evident at least implicitly in the tone, structure, and style of the essay and in your stylistic approach to the essay itself.

The Writing Workshop

Accepting Criticism

One of the most important aspects of developing as a writer is learning to listen to other people discuss your work. Often it's hard to take critical commentary regardless of how gently it is phrased or how well the remark was intended. Even if you've received a lot of positive commentary about your work, it may still be uncomfortable to experience hearing other people discuss it. It's essential to remain objective and listen quietly without feeling defensive or upset.

When other students make critical comments about your manuscript, it doesn't necessarily mean that they are right and you are wrong. It does not mean that you are a weak writer or even that you "missed the mark." People have different ideas and expectations, and different ways of expressing those ideas. *Write everything down*, regardless of whether or not you agree with what's being said. Jot down any questions that come to mind, but wait until the discussion is completely finished before you ask them. Try not to phrase your questions defensively, or spend this time trying to explain things that the workshop members just didn't "seem to get." Ask sincere questions with an open mind, and listen to the answers. Thank your peers for the time and energy they spent on your writing.

After the workshop, don't begin revision work on your manuscript right away. If you need to, put the manuscript with all its commentary in a desk drawer for a few days. Go back and read the comments when you are feeling more objective. You might be surprised—sometimes a remark you strongly disagreed with will turn into a true revelation about the manuscript or about your work as a whole.

As a writer, you will make mistakes and you will sometimes experience criticism and disapproval. This is true for everyone. Don't let these block your growth as a writer or interfere with your passion for writing. It's all part of the process.

Revision Tips and Strategies

Is Plot a Bad Word?

In narrative, whether it's fiction or creative nonfiction, one general rule applies: Something has to happen. Even in highly descriptive nature writing, or writing that is primarily contemplative or reflective, something changes in the mind and heart of the character and/or the mind and heart of the reader.

Plot usually revolves around or builds toward a point of climax or epiphany. Climax and epiphany are not necessarily the same thing. The climax is the point of highest tension, a crucial turning point in a story that then leads to the denouement or resolution. The term

(continued)

Revision Tips and Strategies *(continued)*

epiphany describes a moment in time that represents a sudden revelation, a psychological or even spiritual realization that leads to a greater understanding of the self or the self in relation to others (including nature or a divine entity).

Plot is the order of events in your narrative and how you emphasize and develop those events. Plot is movement: how your story proceeds from A to B to C. A better term, I think, is *narrative arc*. Does your narrative arc have to be chronological or linear? Of course not (although this may be a good place to start). You can begin at a particular point and then move backward and forward in time. Use flashbacks to fill out the details of a story. Consider weaving together several different stories, or different perspectives of the same story. Relate part of one story and then the next and so on, returning to each story in turn. Use a frame: that is, begin and end with the same point in time or the same image.

Plot isn't everything. A narrative that depends too heavily upon plot and neglects other important aspects of literary technique and style can be predictable, clichéd, and unsatisfying. But plot provides the scaffolding for all the other elements of your work: character development, voice, tone, mood, and theme.

Put Yourself in the Picture

One way in which creative nonfiction differs from "noncreative" nonfiction is that the writer is often present in the work in subtle or less-than-subtle ways. This is true in fiction as well, particularly "postmodern" fiction, where the voice of the author can be a part of the story in an ironic or self-reflexive manner.

Think about the relationship that you, as author, have to your story. Do you want to assume an objective, omniscient voice? Do you want to present yourself as a character in the story? Would an intimate, self-revelatory, first-person approach work best? How should you reveal yourself in your work? If you choose to remain invisible and behind the scenes, think about the best and most honest way to achieve this. Is true objectivity possible?

Feel the Beat

Writing prose is like writing music. There is a rhythm and beat to the language that the reader will enjoy. One way you can begin to develop and understand your own style and voice is to pay attention to the natural rhythms that begin to emerge as you write more and experiment with different assignments and structures.

Begin by varying your sentence structure. Try to avoid a simple subject-verb-object construction. Check every sentence in every paragraph to ensure that you're not beginning two sentences in a row with the same word. Avoid repeating words in sentences, even simple words, and avoid repetition in paragraphs unless you intend it for emphasis. Look at the structure and rhythm of your paragraphs. What sentence provides the center or anchor for each paragraph? How does one paragraph lead to the next?

Vary the length of your sentences to reflect what's happening in the story. Short, concise sentences increase the pace and can add drama to a scene involving action or suspense. Longer sentences can provide depth and breadth to scenes dependent upon description.

Read your work aloud to discover the natural rhythm of your style. One of the best exercises I know is to read your work into a tape recorder and then listen while you're driving or relaxing. Odd phrases and clunky sentences suddenly become painfully evident. But the beauty of those passages that really work—where the language flows, the meaning is clear, and the reader or listener can't help but be moved by the style and subject—becomes evident as well. Allow yourself to enjoy the passages that work. Give yourself credit for the progress you've made.

For Further Reading

Conover, Ted. *Rolling Nowhere: Riding the Rails with America's Hoboes*
Didion, Joan. *Salvador* and *Slouching Towards Bethlehem*
Herr, Michael. *Dispatches*
Hersey, John. *Hiroshima*
Kidder, Tracy. *Among Schoolchildren*
Orleon, Susan. *The Orchid Thief* and *The Bullfighter Checks Her Makeup: My Encounters with Extraordinary People*
Larson, Erik. *The Devil in the White City*

Chapter 4

Nature Writing

Introduction

In the last few decades, nature writing has grown dramatically and experienced enormous popularity as well as a great deal of change. Like other forms of creative nonfiction, it is not a new field by any means. People often refer to Rachel Carson's *Silent Spring*, published in 1962, as the first deeply influential work of contemporary nature writing, but of course essays and treatises discussing the relationship of people to their environment go all the way back to the 1700s. Contemporary and classic authors such as Ralph Waldo Emerson, Charles Darwin, Walt Whitman, John Muir, Mary Austin, Aldo Leopold, Edward Abbey, and many others have made significant contributions to the way we think about nature. Henry David Thoreau is perhaps the best-known nature writer in English. "I wish to speak a word for Nature," he writes in 1863, "for absolute freedom and wildness, as contrasted with a freedom and culture merely civil,—to regard man as an inhabitant, or a part and parcel of Nature, rather than a member of society."

What is nature writing? Students sometimes balk at the idea of writing an essay about nature. "It's boring," one student complains. "Just descriptions of landscapes and animals. Nothing happens." Another student notes in her journal, "Most nature writing is about politics and the environment. And I'm just not into politics."

Nature writing, however, is much more than descriptions of beautiful scenery, animal behavior, or persuasive rhetoric—although those categories are an important part of the field. Simply stated, nature writing is a response to the natural world that surrounds us. It falls into the category of creative nonfiction because it is writing that is based on fact, observation, and experience which is then filtered through the perception and sensibility of the writer. Generally speaking, the nature writer combines literary language—an emphasis on style, rhythm, and form—with an interest in scientific, biological, or ecological fact. A nature writer may rely heavily on description, but she might also employ characterization, exposition, climax, and epiphany to make her point.

It's impossible to talk about nature writing without looking a little more closely at the word *nature*. Before you begin your nature writing assignment, take a moment to look up the word in a dictionary and thesaurus. The word contains a multitude of meanings. "Nature" is an idea, a cultural and historical construct, as much as a place or landscape. More than one critic has noted that what we mean when we use the word *nature* says as much about ourselves—our religious and social values, political views, and personal ethics—as it does about a particular plot of land or ecosystem. Consider how the terms *nature, wilderness,* and *frontier* have changed over the course of history, and the weight these words carry in contemporary culture. In early American history, the wilderness was something to be feared, dominated, and conquered. Today, the word tends to help sell a great number of sports utility vehicles. It's easy to fall back on an equation that advertisers like to exploit: Natural things are good, and unnatural things are bad. Next time you go to the market, notice how many products are labeled "natural." Is there any degree of authenticity in the claim?

What landscapes are "natural"? For some wilderness enthusiasts, the only truly natural landscape is one that has been completely untouched by human culture or civilization and must remain so. According to this philosophy, nature is a pure, stable, self-sustaining, homeostatic system that in its entirety represents all that is grievously lacking in our high-tech lifestyles: serenity, spirituality, and balance. The best thing we can do is to preserve nature and leave it alone. In this context, the nature writer might feel like a curator, describing artifacts from antiquity that are carefully stored under glass.

This approach, while appealing in its purity and simplicity, rarely stands up to scientific or anthropological scrutiny. Biological systems tend not to be as balanced and predictable, as we might like to believe, and are also highly susceptible to change. Since the beginning of recorded time, humans have actively participated in and altered ecosystems. Nothing exists in a vacuum. Human history and the history of our planet are irrevocably intertwined.

This is not to say that the wild—and all that it contains—is insignificant, unreal, purely imagined, or strictly metaphorical. In fact, the most important responsibility of the nature writer is to define and deconstruct our relationship to our natural environment and defend aspects of the environment that are far too often overlooked or exploited. It's crucial to keep in mind, however, that we experience reality through our own particular cultural and social lens. We impose our own ideas and imaginings upon the natural world. We like nature to represent what we are not. Thoreau uses extraordinarily detailed prose to allow the reader to feel what it's like to live at Walden Pond. However, he also shows that if we insist upon a distinct difference between "nature" and "humanity," the "wild" and the "civilized," nature becomes abstracted and objectified, an ideological or metaphorical construct. Nature does not exist simply to reflect the human;

indeed, most wild places on our planet exist beyond the reach of direct human interference, and must be protected as such.

Ultimately, nature writing must do what all creative nonfiction attempts to do: embrace ambiguity. This ambiguity may include questioning the assumption that the "natural" environment is limited to pristine, undeveloped landscapes or the outdoors in general. The word *nature* also means the essential characteristics of a person or thing—or, by extended definition—the living system in which that person or thing exists. Does this necessarily mean trees and rivers? Is there such a thing as an "unnatural" or artificial environment? One student attending an urban university argued persuasively that her nature essay should address her observations and experiences at the mall. The result was a wry, witty, and very insightful look at human behavior in an environment common to many.

Another reason why students sometimes struggle with nature writing assignments is what I like to call the "specter of the sublime." Readers often look to nature writing to experience an appreciation of beauty or state of emotional elevation through the author's description of the natural world. This expectation can be intimidating and even self-defeating for both beginning and experienced writers. For an explanation of the sublime, we can go all the way back to the Greek philosopher Longinus, who wrote that it is the experience of the sublime, through emotion and language, that allows us to transcend the limits of the human condition. The sublime takes us beyond the real and the ordinary to what might exist beyond commonplace human, empirical experience. This idea was popular with the Romantic poets, Wordsworth in particular, and has helped shaped our own feelings and expectations about nature and nature writing. "[S]ublimity is a certain distinction and excellence in expression," Longinus writes. "It is from no other source than this that the greatest poets and writers have derived their eminence and gained an immortality of renown. The effect of elevated language upon an audience is not persuasion but transport." That moment of transportation happens suddenly and briefly, "flashing forth at the right moment [that] scatters everything before it like a thunderbolt."

This is not to say that this type of experience does not exist or is not available to those willing to sit, walk, listen, and pay attention. It is true that we often seek escape, refuge, emotional release, or wisdom in nature, or a sense of a higher spiritual or moral experience. Sometimes, perhaps often, we find it. But good nature writing must go beyond the pastoral, the nostalgic, and a naïve—although not necessarily unfounded or misplaced—reverence. Nature writing should explore our relationship with the natural world in all its complexity and ambiguity. It can help mend our connection with the living and nonliving world and, ultimately, our connections with each other. It can help each of us understand our own personal relationship with the natural world and our place within it.

Overuse and exploitation of natural resources, unchecked development, manufacturing, nuclear development, and a score of other issues have led to critical problems in ecosystems around the world. Environmental issues are significant on several levels, from the local or regional to the national and transnational. Nature writing with a strong political or environmental focus is essential and can provide the forum and catalyst for action and real reform. It can lead readers to examine their ethical principles with respect to the world they live in. As an individual and as a writer, what is your role and responsibility to the natural environment?

Think carefully about your subject matter. Are there environmental issues or concerns that you care deeply about, or that you have personal experience with? On the other hand, your essay may concentrate primarily upon story, anecdote, or description. Remember that particular landscapes or animals are often more popular than others. The desert southwest, for example, has inspired many writers. What landscape speaks to you? Many writers describe wolves or bears. What might be an unlikely—and therefore surprisingly interesting—animal topic? Choose a subject that has relevance or meaning to you, not just something that's trendy at the moment.

Do your homework and doublecheck your facts. Understand all the particular details of the landscape you describe: the names of flowers, grasses, and trees. The direction the river flows. The history of the land and the people who occupy it. If you're writing about a hummingbird, ask yourself, how does it get such iridescent wings? How can it hover so perfectly in the air? What type of hummingbird is it exactly, and why does it seek a particular type of flower?

But ultimately you have to go beyond fact. Nature writing seeks to do what all other types of creative nonfiction strive for: to connect. What inspiration and meaning do you find in nature, in the contemplation of the natural environment? How can you convey this to the reader? How can you write this in a compelling way that moves the reader emotionally and intellectually?

In his book *Land of the Spotted Eagle* (1933), Luther Standing Bear writes, "But the old Lakota was wise. He knew that man's heart, away from nature, becomes hard; he knew that lack of respect for growing, living things soon led to a lack of respect for humans too."

All nature writing is, ultimately, a celebration of what is most humane in our world.

Readings with Discussion Questions

Terry Tempest Williams
Refuge: An Unnatural History of Family and Place

Terry Tempest Williams was born in 1955 in Corona, California but grew up in Salt Lake City, Utah. A fifth-generation Mormon, her books reflect not just environmentalism, but an intensely personal view of her place in the world as a human being and as a member of a family, a community, and a religious body of faith. Williams won a Children's Science Book Award from the New York Academy of Sciences for her first book, The Secret Language of Snow, *co-written with Ted Major. She went on to receive a conservation award for special achievement from the National Wildlife Foundation, and a Lila Wallace–Reader's Digest Writer's Award in 2000.*

*   * Refuge: An Unnatural History of Family and Place *chronicles the environmental changes occurring in the Great Salt Lake and juxtaposes the personal story of the death of Williams's mother to cancer, linking the disease to nuclear tests conducted upwind in Nevada in the 1950s and 1960s.*

Burrowing Owls

lake level: 4204.70'

Great Salt Lake is about twenty-five minutes from our home. From the mouth of Emigration Canyon where we live, I drive west past Brigham Young standing on top of "This Is the Place" monument. When I reach Foothill Drive, I turn right, pass the University of Utah and make another right, heading east until I meet South Temple, which requires a left-hand turn. I arrive a few miles later at Eagle Gate, a bronze arch that spans State Street. I turn right once more. One block later, I turn left on North Temple and pass the Mormon Tabernacle on Temple Square. From here, I simply follow the gulls west, past the Salt Lake City International Airport.

Great Salt Lake: wilderness adjacent to a city; a shifting shoreline that plays havoc with highways; islands too stark, too remote to inhabit; water in the desert that no one can drink. It is the liquid lie of the West.

I recall an experiment from school: we filled a cup with water—the surface area of the contents was only a few square inches. Then we poured the same amount of water into a large, shallow dinner plate—it covered nearly a square foot. Most lakes in the world are like cups of water. Great Salt Lake, with its average depth measuring only thirteen feet, is like the dinner plate. We then added two or three tablespoons of salt to the cup of water for the right amount of salinity to complete the analogue.

The experiment continued: we let the plate and cup of water stand side by side on the window sill. As they evaporated, we watched the plate of water dry up becoming encrusted with salt long before the cup. The crystals were beautiful.

Because Great Salt Lake lies on the bottom of the Great Basin, the largest closed system in North America, it is a terminal lake with no outlet to the sea.

The water level of Great Salt Lake fluctuates wildly in response to climatic changes. The sun bears down on the lake an average of about 70 percent of the time. The water frequently reaches ninety degrees Fahrenheit, absorbing enough energy to evaporate almost four feet of water annually. If rainfall exceeds the evaporation rate, Great Salt Lake rises. If rainfall drops below the evaporation rate, the lake recedes. Add the enormous volume of stream inflow from the high Wasatch and Uinta Mountains in the east, and one begins to see a portrait of change.

Great Salt Lake is cyclic. At winter's end, the lake level rises with mountain runoff. By late spring, it begins to decline when the weather becomes hot enough that loss of water by evaporation from the surface is greater than the combined inflow from streams, ground water, and precipitation. The lake begins to rise again in the autumn, when the temperature decreases, and the loss of water by evaporation is exceeded by the inflow.

Since Captain Howard Stansbury's *Exploration and Survey of the Great Salt Lake, 1852,* the water level has varied by as much as twenty feet, altering the shoreline in some places by as much as fifteen miles. Great Salt Lake is surrounded by salt flats, sage plains, and farmland; a slight rise in the water level extends its area considerably. In the past twenty years, Great Salt Lake's surface area has fluctuated from fifteen hundred square miles to its present twenty-five hundred square miles. Great Salt Lake is now approximately the size of Delaware and Rhode Island. It has been estimated that a ten foot rise in Great Salt Lake would cover an additional two hundred forty square miles.

To understand the relationship that exists at Great Salt Lake between area and volume, imagine pouring one inch of water into the bottom of a paper cone. It doesn't take much water to raise an inch. However, if you wanted to raise the water level one inch at the top of the cone, the volume of water added would have to increase considerably. The lake bed of Great Salt Lake is cone-shaped. It takes more water to raise the lake an inch when it is at high-level, and less water to raise it in low-level years.

Natives of the Great Basin, of the Salt Lake Valley in particular, speak about Great Salt Lake in the shorthand of lake levels. For example, in 1963, Great Salt Lake retreated to its historic low of 4191'. Ten years later, Great Salt Lake reached its historic mean, 4200'—about the same level explorers John Fremont and Howard Stansbury encountered in the 1840s and 50s.

On September 18, 1982, Great Salt Lake began to rise because of a series of storms that occurred earlier in the month. The precipitation of 7.04 inches for the month (compared to an annual average of about fifteen inches from 1875 to 1982) made it the wettest September on record for Salt Lake City. The lake continued to rise for the next ten months as a result of greater-than-average snowfall during the winter and spring of 1982–83, and unseasonably cool weather (thus little evaporation) during the spring of 1983. The rise from September 18, 1982 to June 30, 1983, was 5.1', the greatest seasonal rise ever recorded.

During these years, talk on the streets of Salt Lake City has centered around the lake: 4204' and rising. It is no longer just a backdrop for spectacular sunsets. It is the play of urban drama. Everyone has their interests. 4211.6' was the historic high recorded in the 1870's. City officials knew the Salt Lake City International Airport would be underwater if the Great Salt Lake rose to 4220'. Developments along the lakeshore were sunk at 4208'. Farmers whose land was being flooded in daily increments were trying desperately to dike or sell. And the Southern Pacific Railroad labors to maintain their tracks above water, twenty-four hours a day, three hundred sixty-five days a year, and has been doing so since 1959.

My interest lay at 4206', the level which, according to my topographical map, meant the flooding of the Bear River Migratory Bird Refuge.

There are those birds you gauge your life by. The burrowing owls five miles from the entrance to the Bear River Migratory Bird Refuge are mine. Sentries. Each year, they alert me to the regularities of the land. In spring, I find them nesting, in summer they forage with their young, and by winter they abandon the Refuge for a place more comfortable.

What is distinctive about these owls is their home. It rises from the alkaline flats like a clay-covered fist. If you were to peek inside the tightly clenched fingers, you would find a dark-holed entrance.

"*Tttss! Tttss! Tttss!*"

That is no rattlesnake. Those are the distress cries of the burrowing owl's young.

Adult burrowing owls will stand on top of the mound with their prey before them, usually small rodents, birds, or insects. The entrance is littered with bones and feathers. I recall finding a swatch of yellow feathers like a doormat across the threshold—meadowlark, maybe. These small owls pursue their prey religiously at dusk.

Burrowing owls are part of the desert community, taking advantage of the abandoned burrows of prairie dogs. Historically, bison would move across the American Plains, followed by prairie dog towns which would aerate the soil after the weight of stampeding hooves. Black-footed ferrets, rattlesnakes, and burrowing owls inhabited the edges, finding an abundant food source in the communal rodents.

With the loss of desert lands, a decline in prairie dog populations is inevitable. And so go the ferret and burrowing owl. Rattlesnakes are more adaptable.

In Utah, prairie dogs and black-footed ferrets are endangered species, with ferrets almost extinct. The burrowing owl is defined as "threatened," a political step away from endangered status. Each year, the burrowing owls near the Refuge become more blessed.

The owls had staked their territory just beyond one of the bends in the Bear River. Whenever I drove to the Bird Refuge, I stopped at their place first and sat on the edge of the road and watched. They would fly around me, their wings sometimes spanning two feet. Undulating from post to post, they would distract me from their nest. Just under a foot long, they have a body of feathers the color of wheat, balanced on two long, spindly legs. They can burn grasses with their stare. Yellow eyes magnifying light.

The protective hissing of baby burrowing owls is an adaptive memory of their close association with prairie rattlers. Snake or owl? Who wants to risk finding out.

In the summer of 1983, I worried about the burrowing owls, wondering if the rising waters of Great Salt Lake had flooded their home, too. I was relieved to find not only their mound intact, but four owlets standing on its threshold. One of the Refuge managers stopped on the road and commented on what a good year it had been for them.

"Good news," I replied. "The lake didn't take everything."

That was late August when huge concentrations of shorebirds were still feeding between submerged shadescale.

A few months later, a friend of mine, Sandy Lopez, was visiting from Oregon. We had spoken of the Bird Refuge many times. The whistling swans had arrived, and it seemed like a perfect day for the marsh.

To drive to the Bear River Migratory Bird Refuge from Salt Lake City takes a little over one hour. I have discovered the conversation that finds its way into the car often manifests itself later on the land.

We spoke of rage. Of women and landscape. How our bodies and the body of the earth have been mined.

"It has everything to do with intimacy," I said. "Men define intimacy through their bodies. It is physical. They define intimacy with the land in the same way."

"Many men have forgotten what they are connected to," my friend added. "Subjugation of women and nature may be a loss of intimacy within themselves."

She paused, then looked at me.

"Do you feel rage?"

I didn't answer for some time.

"I feel sadness. I feel powerless at times. But I'm not certain what rage really means."

Several miles passed.

"Do you?" I asked.

She looked out the window. "Yes. Perhaps your generation, one behind mine, is a step removed from the pain."

We reached the access road to the Refuge and both took out our binoculars, ready for the birds. Most of the waterfowl had migrated, but a few ruddy ducks, redheads, and shovelers remained. The marsh glistened like cut topaz.

As we turned west about five miles from the Refuge, a mile or so from the burrowing owl's mound, I began to speak of them, *Athene cunicularia*. I told Sandy about the time when my grandmother and I first discovered them. It was in 1960, the same year she gave me my Peterson's *Field Guide to Western Birds.* I know because I dated their picture. We have come back every year since to pay our respects. Generations of burrowing owls have been raised here. I turned to my friend and explained how four owlets had survived the flood.

We anticipated them.

About a half mile away, I could not see the mound. I took my foot off the gas pedal and coasted. It was as though I was in unfamiliar country.

The mound was gone. Erased. In its place, fifty feet back, stood a cinderblock building with a sign, CANADIAN GOOSE GUN CLUB. A new fence crushed the grasses with a handwritten note posted: KEEP OUT.

We got out of the car and walked to where the mound had been for as long as I had a memory. Gone. Not a pellet to be found.

A blue pickup pulled alongside us.

"Howdy." They tipped their ball caps. "What y'all lookin' for?"

I said nothing. Sandy said nothing. My eyes narrowed.

"We didn't kill 'em. Those boys from the highway department came and graveled the place. Two bits, they did it. I mean, you gotta admit those ground owls are messy little bastards. They'll shit all over hell if ya let 'em. And try and sleep with 'em hollering at ya all night long. They had to go. Anyway, we got bets with the county they'll pop up someplace around here next year."

The three men in the front seat looked up at us, tipped their caps again. And drove off.

Restraint is the steel partition between a rational mind and a violent one. I knew rage. It was fire in my stomach with no place to go.

I drove out to the Refuge on another day. I suppose I wanted to see the mound back in place with the family of owls bobbing on top. Of course, they were not.

I sat on the gravel and threw stones.

By chance, the same blue pickup with the same three men pulled alongside: the self-appointed proprietors of the newly erected Canadian Goose Gun Club.

"Howdy, ma'am. Still lookin' for them owls, or was it sparrows?"

One winked.

Suddenly in perfect detail, I pictured the burrowing owls' mound— that clay-covered fist rising from the alkaline flats. The exact one these beergut-over-beltbuckled men had leveled.

I walked calmly over to their truck and leaned my stomach against their door. I held up my fist a few inches from the driver's face and slowly lifted my middle finger to the sky.

"This is for you—from the owls and me."

My mother was appalled—not so much over the loss of the burrowing owls, although it saddened her, but by my behavior. Women did not deliver obscene gestures to men, regardless. She shook her head, saying she had no idea where I came from.

In Mormon culture, that is one of the things you do know—history and geneology. I come from a family with deep roots in the American West. When the expense of outfitting several thousand immigrants to Utah was becoming too great for the newly established church, leaders decided to furnish the pioneers with small two-wheeled carts about the size of those used by apple peddlers, which could be pulled by hand from Missouri to the Salt Lake Valley. My ancestors were part of these original "handcart companies" in the 1850s. With faith, they would endure. They came with few provisions over the twelve-hundred-mile trail. It was a small sacrifice in the name of religious freedom. Almost one hundred and fifty years later, we are still here.

I am the oldest child in our family, a daughter with three younger brothers: Steve, Dan, and Hank.

My parents, John Henry Tempest, III, and Diane Dixon Tempest, were married in the Mormon Temple in Salt Lake City on September 18, 1953. My husband, Brooke Williams, and I followed the same tradition and were married on June 2, 1975. I was nineteen years old.

Our extended family includes both maternal and paternal grandparents: Lettie Romney Dixon and Donald "Sanky" Dixon, Kathryn Blackett Tempest and John Henry Tempest, Jr.

Aunts, uncles, and cousins are many, extending familial ties all across the state of Utah. If I ever wonder who I am, I simply attend a Romney family reunion and find myself in the eyes of everyone I meet. It is comforting and disturbing, at once.

I have known five of my great-grandparents intimately. They tutored me in stories with a belief that lineage mattered. Genealogy is in our blood. As a people and as a family, we have a sense of history. And our history is tied to land.

Questions for Discussion

1. How do you feel about the structure of this essay? How are you drawn into the voice and perspective of the narrator?

2. Is this "environmental" writing? Do you feel moved to take some political or personal action as a result of reading this?

3. Describe the tone of this essay. Is it angry and direct? Intimate and inviting? Analyze the connection between the author and the reader.

Christa Wolf
Accident: A Day's News

East German novelist, essayist, and short story writer Christa Wolf was born in 1929 in Landsberg an der Warthe, Germany (now Gorzow Wielopolski, Poland). Wolf gained widespread recognition in 1963 with her first full-length novel Der Geteile Himmel (Divided Heaven: A Novel of Germany Today) *for which she won East Germany's prestigious Heinrich Mann Prize. Subsequent works caused controversy in East Germany as they gained popularity in the West. Wolf is interested in landscape, both within and without; myth and personality; and the responsibility of the individual with respect to environmental issues.*

Wolf's 1987 novel, Stoerfall (Accident: A Day's News), *juxtaposes the Chernobyl nuclear disaster against the narrator's brother's personal crisis, an operation for a brain tumor.*

On a day about which I cannot write in the present tense, the cherry trees will have been in blossom. I will have avoided thinking, "exploded," the cherry trees have exploded, although only one year earlier I could not only think but also say it readily, if not entirely with conviction. The green is exploding. Never would such a sentence have been more appropriate in describing the progress of nature than this year, in this spring heat, following the endlessly long winter. I knew nothing yet of the warnings that would circulate much later about eating the fruit, still invisible on the branches of the blossoming trees, on the morning when I was annoyed, as I am every morning, by the bustlings of the neighbor's chickens on our freshly seeded lawn. White leghorns. The only good thing you can say about them is that they react to my clapping and hissing with fear, if also confusion. Still, most of them scattered in the direction of the neighboring property. There's a good chance you'll be able to hang on to your eggs now, I thought spitefully, and I intimated to that authority who had begun early on to watch me alertly from a very distant future—a glance, nothing more—that I would not feel bound by anything anymore. Free to do and, above all, not to do as I pleased. That goal in a very distant future toward which all lines had run till now had been blasted away, was smoldering, along with the fissionable material in a nuclear reactor. A rare case . . .

Seven o'clock. Where you are now, brother, they begin punctually. You will have received your sedative shot half an hour ago. Now they have wheeled you from the ward into the operating room. Cases such as yours are usually the first to come under the knife. Now I imagine you feel a not unpleasant dizziness within your shaven head. The point is to prevent you from having any clear thoughts, any all too distinct feelings. Fear, for instance. Everything will be all right. This is the message that I'm transmitting to you as a focused beam of energy before they send you off into anesthetized sleep. Is it getting through? Everything will be all right. Now I summon up your head before my inner eye and seek out the most vulnerable spot where my thought can penetrate to your brain, which they are about to expose. Everything will be all right.

Since you can't ask, the kinds of beams I'm talking about are certainly not dangerous, dear brother. In a manner unknown to me, they traverse the poisoned layers of air without becoming infected. The scientific term is "contaminated." (I'm learning new words while you sleep, brother.) Sterile, completely sterile, they reach the operating room and your body, laid out helpless and unconscious, touching and knowing it within fractions of a second. Would know it even if it were more greatly disfigured than you claim it is. Effortlessly, they penetrate the powerful force field of your unconsciousness in search of the glowing, pulsating core. They retard the ebbing flow of your strength in a way which defies language. This you must rely on; that was the agreement. It still counts . . .

Although unsuspecting, we will not have been unprepared before receiving the news. Didn't it seem familiar to us? Yes, I heard someone inside me think: Why always only the Japanese fishermen? Why not us as well, for a change?

The Birds and the Test.

In the shower I let the water run down my body carelessly, without a second thought. Every single one of the countless experts who are now shooting up out of the ground like mushrooms (mushrooms! inedible this season!) has stated that the groundwater will not be endangered for a long, long time—if at all this time. In a clear brooklet. Singing in the shower is a bad habit. It also makes it difficult to hear the NEWS on my little Sanyo transistor radio chopped up and refashioned every hour into the news. The wayward trout. Fish for storing radioactive waste. Depending on his affiliation with one of the factions into which the public has predictably divided, whether he was an optimist or a pessimist, the expert would say: No. Under no circumstances will the core melt down. Or: But of course. Yes, yes. Even that eventuality cannot be excluded. In such a case, one would have to expect that phenomenon so graphically christened the China Syndrome by scientific wits. As long as the fire hasn't been extinguished—and, brother, you probably don't know that although it may be hard for graphite fires to start, we have been forced to learn that it is incredibly difficult to put them out—as long as the chain reaction continues, the reactor core can remain active, melting through the earth's core until it reemerges in the antipodes. Transformed, perhaps, but still glowing. Brother, do you remember lowering a beer bottle full of hydrochloric acid into the deep hole we dug in the sandpile in front of our house? It was conscientiously pasted over with warning labels, for we were confident that it would eat its way through to the antipodes. Do you remember the letter we wrapped watertight in cellophane and fastened to the neck of the bottle? And its contents? Brothers and sisters, that's what we called the antipodeans, and we urgently requested that they confirm receipt of our bottle post at the return address we had, naturally, included.

We used to be truly thankful whenever we were able to picture an idea. I couldn't dwell on the sudden notion of apologizing betimes to the antipodeans because I had to listen to what a radio announcer was asking a seemingly young expert who had kindly consented to join him in the studio. What was he doing with his children today, if he had any. He did. He said he had told his wife not to give the children any fresh milk, spinach, or salad. Also, to be on the safe side, not to let them play in the park or the sandbox. Just then, as I was squeezing some toothpaste onto my toothbrush, I heard someone say: So, it had to come to this!

The woman who had spoken was myself. Already on the third day, the test of how long I can be alone without starting to talk to myself had loosed the first chunks of audible monologue of this kind: So, now I'll just finish up the laundry and then that's it! Today was the fifth day spent under aggravated conditions and I began talking out loud to people who weren't there. You'd like that, wouldn't you! for example . . .

I don't know what kind of saw is used to cut open the cranium. They say one follows the seams which divide the skull into several segments. If we want to, the doctor told you to reassure you of the perfection of his technique, we can simply lift off the skullcap like any other cap and put it back on again later. But we don't even want to in your case. What they do want to do—fold up a single segment, more specifically, the one over the right temple—they will no doubt have done by now. Your brain matter lies exposed before them. It's getting time for me to concentrate on the hands of the surgeon. On his fingertips. Impulses, for which there are no words. In the deepening wells of your unconsciousness, you shall be soothed. Are you suffering? What comes of the suffering which we cannot perceive . . .

Life as a series of days. Breakfast. Measuring out the coffee with the orange measuring spoon, turning on the coffee machine, savoring the aroma which envelops the kitchen. It hasn't yet occurred to me to try to be more strongly, more consciously aware of smells than I was before. I haven't yet realized that they will be lost to you. Losses cannot always be avoided, your doctor told you, but we try to keep them down to an absolute minimum. Boiling the egg for exactly five minutes, managing the trick, day in day out, in spite of the faulty egg-timer. Imperishable pleasures. The structure that carries life even through dead times. The cutting surface of dark Mecklenburg bread. Sliced kernels of rye. How and when are nuclids—another word I have just begun to learn—actually stored in kernels of grain? From my place at the kitchen table I could see the rich green of the immense field of grain behind our house, since the elderberry bushes were still bare. I was looking for the right word to describe its appearance. "Carpet." A green carpet. In the country, one always risks slipping into archaic imagery.

There wasn't a cloud in the sky that day. (Why did I think "dead time" just now?) In shadows cool and clean / Upon your carpets green / O sweet repose / O sweet repose. Songs which I haven't thought of for years, for decades. I informed that authority who was critically examining everything I ate that the eggs in my refrigerator had grown in the bellies of chickens before the accident. That they had been nourished with grass and seeds free of radiation and delivered right to the store, undated and guaranteed fresh. But not too fresh. Definitely not yesterday fresh.

O heavens' radiant azure.

According to what laws and how quickly does radioactivity spread, at best and at worst? Best for whom? And would those living in the immediate vicinity of the explosion have a slightly better chance if it were spread by a fair wind? If it were to ascend to the higher strata of the atmosphere and there set off on its journey as an invisible cloud? In my grandmother's day the word "cloud" conjured up condensed vapor, nothing more. Probably white and more or less prettily shaped—a picture in the sky to stir the imagination. Hurrying clouds like the ships of the sky / Oh, could I sail with you as you fly . . . You'd end up elsewhere. So said our grandmother, who never traveled anywhere unless she was evacuated. Why are we so addicted to travel, brother?

She would approve of the plum puree which we made ourselves last year, gasping beneath the burden of the harvest. She used to sprinkle hers with cinnamon; we chose not to. She, on the other hand, would never put an old crust of bread in Plaack's feed bucket, as I did after a brief moment's hesitation. She would use the stale bread to make her weekend bread soup with raisins, Polish style, the only one of her dishes I didn't like. It was sinful, she said—a word which she didn't otherwise use—sinful to throw away bread. I should remember that. Her only motto. Our grandmother was a modest woman, brother . . .

We're alive. Not exactly thriving at the moment as far as you're concerned, I'll grant you that. Your life is not exactly hanging by a silken thread, but certainly, I would think, by a suture. To think that a metallic instrument is just now skirting your cerebral membrane, presumably pushing aside the brain matter to make room for another instrument, with a microscope at its end . . . When we spoke on the telephone yesterday, I did not tell you what I recently saw on television: a computer, specially developed for operations on the human brain, programmed to make precise incisions down to one-hundredth of a millimeter. Less fallible than the human hand, they said. But we assured one another that the experience and finesse of your surgeon were one hundred percent reliable . . .

I stood still, in my hand the cup which I meant to put in the sink, and thought several times in a row as intensively as I could: You can rely on the experience and the finesse of your surgeon. On my way to the post office I stopped by old Weiss's place and was reminded once again that he looked rather more like a retired sea captain than a former stable hand. Former? he said. Fat chance. This year as well he would be tending his share of calves along with fishing in the Mildenitz and hunting for mushrooms in the pastures by the village lake. Eighty-three was just a drop in the bucket. But whether he would reach ninety like his father . . . Wait a minute! said his wife as she came out the door, pails of water in hand. Did he want to die all of a sudden! The winter? Oh dear, she said, it had been bad, very bad. Stoking the fire several times a day, and the cold which had seemed to go on forever. And not being able to go anywhere, not even to see their son in town. There hadn't been a single bus running anywhere, and "our father"—that's what she called old Weiss her husband—wouldn't let her go away overnight; she was a prisoner in her own house. To which old Weiss placidly responded: Well, listen to that! A woman belongs in the home. There, you hear, said his wife, this had been going on for forty years.

Questions for Discussion

1. Describe the style of this writer. How does she use parentheticals and seemingly digressive comments to establish tone and an intimate connection to the reader?

2. With respect to radiation, how technical does the author get in this work? Is there enough information to inform the story and allow you to understand the impact of Chernobyl on the characters?

3. Wolf begins her essay with the phrase, "On a day about which I cannot write in the present tense . . ." How does this line set up the story that is to follow? What does it say about the narrator?

Gretel Ehrlich
The Solace of Open Spaces

Gretel Ehrlich was born in Santa Barbara, California in 1946. At age 30, she accepted a PBS assignment that took her to Wyoming and changed her life. Ehrlich so enjoyed the sparsely populated state that she remained there, took up sheepherding, and began writing about the wide-open spaces. Her later works reflect the influence of her solitary and sometimes difficult life in the west.

Her highly acclaimed essay collection on the land and people of Wyoming, The Solace of Open Spaces, *won Ehrlich the Harold D. Vursell Award in 1986 and the Whiting Writer's Award in 1987.*

From a Sheepherder's Notebook: Three Days

When the phone rang, it was John: "Maurice just upped and quit and there ain't nobody else around, so you better get packed. I'm taking you out to herd sheep." I walked to his trailerhouse. He smoked impatiently while I gathered my belongings. "Do you know *anything* about herding sheep after all this time?" he asked playfully. "No, not really." I was serious. "Well, it's too late now. You'll just have to figure it out. And there ain't no phones up there either!"

He left me off on a ridge at five in the morning with a mare and a border collie. "Last I saw the sheep, they was headed for them hills," he said, pointing up toward a dry ruffle of badlands. "I'll pull your wagon up ahead about two miles. You'll see it. Just go up that ridge, turn left at the pink rock, then keep a-going. And don't forget to bring the damned sheep."

Morning. Sagesmell, sunsquint, birdsong, cool wind. I have no idea where I am, how to get to the nearest paved road, or how to find the sheep. There are tracks going everywhere so I follow what appear to be the most definite ones. The horse picks a path through sagebrush. I watch the dog. We walk for several miles. Nothing. Then both sets of ears prick up. The dog looks at me imploringly. The sheep are in the draw ahead.

Move them slow or fast? Which crossing at the river? Which pink rock? It's like being a first-time mother, but mother now to two thousand sheep who give me the kind of disdainful look a teenager would his parent and, with my back turned, can get into as much trouble. I control the urge to keep them neatly arranged, bunched up by the dog, and, instead, let them spread out and fill up. Grass being scarce on spring range, they scatter.

Up the valley, I encounter a slalom course of oil rigs and fenced spills I hadn't been warned about. The lambs, predictably mischievous, emerge dripping black. Freed from those obstacles, I ride ahead to find the wagon which, I admit, I'm afraid I'll never see, leaving the sheep on the good faith that they'll stay on their uphill drift toward me.

"Where are my boundaries?" I'd asked John.

"Boundaries?" He looked puzzled for a minute. "Hell, Gretel, it's all the outfit's land, thirty or forty miles in any direction. Take them anywhere they want to go."

On the next ridge I find my wagon. It's a traditional sheepherder's wagon, rounded top, tiny wood cookstove, bed across the back, built-in benches and drawers. The rubber wheels and long tongue make it portable. The camp tender pulls it (now with a pickup, earlier with teams) from camp to camp as the feed is consumed, every two weeks or so. Sheep begin appearing and graze toward me. I picket my horse. The dog runs for shade to lick his sore feet. The view from the dutch doors of the wagon is to the southeast, down the long slit of a valley. If I rode north, I'd be in Montana within the day, and next week I'll begin the fifty-mile trail east to the Big Horns.

Three days before summer solstice; except to cook and sleep I spend every waking hour outside. Tides of weather bring the days and take them away. Every night a bobcat visits, perched at a discreet distance on a rock, facing me. A full moon, helium-filled, cruises through clouds and is lost behind rimrock. No paper cutout, this moon, but ripe and splendid. Then Venus, then the North Star. Time for bed. Are the sheep bedded down? Should I ride back to check them?

Morning. Blue air comes ringed with coyotes. The ewes wake clearing their communal throats like old men. Lambs shake their flop-eared heads at leaves of grass, negotiating the blade. People have asked in the past, "What do you do out there? Don't you get bored?" The problem seems to be something else. There's too much of everything here. I can't pace myself to it.

Down the valley the sheep move in a frontline phalanx, then turn suddenly in a card-stacked sequential falling, as though they had turned themselves inside out, and resume feeding again in whimsical processions. I think of town, of John's trailerhouse, the clean-bitten lawn, his fanatical obsession with neatness and work, his small talk with hired hands, my eyesore stacks of books and notes covering an empty bed, John smoking in the dark of early morning, drinking coffee, waiting for daylight to stream in.

After eating I return to the sheep, full of queasy fears that they will have vanished and I'll be pulled off the range to face those firing-squad looks of John's as he says, "I knew you'd screw up. Just like you screw up everything." But the sheep are there. I can't stop looking at them. They're there, paralyzing the hillside with thousands of mincing feet, their bodies pressed together as they move, saucerlike, scanning the earth for a landing.

Thunderstorm. Sheep feed far up a ridge I don't want them to go over, so the dog, horse, and I hotfoot it to the top and ambush them, yelling and hooting them back down. Cleverly, the horse uses me as a windbreak when the front moves in. Lightning fades and blooms. As we descend quickly, my rein-holding arm looks to me like a blank stick. I feel numb. Numb in all this vividness. I don't seem to occupy my life fully.

Down in the valley again I send the dog "way around" to turn the sheep, but he takes the law into his own hands and chases a lamb off a cliff. She's wedged upside down in a draw on the other side of the creek. It will take twenty minutes to reach her, and the rest of the sheep have already trailed ahead. This numbness is a wrist twisting inside my throat. A lone pine tree whistles, its needles are novocaine. "In nature there are neither rewards nor punishments; there are only consequences." I can't remember who said that. I ride on.

One dead. Will she be reborn? And as what? The dog that nips lambs' heels into butchering chutes? I look back. The "dead" lamb convulses into action and scrambles up the ledge to find his mother.

Twin terrors: to be awake; to be asleep.

All day clouds hang over the Beartooth Mountains. Looking for a place out of the wind, I follow a dry streambed to a sheltered inlet. In front of me, there's something sticking straight up. It's the shell of a dead frog propped up against a rock with its legs crossed at the ankles. A cartoonist's idea of a frog relaxing, but this one's skin is paper-thin, mouth opened as if to scream. I lean close. "It's too late, you're already dead!"

Because I forgot to bring hand cream or a hat, sun targets in on me like frostbite. The dog, horse, and I move through sagebrush in unison, a fortress against wind. Sheep ticks ride my peeling skin. The dog pees, then baptizes himself at the water hole—full immersion—lapping at spitting rain. Afterward, he rolls in dust and reappears with sage twigs and rabbit brush strung up in his coat, as though in disguise—a Shakespearian dog. Above me, oil wells are ridge-top jewelry adorning the skyline with ludicrous sexual pumps. Hump, hump go the wells. Hump, hump go the drones who gather that black soup, insatiable.

We walk the fuselage of the valley. A rattlesnake passes going the other way; plenty of warning but so close to my feet I hop the rest of the day. I come upon the tin-bright litter of a former sheep camp: Spam cans flattened to the ground, their keys sticking up as if ready to open my grave.

Sun is in and out after the storm. In a long gully, the lambs gambol, charging in small brigades up one side, then the other. Ewes look on bored. When the lamb-fun peters out, the whole band comes apart in a generous spread the way sheep ranchers like them. Here and there lambs, almost as big as their mothers, kneel with a contagiously enthusiastic wiggle, bumping the bag with a goatlike butt to take a long draw of milk.

Night. Nighthawks whir. Meadowlarks throw their heads back in one ecstatic song after another. In the wagon I find a piece of broken mirror big enough to see my face: blood drizzles from cracked lips, gnats have eaten away at my ears.

To herd sheep is to discover a new human gear somewhere between second and reverse—a slow, steady trot of keenness with no speed. There is no flab in these days. But the constant movement of sheep from water hole to water hole, from camp to camp, becomes a form of longing. But for what?

The ten other herders who work for this ranch begin to trail their sheep toward summer range in the Big Horns. They're ahead of me, though I can't see them for the curve of the earth. One-armed Red, Grady, and Ed; Bob, who always bakes a pie when he sees me riding toward his camp; Fred, wearer of rags; "Amorous Albert"; Rudy, Bertha, and Ed; and, finally, Doug, who travels circuslike with a menagerie of goats, roosters, colts, and dogs and keeps warm in the winter by sleeping with one of the nannies. A peaceful army, of which I am the tail end, moving in ragtag unison across the prairie.

A day goes by. Every shiver of grass counts. The shallows and dapples in air that give grass life are like water. The bobcat returns nightly. During easy jags of sleep the dog's dreampaws chase coyotes. I ride to the sheep. Empty sky, an absolute blue. Empty heart. Sunburned face blotches brown. Another layer of skin to peel, to meet myself again in the mirror. A plane passes overhead—probably the government trapper. I'm waving hello, but he speeds away.

Now it's tomorrow. I can hear John's truck, the stock racks speak before I can actually see him, and it's a long time shortening the distance between us.

"Hello."

"Hello."

He turns away because something tender he doesn't want me to see registers in his face.

"I'm moving you up on the bench. Take the sheep right out the tail end of this valley, then take them to water. It's where the tree is. I'll set your wagon by that road."

"What road?" I ask timidly.

Then he does look at me. He's trying to suppress a smile but speaks impatiently.

"You can see to hell and back up there, Gretel."

I ride to the sheep, but the heat of the day has already come on sizzling. It's too late to get them moving; they shade up defiantly, their heads knitted together into a wool umbrella. From the ridge there's whooping and yelling and rocks being thrown. It's John trying to get the sheep moving again. In a dust blizzard we squeeze them up the road, over a sharp lip onto the bench.

Here, there's wide-open country. A view. Sheep string out excitedly. I can see a hundred miles in every direction. When I catch up with John I get off my horse. We stand facing each other, then embrace quickly. He holds me close, then pulls away briskly and scuffles the sandy dirt with his boot.

"I've got to get back to town. Need anything?"

"Naw . . . I'm fine. Maybe a hat . . ."

He turns and walks his long-legged walk across the benchland. In the distance, at the pickup, an empty beer can falls on the ground when he gets in. I can hear his radio as he bumps toward town. Dust rises like an evening gown behind his truck. It flies free for a moment, then returns, leisurely, to the habitual road—that bruised string which leads to and from my heart.

Questions for Discussion

1. How do the details of Ehrlich's descriptions reveal aspects of the narrator's attitude and voice?

2. How does the author use internal dialogue in this essay?

3. Ehrlich is not a published poet, yet her sentences often employ poetic techniques. Analyze the very last line of the essay. How does this line provide practical (i.e., plot) and poetic closure for the essay?

Louis Owens
At Cloudy Pass: The Need of Being Versed in Human Things

Louis Owens was born in 1949 in Atascadero, California. Of Cherokee and Choctaw descent, Owens's work is informed by American Indian life and culture. Owens was the first member of his extended family to graduate from high school and attend college, and he received his bachelor's and master's degrees from the University of California, Santa Barbara and his doctorate in English from the University of California, Davis. Owens's many literary awards include a Fulbright Scholarship (1980), a National Endowment for the Humanities Fellowship (1988), and a National Endowment for the Arts Fellowship (1989). His book The Sharpest Sight *was nominated for the Pulitzer Prize, A National Book Award, and a Poe Award. His book reviews, articles, literary criticism, and essays appeared in numerous periodicals. Owens died at age 53 while on the faculty at the University of California, Davis.*

This previously unpublished essay was an address that Louis Owens gave at the Huxley College of Environmental Studies Commencement at Western Washington University, Bellingham, Washington, in June of 2002.

In my office at the University of California at Davis, I have a small, much battered cedar sign, brown with faded white paint routed into the wood. It reads "Cloudy Pass—Foot Travel Only." I didn't steal the sign. In the late summer of 1976, if my fading memory is correct, one of my jobs as a ranger in the Glacier Peak Wilderness was to remove old signs, replacing some of them with newer signs and leaving some unreplaced. Our goal was to reduce the size of the human footprint in the wilderness, a goal I bought into lock, stock and barrel. I had loved the Cloudy Pass sign from the first moment I saw it in its rocky alpine saddle very close to the Cascade crest. So that sign came home with me and has followed me around for a quarter of a century.

I had initially planned to call this commencement talk simply "The Need of Being Versed in Human Things," a play on Robert Frost's beautiful poem titled "The Need of Being Versed in Country Things." But of course I put off providing a title until one day I was told, abruptly, to stand and deliver. A title was needed then and there. I happened to be sitting in my office at that moment looking at the Cloudy Pass sign. A harmonic convergence took place between Robert Frost and the alpine zone, and my talk took a sudden turn.

Louis Owens, "At Cloudy Pass: The Need of Being Versed in Human Things" is reprinted by kind permission of Polly Owens.

It was natural, of course, that when asked to speak at Huxley College I would think of the Glacier Peak Wilderness nearby, where I worked for several years first on trail crew and later as what back then we called "wilderness' guard." And it may be just as natural that Cloudy Pass asserted its important position at that moment, for Cloudy Pass was nearly as remote and perfect as a place could be for us on trail crew and for me roaming around with a backpack up there. Cloudy Pass meant eleven miles up the Suiattle trail, then seven miles of switchbacks up Miner's Ridge, and then several tough miles along the ridge through the Bear Creek Mining Claim to the pass. Foot Travel Only meant no horses or mules. The government was trying to minimize impact on that fragile subalpine and alpine zone, never mind the mining operation just a few miles back.

In "The Need of Being Versed in Country Things," Robert Frost describes a farm house that has burned, leaving only a chimney "Like a pistil after the petals go" and a barn standing nearby spared from flames by a whim of wind. Birds, Frost says, fly in and out through the broken barn windows and make use of the renewed lilac, the elm touched by fire, the arm of the dry pump flung upward as a roost, and the remaining fence post with a strand of wire. The birds, Frost suggests, find this situation just fine. "For them there was really nothing sad," he says, and then he concludes, "One had to be versed in country things / Not to believe the phoebes wept."

Obviously, in this 1923 poem, Frost is reminding us that Nature does not depend upon us for its equanimity, and we would be making a grave error were we to foist a pathetic fallacy off on the natural world that goes on with its business quite nicely around us, blithely unconcerned with us. Frost undoubtedly felt this point was worth making in a carefully wrought poem because most often throughout the history of humanity, we have shown a need to draw nature up around us like a personal comforter, imagining its significance only in our own image, reading the glyphs of infinity and the measure of our souls' redemption upon its walls, whether that measurement be a divine and supernatural light or an old-growth redwood imagined into someone's Marin County home. We have written the significance of Nature according to the human heart and soul and bank account, and we have imagined an anthropocentric universe in a credo that, if embraced, may be not just misleading but catastrophic.

In the twenty-first century, the message of Frost's poem is certainly far from a new and surprising thought. Those who think and write about humanity's place in the universe, who trouble themselves with concepts such as environment and ecology, have long since gone well beyond Frost's mild admonition. Except for those in powerful acquisitive positions, such as some current politicians who would apparently drill and mine and scrape and cut every inch of the earth for purely human and purely short-term profit, many thinking people in the West seem to have long since abandoned the idea that the earth exists exclusively or even primarily for humankind's use. We have, in fact, frequently gone far in the other direction, replacing the now charmingly archaic Sierra Club notion of leaving nothing but a footprint with the idea of removing humanity as entirely as possible from what we call wilderness: "Cloudy Pass—Mind Travel Only" a current sign might now read.

Like the speaker in Frost's poem, I, too, long ago came upon a ruined structure deep in Nature's embrace. Like Frost's speaker, I drew a lesson from that encounter that has remained with me for more than two decades, a lesson diametrically opposed to Mr. Frost's. Unlike Frost's narrator, however, I was an active agent in the ruin I observed. At the tail end of the 1960s and through the first half of the 70s, I worked seasonally in various capacities for the U.S. Forest Service. On trail crew I helped build and maintain trails through the Glacier Peak Wilderness, heading out with a string of philosophical mules with such names as Kansas City, Kitty, and Festus, with diamond-hitched packs, double-bit axes, pulaskis, two-man crosscut saws, hazel hoes, and shovels— sometimes even dynamite, blasting caps, and plastic explosives—with the purpose of grading trails as flat and smooth and generous as we could make them, of removing windfalls that might bar a horse or strain a backpacker, of turnpiking wet places and building beautiful handsplit cedar bridges over streams and marshes. Our job was to make it easier for human beings to access what had been defined by the federal government in 1964 as "wilderness." Paradoxically, we were paid to let people into a place valued precisely because people had been kept out by resistant nature and the whims of history.

After I left trail crew and took a job as a wilderness ranger, I found myself guarding the wilderness against a nemesis I would without hesitation have unthinkingly named as humanity, and I felt good and not a little smug about that, though had I sat thinking on one of those isolated ridges long enough I would surely have come to the rather disquieting conclusion that I was guarding that wilderness against my own isolate presence.

The human construction that, like Frost's destroyed farmhouse, forever altered my vision of wilderness was a three-sided log shelter built in a lovely pass just off one shoulder of the magnificent glaciated volcano called Glacier Peak. Eleven miles from the nearest trailhead by deep forest trail and killing switchbacks in one direction and even more miles from the nearest road in any other direction, the log shelter was securely deep inside the official wilderness area. In the summer of 1976, I was dispatched from the Darrington District Ranger Station in the Mount Baker-Snoqualmie National Forest to a place called White Pass, with a job to do. I was to burn the shelter that had stood in the saddle of the pass for many more decades than I had been alive. The shelter had buckled under heavy winter snow, and the roof had collapsed. It had to be rebuilt or erased, and the Forest Service had a new policy dictating that man-made objects be removed from wilderness areas. The Forest Service was striving for minimum footprint inside official wilderness while selling timber hand-over-fist and bulldozing logging roads with hysterical speed right up to the borders of those same wilderness areas.

There was no question about what had to be done with the White Pass shelter. I arrived in the midst of a late snowstorm to dismantle what remained and burn it, which I did, an experience I've written about in an essay elsewhere and won't go into detail about here except to say that after five days of fire not a sign of the shelter remained. While the snow raged I took down the old logs and burned and piled until no coal or cinder remained. I bagged and cached the hand-forged spikes in gunny sacks out of sight for later removal by mule, and I spaded and replanted the packed earth with plugs taken from secret, hidden spots along the ridge. The meadow soil that had been beaten down and packed hard and tracked for nearly a century by man and horse and mule and mouse, and every other creature that had sheltered between and within the log walls, had been reimagined, the impact erased. When I finished my task, it was impossible to tell at a quick glance that a human construction had ever been there, that man had ever come to this spot and erected a small monument to his will to exist within and with this challenging world we now called wilderness. I was proud of what I'd accomplished as I surveyed the snow-streaked meadow. I knew that by fall nature would have received the pass back into its fold without measure or reservation.

I packed up my camp and headed out, but a mile or so down the first long switchback I met two old women, two Native Upper Skagit sisters who looked to be in their seventies. They explained that they were hiking those wrenchingly hard eleven miles of river trail and switchbacks in order to camp in the log shelter their father had built at White Pass before they were born. For the Upper Skagit Indians, the pass had been an ideal place from which to hunt and to gather berries. In the late summer and early fall, the meadows between the pass and the slopes of Glacier Peak would be thick with blueberries for miles. The two women had a lifetime of memories of camping in the beautiful shelter their father had built and thousands of backpackers and horse-packers had shared, protected from the kind of bone-chilling weather they were now hiking through.

My meeting with those two ladies altered forever the way I looked at the world and began a process of thought that continues to this day. I realized then that I had been seeing only a small part of the picture. I had learned to rather self-righteously feel myself and all things human to be profanations of this thing called wilderness. In minutes, with smiles and few words, the sisters at White Pass had taught me all that was wrong with what I had come to believe. One needed to be versed in human things, I realized as I followed the North Fork trail to my car, to know that people might weep for the vanished shelter, and that it was right and necessary for them to do so.

For the past twenty years, in several American universities, I have taught something I call Native American literature, and I have given talks on that subject throughout the U.S. and Europe. In my classes we read novels and poems and stories written by authors who identify and are identified as descendents of aboriginal Americans. In these classes, we talk about that impossibly vague and infinitely varied phenomenon called traditional value, the systems of belief that come to us through stories and tell us how to live in the world. It is dangerous and wrong, I always say, to generalize about Native Americans. There are today more than five hundred distinct Native cultures just within the boundaries of the United States. However, there are, nonetheless, shared values across Native cultures articulated throughout the oldest stories. Most important among those values is that of human responsibility and reciprocity. The oldest stories teach us, in all Native American cultures—and very likely all Native cultures around the world—that we are related deeply and inextricably to and with the world we inhabit. We have a natural place within the natural world, just like the mountain goat and marmot and black bear. We belong here, and there.

Fundamental to this writing, I tell my students now, all these years since I burned the White Pass shelter, is the truth that the shelters we build, the footprints we leave, the very thoughts that form within and around us, are natural and acceptable and even, at times, beautiful strands woven within the natural fabric. As we all recognize more and more clearly with every year that passes, through our presence, through our very thoughts and words as well as deeds, we affect and alter our world. If we value the world we inhabit, we must also value our places in that world. If we fail to realize this, we may construct in our imaginations something called wilderness, gather up and remove any human beings who may be native to that space, and then symbolically wall humanity out, leaving it vulnerable to the ravages of whatever devastating forces manifest from the maelstrom of civilization.

The U.S. Wilderness Act of 1964, created by the 88th Congress, describes "wilderness" as "an area where the earth and its community of life are untrammeled by man, where man himself is a visitor who does not remain." As many of you know, I'm sure, the same Wilderness Act contains a section called "Special Provisions," the results of which are loopholes big enough to drive an open-pit mine through.

The Wilderness Act's ramifications and qualifications are well beyond the scope of my expertise or this talk, but the language of the Act should make us wonder. Are we in America living a stressful schizophrenia when it comes to our environment? On the one hand our nation is directed by politicians seemingly bent on exploiting as rapidly as possible every available extractable resource, whether off the nation's coastline or within the Arctic National Wildlife Refuge, while our Congress refuses to make even minimal increase in miles-per-gallon standards for SUV's as big as small busses. On the other hand we debate the reality of ecology and this thing called Wilderness. We smugly remove an ancient log shelter built by an Upper Skagit man whose ancestors had built shelters in the same world for innumerable generations—in order to return nature to a prior "natural" condition, as if we as humans are not natural. Meanwhile, American wilderness areas are vulnerable to hordes of sheep and cattle grazing meadows to brown-out conditions, and to multinational mining corporations with patented claims.

Long ago, with some wonderful people who are in this audience today, I helped build and maintain trails into and through the Glacier Peak Wilderness. In long retrospect, I now believe that what we were doing was attempting to direct humanity both toward the beauty and natural wealth that is the birthright of each human being and away from that which is fragile and too easily perishable. We were engaged in implementing choices: I will build for you this eighteen inch wide strip of earth to trod, to impact, to lay barren with the mark of your passage through life, so that you will see and know and value that which lies off-trail but of which you are, vitally and inextricably, a part. The trail, ideally, will preserve this invaluable part of you from the mark of your own crucial passing. Something will be given so that something may be withheld, and the withholding must be the fruit of mutual assent, reciprocity, and respect. This is the bargain we must learn to make: I will touch the earth with my passage, because I must pass and can do no less, but in passing I will leave all that I may leave unmarked.

Today birds visit the meadow at White Pass, just as they visited Frost's fire-ravaged homestead, and I'm sure none of us would be foolish enough to believe that Nature ever wept for the burned shelter. However, today I understand as I could not understand so many years ago, that something valuable, something perfectly human and therefore perfectly natural, disappeared with the vanished shelter. One needs to be versed in human things to understand why the sisters must have wept.

Questions for Discussion

1. Describe Owens's stance toward wilderness and environmental policy.
2. Does this essay present a convincing argument? How does it move from point to point in the development of that argument?
3. What does Owens say about the responsibility of the individual in environmental preservation?

Student Writing

Detail, Detail, Detail

As you read these two student essays, note how each author brings vivid details about landscape and character to the page. Sensory details are woven into the story in such a way that they don't seem heavy-handed or overly expository.

Melissa Edmunson
The Tolerable Naturalist

Melissa Edmunson, currently finishing her master's degree in English, is beginning to take her writing seriously. She lives in San Jose, California with her husband and three children.

Quail are worth five points. Only past the outhouse, and I already have five points: this is going to be a good hike. Fairly hard to spot, quail are the only animals I can think of that are scored as a group. Usually, individuals have point value—rabbits, deer, lizards, coyote—but quail are always together, so you get five points for the whole covey. Scoring, completely spontaneous and mutable, does at least have to make sense.

I am hiking the Almaden Quicksilver Trail, about five minutes' drive from my house in south San Jose. Just warming up, having passed the trailhead, picnic table, bulletin board, and portable outhouse (anchored into the ground since the last time rowdies toppled it), I advance toward the first gravelly incline, which leads up and away to the main walking path, Guadalupe Mine Hill. The trail winds for several miles, in loops and straights, past the Guadalupe Reservoir, along Los Alamitos Creek, through the old quicksilver mining camps, filtering down into the old part of Almaden (inexplicably called New Almaden) near a French restaurant, La Foret, a great spot to dine. I am on my usual jaunt, a 4.6-mile loop that I like to walk up and run down for exercise.

Walking solo this morning, I recognize some of the regular population of hikers and runners the trail hosts from day to day: the guy with the grey ponytail and the ultra-short shorts; the hard-bodied blonde and her two Dobermans; the Japanese woman with her rice-paper parasol. I enjoy walking alone, sorting my thoughts, keeping my stride, breathing with whatever gusto suits me. I feel perfectly safe, what with all the company on the trail, and do not bring my dogs for "protection"; one is too old, and one too short anyway.

Fall has begun, and the poison oak is turning red. I can identify it now and stay away, whereas I have difficulty picking it out in spring, and walk with suspicious clearance around all things green and leafy. I pause by a healthy clump of the stuff, noting the conspicuous wine-colored stains. "You'll never get me now," I say aloud, my voice cracking and garbling with early morning disuse. A jogger emerges from behind and passes, eyebrows raised; he thinks I am talking to him. "Morning," I say, thick with phlegm. He jogs away, repulsed. I check for more surreptitious passers and, finding none, rid my throat of the annoying residue, hawking a satisfying product smack into the poison oak—sweet revenge.

Not much of a spitter, I am surprised at how smug I feel desecrating the bush. "I guess I'll just start spitting now," I think, mulling the implications. I walk briskly, hands curled in semi-fists to discourage swelling. "Having succumbed to spitting," I think, "I'll probably start tossing my empty water bottles into the ravine, too. Before long, I'll be standing by complacently, not a plastic bag in sight, watching my dog just let it go all over the walking path." On cue, I spot a prominent specimen lying ahead, dried and dusty. I kick it into the bushes.

I think about the times I have seen litter on this path—not very often, as opposed to the dog piles. Sometimes there is a water bottle propped in the fork of a tree; someone might stuff a tissue into the hexagonal holes of the chain link fence above the reservoir. Yesterday, I saw a beer can tucked half-heartedly behind a small weedy bush. What was the thinking there? Is it less a transgression if you *partially* hide the can? Does hiding it a little bit make you *sort of* ecological? Of course, you have to be partly guilty to run by and let it sit there, which is what I did. But I was running—that is my excuse. I can hardly be expected to stop when I am running.

The apex of the slope I am grappling looms ahead, and I crane my neck in anticipation of the coming downhill, preparing to sprint.

I can only run downhill. Even the smallest upturn switches my system to walk mode. Truth be told, downhill running is easier than downhill walking—something I do not tell wide-eyed admirers who, toiling upward, gasp at my daredevil passing speed. I'm out of control really, and the flailing pace—along with my decidedly un-Olympian demeanor—probably makes this quite apparent.

But I keep mum. I blaze by, a veteran runner, in training for the next charity marathon: Don't have time for chitchat; I've got a race to prepare for! I love the puffs of dust my feet arouse in pounding staccato; love the flap, flap, flap of that one sweaty-wet strand of loosened hair on my cheek; love the rhythm of my breath—a wind song of my own making, inexplicable in words. What strength!

What power! Then, a slight tick of elevation in the road brings the whole scenario to a crashing halt, but I am spent anyway, and glad for the respite.

I sweat; I am a sweater—a sweater and a panter—which makes for quite an ungainly picture at the end of one of my marathon dashes. Thankfully, no one is around as I slow to a stagger, heaving and sighing, my forehead in rivulets. I drag the hem of my t-shirt up over my face, dabbing the wet pockets under my eyes and nose, and catching the droplets off my chin. My immodest recovery startles a brown rabbit—exactly the color of the brush from which he springs—that zigzags across the path in frantic escape. I watch him ricochet into the brush. "Four points," I think.

Not one to gape at Nature, lately I have been pondering the whole idea of it—the outdoors, wildlife—God, in a way—and have surprised myself in realizing the sway Nature holds on my life. What was a faint, fondly remembered lure of childhood is now a fairly commanding pull on my senses, and I wonder at this force, which fortifies and humbles me in concert. What beckons me here, outside, of all places, in the chill and dust? I know it is not just the exercise; I anticipate the trail itself, what will happen, what new denizen will appear. I feel good up here, and if it weren't for the plodding dog-walkers coming up on my left, I might skip a little, or twirl, or make some other inappropriate gesture of joy. Instead, I squeak exuberantly, addressing the dogs, "Did you see the bunny?"

While I forge this curious partnership with Nature, I still gag when I hear people wax rhapsodic about it, and have trouble understanding tree-huggers and whale-savers; it all seems a bit forced—*un*natural, in a way, and faintly arrogant, as if these people understood enough of Nature's mystery to "save" it. As if they could.

I remember one time on this trail my husband and I saw a wild boar. My husband saw it initially (fifty points); I thought it was just a log. Standing with its head down, rooting, about 45 yards away, it huffed in short, muffled grunts, pushing its snout into the ground. My husband made some sort of bellowing noise—his rendition of the wild boar call—and the boar glanced up momentarily, probably just to roll its eyes, then resumed its foraging.

Some hikers approached and we pointed out the creature. They exclaimed and carried on as if we had discovered King Tut's tomb, bobbing their heads for a better view and tapping one another excitedly. That did it for the boar, which, snorting and turning, walked with cool, swinish, stubby-legged dignity into the brush. I remember looking to the hikers, thinking, "These yahoos better not try and follow him." They did not follow, but ambled on, expounding loudly on the beauty of the creature, the serenity, the nobility, and how seeing him had made their day, absolutely made their day.

A wild boar does not make my day. On the other hand, it is not a shabby beginning. What I would really like to see is a rattlesnake; I know they are here—my husband has seen them. Unlike the artless, nonchalant boar, the rattler winds with rapt and cagey attention through his low-lying realm, camouflaged and slippery. But sometimes, drugged with sunlight, they can be found dozing alongside the trail, and a perfect time for spotting them is right about now, Indian Summer. Always on the lookout, I hardly know what I would do if I actually saw one: poke it with a stick? That is what my husband does, not aggressively, but just enough to get the snake moving so he can see it better. A nice bit of moxie is required for such maneuvers, and I am not sure I need to test those boundaries. Just spotting a rattler would be a coup—and twice the point value of a boar.

Coming upon the last leg of the trail, I recognize that it is mostly downhill from here. The decline falls pretty steeply in places, and I am going to have to watch it if I want to maintain my pretend marathon status. I take a forceful breath and start running. My eyes, alternating between the ground and the tangle of trees and cliff-side bushes to my right, turn bleary with sweat and wind tears. Birdseye views of the town below pass in snatches through the oaks as I pound by: brown and white houses with tile roofs and backyard pools, neat squares of lawn divided by driveways with their cars. Nobody is out. "That's because they're all up here," I think, passing a trail-hogging trio of chatting hikers. A lizard brazenly skitters across the path in front of me. One point, and I almost squished it.

Contrary to what I anticipated starting out today, my point total is less than astounding: an average ten. Of course, the tally is never complete until I reach the park gate, and one never knows what might be scurrying along the outback of the trail, even near the civilized end. One time, I saw a buck, halting and starting, along the barbed-wire fence that circles a barn at the onset of the trail. Head tilted back, black eyes huge and afraid, he seemed perplexed by the sudden termination of woods, and wary of the distinct, voluminous presence of human beings. There must have been a dozen or more people converged at the gate, all standing back, hushed in anticipation, watching for what the creature would do. Presently, as more people appeared, the buck reared slightly, then plunged through a gap in the wire, disappearing into the landscape.

I often think of that buck. He was a juvenile, with a short, unmarred rack, still smooth in its velvety covering. I am fairly certain I have seen him before—how many juvenile bucks could be roaming this patch of land? Even in his confusion, he had that air of winsome gentility so kindred to deer. At the risk of sounding like a boar-gawker, I must admit to a certain noble majesty in the buck, a natural grace sorely lacking in my heaving, panting self.

The side-ache that has been threatening for several minutes materializes in a slow, steady burn, but I refuse to stop running. I have to keep running until the very edge of the gate, and slap my palm on that mossy gatepost, or none of my run will count—another random, mutable rule. Pushing past the bulletin board, the picnic table, the outhouse, I raise my hand flat and ready for the post, smacking it with precision: done. I did it.

The shady gravel pathway to the car is just long enough for me to regulate my breathing and mop most of the sweat from my face. Endorphins, or trail dust, or something, has worked its magic on me: I feel good. I breathe in and out, thinking clear, uncomplicated thoughts.

Approaching the car, I notice that a certain cinnamon-colored cat has made itself at home in the shade of my bumper while I was gone. Seeing me, the cat leaps up, spooked, and tears away to a nearby house, up and over the latticework fence, mortified for being spotted.

Shrugging, I flop onto the seat of my sun-baked car, indifferent to the frenzied getaway. Cats, naturally, are zero points.

Daphne K. Jenkins
Naupaka in Bloom

Daphne Kauahiilani Jenkins was born and raised on the island of Oahu in Hawaii. She did her undergraduate work at Rice University where she double-majored in English and Sports Medicine, and threw the shot put for the Varsity Women's Track and Field Team. Currently she is completing her master's degree in English. She enjoys writing, yoga, and playing with animals.

Summer had seized me, and I was better and browner for it. I sped in my mom's Nissan Sentra along the two-lane highway, determined to continue my fling with the island of Oahu. I had been leading a double life. Except for Christmas break and summertime, I was a mainlander, a virtual haole. But, for the couple weeks or months that I returned home to Oahu, I plunged back into being a kama'aina—a kama'aina who knew how to dance hula, but hated to be put on the spot at family gatherings to perform—a kama'aina who spoke pidgin when she needed to, "Eh, I like one teriyaki beef, chicken katsu mix plate an one shave ice wid da iceshcream in sidem, thanks ahh brah,"—a kama'aina girl who just happened to attend a college in Texas, where she was majoring in English.

I careened around the rock cliffs, hugging each curve, before turning down a steep decline into the yellow-sand cove of Makapu'u Beach. Shards of black porous reef jutted up through the white foam flanking the cove; a warning to all toes of the crags, crannies, cuts, and scrapes awaiting a misjudged frog-kick. I pulled in next to a white convertible Mustang with a license plate starting with an "E" and no personal bumper-stickers or decals—obviously a tourist car, or military. No kama'aina owned such a haole car.

Concrete slabs piled down the slope like fallen dominoes. The sound of my footsteps against the slabs was like the scuff, scuff, scuff of a Texas two-step danced on sandpaper. At last, the domino-steps sank into the fine yellow sand, and then there was only the soft give of a billion fine granules between my toes.

The beach was what locals would call empty. Only three clusters of towels, slippers, sunscreen, and snacks were visible among the dunes. A

Japanese couple wearing matching red aloha print held hands and walked along the water's edge where the sand had the properties of cool packed mud. The woman held a flimsy straw hat to her crown with her free hand, and the man trudged beside her, camera slung round his neck. A haole family of four stood in a descending height order, rubbing milky white sunscreen on one another's backs. I imagined the family's delight at finding a beach "off the beaten path"—for the most part. What a contrast to Ala Moana or Waikiki; their opaque waters white with the wash of too much sunscreen, too many, too much.

In search of the perfect spot, I passed two pairs of flippers plopped on top of two pairs of rubber thong slippers—a pile of amphibian shoes. Two body boarders cruised in the water. Their slick board bottoms slid over each swell as they waited for the biggest nalu.

I flicked my towel out into the wind before setting it down over the footprint-pocked sand. Among the dunes, naupaka bushes clawed their roots into the mealy sand like shipwrecked clumps of seaweed determined to survive on the dry shore. Sprawling out in front of a naupaka bush, I made my own imprint in the sand. I raised my eyes to admire the naupaka bush with its green, waxy leaves and delicate white half-flowers which bloomed, complete, in the shape of miniature Japanese fans.

Perhaps it was in grade school that I learned about the naupaka legend—the Hawaiian story of how the hapa-flower came to be. A Hawaiian princess and Pele, goddess of the volcanoes, had both fallen in love with the same man—a commoner. But the man returned only the princess' love and resisted all of Pele's attempts to win his affection. The enraged goddess Pele, in the form of a lava flow, chased the man to the sea shore and consumed him in her fiery wrath. The princess fled up into the mountains, believing that Pele's lava flow could not chase her there. But, Pele prevailed. Her lava flows scorched the princess high in the mountains, where the mountain variety of the naupaka now grows. To this day, both naupaka kahakai (the beach variety) and naupaka kuahiwi (the mountain variety) continue to produce half-flowers—symbols of the lovers' eternal separation. It had been a childhood dream of mine to retrieve one flower from each naupaka and unite them. But now, as I studied the tiny blossoms, I felt a sense of contentment with the hapa-flowers which continued to bloom and thrive without their other halves.

"Excuse me, Miss?" I flipped over and stared into the pink face of the haole father.

"Yeah?" I squinted up at him.

"Are you from here? I'm assuming you're local."

"Born and raised."

"Know anything about that park across the street? Sea Life Park, I think it is?"

"Yeah, it's pretty cool."

"Dave. We're visiting from Arizona." He stuck out his hand, and I shook. "So you think it's worthwhile?"

"Well, it's got a reef tank, dolphin exhibits, sea lions. It's not a Sea World. But it's pretty neat."

"Thanks, we'll go check it out. I appreciate it." He walked away, the heels of his Tevas flicking up sand.

Itching from the heat of the sun, I sat up and looked at the water. The body boarders had retrieved their fins and were floating on their boards, bellies flat and flippers up at a right angle. I tiptoed toward the water, noticing the Japanese couple wading in the tide pools. The man was holding the camera in front of his eyes while the woman shouted excitedly, pointing at what must have been a crab or fish. They had donned reef-walkers, a rubber-soled variation of Japanese tabe—funny white canvas socks that separate the big toe from the others. We had to wear them at our high school graduation with our white missionary holoku dresses. The boys wore khaki slacks, blue blazers, and the traditional Punahou School tie.

With the pummeling shore-break, there was no way to wade in and slowly submerge an inch at a time. I timed a breaking wave, and plunged into the thickened water. Clumps of greenish brown limu brushed against me in the swirling water. Bits of sand made their way under the spandex material of my swimsuit, and I'd find them there unbudged when I peeled the suit off to take a shower.

In the midst of the surf zone, I emerged among sand particles and air bubbles stirred up by the waves. Seaweed clumps and driftwood splinters bobbed around me like the nerve endings of the churning sea. I bounced out to where the crests and troughs of the waves were glassy and unbroken. There, I treaded water, my legs spinning like egg-beaters and my arms flailing beneath the surface. I could see the shore before me, the tide pools, the road wrapping around the cliff, and beyond it, the wooden mast of a whaling ship peaking above the cars that whizzed by.

Grade school field trips had familiarized me with Sea Life Park's whaling ship and its other exhibits. Trained bottle-nose dolphins swam in a tank surrounding the whaling ship's hull, their lives on display through portholes in the ship's belly. Across from the ship, sea lions barked and sunbathed on brown slabs of concrete. Near the park's entrance was the reef tank, complete with hammerhead mano and honu, endangered sea turtles. At specified feeding times, a scuba diver swam through the tank, emptying buckets of chum. Across the park, a tourist favorite—the "dolphin princess show"—took place on a tiny island in the middle of a lagoon, no deeper than a backyard swimming pool. A beautiful local girl with long hair played the part of princess, pretending to live on the island in a crate-size grass hut with her dog. She commanded the dolphins to take her to and from her island. She paddled her canoe and the dolphins flanked her. She stood on the island, waved a command and they jumped and flipped and even waved back.

My gaze wandered back from the whaling ship just in time to glimpse a wave building in the distance. It was huge—must be high tide. I glanced at the tide pools. The Japanese couple was gone and the tide pools were covered in white froth. The face of the wave grew steadily taller as it approached. The best thing to do was to swim out toward it, in hopes that it would not break on me before I could duck beneath it.

I began a freestyle stroke out toward the wave. A few feet away, the body boarders, their fins like propellers, coasted into position to catch the wave. I watched them in envy as the wave, hoarding more water into its mass, pulled me toward it. The crest of the wave lurched and a seam of white ripped down its face. I dove into the turbulence, hoping not to be tossed and bent and held under. Gallons tumbled over me, rolling me beneath the water. Crumpled into a ball of arms and legs, I whirled around, my hair collecting seaweed, sand and what else? When I could, I extended my legs and poked for the sandy floor. My feet found the bottom and launched up, knowing that another monster might interrupt my first new breath.

My head pierced the surface and I sucked the air into my lungs fast and hard. No monster coming, at least for now. Millions of air bubbles surfaced around me as I thrashed around to face the shore. I bounded and flopped in a half-swim-half run, fighting the current's suction. Water peeled away from me, forming little waves just behind me. They pummeled me, pushing me forward like a high school bully picking a fight. Finally, my thighs broke the surface and with careful strides I muscled through the knee deep water and onto shore. Exhausted, I plopped down on my beach towel and stretched out flat, face down. The sand pressed against me like a full body orthodic. After a few minutes of deep breathing, I gathered myself and trekked to the shower.

At the end of a bush-lined path four tall pipes stood in the middle of a concrete island like a perfectly centered metallic palm tree. A moat of wet sand and soap bubbles lapped around the shower's base. As I twisted one of the metal knobs, I heard the dolphin princess show starting across the street at Sea Life Park.

"Everyone give a warm ALOOOOHA to Princess Kanani and her dog, Poi!"

The audience hollered in unison, "ALOOOOHA!" *There are no big waves in Princess Kanani's life,* I thought.

I raked my fingers through my hair and scratched my scalp. Bits of sand wedged deeper under my fingernails with each stroke. Next time I'd bring some shampoo and conditioner. I ducked under the water, letting it cascade down my blushing shoulders. I'd also use a higher SPF.

Finished with my shower, I wrapped beach towel twice around my waist—protection for the car's upholstery—and then climbed the remaining domino stairs to the parking lot.

"Eh, sista. Dat one yo Mustang?" I turned to face a dark Hawaiian guy wearing aloha-print swim trunks. I recognized him—one of the body boarders.

"No. I think it's a rental. One of the tourists'. The Sentra's mine." I clicked the car remote, unlocking the driver's side door.

"Nah, dat Mustang one nice bugga! Whoa, one convertible and ereting! I like get one li-dat! Hoa I be cruisin'!" He swung his arms to exaggerate his walk and poked his neck out and back like a pidgin.

"Yeah. It's a nice car."

"Hoa, da waves was pumpin', no? I saw you wen wipe-out one time, yeah?"

I slinked into the front seat of the Nissan and pulled down my sunglasses.

"I'll bring a board and fins next time," I said.

"Bum by I tink dat way mo betta next time."

"Take it easy," I told him through my half-opened window.

"Kay sista. Take care." He gave me a shaka and I waved back. I clicked the car doors locked and started the engine. The body boarder lifted his chin toward me as I reversed. I nodded back.

My fingers throbbing with the pressure of the sand still wedged under my nails, I turned the car back onto road and rolled down my window to breathe the salty air. I stroked my hair, sure that a stowaway clump of limu was tangled somewhere in the strands. More than souvenirs, the sand and seaweed assured me that on Makapu'u Beach's golden shore the imprint of my body pressed into the sand, inseparable.

■ Writing Exercise ■

Write an essay from the first person point of view that celebrates, illuminates, reveals, or interrogates a connection you feel with a specific place or landscape, rural or urban. Illuminate your points through attention to small detail, and imply greater connections as the essay builds. Move from the experience of the individual to a greater, more universal experience. Experiment with structure. Do you need a plot? Have a specific reason for structuring your essay the way you do.

The Writing Workshop

Workshop Goals

Most writing workshops seem to work optimally with about twelve people. Groups larger than this can work well, too, although it takes a little more effort to ensure that everyone participates equally. Regardless of the size of your workshop, occasionally break into smaller groups of two or three. In these smaller groups, each person can read his or her work aloud and participate in the review and analysis. This is a good exercise for the first draft of an assignment. After a small-group workshop, each person can then take home their group's comments, revise the manuscript, and bring in a more polished piece for the larger group to workshop as a whole.

Regardless of the size of the workshop, begin each session with a brief discussion of the goals for the particular type of assignment you are about to discuss. What should you concentrate on? Consider the guidelines of the assignment. Come up with six specific things to discuss. Examples might be higher-level issues such as tone, structure, and theme. What is the tone? How is the piece structured? Is there a theme? (More than one?) Then you might want to discuss specific issues like dialogue, paragraph structure, and transitions between scenes or episodes. Should there be dialogue? Does it work? Are the paragraphs clear and cohesive, leading logically from one to the next? Are there clear transitions between the literary movements in the piece?

This doesn't preclude or prevent workshop members from bringing up other aspects of the work at hand, but it helps focus the discussion and often leads to very concrete suggestions for the author to work on.

Revision Tips and Strategies

Write with All Your Senses

Whether you're describing a desert landscape or an urban jungle, use all of your senses when you write. Strive to invoke all the senses of your reader. How things look, sound, taste, smell, and feel—physically and even metaphysically—is of utmost importance to creating a vivid world in which the reader can share. Abstract words appeal obliquely to the intellect, to the rational mind. Concrete, specific words that reveal sensory experience appeal directly to the imagination. "She was a beautiful girl" doesn't carry nearly as much appeal as a description of the girl's braid as it hangs down the back of her neck, or the scent of her fingertips as they brush across a cheek. "It was a nice day" reveals nothing but the author's inclination for clichés. A description of how the reeds lean into the curve of the river as the sun glints off the water will leave an indelible image in the reader's mind. Try to describe people, settings, and events as if you were seeing and experiencing them for the first time. What makes your perspective fresh and enlivening?

But don't let yourself get carried away with description. Keep it concise and to the point; keep it relevant to the story. Keep things moving.

What Kind of Nut?

In the movie *Best in Show,* a spoof on dog shows, one character—in perfect deadpan—describes how as a child he used to drive his mother crazy by "naming nuts." "We grew up in the town of Pine Nut," he notes, "but of course there are many other types of nuts." He names them in succession: the peanut. The chestnut. The pistachio nut. The white pistachio nut. The result is a hilarious snapshot of a down-to-earth rural character, his family, and the town in which he grew up.

Does it truly matter what kind of "nut" is described in your essay or story? In nature writing or any other genre of creative nonfiction, the writer bears a responsibility to know her subject. Identify and state the names of birds, trees, flowers, animals, or other elements that populate the landscape you're recreating for the reader. Do you mean a sunflower or a stalk of Indian paintbrush? A great egret or a goldfinch? A thoroughbred or a quarter horse? If you're not sure or can't remember clearly, make a trip to the library. It doesn't matter if your reader is familiar with the particular species you describe; the writing will be more vivid and alive for all the detail you can muster.

Details like these can also lend a certain deftness in style, as demonstrated in the example mentioned previously. Naming, and the use of specific detail, can add to or deepen the tone of your work. Whether your essay or story is high-minded or ironic, serious or comic, informative or subversive, use the particular details of landscape to reveal the broader theme.

But I Like It Just the Way It Is

This phrase is often repeated in writing groups and workshops. It can bring a workshop to a dead halt. It can stop a piece of writing in its tracks.

A mature writer is one who can approach the work of revision objectively, without self-pity or attachment. This is very difficult to do, but like many other aspects of writing, it gets easier with practice. The first thing to do is to try to check your ego at the door. In your writing group or writing workshop, jot down what everyone says, whether you agree or not. Listen carefully—without emotion, if you can manage it. Try to hear what it is that people are getting out of your work. Some of their comments will turn out to be relevant; some not. Ultimately it is up to you to decide what to use and what to discard.

Put a little space between you and the work and the comments that the work has generated. Give yourself a rest. Put the manuscript in a desk drawer for a day or two. When you feel somewhat refreshed, take the work out again and brace yourself. This is where

(continued)

Revision Tips and Strategies *(continued)*

you have to be ruthless. But this can also be the most exciting phase of the process.

Begin by throwing out your best line, the one you really love. See what happens to the rest of the piece. Or take that one good line and start over, using that line as a high-water mark. Try to make every new line come up to the same quality.

Try removing the first paragraph, or the first page. What happens if you begin at the top of your second page ? Or your third—or your tenth? Take the last paragraph and put it at the beginning. Take the first paragraph and put it at the end.

The act of revising and re-visioning inevitably brings up many of the doubts and insecurities that were present when the piece was first conceived. Remember the voice of the Destroyer? It's important to extinguish that voice and let the mature voice of the Editor take over instead. One way you can do this is to trick your rational mind. Walk into the center of the room and toss your manuscript into the air. Let the pages fall where they may. Pick them up randomly, and rewrite the piece in the order you've just created. Or, cut apart the paragraphs. Turn them over so you're looking at blank paper. Rearrange the pieces of paper and then turn them over. Again, rewrite the piece in the new order.

These exercises help remove, at least temporarily, the emotional attachment you may feel to a particular piece of writing. Ironically, it is often through radical restructuring that you discover the real heart and soul of a story.

Some authors claim to write without revision. No doubt this is true, especially if the writer has been formulating a piece in her heart and mind for a long time. Writing doesn't happen only when you're sitting at your desk or in front of your computer. It happens all the time: when you're cooking, reading, exercising, or discussing a movie with a friend. Writing is not a single act or static event but an ever-changing process.

Learn to love revision, not to fight it. Keep yourself open to creative possibilities.

For Further Reading

Abbey Edward. *Desert Solitaire* (1968)

Austin, Mary Hunter. *Land of Little Rain* (1903)

Carson, Rachel. *Silent Spring* (1962) and *The Sense of Wonder* (1964)

Clarke, Jeanne Nienaber, and Hanna J. Cortner, eds. *The State and Nature: Voices Heard, Voices Unheard in America's Environmental Dialogue* (2002)

Dillard, Annie. *Pilgrim at Tinker Creek* (1974)

Ehrlich, Gretel. *The Solace of Open Spaces* (1985)

Emerson, Ralph Waldo. "Nature" (1836)

Finch, Robert, and John Elder, eds. *The Norton Book of Nature Writing* (1990)

Griffin, Susan. *Woman and Nature* (1978)

Kingsolver, Barbara. *Prodigal Summer* (2001)

LaDuke, Winona. *All Our Relations: Native Struggles for Land and Life* (1999)

Leopold, Aldo. *A Sand County Almanac* (1949)

Lopez, Barry. *Arctic Dreams* (1986)

Muir, John. *The Mountains of California* (1894) and *Our National Parks* (1901)

Murray, John, ed. *American Nature Writing 2001* (2001; an ongoing series)

Reuther, Rosemary Radford, ed. *Women Healing Earth: Third World Women on Ecology, Feminism, and Religion* (1996)

Silko, Leslie Marmon. *Ceremony* (1977)

Snyder, Gary. *Practice of the Wild* (1990)

Thoreau, Henry David. *Walden* (1854) and "Walking" (1863)

Walker, Clare Leslie, and Charles E. Roth. *Keeping a Nature Journal: Discover a Whole New Way of Seeing the World Around You* (2000)

Warren, Karen J. *Ecofeminist Philosophy: A Western Perspective on What It Is and Why It Matters* (2000)

Chapter 5

Biography and History

Introduction

If often seems that Americans today aren't interested in history or historical figures. We replace historic buildings with high-rises and parking lots. We pack up and move more often than any other culture, relocating from city to city in search of new jobs and opportunities. With the explosive growth of chain restaurants and hotels, cities tend to look alike. American ideology is based on growth, change, and improvement. We like to think of ourselves as free not only from political oppression but also from the constraints of tradition, custom, and habit.

But our fast-paced lifestyle is illusionary.

History and biography are experiencing a renaissance. It just looks a little different these days. Books, of course, are a significant part of how most people learn about the lives of others—the famous and the not-so-famous—and the historical past. Recent bestsellers include the biographies of John Adams, Frida Kahlo, and Benjamin Franklin. But biographies aren't limited to famous politicians or artists. *Seabiscuit,* a recent bestseller by Laura Hillenbrand, profiles the life of a racehorse.

What is new within the last decade or so is that history and biography have exploded into other media. From the History Channel and the Arts & Entertainment Biography Channel to E! Entertainment Television and Lifetime for Women's *Intimate Portrait* series, stories about people's lives, both contemporary and historical, stream into our living rooms on a daily basis. Some of these stories are entertaining; others provide a moral or cautionary tale. Documentaries such as Ken Burns's "Not For Ourselves Alone: The Story of Elizabeth Cady Stanton and Susan B. Anthony," the story of two founders of the women's movement, bring to light important stories that have profoundly changed and shaped our lives today.

More than ever, people are interested in understanding the lives of historical figures and connecting to those lives in a meaningful way. We want to know history through the life story of someone who lived it, and we want to understand what historical events mean to us now. Our fascination with history goes beyond books and television and is evident in our renewed interest in geneology, family history, and memoir. Popular hobbies such as antiquing (seeking out historic objects and restoring them) and historical reenactment (researching, re-creating, and reenacting a particular historical event) reflect our connection to the past and the need to integrate it into our lives today.

What is the difference between biography and history? Essentially, biography is the study of a particular person, and history the study of a particular event or series of events. Conventional works of history and biography generally focus on a chronological development of fact. The facts are presented in a straightforward, objective manner in which the author is usually invisible and makes no reference to personal feelings or perceptions. The language is clear and well structured but generally not concerned with literary style. Conventional biographies tend to take a "womb to tomb" approach, relating the story of a historical figure from birth to death.

Literary history and biography are a balance of fact and invention, reality and imagination. Writers of literary biography and history tend to tell a more personal story, showing how an individual life (or lives) is shaped and influenced by historical experience. There is a poetic sensibility toward language and a greater freedom in structure; the story may be chronological or nonlinear. The author may be present in the text as a voice or character, or may simply provide distinct commentary on the people and events being described. The tone may be serious or ironic, light or tragic. Literary biography and history explore context and subjectivity. They examine the position of individuals within their societies and broaden their personal story into the story of their place and time, thus revealing what that story means to us today. Solid research, a canny sense of detail, and a novelistic imagination are all essential tools of the biographer or historian who chooses to write creative nonfiction.

Just like "straight" nonfiction, literary history and biography is based on research that might include documents, letters, newspaper clippings, and interviews. Again, we must ask, How much—if anything—can be embellished or invented? To what ethical truth is the writer bound?

History and biography are, above all, modes of storytelling. We would like to think that the historian and biographer are purely objective and report only what really happened. But is true objectivity possible? The writer must rely upon the information and historical artifacts available at the time he or she is writing. This information may be limited or may reflect only one viewpoint or perspective. Further, the writer brings his or her own set of expectations to how this information is viewed, interpreted, and then relayed to the reader. All research and writing is a process of selection, inclusion and exclusion, interpretation, and narrative structuring. Even the historian, intentionally or not, distorts to a certain extent. Consider how many different versions of a particular event, or a particular person, have been written. How many biographies of John F. Kennedy have been written? How do you determine which one is the most "correct"?

This is not to say that historical or biographical fact does not exist, or that we do not bear a responsibility to present facts as fully and truthfully as possible. The process, though, is complicated—even more so with historical figures who have reached almost mythic proportion in our cultural consciousness. Think of Elvis Presley, Abraham Lincoln, or Marilyn Monroe. The myths and legends surrounding these names are almost more tenacious than the truth and perhaps tell us more about ourselves as a culture than about these people as individuals.

Some writers and critics believe that creative nonfiction can be more "truthful" than a so-called straight journalistic approach since it tends to recognize the role of storytelling in history and biography, and the role of the individual and collective imagination in how we tell those stories. Creative nonfiction tends to be more aware of our own particular biases and the cultural or historical lens through which we examine history and historical figures.

The first step in writing literary biography or history is deciding on a subject. This step alone can feel overwhelming. Think about aspects of history or place that have fascinated you. Perhaps on a summer trip to Greece, you visited the island of Delos and were captivated by the ancient stone lions. Or—a little closer to home—you might recall stories your grandmother used to tell you about living through the Depression. A few hours of research would reveal a wealth of storytelling opportunities. Libraries and historical societies are filled with stories waiting to be told. Take the time to hunt for overlooked odds and ends of history, of stories that have been hidden or obscured. If you are writing biography, make a list of people whose lives have fascinated or influenced you. They don't necessarily have to be famous historical or literary figures—friends or relatives work, too. Your topic will likely be quite broad to begin with; you'll need to limit the subject to something that is manageable as you proceed with your research and writing. As you consider your subject, keep asking yourself, What is my connection to this story? Why is this story relevant now, to me and my reader? What is the parallel to our times?

Begin your research by gathering as much information as you can about the subject and the historical period. Strive to understand the context of the historical person or event you are writing about and the cultural and social issues that were relevant at the time. As much as possible, begin your research with primary sources. Thanks to the Internet, interlibrary loan services, and university databases that are now online, these sources may be more available than you realize. Even with primary sources, try to have at least two solid sources for each fact that you use in your story, and then make it clear to the reader—implicitly or explicitly—what aspects of the story you are developing beyond fact. As you move to the next stage of researching secondary sources (books and articles written *about* your subject), keep in mind that with secondary sources, every writer has a different approach.

Be a sleuth. Go to your local historical society and peruse old files. Look for letters, journals, newspapers (beyond what's on the Internet), and microfiche. Visit a nursing home and interview someone who lived through the event you're researching. Check genealogical records. Your research might extend into matters of dress, style, dining, or even dance steps. What were people wearing in 1898? Remember that your job is to get into the dirt and grit of the past. What was life like back then? As in other types of creative nonfiction, the story lives in the details. You need enough solid research to paint a deeply intimate portrait of what it was like to live at that time.

At the same time, you must keep in mind the broader perspective of your work. What approach will you take to the story? What point of view is most appropriate? Keep thinking about your characters and develop them as fully as possible. What drives your characters? What are the influences on their lives? Why is this story relevant today?

Once you begin writing, you'll discover that you have many decisions to make. How much information should you include, and what should you leave out? You may need to eliminate trivial details and develop scenes that at first seemed unimportant. You might decide to create composite characters and write dialogue to create an emotional and physical experience for the reader. Some scenes require a lot of time and development; in other places in the text you will need to compress time. If you write about past events in the present tense—as if they are unfolding right before our eyes—your story is no longer a narration but an actuality. The reader experiences the events as they happen and feels a sense of immediacy and a deeper connection with the character and story.

News or "straight" fact is the first draft of history. Now your job is to bring perspective to the people and events that you're writing about, to make the story come alive and teach us something about history—and about ourselves—in the process.

Histories and biographies are the stories that bring us together. We read these stories to share the joy and grief, the discoveries and disappointments, the obstacles and triumphs that others have experienced. No life story is ever quite so unique as we would like to believe—through storytelling, we find connection with and compassion for people from all walks of life. Not only do these stories provide us with a lens through which we can look at specific events in history, but we can learn about our own lives by reading the lives of others. And as writers, we learn by telling. Often we discover our own greatest revelations by researching and relating the stories of other people. Writing literary biography and history is a way of connecting our own individual life to the wide human experience, of locating ourselves within the stream of human history.

Readings with Discussion Questions

Jacob Silverstein
The Devil and Ambrose Bierce

Jake Silverstein, a resident of Marfa, Texas, is a graduate of Wesleyan University in Connecticut and a graduate student in English and creative writing at Hollins University in Roanoak, Virginia. He was formerly a reporter for the Big Bend Sentinel *in Marfa, Texas. Silverstein was awarded a Fulbright Student Scholarship for research and writing in Zacatecas, Mexico.*

    Silverstein's essay "The Devil and Ambrose Bierce" appeared in the February 2002 issue of Harper's *magazine.*

    SATAN, n. One of the Creator's lamentable mistakes, repented in sashcloth and axes. Being instated as an archangel, Satan made himself multifariously objectionable and was finally expelled from Heaven. Halfway in his descent he paused, bent his head in thought a moment and at last went back. "There is one favor that I should like to ask," said he.

    "Name it."

    "Man, I understand, is about to be created. He will need laws."

    "What, wretch! you his appointed adversary, charged from the dawn of eternity with hatred of his soul—you ask for the right to make his laws?"

    "Pardon; what I have to ask is that he be permitted to make them himself."

    It was so ordered.

                     —Ambrose Bierce, The Devil's Dictionary

    "Where is the grave of Ambrose Bierce?"

    "It's behind you. . . ."

                     —graffiti in a toilet stall at Big Bend National Park

In Far West Texas, on the side of the highway that runs south from Marfa to Presidio and across the Rio Grande into Ojinaga, Mexico, there is a small green sign that reads, PROFILE OF LINCOLN. Under these words an arrow points west at the jagged foothills of the Chinati Mountains, where you can make out the sixteenth president's profile in the ridges of rock. He lies on his back, forever staring at the sky, his gigantic head inclined gently, as if on a pillow. The short brim of his stovepipe hat has afforded him little shade over the years, and his brow is black from the scorch of the sun. His lips, such as they are, appear cracked and turned down, his forehead wrinkled with worry, his gaze fixed ahead as if in contemplation of some profound bafflement. He seems to wonder, "How in God's name did I end up here?"

    The term "Far West Texas" refers to that portion of the state that lies west of the Pecos River. It is a dry and sparsely populated portion. The urban centers are El Paso, a city of 600,000, which recently announced that it may run out of drinking water by the year 2025, and Midland-Odessa, a two-city metropolis of around 180,000. Midland's nickname is The Tall City. It is not tall, but the plains that surround it are flat and empty. Odessa's nickname is The City of Contrasts.

All three cities are located about three hours from Marfa, the little town where this story begins. On the road, you pass through vast cattle ranches, though you do not see many cows. This is the Far West Texas range-cattle business. Since the first boom, in the years after the Civil War, it has been a business in decline. Encouraged by cheap land, and then discouraged by the never-ending drought, Far West Texas cattlemen went about setting up some of the largest and emptiest ranches in the West. As you drive south the situation worsens. Last year some ranchers in Presidio County, where Marfa is located, reported herds as small as one cow per 200 acres.

The human population throughout the region is as sparse as that of the cow. In five Far West Texas counties that cover as much ground as Massachusetts, Connecticut, and New Jersey combined, there are barely 50,000 people, most of them clustered in small, dusty towns scattered over an emptiness that would be absolute were it not for the occasional thirsting cow. The scout W. B. Parker appraised the area thusly in his 1856 account *Through Unexplored Texas:* "For all purposes of human habitation—except it might be for a penal colony—these wilds are totally unfit."

Parker's appraisal was meant for the human settler, but there was another to whom this desolation appealed. His story is one you will not hear the civic boosters tell, but in the bars and fields you might ask a friend. When he was falling toward earth from heaven, the devil wished to prove a point. He searched the globe for the least heavenly place he could find. Green valleys, cheerful streams, and lush forests did not interest him. With a sneer, he flew over orchards and farms. Too pleasant. Then he came to West Texas. There are numerous topographical features named for him here: Devils River, Devils Lake, Devil's Backbone, Devil's Ridge, Sierra Diablo, Diablo Plateau, Cerro Diablo. Many of the county's older residents believe that he still lives here, in a mountaintop cave with a nice view of Presidio and Ojinaga.

Four years ago I passed through Marfa as a tourist. I had read an article about an art museum there that sounded interesting. I looked up Marfa on the road atlas—a little speck in the blankness—and made my way there for a one-night stay. A year later, occupied with fantasies of the open range, I headed back. I left my home in California on the day after Halloween, my dashboard covered with leftover candy that melted in Arizona. I arrived in Marfa on a Saturday night. A crowd of girls asked me what I was doing.

"I'm moving here," I announced.

"You'll never make it," one of the girls said. "The boredom will drive you crazy."

I got a job with the *Big Bend Sentinel,* Marfa's weekly newspaper. I covered the school board, the city council, the drought, the Border Patrol, crime, art, rain, the post office, the Amtrak line, the D.A.'s race, and anything noteworthy in Valentine, a flyspeck town nearby. I wrote a long story about a local man who spent six months each year working as a helicopter pilot in Antarctica. "Write that what I miss most is the chile verde at Mando's," he told me.

I found a position as a caretaker on a bygone cattle ranch at the edge of town. The new owners, a couple from Houston, were frequently out of town. It was my job to keep their flowers and fruit trees alive and their paths weeded. I lived in a small adobe building with cold tile floors. Behind my little house was an even littler house, a miniature built by the previous owners for their daughter to play in. It had a miniature broom and a miniature stove. When I watered the pansies around its porch I liked to stick my head in the miniature windows, pretending I was a giant.

About six months after I started working at the *Sentinel* I got a phone call from an old Marfan who wanted me to find an article about him in the newspaper archives. He had been a war hero. He'd misplaced his old clipping, and it was getting yellow besides. He didn't remember the date of the article, but there was a big picture of him on the front page. Could I look for it? This sort of request was common at a newspaper that sometimes felt like a huge community scrapbook, and I had performed the same service many times before. On this day, though, I got sidetracked. In one of the giant archive books, I came across a letter to the editor from the December 20, 1990, edition of the *Sentinel* that contained, after some opening remarks, the following sentences:

> [N]either [Pancho] Villa or his men had any involvement in the disappearance of Ambrose Bierce. Bierce died on the night of January 17, 1914, and was buried in a common grave in Marfa the following morning. In a cemetery then located southwest of the old Blackwell School and across from the Shafter road.

I knew a few things about Bierce—that he had written *The Devil's Dictionary* and *In the Midst of Life,* that he was considered a great misanthrope, that he had disappeared somewhere in northern Mexico, and that his disappearance had never been explained. I read on. The author of the letter was a man named Abelardo Sanchez, from Lancaster, California. He was born in Marfa in 1929 and lived here until he was sixteen, when he joined the Air Force. In 1957 he was driving from California back to Marfa on a Mexican highway when he picked up an old hitchhiker named Agapito Montoya in San Luis, Sonora. When Montoya found out his driver's destination he piped up, "I been there, during the revolution." Sanchez, who had a keen interest in the history of that war, encouraged his passenger's tale.

As Sanchez's letter explained, Montoya had been a soldier in Antonio Rojas's army, which fell to Villa's at the Battle of Ojinaga in January of 1914.

Montoya survived the battle and with four friends began to head south, toward Cuchillo Parado. Along the way they came across an old man who "appeared quite sick from a cold." He was trying to fix a broken wheel on a horse cart.

The old man asked the troops, of which Montoya, at seventeen, was the youngest, if they could help him find Pancho Villa, about whom he intended to write an article. They laughed at him and told him they were trying to get away from Villa. The old man's condition worsened through the night, which the soldiers spent nearby, and in the morning he shifted his aim and asked if they might help him get back across the border and up to Marfa. He offered to pay them twenty pesos apiece. The soldiers agreed.

Sanchez's letter continued:

> During the trip they heard of different books he had written including one that my narrator recalled with the word devil in its title he said his name in Spanish was Ambrocio. My narrator also recalled that years later while visiting in El Paso, he recalled the name of a dairy milk that sounded just like Ambrocio's last name. On the second day after crossing the Rio Grande they were captured by elements of the Third Cavalry which was rounding up stragglers who had crossed the border. Bierce by this time had pneumonia and could hardly speak, my narrator recalls him repeating a doctor's name in Marfa that began with the letter D.

Neither the soldiers, whose English was poor, nor the old man himself, whom sickness had rendered almost mute, could convince the troops that he was an American, and he was loaded into a wagon full of wounded and dying Mexicans. Several days later, while interned in Marfa, Montoya and his friends found out from a cavalryman that the old man had died and was buried in a common grave.

I photocopied the letter. Later that night I reread it. It seemed entirely believable. Why would Sanchez make this story up? The next day I ran down some of the letter's clues. A Price's Dairy had existed in El Paso from 1904 until 1970. In 1908 a doctor named Joseph Calhoun Darracott moved to Marfa from Tyler and opened a practice.

In the next few weeks I learned more about Bierce. There were various theories regarding his end. A writer named Sibley Morrill contended that Bierce had gone into Mexico as a secret agent, dispatched by Washington to spy on the Germans and Japanese, who were plotting a sneak attack with the Mexicans. Joe Nickell argued that the whole Mexico story was meant to give Bierce the privacy he needed to go to the Grand Canyon and shoot himself. The most popular theory had Bierce killed in the Battle of Ojinaga, his body burned with the other dead to curb an outbreak of typhus. What is certain is that he departed Washington, D.C., on October 2, 1913, with northern Mexico as his stated destination. "Don't write," he wrote to a San Francisco acquaintance on September 30. "I am leaving in a day or two for Mexico. If I can get in (and out) I shall go later to South America from some

Western port. Doubtless I'm more likely to get in than out, but all good Gringos go to Heaven when shot." All his final letters had this macabre tone. He was seventy-one years old, and his health was failing. To his niece he wrote: "Good-bye—if you hear of my being stood up against a Mexican stone wall and shot to rags please know that I think that a pretty good way to depart this life. It beats old age, disease, or falling down the cellar stairs. To be a Gringo in Mexico—ah, that is euthanasia."

In 1861, about two months prior to his nineteenth birthday, Bierce had shipped off with the Ninth Indiana Volunteer Infantry Regiment. During the war he was promoted to second lieutenant and shot in the head by a rebel marksman. Without a doubt the fighting had a profound effect on Bierce, forever tilting his humor toward the dark. Forty-eight years later, along the way from Washington to Mexico, he visited all the battle sites of his youth. He toured Orchard Knob and Missionary Ridge, Chickamauga, Snodgrass Hill, Hell's Half-Acre, Franklin, Nashville, and Corinth. At Shiloh he spent a whole day sitting alone in the sun. In New Orleans he let himself be interviewed by a newspaper reporter, who observed, "Perhaps it was in mourning for the dead over whose battlefields he has been wending his way towards New Orleans that Mr. Bierce was dressed in black. From head to toe he was attired in this color." From New Orleans he made his way across Texas. The final letter to his niece, dated November 6 from Laredo but sent November 5 from San Antonio, said, "I shall not be here long enough to hear from you, and don't know where I shall be next. Guess it doesn't matter much. Adios." For most of November and December he was silent. His last letter was posted from Chihuahua City, Mexico, on December 26, 1913. It was addressed to his secretary and outlined his plan to leave for Ojinaga the following day.

The gloom of Bierce's last letters would not have surprised his friends and readers. Death haunted nearly all of his work, from the war-mangled bodies in his Civil War stories to the mysterious demises in his collection of ghost tales, *Can Such Things Be?* He favored the *coup de foudre*. A man is buried alive, then dug up by two medical students, then bludgeoned to death when he sits up panting in his coffin. An inventor is strangled by his automaton chess player. A killer is pardoned, but the man carrying his pardon can't transmit the message as everyone in the capitol has left to watch the hanging. In "An Occurrence at Owl Creek Bridge," the reader is duped into believing a hanging man's fantasy of escape. In "Chickamauga," a little child wanders out to play in the forest. He comes upon a clearing where a plantation is on fire:

> [S]uddenly the entire plantation, with its enclosing forest, seemed to turn as if upon a pivot. His little world swung half around; the points of the compass were reversed. He recognized the blazing building as his own home!

One of Bierce's many nicknames was "The Laughing Devil."

Sanchez's version of Bierce's end seemed so Biercian. It did not swerve from the expected with quite the velocity of a Bierce story, but it did swerve. Bierce had high hopes for a heroic death before a firing squad or in the heat of battle. Was there not a certain devilish poetry in this unglamorous business with the horse cart and the soldiers, in the confusion of identity, in the common grave?

One morning I called Sanchez at his home. He did not demonstrate much familiarity with Bierce, referring to him repeatedly as "Bryce" and to his masterwork as "*The Devil's Advocate.*" He said that before his conversation with Montoya, he "didn't know Ambrose from shinola." Even after that, he had no idea that Bierce's death was an unsolved mystery. What prompted his letter to the *Sentinel* was the 1989 movie *Old Gringo*—starring Gregory Peck as Bierce—based on Carlos Fuentes's novel of the same name. Sanchez told me how his letter was briefly picked up by some local historians and then dropped. "But there is no question in my mind," he said, his voice rising: "Ambrose Bryce, the author of *The Devil's Advocate,* is buried in Marfa."

Archaeologists say the desert is one of the best places to dig for remains. In the arid soil, clothing may remain intact, free of rot and rain, for hundreds of years. The only preferable places for grave digging are the Arctic Circle and Mt. Everest, where even bits of flesh stand a chance against decay.

Sanchez's letter stated that Bierce's grave was southwest of the old Blackwell School and across from the Shafter road, which runs down to Ojinaga. But how far southwest of the school? Past the trailer park? Before Jerry Agan's house? *Under* Jerry Agan's house? And what did "across from the road" mean? A horse pasture that ran along the west side of the old Shafter road looked promising, but my late-night investigation there yielded nothing. Across the road from the horse pasture is a Mexican restaurant without a public rest room called La Carreta, which means The Cart. Was this a clue?

A friend of mine named Michael Roch said that he had heard I was looking for a graveyard near the Shafter road.

"Oliver Cataño took me down there once on horseback," he said, "and I remember my horse stepping over a grave. There wasn't much there. I don't know if I could find it again, but I could try."

We drove down along Alamito Creek and parked the car. Alamito is a dry creek that runs beside the Shafter road. If there has been rain in the Davis Mountains, it gushes a brown torrent for a day or two, but that is a rare occurrence. A few months before, a man had inadvertently drowned his horse in the creek. He had gotten into the habit of staking the animal at various spots along the creek bed where there was something to graze. During that same rain, I saw a telephone pole go flying past on the current, pursued by a live goat.

Michael and I walked down the dry bed. I had thought about carrying my gardener's trowel but decided instead on a wooden stake and some orange surveyor's tape. The desert soil is corky and dense; a trowel will barely scratch your initials. If we found anything, we would need to return with picks and spades and a bar. Michael stopped and scanned the horizon. "It was somewhere down this way," he said, climbing up the east bank of the creek.

We walked through a field of abandoned cars and other weathered artifacts. The junk thinned as we walked. We ducked through a barbed-wire fence and into a large dusty field, then through another fence and into another field. Two horses wandered around listlessly. It was quiet and hot. Discarded bottles had filled up with dust. Michael looked disoriented. "I think this is the spot," he said. We scanned the field before us. It was wide and empty. Michael said, "I guess it could be another field, but this field feels right." We walked up and down, running our eyes over each contour of the ground, each nub of desert grass and greasewood bush. I looked underneath a mesquite tree. Michael snapped a bean pod off a *largonsilla* bush. We looked at each other. "It's strange," he said. "I really thought it was over here."

None of the other Marfans I talked to seemed to know exactly where the old cemetery southwest of Blackwell School was located either. Some of them seemed to think it had been moved.

Talk of graveyards led to talk of devilry. A friend of mine named Frank Quintanar told me about the time, thirty years ago, that a stranger showed up at a Marfa dance. This stranger was handsome and well dressed, and he quickly found a girl to take his arm. Laughing and shrieking, they spun around the floor. As the dance wound down, a boy in the crowd noticed that the stranger had the feet of a rooster. The boy screamed and pointed. The stranger vanished in a puff of smoke. It was the devil.

"And that is why Marfa will never be prosperous," Frank said. We were at the bar.

In another of Frank's stories the devil appeared as a little red demon with horns. He stood outside the kitchen window of one of Frank's friends, steaming. Then he drifted off. Neither of these little episodes seemed very devilish to me, but I was missing the point. This devil was not interested in death and mayhem. He liked to play games with people. He once appeared to a group of Presidio children as a burro with no tail. The children ran to tell their parents. When they returned the burro had vanished. Another time, a woman saw a dancing rabbit with no front legs. She reached for the rabbit, the rabbit disappeared, and she grabbed a cactus. The cactus gave her a minor infection.

It all made a kind of hell-born sense—the Laughing Devil bungling his end, the actual devil laughing. Was not the devil's mountaintop cave said to overlook the very spot where, according to Sanchez, Montoya and his friends found the old gringo fumbling with his broken cart? Would not the devil's trail lead me to Bierce?

To find the devil I went to see Saul Muñoz, a man old enough to know him. Don Saul lived down on the border, in a blink-and-you-miss-it town called Redford. Many people say that Highway 90, which runs east-west through Marfa, is the real border, and that everything south of it might as well be Mexico. Redford would not dissuade you from this notion. I found the small crumbling house perched on a crumbling hill.

Don Saul was born just across the river in El Mulato. Most of his life he was a shepherd. On the mammoth ranches to the north and east, he would spend up to eight months at a time wandering with a herd of sheep. He worked alone, slept in caves, and now and again he would slaughter one of his own flock to feed himself. In later years he was a ranch cook. Around the time I went to see him, he was spending much of his time at home, watching a black-and-white television with a broken contrast knob and smoking pack after pack of Fiesta cigarettes.

He was happy to have the visit, and we sat in his dark, cool kitchen, drinking water from chipped coffee mugs, talking softly in Spanish. Then I brought up the devil.

"What?" he said, surprised.

I repeated my question. Had he ever seen the devil?

"There is no death and no devil," he told me, speaking slowly so I could understand. "We make death and we are the devil."

He started talking about water—how important it is, how to find it, what to do when there isn't any. He rattled off a series of maxims about hydration: "Water brings work." "No water means no life." "When it rains on a man's land, he's got everything."

Why had he been so quick to change the subject? He cursed the drought awhile longer and lamented the slipping away of the old ranch life. What did any of this have to do with my question?

"I was once a cook for thirty men," he sighed. "Those days are over." As he spoke, a polite young man stuck his head in the room. He was tall, with a friendly smile. Don Saul got up to pour him a mug of water. The young man nodded his thanks and sat on the bed in the corner. Don Saul fished another Fiesta from his crumpled pack and sat back down.

"What about animals?" I asked him. There were many folktales in which the devil took the form of an innocent creature. Perhaps I could help him to remember. "Have you ever seen an animal that seemed strange in one way or another?"

He thought about this for a while, burning down his cigarette with long, slow intakes of smoke.

"Owls have their own language," he said, as if he had finally found something that would interest me.

The young man nodded.

I knew that it was common for witches to take the form of owls in local folktales. I asked if he had ever seen one.

"A witch?" he said.

"Yes," I said, glancing sidelong at the young man. Why was he smiling at me?

Don Saul gave me a disappointed look, then launched into a long argument about how every supposedly extraordinary phenomenon has an ordinary explanation. I could understand only about half of what he said, since in his eagerness to make me see his point he had begun to speak more quickly, his hands gesturing wildly. The last thing he said was, "An owl is just a bird." A silence fell over the room, and we listened to his dry tobacco crackle. I sat back in my chair. The young man was still smiling at me. What did he know?

"A friend of mine did see a witch one time," Don Saul said after a while, exhaling a large cloud of smoke. "She was flying around in front of his campfire."

"A real witch?" I asked, sitting up.

"Of course not," he said. "It was his hair hanging in front of his eye. We are the witch. We trick ourselves."

Don Saul walked me outside into the scorching midafternoon sun. I thanked him for his time and asked if we might take a photograph. The young man took my camera, lined us up against the remains of an adobe wall, and silently shot two pictures of us squinting into the sun.

I began to look for area historians who might be of some help. It seemed unlikely that I would have been the first to investigate Sanchez's letter. I needed the guidance of a trained professional.

After two annoying conversations ("Don't chase fireflies," one man told me), I found my way to Glenn Willeford, a professor at the Center for Big Bend Studies at Sul Ross State University in Alpine. He referred to himself as a "Bierce-chaser." I made an appointment to see him the next day.

Alpine is twenty-six miles from Marfa. Most towns in Far West Texas are about thirty miles apart, since they were water stops on the railroad before they were towns. Alpine has a population of around 5,800, a two-screen movie theater, a lumber store ("We Put The Pine Back In Alpine"), an Amtrak station, and a state university. The university's mascot is the *lobo*, or wolf, but a cast-iron longhorn with a gigantic rack stood at the campus gate, calling to mind a passage I had just read from Colonel Richard Irving Dodge's account of life in nineteenth-century Texas:

> Every bush had its thorn; every animal, reptile, or insect had its horn tooth or string; every male human his revolver; and each was ready to use his weapon of defense on any unfortunate sojourner, on the smallest, or even without the smallest, provocation.

I parked in the visitor lot. A teenager was picking cigarette butts out of the university's flower beds with a spearlike implement. I tried not to provoke him.

Willeford's office was in the basement of a brick building, in a corner of a large storeroom full of archaeological artifacts and office supplies and boxes of brand-new novels from a Westerns series with titles like *Pony Express, Carry My Message,* and *Across the Crevasse.* His desk was wedged between two crates. "No one bothers me down here," he told me. Willeford was first drawn to Bierce by the Civil War stories. "I think his experiences in that war embittered him," he said. "But they made him think about the hereafter, and what men are like, and God. Vietnam did the same thing to me." Willeford had just finished writing a short paper on the Bierce mystery, and one of his central projects had been to refute the Sanchez letter. He handed me a copy. Mortified, I accepted it. Three things became clear in rapid succession: 1) Sanchez's letter was full of holes, some of them serious, some minor; 2) It was unlikely that Ambrose Bierce's bones would ever be found; and 3) I would make a terrible historian. The historian must develop an immunity to the poetry of coincidence. But has he no use for intuition?

I put this question to Willeford, but he dismissed it and proceeded to annotate the errors in my copy of the Sanchez letter: "One week after the battle? Pneumonia kills a lot faster than that." "This was $10 U.S. at the time. Not much inducement." "Unlikely." "Contradictory." "Impossible!"

"I don't think he'll ever be found," he said at last, "but I'm not going to quit looking. You don't know anything until you look."

By the time I left Alpine, night had fallen. Where the road comes down out of Paisano Pass, I pulled over. This is where tourists come from all over the country to watch the sky over Mitchell Flat for the so-called Marfa Mystery Lights. The lights streak across the horizon; they hover in the air; they have, on occasion, approached certain viewers like friendly ghosts ("The Lights of God," Capt. Manuel Pedro Vasco called them in 1617). Science has never explained the lights, and many people who have lived in the vicinity their whole lives have never seen them. I sat on the hood of my car. Some tourists had parked an RV nearby and set up for their all-night vigil. "Do you see anything?" I heard one ask another. I knew that the odds were against them getting any more out of the experience than videotape of the headlights on the Shafter road. Yet every week more tourists came, fooled themselves, slept in their cars with binoculars, bought T-shirts.

The prairie before us was empty and black. Willeford could annotate till dawn; I still believed Sanchez.

It was noon when I arrived in Mexico, and after a quick lunch and some sketchy directions from the woman who had sold me the lunch, I got in my car and drove toward the mountain on which, legend told me, I would find the devil in a cave. I turned right at the decrepit Hotel Ojinaga and rumbled along a terrible road, past the military *campamento* and the *tortillería* and over the railroad tracks. The outskirts of town were a mess of sad old adobe houses, satellite dishes, chickens, and faded political slogans painted on cinderblock walls, with shards of broken glass in place of barbed wire. At the end of the road I could turn either right or left. My lunch lady's directions did not include this fork. The mountain was straight ahead, a small white cross shining from its summit in the fierce sun. I stopped in at a small market called Abarrotes "Nellie."

The butcher in the back of the store was mindlessly working some sort of awful-looking meat product in a huge tub. His arms were bloody up to the elbows. I couldn't take my eyes off him as the woman behind the counter (Nellie?) gave me directions. From the look on the butcher's face, you would have thought he was icing cakes. When a girl walked into the store he raised one gore-encased arm and waved.

Following Nellie's directions, I took the right turn and drove along a road far too wide to be a real road, kicking up a cloud of dust that had completely obscured the store by the time I was a hundred feet beyond it. Past the last house, the road turned left and crossed half-buried train tracks. A small cemetery, overgrown with mesquite trees, marked the beginning of the way to the mountain.

The road began to fork continuously. What looked like flags marking the route to the mountain turned out to be white plastic bags blown into the thorny *ocotillos* along the road, and although their distribution was by no means uniform, one seemed to appear before me each time I thought I'd picked the wrong fork, as if some unseen hand had called together wind, trash, and flora to lead me straight to hell.

I parked at the base of the mountain. The parched prairie spread around me. A breeze blew, but it blew hot and dusty. I started up the trail, which split into two trails, which split into four trails, and although each trail led to the same place, the one I chose always seemed to take the most difficult ascent. I clambered up a steep devil's slide, kicking loose rocks that crashed violently down the mountain to settle in the talus below. I grabbed a root and pulled myself over a small cliff on my stomach. All I could hear was my breath and the wind. I had come alone because I thought these terms would suit my host, but in the emptiness and silence I began to fear that they would suit him too well. When I reached the summit, I sat at the base of the twenty-foot cross and caught my breath. This was a serious cross, designed to protect a lot of people from something very bad. Pieces of cinderblock kept the votive candles around it from falling down the mountain.

The wind picked up. Chinati Peak looked across from the other side of the valley. They say the devil used to string a tightrope between these two summits and prance back and forth, tormenting the villagers below. I gazed down from his perspective. There was the gully where the gringo writer's cart broke; there, the clearing where he found the soldiers, the thicket where they slept; across the river, the hillside where they were captured by the cavalry and loaded into the wagons.

It was all very devilish, but where was the devil? I searched the summit for his cave. The spines on a cactus pointed me in opposite directions.

From the dust, an old Fanta bottle cap stared up at me like a dead eye. I did not find the cave.

I got back to Ojinaga just as the stores reopened after siesta and went looking for Bryant Eduardo Holman. Holman was an old mud logger—an oilfield hand—who had moved to Presidio from Roswell, New Mexico, years before, married a Mexican orthodontist, and opened up a native crafts store in Ojinaga called Fausto's. He always kept a close eye on local politics, and I was in the habit of stopping in on him to hear the newest plot he had uncovered; on occasion they held enough water to warrant an article.

"You want to find the cave?" he said. "Sure, no problem."

We took his car, a brown Isuzu Trooper. He drove as fast as he talked, spinning another outlandish tale about municipal corruption and swaggering drug kingpins, and in what seemed like an impossibly short time we were back at the base of the mountain.

"It's just up here," Holman said, waddling up the path.

I had been all wrong to head for the summit. Only a quarter of the way up the mountain, Holman veered off the left side of the path, climbed down a rock to a sandy ledge and announced, "*This* is the *cueva del diablo*," in a spooky voice. He then jumped down inside the cave and launched into a confusing account of the devil legend, which involved Cabeza de Vaca, Pancho Villa, the Aztec god Smoking Mirror, and John Reed, "the father of American journalism." He hopped while speaking.

"To really understand what's going on here," he said, rubbing his hands, "you need to know about the four unlucky days and the powerful syncretism that De Vaca brought to this region. But even then, this is really ancient stuff. It goes back to the Uto-Aztecans and their tales about spiders in caves. Before that even."

The cave was L-shaped, opening out to the valley and up to the sky. It was about ten feet deep and ten feet tall. *Hello? Devil?* Here was the mountain; here was the cave. Where was he? I had come for the devil and found a folk-art dealer. When I turned back to him, Holman was explaining his decision to become a pagan. *Should I check his pant cuffs for chicken feet?*

Down at the Trooper a police truck had pulled up. The road was a dead end, miles and miles from town, but the two fat cops in the cab were not interested in us. They were looking for a stolen Mustang with doors that were a different color from the body.

Several days later I was sitting at home reading a story of Bierce's entitled "The Stranger." In the story, the ghost of an old prospector visits the campfire of a group of "gentleman adventurers." This is in the Arizona desert. The men do not know he is a host straightaway. His behavior is strange but they take him for a "harmless lunatic," driven crazy by the solitude of the desert. The narrator observes,

We were not so new to the country as not to know that the solitary life of many a plainsman had a tendency to develop eccentricities of conduct and character not always easily distinguishable from mental aberration. A man is like a tree: in a forest of his fellows he will grow as straight as his generic and individual nature permits; alone in the open, he yields to the deforming stresses and tortions that environ him.

Is this what had happened to me? Once I left Marfa would I care where Bierce was buried? Outside my window a work crew from the local nursery was toiling away, installing an automatic irrigation system for my landlords that would fulfill all my watering duties with the flip of a switch and the punch of a code. The sound of their work punctuated Bierce's sentences with clangs and grunts. As I read, I let them supply each grammatical mark—a clang for a comma, a grunt for a period.

Suddenly a cry went up from one of the crew: "Hey! Get over here! Tony hit something!"

I peered through the blinds. The crew gathered around Tony as he pointed at the ground and gestured with his bar. A younger man with a shovel began to dig; the rest stood around with their hands on their hips waiting to see what he would uncover. In no time the young man was standing in a hole that obscured the bottom half of his legs. He dropped out of sight completely, and from the instructions I saw the others giving I understood that he was on his hands and knees, sweeping dirt off something down there. In time he stood up and stepped out of the hole. The whole crew then stood, it seemed, in silence and beheld what he had uncovered. One man crossed himself. Another said something that made the whole group laugh.

It was evening before they left. I had spent the afternoon pacing my room. When the work trucks had finally bounced off the property, gravel crunching beneath their heavy tires, and rolled smoothly onto the blacktop toward town, and when the music from their radios had faded into the night, I stood outside on the open plain.

The wind blew. Along the northern horizon, at intervals, great flashes of silent heat lightning surprised the sky. Swirling over the path, the dried leaves rasped out a greeting. One window of the miniature house had been left open, and the white curtains behind it fluttered softly, hung still, and fluttered once more, like a lady being seated at the theater.

I crossed the yard to the area where the hole had been dug. The practical foreman, blind to the potential historical import of the discovery, had directed his crew to cover it back up. But I had no trouble finding the spot where the digging had been done. In the center of the dirt yard, by a tree stump, a multitude of boot tracks pointed inward, as if the men had stood there for a moment before turning away.

I fell to my knees and began to dig. The dirt had been shoveled already, and once I had broken it up with the trowel it came away easily in my hands. The dirt pile grew at my side. The moonlight brightened. Finally, my fingertips met with that which would not give—a wide, flat stone. I scooped out the dirt to find its edges. It was a large rectangle, made roughly from cement, three feet wide and six feet long. I swept the surface clean with my hands and, bending low, blew down on it, my cheeks filling and emptying with air, the dirt particles flying up off the stone and into my face and hair. I staggered to my feet and stood on the stone. The wind died. The plain was quiet. The stone was blank.

In Far West Texas, on the side of the highway that runs south from Marfa to Presidio and across the Rio Grande into Ojinaga, Mexico, there is a small green sign that reads, PROFILE OF LINCOLN. Under these words an arrow points west at the jagged foothills of the Chinati Mountains, where you can make out the sixteenth president's profile in the ridges of rock. It is not so easy to see—the vast sameness of the landscape's color confuses the eye—and many travelers who stop fail to find the accidental monument. Sometimes I pass them on my way up and down the Shafter road. Their cars are parked along the shoulder, fifty feet past the sign, in positions that testify to the abruptness of the stop; cameras hang idly by their sides; they stare for a while, squinting, furrowing their brows, their lips curling into profoundly baffled grins.

Questions for Discussion

1. How much of this story is based on fact? How much on speculation? How does the author's tone reflect the tension between these two things?

2. How does this author incorporate historical documentation into the essay?

3. This story is, in many ways, a quest. Does the writer find what he is seeking?

Evan S. Connell
Son of the Morning Star

Evan S. Connell is a multifaceted writer of both fiction and nonfiction. His subjects range from the Midwest world of Mrs. Bridge *to the sixteenth-century European world of* The Alchemist's Journal. *Born in 1924 in Kansas City, Missouri, Connell received his bachelor of arts degree from the University of Kansas in 1947 and went on to graduate study at Stanford University. His literary awards include a National Book Critics Circle nomination for general nonfiction (1984) and a* Los Angeles Times

Book Award (1985), both for Son of the Morning Star: Custer and the Little Bighorn, *and a Lannan Foundation Lifetime Achievement Award in 2000.*

Son of the Morning Star: Custer and the Little Bighorn *is Connell's account of the Battle of Little Bighorn, where Sitting Bull and his Sioux warriors overwhelmed General Custer's troops. Note Connell's extraordinary attention to detail.*

All three bluecoat armies—Crook, Terry, Gibbon—were under surveillance by Sioux and Cheyennes. The Terry-Custer column might have been watched from the day it left Fort Lincoln, and there is no doubt that hostile scouts observed the *Far West* at the mouth of Rosebud Creek several days before the battle. They also reported soldiers traveling up the Rosebud; and on the morning of June 25, two or three hours before Custer crossed the fatal divide, it is almost certain they knew exactly where he was and the size of his regiment. The only thing that surprised them was the speed of his advance.

Not many Indians were alarmed. Just a few days earlier they had fought Three Stars Crook, and although they had defeated him there was a chance he might return. Yet they could not imagine that Crook, or any white general, would attack such a large camp. It is said that about noon of the twenty-fourth a Sans Arc herald went around crying: "Soldiers will be here tomorrow!" Nobody paid much attention.

A Cheyenne prophet named Box Elder saw the advancing regiment in a dream and when he awoke he tried to warn everybody, but other Cheyennes mocked him by howling—implying that he had gone mad and should be fed to the wolves.

A Miniconjou named Standing Bear went for a swim on the morning of the fight. When he got back to his lodge one of his uncles advised him to collect the horses right away because something might happen.

An Oglala named Joseph White Cow Bull slept late. When he got up he asked an old woman for breakfast and while he was eating she told him there would be a battle. "How do you know, grandmother?" he asked. She refused to talk about it. Not long after this he was visiting friends at the Cheyenne camp when they heard shots and saw dust in the air and an Oglala rode by calling out that soldiers had attacked the Unkpapa circle. Joseph and three Cheyenne friends were getting ready to join the Unkpapas when they saw Custer's battalion on the ridge, so instead of riding south they went east toward the river. An old warrior named Mad Wolf tried to stop them, saying there were too many bluecoats, but a Cheyenne—Bobtail Horse—replied: "Uncle, only the earth and the heavens last long." Joseph and his friends then continued east, all four singing their death songs.

Soldiers—pink and hairy—came riding down a coulee. Joseph noticed one in a big hat and a buckskin jacket who rode a blaze-faced sorrel with white stockings. Beside him rode a soldier with a flag. This man in buckskin looked across the river and shouted, which caused the bluecoats to charge. Joseph and the Cheyennes slid off their ponies and began to shoot. Bobtail Horse hit a soldier who fell out of the saddle into the water. Joseph hit the one in buckskin. He, too, fell out of the saddle and when this happened many soldiers reined up, gathering around him. After that it was difficult to see anything because other Indians were arriving and the air filled with smoke.

This story of four braves challenging Custer's battalion has been told various ways. They might have been searching the valley for injured warriors when Custer appeared on the ridge, so they splashed across a ford and rode some distance up Medicine Tail coulee before starting to fight.

Just what occurred is now forgotten, but almost certainly three or four young Indians did confront five picked companies of the elite Seventh—an act of suicidal defiance which may have affected Custer's battle plan. Not that they could intimidate him, but he had no way of knowing how many other hostiles lay in wait. Those four might have looked like decoys, so he withdrew.

How surprised the Indians were by almost simultaneous assaults on opposite ends of the village is impossible to say. Ten or fifteen thousand people had camped beside the river and there is no reason to suppose they would all agree. Most of them were startled and disconcerted. Others probably had been wondering if Crook would try again. Some must have realized it was not Crook's army. Some had heard about Custer and might have guessed this was his regiment.

Tribal leaders had talked about what to do if the camp was threatened. Their decision seems to have been that they would wait to see how the soldiers behaved.

Scouts watched the regiment cross the divide and later observed it separate into battalions. Gall himself watched Custer's five companies ride along the bluffs east of the river. He said they kicked up a lot of dust. They rode out of sight but soon reappeared. He said they were mounted on white horses, which must be an incorrect translation of his words, or else he was referring to Lt. Smith's gray horse company, or to the fact that among the grays and browns were a few white horses belonging to musicians who dismounted at the Powder River depot. Gall thought these soldiers looked nice, riding as if they were on parade. He and his Unkpapas continued to watch them, meanwhile rounding up the pony herd in case the bluecoats meant to cause trouble. He had no idea who was leading these men, or if they intended to start a fight.

In 1919 a Miniconjou, Feather Earring, said to General H. L. Scott: "If Custer had come up and talked with us, we had all agreed we would have surrendered and gone in with him." During subsequent conversations

Feather Earring emphasized that if Custer had approached diplomatically the Indians would have gone back to the reservation. This was confirmed years later by other Indians. General Scott observed that such a method of dealing with the hostiles had not occurred to anybody.

The entire expedition might have been unnecessary. A Sioux chief whose name has been awkwardly translated as Pretty Voice Eagle spoke with Custer just before the army left Fort Lincoln. Whether this chief also spoke with General Terry is not clear, but he was very clear about the fact that he led a delegation of his people to Custer in an attempt to avoid a battle. He asked Custer to promise that he would not fight the Sioux. Custer promised.

> . . . and we asked him to raise his hand to God that he would not fight the Sioux, and he raised his hand. After he raised his hand to God that he would not fight the Sioux he asked me to go west with my delegation to see these roaming Sioux, and tell them to come back to the reservation, that he would give them food, horses, and clothing. After we got through talking, he soon left the agency, and we soon heard that he was fighting the Indians and that he and all his men were killed. If Custer had given us time we would have gone out ahead of him, but he did not give us time. If we had gone out ahead of Custer he would not have lost himself nor would his men have been killed. I did all I could to persuade the Ree scouts not to go. . . .

Capt. Bourke once remarked that some people learn quickly, others learn slowly, "preachers, school-teachers, and military people most slowly of all."

Many Indians at the Little Bighorn were so convinced of trouble that tribal leaders posted guards east of the river to prevent ambitious young men from riding out to locate the troops and drench themselves in glory by being the first to count coup. About sundown on the evening before the fight these guards made themselves visible on the ridge. Despite this warning, several braves sneaked across the river and got up into the hills. The next day they were riding around looking for soldiers when they heard the shots fired by Reno's troops in the valley.

Crazy Horse did not behave as usual. Ordinarily he was composed, even when battle was imminent, but it is said that this morning he rode back and forth, hurried into his lodge, and quickly reappeared with his medicine bag. After moistening one hand he dipped it in maroon pigment and printed a hand on each side of his pony's hips. On both sides of the neck he drew an arrow and a bloody scalp. All of which suggests intuitive knowledge of things to come, or else he had been talking with Oglala scouts who told him what to expect. Most Indians, however, seem to have felt secure in the belief that only a great fool would attack.

Low Dog thought it must be a false alarm when he heard about soldiers charging the Unkpapa circle.

Iron Thunder could not believe the truth until a few bullets whizzed by.

Chief Red Horse and several women felt so unconcerned that they were away from the village digging tipsina—wild turnip—a knobby root filled with starch, when they noticed a dust cloud and saw Reno's troops.

A female cousin of Sitting Bull, Pte-San-Waste-Win, usually translated as Mrs. Spotted Horn Bull, said that by the time the turnip diggers got back to the village everybody could see the flash of sabers, which is a puzzling remark. Not one cavalryman, with the possible exception of DeRudio, carried a saber. What she saw might have been sunlight glinting on gun barrels.

Rain in the Face had been invited to a feast. The guests were eating when they heard bluecoat guns, which did not sound like their own. Rain habitually carried a stone-headed war club, even to parties, but he rushed back to his lodge for a gun, his bow, and a quiver of arrows. Then he hopped on his pony and was about to ride south when he and his friends saw troops on the eastern ridge. While riding against these troops they discovered a young woman—Tashenamini, Moving Robe—riding with them. Her brother had been killed during the fight with Crook and now she was holding her brother's war staff above her head. Rain declared that she looked as pretty as a bird. "Behold, there is among us a young woman!" he called out, because this would make everybody brave. "Let no young man hide behind her garment!"

Custer's soldiers were almost surrounded by the time Rain got there. They had dismounted, he said, but climbed back on their horses, dismounted again, and split into several companies. They were shooting very fast. After a while some of them began riding toward Reno's troops, but Indians followed them like blackbirds following a hawk.

The Cheyenne chief Two Moon told Hamlin Garland in 1898 that he was trying to reassure a bunch of frightened women when Custer's men arrived, cloaked with dust: "While I was sitting on my horse I saw flags coming up over the hill to the east. . . ."

When it was all over Two Moon and four Sioux chiefs rode through the valley and across the hillside counting dead bluecoats. He explained through an interpreter, Wolf Voice, that one Indian carried a little bundle of sticks: "When we came to dead men, we took a little stick and gave it to another man, so we counted the dead. There were three hundred and eighty-eight." However, Two Moon told a different story sixteen years later. This time he said they went to the river to cut willow sticks. An Indian was assigned to throw down a stick beside each dead soldier, then the sticks were picked up and counted: "It was about six times we had to cut willow sticks, because we kept finding men all along the ridge. We counted four hundred and eighty-eight. . . ."

Either way the number has been inflated, but how to explain this seems impossible. As Robert Utley points out, meanings are difficult to convey from one language to another. "Testimony delivered from an aboriginal frame of reference risked serious distortion in the process."

Three hundred and eighty-eight. Four hundred and eighty-eight. What did Two Moon actually say? What did he mean?

In a communiqué from the north bank of the Yellowstone, dated July 9, 1876, General Terry wrote that two hundred sixty-eight officers, men, and civilians were killed, fifty-two wounded—which may or may not be accurate. Company rosters were kept by first sergeants and five of these sergeants—Edwin Bobo, James Butler, Frederick Hohmeyer, Michael Kenney, Frank Varden—died with Custer. When the bodies of these men were stripped the company rosters disappeared.

In 1927 a Northern Cheyenne woman, Kate Bighead, told Dr. Thomas Marquis about the battle. She spoke in sign language, which Marquis had learned while working as a government doctor on the Cheyenne reservation. He transcribed the story she delivered with her hands.

When she was young, she related, she lived with the southern branch of the tribe in Oklahoma. Early one morning during the winter of 1868, after a big storm, soldiers led by General Custer attacked Black Kettle's village on the Washita. She ran barefoot across the snow to escape being killed. Next spring, while the Cheyennes were camped on a branch of the Red River, General Custer returned. He smoked a peace pipe and said he would not fight anymore. The chiefs told him that if he broke this promise he surely would be killed, and they gave him the name Hi-es-tzie, which means Long Hair.

She saw him often, she told Dr. Marquis. One time the general came very close while she was mounting her pony and she looked at him. He had deep eyes and wavy red hair. He wore a buckskin suit with a big white hat. She was then twenty-two years old and she thought he was handsome. She admired him. All the Cheyenne women thought he was handsome.

She had a cousin, Me-o-tzi, who sometimes went riding with General Custer. The Cheyennes were pleased that Me-o-tzi was important to him. Later, after he went away, quite a few young Cheyennes wanted to marry her but Me-o-tzi said General Custer was her husband. She told them he had promised to come back for her. She waited seven years. During those years Kate Bighead joined the northern branch of the tribe so she did not know what happened when Me-o-tzi learned of Custer's death, but she was told that the girl gashed her legs and chopped off her hair.

Joseph White Cow Bull also gave an account of Me-o-tzi, which differed from the story told by Kate Bighead. According to Joseph, Me-o-tzi was at the Little Bighorn with her seven-year-old son—called Yellow Hair or Yellow Bird because of light streaks in his hair. Joseph said he knew her. In fact, he said, he was courting her.

This legend of Custer's child by a Cheyenne woman turns up again and again, like a will-o'-the-wisp at dusk, as though the Indians did not want their enemy absolutely eliminated, and it cannot be proved or disproved. Nor is it possible after such a long time to establish the presence or absence of Me-o-tzi at the Little Bighorn. This comely girl whose silken tresses, the general said, rivaled in color the blackness of a raven—was she in Oklahoma or with northern relatives in Montana? Kate Bighead told Dr. Marquis that about a year after the battle Me-o-tzi married a white man named Isaac. They had several children and Me-o-tzi died in Oklahoma in January of 1921, but among the Cheyennes her name lived on. One of Kate's granddaughters was called Me-o-tzi, and friends liked to tease this girl by saying she was Custer's Indian wife.

Questions for Discussion

1. Does this narrative read like history or like a novel? How does it keep the reader moving forward through the story?
2. Note some of the detail Connell uses to create his characters. How much of this is historically accurate? How much is imagined?
3. Describe Connell's tone in this piece. How does he present historical fact?

Barbara Tuchman
In Search of History

American popular historian Barbara Wertheim Tuchman was born in New York City in 1912. She received her bachelor of arts degree from Radcliff College in 1933, followed by years as a foreign correspondent for various publications. Tuchman's distinguished writing career spanned fifty years, during which she was the recipient of many prestigious literary awards, including two Pulitzer Prizes for The Guns of August *in 1963 and* Stilwell and the American Experience in China *in 1972. Her imaginative and entertaining prose brought history alive to the reader. She died after suffering a stroke in 1989.*

One learns to write, I have since discovered, in the practice thereof. After seven years' apprenticeship in journalism I discovered that an essential element for good writing is a good ear. One must *listen* to the sound of one's own prose. This, I think, is one of the failings of much American writing. Too many writers do not listen to the sound of their own words. For example, listen to this sentence from the organ of my own discipline, the *American Historical Review:* "His presentation is not vitiated historically by efforts at expository simplicity." In one short sentence five long Latin words of four or five syllables each. One has to read it three times over and take time out to think, before one can even make out what it means.

In my opinion, short words are always preferable to long ones; the fewer syllables the better, and monosyllables, beautiful and pure like "bread" and "sun" and "grass," are the best of all. Emerson, using almost entirely one-syllable words, wrote what I believe are among the finest lines in English:

> By the rude bridge that arched the flood,
> Their flag to April's breeze unfurled,
>   Here once the embattled farmers stood
> And fired the shot heard round the world.

Out of twenty-eight words, twenty-four are monosyllables. It is English at its purest, though hardly characteristic of its author.

Or take this:

> On desperate seas long wont to roam,
>   Thy hyacinth hair, thy classic face,
> Thy Naiad airs have brought me home
>   To the glory that was Greece
>   And the grandeur that was Rome.

Imagine how it must feel to have composed those lines! Though coming from a writer satisfied with the easy rhythms of "The Raven" and "Annabel Lee," they represent, I fear, a fluke. To quote poetry, you will say, is not a fair comparison. True, but what a lesson those stanzas are in the sound of words! What superb use of that magnificent instrument that lies at the command of all of us—the English language. Quite by chance both practitioners in these samples happen to be Americans, and both, curiously enough, writing about history.

To write history so as to enthrall the reader and make the subject as captivating and exciting to him as it is to me has been my goal since that initial failure with my thesis. A prerequisite, as I have said, is to be enthralled one's self and to feel a compulsion to communicate the magic. Communicate to whom? We arrive now at the reader, a person whom I keep constantly in mind. Catherine Drinker Bowen has said that she writes her books with a sign pinned up over her desk asking, "Will the reader turn the page?"

The writer of history, I believe, has a number of duties *vis-à-vis* the reader, if he wants to keep him reading. The first is to distill. He must do the preliminary work for the reader, assemble the information, make sense of it, select the essential, discard the irrelevant—above all, discard the irrelevant—and put the rest together so that it forms a developing dramatic narrative. Narrative, it has been said, is the lifeblood of history. To offer a mass of undigested facts, of names not identified and places not located, is of no use to the reader and is simple laziness on the part of the author, or pedantry to show how much he has read. To discard the unnecessary requires courage and also extra work, as exemplified by Pascal's effort to explain an idea to a friend in a letter which rambled on for pages and ended, "I am sorry to have wearied you with so long a letter but I did not have time to write you a short one." The historian is continually being beguiled down fascinating byways and sidetracks. But the art of writing—the test of the artist—is to resist the beguilement and cleave to the subject.

Should the historian be an artist? Certainly a conscious art should be part of his equipment. Macaulay describes him as half poet, half philosopher. I do not aspire to either of these heights. I think of myself as a storyteller, a narrator, who deals in true stories, not fiction. The distinction is not one of relative values; it is simply that history interests me more than fiction. I agree with Leopold von Ranke, the great nineteenth-century German historian, who said that when he compared the portrait of Louis XI in Scott's *Quentin Durward* with the portrait of the same king in the memoirs of Philippe de Comines, Louis' minister, he found "the truth more interesting and beautiful than the romance."

It was Ranke, too, who set the historian's task: to find out *wie es eigentlich gewesen ist,* what really happened, or, literally, how it really was. His goal is one that will remain forever just beyond our grasp for reasons I explained in a "Note on Sources" in *The Guns of August* (a paragraph that no one ever reads but *I* think is the best thing in the book). Summarized, the reasons are that we who write about the past were not there. We can never be certain that we have recaptured it as it really was. But the least we can do is to stay within the evidence.

I do not invent anything, even the weather. One of my readers told me he particularly liked a passage in *The Guns* which tells how the British Army landed in France and how on that afternoon there was a sound of summer thunder in the air and the sun went down in a blood-red glow. He thought it an artistic touch of doom, but the fact is it was true. I found it in the memoirs of a British officer who landed on that day and heard the thunder and saw the blood-red sunset. The art, if any, consisted only in selecting it and ultimately using it in the right place.

Selection is what determines the ultimate product, and that is why I use material from primary sources only. My feeling about secondary sources is that they are helpful but pernicious. I use them as guides at the start of a project to find out the general scheme of what happened, but I do not take notes from them because I do not want to end up simply rewriting someone else's book. Furthermore, the facts in a secondary source have already been pre-selected, so that in using them one misses the opportunity of selecting one's own.

I plunge as soon as I can into the primary sources: the memoirs and the letters, the generals' own accounts of their campaigns, however tendentious, not to say mendacious, they may be. Even an untrustworthy source is valuable for what it reveals about the personality of the author, especially if he is an actor in the events, as in the case of Sir John French, for example. Bias in a primary source is to be expected. One allows for it and corrects it by reading another version. I try always to read two or more for every episode. Even if an event is not controversial, it will have been seen and remembered from different angles of view by different observers. If the event *is* in dispute, one has extra obligation to examine both sides. As the lion in Aesop said to the Man, "There are many statues of men slaying lions, but if only the lions were sculptors there might be quite a different set of statues."

The most primary source of all is unpublished material: private letters and diaries or the reports, orders, and messages in government archives. There is an immediacy and intimacy about them that reveals character and makes circumstances come alive. I remember Secretary of State Robert Lansing's desk diary, which I used when I was working on *The Zimmermann Telegram*. The man himself seemed to step right out from his tiny neat handwriting and his precise notations of every visitor and each subject discussed. Each day's record opened and closed with the Secretary's time of arrival and departure from the office. He even entered the time of his lunch hour, which invariably lasted sixty minutes: "Left at 1:10; returned at 2:10." Once, when he was forced to record his morning arrival at 10:15, he added, with a worried eye on posterity, "Car broke down."

Inside the National Archives even the memory of Widener paled. Nothing can compare with the fascination of examining material in the very paper and ink of its original issue. A report from a field agent with marginal comments by the Secretary of War, his routing directions to State and Commerce, and the scribbled initials of subsequent readers can be a little history in itself. In the Archives I found the original decode of the Zimmermann Telegram, which I was able to have declassified and photostated for the cover of my book.

Even more immediate is research on the spot. Before writing *The Guns* I rented a little Renault and in another August drove over the battle areas of August 1914, following the track of the German invasion through Luxembourg, Belgium, and northern France. Besides obtaining a feeling of the geography, distances, and terrain involved in military movements, I saw the fields ripe with grain which the cavalry would have trampled, measured the grain which the cavalry would have trampled, measured the great width of the Meuse at Liège, and saw how the lost territory of Alsace looked to the French soldiers who gazed down upon it from the heights of the Vosges. I learned the discomfort of the Belgian *pavé* and discovered, in the course of losing my way almost permanently in a tangle of country roads in a hunt for the house that had been British Headquarters, why a British motorcycle dispatch rider in 1914 had taken three hours to cover twenty-five miles. Clearly, owing to the British officers' preference for country houses, he had not been able to find Headquarters either. French army commanders, I noticed, located themselves in *towns,* with railroad stations and telegraph offices.

As to the mechanics of research, I take notes on four-by-six index cards, reminding myself about once an hour of a rule I read long ago in a research manual, "Never write on the back of anything." Since copying is a chore and a bore, use of the cards, the smaller the better, forces one to extract the strictly relevant, to distill from the very beginning, to pass the material through the grinder of one's own mind, so to speak. Eventually, as the cards fall into groups according to subject or person or chronological sequence, the pattern of my story will emerge. Besides, they are convenient, as they can be filed in a shoebox and carried around in a pocketbook. When ready to write I need only take along a packet of them, representing a chapter, and I am equipped to work anywhere; whereas if one writes surrounded by a pile of books, one is tied to a single place, and furthermore likely to be too much influenced by other authors.

The most important thing about research is to know when to stop. How does one recognize the moment? When I was eighteen or thereabouts, my mother told me that when out with a young man I should always leave a half-hour before I wanted to. Although I was not sure how this might be accomplished, I recognized the advice as sound, and exactly the same rule applies to research. One must stop *before* one has finished; otherwise, one will never stop and never finish. I had an object lesson in this once in Washington at the Archives. I was looking for documents in the case of Perdicaris, an American—or supposed American—who was captured by Moroccan brigands in 1904. The Archives people introduced me to a lady professor who had been doing research in United States relations with Morocco all her life. She had written her Ph.D. thesis on the subject back in, I think, 1936, and was still coming for six months each year to work in the Archives. She was in her seventies and, they told me, had recently suffered a heart attack. When I asked her what year was her cutoff point, she looked at me in surprise and said she kept a file of newspaper clippings right up to the moment. I am sure she knew more about United States–Moroccan relations than anyone alive, but would she ever leave off her research in time to write that definitive history and tell the world what she knew? I feared the answer. Yet I know how she felt. I too feel compelled to follow every lead and learn everything about a subject, but fortunately I have an even more overwhelming compulsion to see my work in print. That is the only thing that saves me.

Research is endlessly seductive; writing is hard work. One has to sit down on that chair and think and transform thought into readable, conservative, interesting sentences that both make sense and make the reader turn the page. It is laborious, slow, often painful, sometimes agony. It means rearrangement, revision, adding, cutting, rewriting. But it brings a sense of excitement, almost of rapture; a moment on Olympus. In short, it is an act of creation.

Questions for Discussion

1. According to Tuchman, what are the duties and responsibilities of the writer of history? What is the relationship between fact and creative imagination?

2. Does Tuchman believe that the historian should be an "artist"? Do you agree or disagree?

3. The author states that she tries to stay "within the evidence." What is evidence, and how many different types of evidence might you come across in researching a topic? How should evidence be judged? How does the writer's own cultural background, values, and experiences influence judgment?

Kristen Iversen
Molly Brown: Unraveling the Myth

Molly Brown: Unraveling the Myth *is a book that dispelled popular myths and stories about the woman known as the "Unsinkable Molly Brown." Many of these tales stemmed from the popular Broadway play* The Unsinkable Molly Brown *starring Tammy Grimes and the later film version of the same name starring Debbie Reynolds. One part of the legend is true: Margaret Tobin Brown (never known as "Molly" in real life) was indeed a heroine of the* Titanic. *However, her life as a suffragette and human rights activist extends far beyond the "belly-up-to-the-bar" saloon girl portrayed on stage and in film.* Molly Brown: Unraveling the Myth *won the Colorado Book Award and the Barbara Sudler Award for Nonfiction and was a finalist for a* WILLA *Award.*

This book is a combination of straightforward narrative and description, with the beginning and ending chapters written in a novelistic fashion. This excerpt is from the last chapter of the book and takes place just as the rescue ship Carpathia *is entering New York harbor.*

Envoi
April 18, 1912

On a cold, rainy night four days after the *Titanic* hit the iceberg, Margaret Tobin Brown stood on the deck of the *Carpathia*, still wearing the black velvet suit she had put on the evening of April 14. The shoreline of New York Harbor was barely visible in the driving rain. Margaret reached into her pocket and curled her fingers around the tiny turquoise statue from Cairo— her good-luck charm, all she had left from the trunks of clothing, art, and

Kristen Iversen, excerpt from *Molly Brown: Unraveling the Myth,* Johnson Books, 1999, pp. 253–257. Reprinted by permission of the author.

souvenirs from her trip across Europe that now lay at the bottom of the sea. Looking toward the shore, she saw a moving blanket of lights, blurred in the black mist, slowly advancing toward them as if pulled by a magnet. "Ah," gasped the young woman standing next to her, but whether in awe or terror Margaret couldn't tell. She was one of three Irish girls whom Margaret, along with the others who had combed the ship for extra blankets and clothing, had found hiding in a steerage corridor. Now wrapped in makeshift clothes and blankets, the three girls stood next to her in the driving rain. The last few days had seemed eternal. Of the hundreds of *Titanic* survivors the *Carpathia* had plucked from the icy waters off the coast of Newfoundland, a few had died in the hours and days following their rescue. Hypothermia, shock, broken limbs, and frostbitten feet and hands were common afflictions. Some people had bouts of hysteria; others withdrew into silent shells. Only 705 of the *Titanic*'s estimated 2,227 passengers lived to see the black skies and freezing rain of New York Harbor.

Suddenly from the dark mist the boats emerged: a flotilla of tugs, pleasure boats, skiffs, and ragboats. The lights split the darkness, and the deck of the *Carpathia,* somber and resolute in its steady progression toward shore, broke into chaos.

A voice bellowed from the water's surface. "*Titanic!*" barked a man through a megaphone, standing on the prow of a skiff. "*Titanic* survivors!"

Rushing to the edge of the deck, an officer leaned out over the rail. "Get out of the way!" he shouted. "We can't make our way!"

A beam of light reached up to the deck from a boat where a figure stood with a huge placard. Margaret could barely read the hand-lettered names: Astor. Guggenheim. Strauss.

"Mrs. Astor!" a man shouted from below. "Is Mrs. Astor on board?"

"Fifty dollars for the first survivor's story!" a voice roared through a megaphone.

"Get back!" cried the officer. "Let us through!" He waved his arms broadly in the air.

"One hundred! One hundred dollars for a story!" The skiff drew alongside. "Survivors, come aboard!" the megaphone shouted. Popping lights splintered the darkness as photographers' flashbulbs snapped like firecrackers. Margaret drew the women closer to her, and they pulled back, away from the lights. A commotion arose on the other side of the ship; a reporter had scrambled up through an open cargo door in the side of the ship. He sprinted across the wet wooden planks toward the group of survivors, now grown to almost two hundred, who had gathered on the deck.

"Get him!" shouted an officer, and several men sprinted toward the man, tackling him and knocking him to the ground. Captain Rostron appeared. "Put him under close arrest immediately," he barked. "Lock him in my cabin." He positioned crew members along the rail and ordered everyone back inside.

Margaret, who like many others had barely slept in the past four days, felt the thin crust of self-control that had served her so well begin to crack slightly. No one could have anticipated the fracas that welled around the ship. Who would meet her at the shore? Did her family know she was alive? Her eyes met those of Emma Bucknell, who had worked side by side with Margaret over the past three days. A different kind of terror now shone in Emma's eyes as the ship slowly parted the swarming flotilla. Margaret's face felt windburned and beaten; her arms and legs were sore; she longed for a bath and a change of clothing. This part of their journey could be no worse than what they had already endured—shock and exhaustion had turned into a ribbon of adrenaline that had pulled her through the past four days, and she couldn't stop now. "Come now." She turned and spoke to her Irish companions. "Who is to meet you on shore? Do you have family or friends here? We have to ready ourselves." She bustled them back inside.

Tens of thousands of people crowded the long Cunard pier awaiting the first glimpse of the *Carpathia,* the high whine of ambulance sirens and the occasional blast of an auto horn rising above the noise of the crowd. A glistening wet canopy had been drawn up over the pier, and a group of several hundred—most of whom had relatives or friends on the *Titanic*—pressed up against each other as if poised to spill right over into the harbor. Police had arranged the pier into alphabetically designated sections, with family and friends of known survivors allowed to stand nearest, but few paid attention to the rules. For more than three hours people had waited and cried and fainted and argued and commiserated with one another. And then waited some more. A line of customs officials stood shoulder to shoulder, forming a human line of defense against the pushing throng. Their faces were wooden and exhausted.

A short, stocky man with a puffy, florid face stood next to a Denver reporter, nervously chewing his cigar. "I have five on board," he said. "I don't know if they're all alive—I can't tell. They've taken their names off the lists and put them on again—"

The chugging of a tugboat sounded from out in the North River. The man's ruddy face went white. "My God!" he said. The crowd suddenly fell silent. The sound of the tug's lusty churning filled the air. People strained to see beyond the canopy; a long wooden spar appeared, followed by a mast gliding silently past. Then the white bow of the *Carpathia* appeared.

"They're smoking!" shrieked a woman, her voice startling everyone. The incongruity of the remark fit the peculiar sight of a solid row of faces streaming past as the *Carpathia* slid into view. Like tiny bright stars, lighted cigars glowed in the mass of humanity standing on the deck. No single face emerged from the dark apparition, only dark bodies pressed together.

"Guess there are lots of them able to smoke," the florid man quipped, and then stopped. "My sister was drowned," he added after a moment, as though in apology. The reporter nodded and steadied his camera. He still felt a little awkward with the magnesium flash.

The crew of the *Carpathia,* unresponsive to the shouts of reporters and the whistles of police officers in their wake, solemnly let down *Titanic*'s thirteen lifeboats at the White Star pier. The lifeboats, now all that remained of the ship that had been as large as a stadium, knocked against each other with each slap of a wave and hardly looked capable of saving the lives of hundreds of people. *Carpathia* completed its duty and allowed itself to be pulled up to Pier 54, the Cunard pier, where tens of thousands turned their faces to the glistening bow. The ship was warped into the berth and stood steaming at the dock. For a long, tense moment the two throngs of people looked upon one another, searching, and then the dock exploded into pandemonium. The gangplank was swung aboard. Countless cameras stood poised to capture the first *Titanic* survivor to walk down the plank.

There must have been some consideration regarding who would take this place in history, for the crowd grew restless. At last a figure appeared. Dr. Henry W. Frauenthal, a distinguished surgeon from New York, emerged in fine form. His wife, young enough to be his daughter, balanced herself with his elbow and matched him stride for stride. Dr. Frauenthal's red beard was neatly combed, and his shoes and hat "bespoke careful attention." His wife was equally well coifed. He smiled tightly, nodding left and right to the burst of photographers' magnesium bulbs, and with measured gait the couple strolled toward the exit. The Denver reporter noted that Dr. Frauenthal might have been "alighting from a ferry boat after a day in Jersey City."

The next passenger was not as composed. A young woman emerged alone, her hair wild and loose about her face, her cheeks flushed and eyes red and swollen. She wore odds and ends of unmatched clothing and didn't seem to notice the fact that thousands of eyes were trained upon her. She walked straight toward the crowd, now beginning to break free from the customs officials. Abruptly halting, she thrust her hands out into the air, the fingers clutching at nothing, the cords in her thin wrists "standing out like strings on a violin." Not a single word or sob escaped her throat, but at last her eyes found what they sought, and she staggered headlong into the arms of an elderly woman and wilted into a quiet heap on the ground.

The procession was halted while a tidy group of white-coated physicians, dutifully followed by white-capped nurses bearing "great packages of surgical bandages and cases of evil-looking little knives and saws," entered the ship. Ten minutes later the first physician emerged to calm the mounting tension outside. "Thank heaven," he announced, mopping his brow. "There was nothing for me to do."

A nurse carried out a chubby baby boy who began wailing at the top of his lungs. Four small children were brought out on miniature stretchers. Two burly men made a chair of their arms and shoulders and brought out a man whose feet were so frozen he couldn't walk—despite his disability, the man deftly smoked a cigar as he made his exit.

Suddenly it seemed as if a dam had broken, and the passengers streamed out in groups of five and ten. Nearly all of them wore clothing that was ill sized, ill matched, torn, and dilapidated. One after another they fell into the arms of frantic relatives and friends. Customs officers, some of them overcome with as much emotion as those who had been reunited, allowed people to break rank and fall forward into the surging path of survivors. They made way for couples and families with arms locked about each others' necks, sobbing in grief and joy, and the anxious ones who still waited.

Madeleine Astor, despite rumors that she was critically ill, walked steadily on her own down the gangplank and into the arms of her father. Wearing a heavy white sweater that had been given to her, she declared to reporters that she held faith that John Jacob had not perished. "I hope he is alive somewhere," she said. "I cannot think of anything else, but I am sure he will be saved." Her husband's last words to her, she said, had been "I will meet you in New York, dear." The Astor family quickly bundled her into an automobile and took her to the Astor home on Fifth Avenue. For a full hour and a half, *Titanic* survivors straggled down the gangplank and were met by family and friends as well as a sea of newspaper reporters "pouring queries faster than tongues could answer."

After the first wave of survivors had emerged, Margaret darted out, frantically searching the crowd for her family. Her brother Daniel Tobin and friend Genevieve Spinner quickly materialized. "Margaret!" Genevieve cried, and broke into sobs. Margaret held her tightly. "I'm fine, dear, fine," she said, and turned to her brother. "What about Pat?" she asked. "Is the baby all right?"

"The baby's fine," he said, trying to keep the tears from his eyes. "Healthy as can be. It was the milk—something about the milk disagreed with him."

"And Helen, and Lawrence, and the girls?"

"Grace, Florence, and Helen are still at the house in Denver, and they know that you're okay. We'll wire them again tonight. Helen is waiting in Paris and knows you're safe. Lawrence is on his way to meet you in Denver."

"Thank God!" Margaret cried, and hugged them both.

"Let's get you to the hotel," Genevieve cried. "You look completely worn. Look at your dress!"

"No, no, I can't," Margaret said, and pulled back. "All these women and children, and some men too—they have no place to go. They can't speak English, and we can't just turn them out on the street. Emma and I are standing there at the door with a list and marking off names, only allowing people off the ship if they have someone to meet them. Otherwise we are making arrangements for them."

"But you must be so exhausted yourself," Daniel said. "Your health is ruined." The rain still pounded steadily; the night air had grown so cold they could see their breath.

"Listen," Margaret said. "You must go to the Ritz-Carlton and get my room. I will be coming with some people—there's a Russian woman in particular who has lost everything, and is so terrified she won't leave the ship. I'm bringing her with me. And there are so many others who need help. From the room we can begin to make arrangements with embassies and the like. And they all need clothes. And money. We've got to—"

"I know," Daniel interrupted gently. He knew his sister well. "Go back inside. We'll go and get the room. But don't be too long, or we'll send the Ritz-Carlton cab after you."

By five A.M. on the morning of April 19, 1912, the last *Titanic* survivor had disembarked. The crowd was gone and the dock deserted. The rain beat down steadily in the cold gray dawn, and the crew and passengers of *Carpathia* slept. Just hours before, Captain Rostron had met with the officials of the Cunard Line and agreed to have his ship ready to sail again at four that afternoon, despite the fact that his crew was exhausted. U.S. government officials had issued orders that no one was to be allowed on *Carpathia*'s pier, but now nearly twenty drays stood at the docks, ready for cargo to be transferred. Soon the city began to rouse itself, but the ship was still silent. In an act of kindness, Cunard Line officials had relented—despite their obvious desire to get the *Carpathia* on its way back to Gibraltar as soon as possible, the crew was allowed to sleep in.

Margaret Tobin Brown was asleep in her room at the Ritz-Carlton, her new Russian friend slumbering nearby. By the time the sun rose above the horizon she would be up with Genevieve and Daniel, another list in hand, organizing a buying party to replace the wardrobes of passengers and crew who had lost or given away their clothing. She slept fitfully, already haunted by the faces of those she had watched go to their deaths—particularly Ida and Isidor Straus. But the dawn would bring a whole new wave of troubles to solve.

In hospitals and hotel rooms and shelters and boardinghouses, the 705 people who had survived the sinking of the *Titanic* awoke, gathered their belongings and the remnants of their lives, and slowly filtered out of the city. Despite the flurry of media that surrounded them at the time, America would eventually forget them in the unfathomable tragedy to come: the first World War. Death would assume a new face.

Decades later Americans would begin to question why the *Titanic* still obsessively occupies our imaginations and fuels our greatest fears. But in late April 1912, as New York City was just beginning to feel the spring, most *Titanic* survivors left little trace of who they were or where they were going. Or how they would carry the grief of 1,500 souls lost one frigid night in the icy waters of the north Atlantic.

Questions for Discussion

1. Should history be written in novelistic fashion? What are the benefits? What are the pitfalls?

2. What are the possible methods by which a story might make reference to the research that it is based on? Footnotes? Citations? Is it important for the reader to be aware of the sources of historical information?

3. How much character development should go into the writing of history? Does the author have a responsibility to develop characters as fully as the fiction writer does?

Student Writing

The Element of Surprise

In these two student essays, the reader is led into a journey of discovery. How do these two "quests" differ in style, tone, and structure? How do these authors build tension and suspense?

Robert F. James
Rebecca Tucked Away

Robert F. James enlisted in the Navy as a journalist in 1989 and spent eight years serving in Japan, Diego Garcia, and Washington, D.C. In 1996, James separated from the Navy as a Journalist Second Class (Enlisted Aviation Warfare Specialist) and served as Editor-in-Chief of Surface Warfare Magazine *through the spring of 2001. He then completed his undergraduate degree at George Mason University, graduating with honors in English (Creative Writing) with a minor degree in Folklore/Mythology. James is currently completing his master of fine arts degree and working on a novel.*

My fingernails clicked on the coffee table in the drab hospitality room of the John D. Lucas printing plant. My magazine printed at the facility every two months, and this dreary Tuesday in January was no different. I was a clean-cut businessman pressed to fit into the dress-down casual world of Northern Virginia tech firms and corporations. I loved the pressure demanded by the editing environment, but at that particular time, I was bored. I usually brought along a book of short stories to pass the interval between inspecting signatures, but I had left in a rush.

I thought about the collection of Edgar Allen Poe stories sitting on my coffee table. Through the years, I've endured a good deal of ribbing for my love of Poe. People say he's not literary—too commercial. "Real writers don't like Poe." But I secreted my admiration for his writing nonetheless. It's not that I am a macabre man but I've always enjoyed the occasional tale of the supernatural or touch of gothic. Poe won my heart in high school, "Ligeia" being the first short story I remember enjoying. The love affair tapered off with time, but it never disappeared entirely. Even at this point, 30 years old and climbing the corporate ladder, Poe had a firm niche carved out for himself in my life.

I got lost thinking about all of Edgar's literary credits, his influence on the genres of murder mystery, science fiction, and horror. Edgar was a thinker. For instance, when he published "The Murders in the Rue Morgue," he not only showed the crime, but also revealed the ingenious solution. Murders and dead bodies had appeared in fiction well before Edgar's, but he shifted the focus from the body to the act.

While his intellect was evident, his imagination was equally intimidating. "The Unparalleled Adventure of One Hans Pfaall" and "A Descent into the Maelstrom" made for compelling pieces of fiction that inspired Jules Verne, Isaac Asimov and even Arthur Clarke, just as Poe's murder mysteries fertilized the sleuthing styles of Arthur Conan Doyle, Agatha Christie and Erle Stanley Gardner.

His fiction astounded me, but his literary analysis, his ability to delve into and explicate a work was baffling. He not only critiqued stories when he became editor of the *Southern Literary Messenger* in Richmond, Virginia, but also established the working definition of the short story still influencing writers and critics to this day.

Truly, Edgar was a man ahead of his time and centuries ahead of me in my writing. Edgar connected with me unlike any other writer. I thrived on every detail I gleaned about his life. His mother died when he was only two, by which time his father, David Poe, had already disappeared. He signed a two-year enlistment in the Army just after publishing his first volume of poems at the age of 18. He even secured an appointment to West Point. Even though his stint in the service didn't work out so well his time in service, much like mine, spring boarded him into his writing.

Edgar was 22 by the time he was through with the Army. He started writing stories and selling them to journals in Baltimore and Philadelphia before becoming editor of the *Southern Literary Messenger.* I took inspiration from the fact that even though he struggled in his personal and financial life, he found solace in his words.

As I sat thinking about the influence those words had on my life and on my writing and reading habits, the irony of my presence in Baltimore finally dawned on me. I looked through the front pages of a phone directory to find local attractions. The Edgar Allen Poe House was only a few miles down the road. From there, I figured I could get good directions to his grave—where, if I was fortunate, I could spend some quality time alone with my favorite writer. I figured I'd be back in plenty of time for the final press sheet inspection at 5:00.

The hair-pullling stress of the press sheet inspections wasn't the ideal time for a field trip. The proofreading process is too controlled, too precise. Each detail, each tantalizing morsel of minutiae, was my responsibility. I reveled in that control. In that moment, with a room of on-lookers gawking behind me, holding their collective breath for my approval, I was alive. An unwieldy project—48 pages and two months of nail-biting writing and editing—culminated in those moments on the drafting table. I couldn't focus on the job in those moments, though. The impulse to visit Poe's grave had to be indulged.

It was already past lunchtime, but I didn't want to eat first. An impromptu excursion to visit a dead writer whose grave was located in a questionable neighborhood was completely out of my character, and I wanted to get there before I lost my nerve or someone questioned me about my plans. It shouldn't have bothered me, but it did. I felt like I was buying pornography in a neighborhood where everyone knew me.

It wasn't long into my trip before I was lost. Holabird turned into Ponca Street, which crossed with Boston. Boston became Fleet Street from which I took a right onto Presidents. Road construction messed me up and I ended up in a maze of one-way streets. I went with the flow of traffic onto North Howard, across a bridge—each span prominently spray-painted with a "Free Mumia" stencil.

I was in trouble. My heart pounded. My hands clenched the steering wheel. I had to get out. I had to get safe, and safety meant turning around and going back the way I'd come. I somehow made it back onto Martin Luther King Boulevard and even thought briefly about trying again to find the Poe House, but my fear proved stronger than my desire.

"Edgar Allen Poe can wait," I thought.

Lunch was sounding like the better option after all. There was a McDonald's near the printing plant, so I headed in that direction wondering what kind of Extra Value Meal Poe would have liked. I didn't figure Edgar as the Big Mac sort, and the Big Extra or any of the Quarter Pounder varieties seemed too grand for his reputation. I figured it would be the two-cheeseburger meal, small water instead of soda, no ketchup for the fries and some eccentricity about the burgers—extra pickles, maybe, or a big dollop of mayo that oozed out of the bun when he took a bite.

I was laughing at the image of Edgar's hamburgers when I came to O'Donnell Street and saw the cemetery. There was no humor here. Mismatched headstones, Virgin Mary statues, crosses and angels—everything tilted at odd angles or fallen on the ground—littered the cemetery. I steered my rented Chevy Corsica to the curb at the corner of Bonsal and O'Donnell, the sound of nearby Interstate 95 mingling with the loudspeaker of the Greyhound bus terminal and travel plaza around the block. I got out of the car and pushed through the cemetery gates and into the waist-high weeds. The sun had finally melted through the cold drizzle of the afternoon providing a theatrical lighting to the harbor cranes peaking up over the horizon of factory buildings.

Inside the cemetery, the sounds of the city faded to a low hum. I almost left. I didn't want to be here in the first place. I had been searching for a grave, but not here. Then one broken stone called to me.

Tucked away into a shadowed corner of the cemetery, even more desolate and overgrown than the rest, stood her pitiful marker. I felt drawn to it. It may have been white once, but the stone and the angel on it were so badly decayed and covered with other organic material it was hard to say for sure. The angel's face had eroded inward so that barely a bump served as a head on the crippled, wingless body. Half the statuette was gone—split cleanly down the middle. The stone base listed ominously, the right half subsiding into the soft grave underneath. A tangle of brambles and weeds obscured the preponderance of the marker. The headstone was visible only from where I stood. I pushed my way through the growth and around the grave, pulling it back enough from the marker's face to read the inscription: Rebecca Faherty, Daughter, 1876–1896, God Forgive Her Wickedness.

I couldn't get the phrase out of my mind: "God Forgive Her Wickedness." These four words on a broken angel were all that Rebecca Faherty would be remembered for. I couldn't help wonder how I would be remembered. The thought of wasting away in a corner like Rebecca was startling. I wanted to be gone from her presence. I wanted to let go and to quit staring, but I couldn't help myself from being with her. I felt like I was meant to know her—had to know her. It didn't matter to me that the afternoon light in this corner of the cemetery looked closer to twilight. The ominous black angels resting on their obelisks didn't concern me. I was here for Rebecca, and somehow I knew that.

Knowledge and comfort, though, are two different things. I wanted to see Poe's grave, not Rebecca's. Through her eyes, I had to admit the brevity of *my* life and the severity of its judgments. What loss of control for her, not only giving up the ghost, but also giving up her reputation. She had no tongue to speak in defense of the accusations. And I had to take the word of the faceless stone carver as to her "wickedness." Into whose hands would my final words be entrusted?

The thought of being a faded inscription chilled me. The air seemed oppressive, the sun duller in this section of the cemetery. I became more uncomfortable standing in the weeds and overgrown graves and I regretted ever coming inside. I tried to whistle on my way out, but my lips were too dry. I hadn't realized I was so far into the graveyard, the rental car barely visible on the other side of the fence. No one was around to see me emerge from the graveyard. I was relieved by that fact. I felt foolish enough without there being witnesses.

I got into the Corsica and drove the two blocks to the travel plaza. Poe entered my mind again and I feigned a smile for my own benefit. I didn't see Edgar that day at lunch as I had hoped, but I couldn't help thinking he was somewhere close by the entire time, enjoying my discomfort. But it was too much of an effort to keep my thoughts on Edgar. I couldn't shake the company of Rebecca now. I hadn't set out wanting to meet her, and I wanted to forget her, to crawl back to the periods and commas of editing, to lose myself in registrations and blending colors. I wanted to read boring articles and edit them into something substantial. I wanted that of which I had lost control.

Even in that moment, so soon after meeting the beguiling Rebecca, I knew that I would not be able to let her go. I knew that she would not let me go, either. She had lain in her corner of condemnation long enough. She didn't seem to care that we were separated by time and mortality. I was the vehicle through which she had chosen to reveal herself, the faithful suitor wooed to her chamber. How I longed for this episode to be one of Edgar's tales, a clever few pages that I could close up and tuck away, momentarily disturbed, but not permanently shaken. Even my old confidante, though, would have to step aside and acquiesce to Rebecca, who was weaving her own tale—personal, real, and anything but temporary.

Ellen Young
Dear John Barry

Ellen Young grew up in the Napa Valley of California and has traveled through almost all fifty states. She's managed a food coop, run her own housecleaning business, worked as a massage therapist, been the night manager of a homeless shelter, and is now using her life as grist for her first novel.

The author writes, "This piece had me struggling until I found the angle that made it easy. I'd chosen the subject not because of any interest in the Revolutionary War or war heroes in general but because I'd thought I was descended from this particular hero. In researching him, I found out that he had a life much more fascinating than I'd suspected but that I was, alas, not descended from him: he had no children. Now that my personal connection was gone, I felt intimidated by the idea of writing the piece. It was History, and he was a Hero. I tried to make it interesting, but every paragraph I wrote seemed duller than the one before. In frustration, I began to write directly to my character, Commodore John Barry, as an exercise to get me moving. I then had him respond in character, and I soon had a lively imaginary exchange going on between him and me, through which the true story of his life unfolded."

Dear John Barry

I understand from my father that you are my ancestor and that you are the Father of the American Navy. When I was young, my sister and I worked out the generational span between you and us, and it looks like you're probably my great-great-great-great-great-grandfather. I'm very honored to be part of your family line. I don't know much about you though. Were you a rich Irishman who paid for the ships used in the war? That's what I was told. I'm sure you were very brave too, of course!

Sincerely,
Ellen Young

Miss Young,

I was not a rich Irishman. Where did you get this bilge? And please desist in claiming me as your ancestor. Whoever you are, you are certainly not my descendant. I have no descendants. Perhaps I might be a great-great-great—oh good lord—your distant uncle or cousin or such. But I had no children. I'm sorry to disappoint you, but you must look elsewhere for your glory.

Rich Irishmen! Why, if there'd been even one rich Irishman on that whole island, he would have given all his wealth over to outfit a navy for the patriotic cause of American freedom. We all hated the damn British bastards and wanted them whipped. As it was, the navy never did get off the ground properly during the war. Who told you this tripe? My lord, what's going on in America these days? Such ignorance would never have been tolerated in my day.

> Patriotically yours,
> Commodore John Barry

Dear Commodore Barry,

Oh, I'm terribly sorry! About everything! You had no children? No descendants? You weren't a rich Irish capitalist? How could my family have got this so wrong? I'm so disappointed. I mean, I wasn't just looking for glory by saying I was related to the Father of the American Navy. I really thought I was. I've told a lot of people I was. I mean, it wasn't the first thing out of my mouth. No one's ever heard of you, so I had to explain. I waited until I got to know someone and then told them.

But I always told them as if it didn't really matter, as if it was just a funny tidbit. Not that you yourself are a funny tidbit, but it was funny, when my parents were anti-war liberals, to think that I could register as a Daughter of the American Revolution. That sort of thing. I just took it for granted.

I'm sorry to have bothered you. This is not your fault, of course. Please forgive me. And I guess I didn't properly introduce myself. I'm just a curious American citizen who thought she had an in with history. Darn. I'm also a student in a writing program, and I chose you to write a paper on. But I'm not sure if I'm all that interested now that we're not related. Not that you're not interesting, I didn't mean that, but you know, it's different now. Oh, and I'm not a Miss. I'm married. If you feel like writing back again, I guess you can address me as Ms.

> Sincerely,
> Ellen Young

Dear Mz. Young,

I apologize for my rudeness in my previous letter. You simply startled the wind out of me. I was known as "the gallant John Barry" during my career, but I have probably not struck you as such. Please don't take this so hard. I'm sure your real ancestors are fine people. You might find you come from healthier stock than I. I had asthma, you know. Died of it.

Best wishes,
John Barry

Dear Mr. Barry,

Thank you. I'm feeling okay. I told my brother, and he didn't believe you weren't related to us. He's such a romantic. We're still going to search our genealogy, though, because you might be my great-great-great—well, uncle or cousin. The asthma is coincidental. My father and brother both have asthma too. Maybe it's a genetic link?

I guess I'm still kind of interested in your history, now that I've made your acquaintance. You know, people don't know much about the Revolutionary War these days. I mean, it was an important war, I know that. Everybody knows that. But I'm kind of shocked to hear that the navy didn't get off the ground for that war. I'm sure that would have helped quite a bit.

Well, if I haven't made you too angry to ever talk to me again, could you explain what you mean about the navy not getting off the ground? And now I'm really curious to know what you did in the war.

You really were Irish, right? Do I have that part right, at least? Because I'm Irish, mostly. I like Ireland, although I've never been there.

What did you do before you were in the Navy?

Don't be mad. Oh, and it's "Ms," not "Mz."

Very sincerely,
Ms. Ellen Young

My dear Misses Young,

You sound very young. Do they teach nothing in schools these days? These questions are preposterous. And many people have asthma. But because I am a gentleman, I will assume you to be a lady and calm my temper. For the moment. But please consider whom it is you are speaking with. *Am I really Irish?* Bah!

People didn't go around shouting from the rooftops how Irish they were in my day, missy. As if being born on the dear old Emerald Isle would give one status back then. My father, god rest his weary soul, was the typical Irishman of his time—devout, hard-working, poor as a church mouse. He farmed the soil as a tenant, couldn't even call the bit of land his own. The dirty British evicted him from it anyway. We had to move from Ballysampson, the town of my birth, to Rosslare then, and start over.

It was in Rosslare that I fell in love with the sea. You want to know about my life? You must understand the love of the sea then. People don't know that sort of love nowadays, I don't expect. Oh, I don't mean the beauty and romance of sea-faring novels. Bilge. There's no romance on the sea, and whatever beauty is found, well, let's just say that some people see it and some people don't. The sea can be ugly too. Never forget that. But I was lucky to come to know her at an early age, and she captured my heart forever.

It was my uncle Nicholas, captain of his own fishing skiff, who started me on a life at sea. As soon as I could, I signed up on a merchant ship as a cabin boy, and oh, the life was dirty and hard. I don't want to upset your female sensibilities, so I won't go into detail about the stench and rats and maggots and disease. Scurvy too. Severe rheumatism, oh yes, that too. And of course, death and dismemberment from accidents were not uncommon. Still, I wouldn't have had anything else. You worked hard, and there was no more exciting thing in the world than taking a finely rigged ship into port.

I worked my way up to seaman and then able-bodied seaman and I achieved a mate's rating at a younger age than most. Does significant stature run in your family today? I was six feet four, with muscles like an ox. As soon as I could, I emigrated to America and settled in Philadelphia with all the other Irish rabble. You could be Catholic there and no one would bother you too much about it. Did you know that Philadelphia was the second largest city in the British Empire then? It was larger than Boston or New York and growing bigger all the time. I captained my first ship out of Philadelphia in 1766. *The Barbadoes,* a schooner. I took her back and forth to and from the West Indies mostly.

Ah, that was a fine time to be a captain. The commerce of the day depended on ships, and the harbors were busy day and night. My skills were in demand, and I could make the kind of living my father and all my countrymen had been denied by the British thieves. The only low point of these days was the death of my dear wife, Mary, while I was at sea. Even if a man loves the sea, you know, he also yearns for the softer climes found on land. I was not the kind of sea-faring man who did not enjoy society. When my heart healed, I married again, to a fine Philadelphia girl.

And that's what I did "before the war." What a silly question. When my new country needed captains to defend and fight for its liberty, I did not hesitate. I could have been a much richer man if I had kept working for the merchants, as many did. The Continental Congress could barely maintain an army much less a whole new navy. I was a patriot though. I was convinced of the rightness of our cause.

As for why the navy didn't get off the ground during the war for independence, that's a big enough subject that people could write books about it. I'm sure they have. Look it up. You shouldn't pester your elders so. Is America so soft now that its citizens don't do anything for themselves?

My proper title is "Commodore," not "Mr."

Regards,
Commodore Barry

Hey Commodore,

Um, you could have mentioned in one of these letters that you're *not* in fact the Father of the American Navy? You know, I'm not as lazy as you think, and it turns out that you're not so gallant. I spoke with an expert. He used to work for the navy as a journalist. The American navy, the one you supposedly fathered. I told him that I had thought I was descended from Commodore John Barry, the Father of the American Navy, and that I'd been mistaken and was feeling rather bad about it.

"I wouldn't exactly call Barry the father of the navy," he said.

My face, of course, fell to the floor. I thought I had at least that part right. So what do you say to that?

Ms. (not Mz.) Ellen Young

MS. Young,

May the Lord in heaven restrain me from throttling you. I understand that John Paul Jones has had thirty biographies written about him. Perhaps he's your flaming ancestor.

John Barry

Dear Commodore Barry, sir,

Wow, did I screw everything up. I did some real research on the history of the Revolutionary War, and I found out what a great guy you were. I apologize! John Paul Jones was no slouch as a war hero, but neither were you. Apparently, Jones was more of the spotlight-hogging war hero type, and you were the constant but modest war hero type. You stuck around after the war was over, too, while Jones left for Europe and never came back. And George Washington himself made you the commissioner of the entire navy when it did take off a few years later. That sounds like "Father of the American Navy" material. Please forgive me. I'm really sorry.

Let me tell you what I've found out at the library. Okay, your ship took the first naval victory of the war. In fact, the initial impetus for creating a navy in the first place came because you brought a report to the Continental Congress regarding a secret British cargo heading for Canada laden with ammunition and just ripe for attacking. The Congress then had to go and have endless meetings about it, but a naval committee was formed. I think that part's rather hilarious, because the entire headquarters of this new navy was nothing more than a rented room in a tavern. I'm beginning to understand what you mean by the lack of funds.

By the war's end, you were the captain of the only ship we had left—the *Alliance*. You were there at the start and at the finish and fought bravely and, yes, gallantly all the way through. I'm very impressed. And! You were being called the Father of the American Navy for many years after your death. It was said that the War of 1812 owed a great debt to you, because so many men received their naval training under you. Oh, and you wrote a signal book for communications between ships at sea. That's very fatherly also.

You know, you can call me whatever you want. I just thought, since we were being so proper and all, I'd tell you what title to use. But I don't really care.

Apologetically yours,
Ellen Young

Misses Young,

You are mostly Irish, I can see that now. You want stories! And you are willing to learn. All right, miss. Stories.

When the War for Independence began in 1776, I was raring to fight. I offered my services to the Continental Congress when they decided, too reluctantly, you're quite correct about that, to form a navy. To be fair to the Congress, though, mustering an army on land was difficult enough, and outfitting a navy was an expensive proposition. But a handful of ships were commissioned. I was directed to convert a small fleet of four merchant ships into man-of-wars, and then I was given the command of one, the *Lexington.* You might have read that I should have been given the *Alfred,* a much more impressive ship, but I didn't have strong enough connections yet, and commands were given through patronage. Or perhaps you didn't read that. Perhaps *Chevalier* John Paul Jones is the only one getting such close scrutiny nowadays. Well, at any rate, I held my tongue about being slighted. What mattered the most to me was the freedom and liberty of the republic. I knew that I would receive what was due me in time, and this turned out to be correct. Patience, my dear, is a necessary virtue for a life given over to sailing the seas.

Once we had a few ships ready for fighting, there was another problem—signing up able seamen. This might sound strange to you, but when the great fight for liberty began, the merchant ships of the colonies found another pastime more lucrative than fighting. They went into the business of what we called "privateering," and if that sounds like pirateering, well, you've got the right idea. The idea was to take over any British merchant ship we could get our hands on. This contributed to the war effort too, for the British empire was dependent on its commerce over the sea, so our raiding weakened them.

On the private merchant ships, the captured booty was then distributed among the officers and seamen, providing a nice bit of pay for all involved. The fledging navy fleet engaged in this raiding too, but the part shared with the crews was less than that of private merchant ships. On private ships, riches could be made, although the actual riches were more meager than the dream of it in most cases, so able-bodied seamen found privateering much more profitable than joining up with some rag-tag navy where you had to contend with military discipline and low pay. Not everyone was a patriot, you know. Not everyone ate and slept and dreamt freedom or believed that the world's largest empire could be defeated. Men might have been sympathetic to the patriot cause, but they had families to feed too.

On the other side, the British navy was the biggest and finest in the world, and their men well disciplined and experienced. They had the most trained seamen of any nation and the best shipyards, and their naval fleet consisted of one hundred and thirty ships. Christ, the nerve it took to fight them! The Lord gave us strength. We did the best we could with what we had, which wasn't much. I was valued because of my patriotism, my courage, and my experience in handling a ship. A captain was the lord and master of his crew while out at sea, and that was a charge I took very seriously. The men labored under hard conditions, but I was fair and honest with them, and I had less trouble than some, Jones, for instance, in recruiting a crew.

Still, there were times when it was near impossible to man my ship. There were two levels of seamen required—able-bodied seamen trained in the ways of sailing, and unskilled workmen. Enlisting captured British rabble into the Continental Navy as unskilled labor was a risky venture, but we were desperate for hands. I well remember one miserable, mutinous crew who sailed with me on my most important cruise, to bring Washington's envoy safely to France. My ship, the *Alliance*, still needed repairs from her last battle and was, as I said back then, "barely in condition to go to sea. There were not ten men, officers included, that could steer her, and no seamen but disaffected ones."

Imagine, my dear Misses Young, contending with the conditions I described to you earlier, the rats and the scurvy and such, on a long voyage of many months, made more difficult by the lowest bunch of scheming bastards to ever swab a deck. As much as I hated to use the cat-o-nine-tails on any hand under my leadership, I did not hesitate to do what I had to do to bring order. I could not tolerate the questioning of authority, no captain could, and we were at war, by God. I did what had to be done. When I remember that day, I remind myself that I requested that their lives be spared when they were condemned to death at their ensuing court-martial. I was a god-fearing man; such final judgment was not mine to give.

If you'll excuse me, I am tired. It's been a long time since I last visited these scenes in my mind.

Sincerely yours,
Jack Barry

Dear Commodore,

Wow. How on earth did you all win the war? No wonder it tuckers you out just to remember it. I'm not sure I would have rebelled against England, myself. On the other hand, I'm kind of independent, so maybe I would have. I don't suppose they let women fight in that war though, just sew flags.

These stories are great, but I probably have enough to go on for my paper, between what you've told and the books I found at the library. I'm kind of too busy to write letters right now. Lots of schoolwork to get done.

Sincerely,
Ellen Young

Dear Ms. Young,

Perhaps you're descended from my sister's children, who I raised with my second wife, Sally. I'm starting to see a resemblance.

I understand that you are busy, but in thinking about my last letter, I'm afraid I left you with the impression that seamen were nothing but wastrels and mutineers. All in all, able-bodied seamen tended to be patriotic, and they rallied to the cause well enough. They came through in battle, I'll say that for them. On our return home on that same mutinous voyage, we were attacked by two British ships. I'd restored order by then, thank the Lord, but we'd been badly battered about by a storm and were lying like a log in the water unable to move until a good wind came up. Our situation was dire, but we were determined. Even when some well-aimed grapeshot hit me in the shoulder, I wouldn't be stopped, and I moved among my men spurring them on. They needed me to keep up their fighting spirit even if I was wounded.

They took me below when I could no longer get about from loss of blood, but even then I wouldn't let them give up. Our flag had gotten shot down, and the British mistook that for our surrender, as if we'd taken it down ourselves, and so they came around and got ready to board. Well, my men wouldn't let them! They kept firing even when it looked hopeless. I wouldn't give them permission to surrender, and by God, they didn't. I ordered another flag hoisted and cried, "If the ship cannot be fought without me, I will be brought up on deck!" God answered my cry with a good stiff wind that filled our sails, and we were able to maneuver into fighting position at last. With a few proper salvos from the *Alliance*, the tide of battle turned until both the British ships hauled down their colors. From down below, I heard my men cheer. That, missy, was the spirit of '76 in all its glory! I was proud to be a part of it, and I just thought you might like this story.

Yours in spirit,
Jack Barry

Hi Jack!

Wow! This is great stuff, you're right! I've got my whole class reading these letters. I told you, no one knows much about that war anymore, and actually, when you get right down to it, I don't think anyone's known much about the navy's part in it for a very long time.

Say, you must have known a Captain Biddle. I've read that he was also a naval captain in the war, so you would have been fellow captains, right?

Did you ever hear about what *his* descendant got herself up to? She called herself the Mayflower Madam. Sydney Biddle-Barrows. She had the entrepreneurial spirit that America is so famous for these days. Anyway, I just think it's kind of funny to come up against one's descendants, or ancestors. If you got to know me better, you might not want me as a descendant, hee hee.

Gotta run.

Sincerely,
Ellen

Dear Ms. Ellen the Young,

Your letters to Barry are the sweetest missives from beyond the grave any of us have received in a good long while. We all thank ye! But you don't want to be that old guy's descendant. How about being mine? I've got good looks and daring both.

I've got something for you. I bet you didn't know where the tune came from for Yankee Doodle Dandy. You're going to love this. It was from a song about a whore. Here 'tis! You know the tune.

> O! how joyful shall I be,
> When I get de money,
> I will bring it all to dee;
> O! My diddling honey.

Except we sing, "O! My diddling Sydney." Ha ha! Poor Biddle.

Your adoring servant, if you wish,
Chevalier John Paul Jones

Madam Young,

Who in bloody hell do you think you are going around digging up this worn-out story about my lineage? Jack Barry's got the whole mess of them riled up again. It's nothing but jokes about Sydney and sailor boys day in and day out. I would think a little respect is in order.

Captain Biddle

My dear Ellen,

A thousand apologies for the boorish behavior of some of my compatriots. Biddle's been through this before. He shouldn't blame you for an innocent comment. As for Jones, well, he still thinks he's the ladykiller of the continent, both here and abroad.

I understand that you're very busy, but would you like to hear about my last battle of the war, the one I fought against the British ship *Sybil?* When they demanded that we identify ourselves, I shouted, "This is the United States ship *Alliance,* saucy Jack Barry, half Irishman, half Yankee, who are you?" We were winning the war by then, by golly, and we gave them no quarter. We beat them thoroughly, no thanks to that cowardly French ship that just stood by and watched and then tried to claim half the booty. That victory was ours, and with it, the war ended. The British were beaten on land and on sea. Back home, the bells rang out as we sailed into port. Tears come to my eyes as I recall that day.

Most sincerely yours,
Jack

Captains courageous,

Gee, settle down, boys! I'm in finals week. I don't really have time for all this. Captain Biddle, I'm sorry I got them on your case. Didn't mean to. John Paul, you're a little old for me. And dear Saucy Jack (I love that), I've got all I need to know for now, but I promise I'll return later on someday to hear more. It's really interesting. And I'll let you know the results if I ever look into being descended from your sister's kids. Thanks for everything. Okay, adios!

Your pal,
Ellen Young

Dear Ms. Ellen,

I haven't heard from you in a while. I hope your schoolwork went well. There's much more to tell whenever you're interested in hearing more. And I wanted to tell you that one of my sister's children was quite a scholar, like you. It's quite possible we are part of the same bloodline. I would be honored if that were so.

Sincerely,
Jack Barry

Dear Ms. Young,

Have you forgotten me then? I've been remembering more stories, and I think you'll like them. I look forward to your return to active correspondence. Until that day, I am at your service.

Your proud prospective uncle,
Commodore John Barry
Father of the American Navy

■ Writing Exercise ■

Choose a significant historical or literary figure or event and research it as fully as possible. Seek out primary and secondary sources, as well as what other writers and critics have written about this person or event. Consider your own relationship to this topic and the cultural or social lens you bring to its interpretation.

The format of this assignment can include many elements: quotes; photographs; fragments of journals, letters, or diaries; lines from poems or excerpts from stories or novels; literary reviews of this person's work; and so on. Be creative in your approach and presentation.

Your own voice—as author, as individual—should enter into the text in some way. Don't be afraid to experiment with tone (especially irony, if appropriate) and voice.

The Writing Workshop

When Things Tilt

Usually by the second or third session of a writing workshop, the group is cohesive, efficient, and takes on an energy of its own. Everyone begins to see the progress made by individual writers and the group as a whole. Members look forward to coming each week, sharing their work, and talking about the work of their peers.

But sometimes things go wrong. One writer may turn in a piece that some workshop members find off-putting or even offensive in its tone or subject matter. Perhaps a reader monopolizes the discussion by focusing on a relatively small or very particular aspect of the piece (incomplete sentences, for example, or the use of semicolons). Sometimes—hopefully very rarely—the discussion will turn to an analysis of the subject or background of the work that feels personally uncomfortable for the author.

Good writing workshops are a balance of honest critique and sincere praise. It's important not to back off from this. On the other hand, when things begin to feel a little off-kilter, the instructor or one of the workshop members should say: Stop. Wait. Let's take a look at our goals again. Perhaps the best thing to do at that point is to simplify your comments into two categories: things that seem to work about the piece, and things that don't. Look at both sides equally. If a manuscript is disconcerting in any way, talk about audience response and receptivity. How do different members of the group feel about the subject and how it's written? How might this piece, if it were published as an essay, a story, or a book, be received by publishers? Readers? Critics? Sometimes the most effective creative nonfiction is surprising, even shocking. Is it the intention of the author to "wake the reader up"? Does he or she do so effectively? How could the structure of the piece be more effective?

A good workshop can embrace controversy and disagreement as comfortably as it includes praise and admiration. Keep things on track.

Revision Tips and Strategies

Why You Shouldn't Tell the Reader Everything

Or at least not all in the beginning.

Sometimes as a writer you have to hold your cards close to your chest. It's important to think about when and how you reveal information to the reader even as you strive to stay true to the facts and chronology of a particular story or a particular life. What makes a good story in fiction or nonfiction? What keeps a reader turning the page? Think about the last really good biography or history book you read. Perhaps the author made the character and the historical time come alive in such a way that you really felt as if you were there. And there was something about the story—yes? You couldn't put the book down. The sense of anticipation, of wondering what would happen next, kept you moving from one chapter to the next.

Narrative tension or narrative "pull" is just as important in creative nonfiction as it is in fiction. This is not to say that a story should be contrived or false in any way. Rather, as an author you need to think about when to withhold information and when to reveal it. If you tell the whole story in the first chapter, there is little reason for the reader to proceed to the end. Even if you tell your story in a nonlinear or nonchronological manner, it still requires the conscious recounting of events and revelation of the significance of those events. It's easy to feel enthusiastic about your research and want the reader to "get the point" right off the bat.

This is a little more complicated than merely thinking about plot. Create a sense of discovery and anticipation for your reader. Perhaps the reader learns of particular facts and details as the character does. Consider using foreshadowing to subtly hint at what may happen in later chapters. Be careful not to repeat yourself but allow circumstances and events to build slowly toward the end of the book.

Falling in Love with Your Subject

A funny thing happens when people begin to research the lives of others. Through letters, diaries, reminiscences, interviews, court documents, newspaper clippings, and the myriad of other sources you may have available to you, your intellect and intuition become finely tuned to your subject. You begin to anticipate the language in the next letter, the photograph in the next file, the next telegram or journal entry. You feel intimately connected to your subject. This is a good and necessary

(continued)

Revision Tips and Strategies *(continued)*

thing, for it helps you write with confidence and authority. And a bit of intuition doesn't hurt.

Nevertheless, it's important to remember that you are a researcher, a historian, and a journalist as well as a creative writer. You bring to the project your own particular social and cultural lens, some of which you are likely aware of and some of which you are likely not. What does it mean to be a writer living in 2003, writing about a character who lived, say, in 1903? Or 1803? It's a tough balancing act to write well and intimately about a character—to bring a character and his or her historical context to life on the page—and still maintain a healthy objectivity.

The Red Ashtray Rule

As any psychologist will be quick to note, symbolism is an important aspect of how we interpret our lives. The way we think, the way we dream, and the way we interpret our day-to-day lives often revolves around symbols. This is also true of how we read and write literature. As a physical or material object representing something *immaterial*, such as an emotion, an idea, or a belief, a symbol can be an effective way to subtly communicate to the reader the essential themes or strategies of your creative work. Rarely is there a one-to-one relationship between the symbol and what it represents; a particular physical object often carries a complex web of associated meanings.

Similarly, simile and metaphor can enhance the impact and meaning of your work. By making a comparison between a concrete, physical object and an abstract concept, idea, or feeling, either directly (as in simile, which uses *like* or *as*), or indirectly through metaphor (which implies the connection), you can communicate feelings, emotions, and subtleties of description to the reader that otherwise might be difficult to convey. For example, note this passage from *The Great Gatsby*, where Nick Carroway is describing his impression of a summer evening: "The wind had blown off, leaving a loud, bright night, with wings beating in the trees and a persistent organ sound as the full bellows of the earth blew the frogs full of life."

Are these literary techniques that are available only to the fiction writer? Do they operate merely as "window dressing" for stories and poems? Certainly not. Use symbol and metaphor—carefully and artfully—to help convey the most essential descriptions, feelings, and images in your work. But keep a light touch. Metaphors must be original but not absurd, meaningful but subtle and simply stated. When you use symbols in your work, remember that much can be implied, particularly through repetition. If you have a red ashtray in your opening scene, for example, and it reappears on page seven and again on page twelve, by page twelve the red ashtray has become symbolic of something. Each time an object is mentioned, it attracts greater meaning. What does that red ashtray represent? That's up to you as the writer to decide and to imply through characterization, description, and nuance of language.

Chapter 6

The Nonfiction Novel

Introduction

The term *nonfiction novel* may seem like an oxymoron. How can a book be based on a real story and still be a novel, employing all the devices of fiction? In many ways, the nonfiction novel defies categorization and often arouses controversy among critics and booksellers. No other category of creative nonfiction so readily brings to mind all the ethical questions about the line between fact and imagination.

The nonfiction novel begins with an actual or "true" story or anecdote and then, through the dramatic imagination and literary skill of the writer, expands into the emotional drama and broad themes of the novel. Despite its controversy (or perhaps partially because of it), the nonfiction novel has enjoyed significant growth since the 1960s, when writers such as Truman Capote, Norman Mailer, and Tom Wolfe began to experiment with the conventional boundary between traditional journalism and fiction or imaginative writing. As in other types of creative nonfiction, however, this genre is not as "new" as it may seem. "True crime" novels and historical fiction have been two of the most popular and best-selling genres in America since the early 1900s. There is a difference, however, between historical fiction and the nonfiction novel, although many people use the terms interchangeably. As a best-selling genre in today's publishing environment, historical fiction as a marketing category generally relies less on literary style and solid research than on formulaic plotlines and stereotypic characters. The nonfiction novel is distinct in that it is based—at least loosely—on a real story; it engages the imagination of the writer and the reader; and the author takes a consciously literary approach to language.

Throughout history there have been countless narratives that begin with a "real" story and involve plot and character development that take the story beyond established fact. Readers have always enjoyed the dramatic thrill that comes from an engaging and well-told story that contains the added punch of knowing that it's all—or at least partially—true. One could even argue that *Moby Dick,* one of the greatest and most imaginative novels ever written in English, qualifies to a certain extent as a nonfiction novel. Melville's tale stems from his own experiences on the sea as well as the stories he heard others tell, and then through dramatic characterization and richly symbolic language he weaves a narrative that ultimately engages the triumphs and defeats of the human spirit. Few novels are strictly products of the imagination with no basis in fact or experience.

The nonfiction novel can be a blend of history, biography, science, politics, or memoir. A writer will often use a relatively small or local story to illuminate larger, enduring themes of the human condition. The author may be a distinct voice or character in the story, as in Melanie Thernstrom's deeply emotional elegy of her murdered best friend in *The Dead Girl,* or the author may be tacitly silent, as in Truman Capote's classic nonfiction novel *In Cold Blood.* The narrative structure can follow a traditional narrative arc involving exposition, climax, and dénouement, or it may consist of concurrent but distinct plot lines, as in Michael Cunningham's *The Hours,* based on the life of Virginia Woolf and one of her characters. Some nonfiction novels use a nonconventional or nonlinear approach and include actual or imagined letters, newspaper clippings, journal excerpts, poems, remembrances, and even photographs. A writer of a nonfiction novel combines the objective, analytical eye of the reporter or journalist with the inventiveness, creative imagination, and moral vision of the novelist. This is often reflected not only in the story but the structure of the story as well.

Critics sometimes accuse books in this category of "masquerading" as works of history, memoir, or biography, and feel that the author is taking an unethical stance toward the reader by weaving together fact and imagination. They feel that fact—solid and irrefutable—is compromised by embellishment of any sort. Many writers of nonfiction novels, perhaps weary of the fray, turn aside and say all that truly matters is a good story and how that story leads us to a greater understanding of the human spirit. Emotional drama and narrative technique must both be in service to one final goal: a story that moves the reader to a broader knowledge of ourselves and the world around us. Many readers would agree.

As you begin the research for your nonfiction novel—or the scene that may ultimately lead to a book-length work—keep all these questions in mind. What is the distinction between fiction and nonfiction? Is the only real goal to write a good story, to create a "good read"? What decisions about your story and your characters will you have to make along the way? The only person who can decide is you.

No doubt it will seem overwhelming to consider writing a narrative that may turn out to be several hundred pages long. There will be many digressions and forks in the road. You may be fifty pages into your manuscript before you discover that you need to tell the story from a different point of view. Perhaps your main character isn't the main character after all. A subplot may abruptly become the main plot. Who knows? Give yourself time and faith. Work steadily on your project, even if it's only half an hour a day. Big things happen in small steps. As you proceed, place your faith in your own sense of intuition. Be thorough and precise in your research, but depend on your own creative imagination. You have a story to tell. Now tell it.

Readings with Discussion Questions

Truman Capote
In Cold Blood

Truman Capote, born Truman Streckfus Persons in 1924 in New Orleans, Louisiana, was a flamboyant self-promoter as well as a gifted storyteller. Although his most original contribution to the literary world was his "nonfiction novel," which sought to combine the artistry of fiction with the technique of journalism, he was also a talented fiction stylist. Capote's body of work consists of novels, mystery/crime/suspense fiction, plays, screenplays, nonfiction, short stories, and film. His many awards include the O. Henry Award in 1948 for "Miriam," a National Institute of Arts and Letters creative writing award in 1959, a National Book Award nomination in 1967 for In Cold Blood, *and an Emmy Award in 1967 for the television adaptation of* A Christmas Memory.*

In Cold Blood *is Capote's nonfiction novel detailing the brutal multiple slayings of a wealthy family in a small Kansas town by two young men.*

The village of Holcomb stands on the high wheat plains of western Kansas, a lonesome area that other Kansans call "out there." Some seventy miles east of the Colorado border, the countryside, with its hard blue skies and desert-clear air, has an atmosphere that is rather more Far West than Middle West. The local accent is barbed with a prairie twang, a ranch-hand nasalness, and the men, many of them, wear narrow frontier trousers, Stetsons, and high-heeled boots with pointed toes. The land is flat, and the views are awesomely extensive; horses, herds of cattle, a white cluster of grain elevators rising as gracefully as Greek temples are visible long before a traveler reaches them.

Holcomb, too, can be seen from great distances. Not that there is much to see—simply an aimless congregation of buildings divided in the center by the main-line tracks of the Santa Fe Railroad, a haphazard hamlet bounded on the south by a brown stretch of the Arkansas (pronounced "Ar-kan-sas") River, on the north by a highway, Route 50, and on the east and west by prairie lands and wheat fields. After rain, or when snowfalls thaw, the streets, unnamed, unshaded, unpaved, turn from the thickest dust into the direst mud. At one end of the town stands a stark old stucco structure, the roof of which supports an electric sign—DANCE—but the dancing has ceased and the advertisement has been dark for several years. Nearby is another building with an irrelevant sign, this one in flaking gold on a dirty window—HOLCOMB BANK. The bank closed in 1933, and its former counting rooms have been converted into apartments. It is one of the town's two "apartment houses," the second being a ramshackle mansion known, because a good part of the local school's faculty lives there, as the Teacherage. But the majority of Holcomb's homes are one-story frame affairs, with front porches.

Down by the depot, the postmistress, a gaunt woman who wears a rawhide jacket and denims and cowboy boots, presides over a falling-apart post office. The depot itself, with its peeling sulphur-colored paint, is equally melancholy; the Chief, the Super-Chief, the El Capitan go by every day, but these celebrated expresses never pause there. No passenger trains do—only an occasional freight. Up on the highway, there are two filling stations, one of which doubles as a meagerly supplied grocery store, while the other does extra duty as a café—Hartman's Café, where Mrs. Hartman, the proprietress, dispenses sandwiches, coffee, soft drinks, and 3.2 beer. (Holcomb, like all the rest of Kansas, is "dry.")

And that, really, is all. Unless you include, as one must, the Holcomb School, a good-looking establishment, which reveals a circumstance that the appearance of the community otherwise camouflages: that the parents who send their children to this modern and ably staffed "consolidated" school—the grades go from kindergarten through senior high, and a fleet of buses transport the students, of which there are usually around three hundred and sixty, from as far as sixteen miles away—are, in general, a prosperous people. Farm ranchers, most of them, they are outdoor folk of very varied stock—German, Irish, Norwegian, Mexican, Japanese. They raise cattle and sheep, grow wheat, milo, grass seed, and sugar beets. Farming is always a chancy business, but in western Kansas its practitioners consider themselves "born gamblers," for they must contend with an extremely shallow precipitation (the annual average is eighteen inches) and anguishing irrigation problems. However, the last seven years have been years of droughtless beneficence. The farm ranchers in Finney County, of which Holcomb is a part, have done well; money has been made not from farming alone but also from the exploitation of plentiful natural-gas resources, and its acquisition is reflected in the new school, the comfortable interiors of the farmhouses, the steep and swollen grain elevators.

Until one morning in mid-November of 1959, few Americans—in fact, few Kansans—had ever heard of Holcomb. Like the waters of the river, like the motorists on the highway, and like the yellow trains streaking down the Santa Fe tracks, drama, in the shape of exceptional happenings, had never stopped there. The inhabitants of the village, numbering two hundred and seventy, were satisfied that this should be so, quite content to exist inside ordinary life—to work, to hunt, to watch television, to attend school socials, choir practice, meetings of the 4-H Club. But then, in the earliest hours of that morning in November, a Sunday morning, certain foreign sounds impinged on the normal nightly Holcomb noises—on the keening hysteria of coyotes, the dry scrape of scuttling tumbleweed, the racing, receding wail of locomotive whistles. At the time not a soul in sleeping Holcomb heard them—four shotgun blasts that, all told, ended six human lives. But afterward the townspeople, theretofore sufficiently unfearful of each other to seldom trouble to lock their doors, found fantasy re-creating them over and again—those somber explosions that stimulated fires of mistrust in the glare of which many old neighbors viewed each other strangely, and as strangers. . . .

The two young men had little in common, but they did not realize it, for they shared a number of surface traits. Both, for example, were fastidious, very attentive to hygiene and the condition of their fingernails. After their grease-monkey morning, they spent the better part of an hour sprucing up in the lavatory of the garage. Dick stripped to his briefs was not quite the same as Dick fully clothed. In the latter state, he seemed a flimsy dingy-blond youth of medium height, fleshless and perhaps sunken-chested; dis-robing revealed that he was nothing of the sort, but, rather, an athlete constructed on a welterweight scale. The tattooed face of a cat, blue and grinning, covered his right hand; on one shoulder a blue rose blossomed. More markings, self-designed and self-executed, ornamented his arms and torso: the head of a dragon with a human skull between its open jaws; bosomy nudes; a gremlin brandishing a pitchfork; the word PEACE accom-panied by a cross radiating, in the form of crude strokes, rays of holy light; and two sentimental concoctions—one a bouquet of flowers dedicated to MOTHER-DAD, the other a heart that celebrated the romance of DICK and CAROL, the girl whom he had married when he was nineteen, and from whom he had separated six years later in order to "do the right thing" by another young lady, the mother of his youngest child. ("I have three boys who I will definitely take care of," he had written in applying for parole. "My wife is remarried. I have been married twice, only I don't want any-thing to do with my second wife.")

But neither Dick's physique nor the inky gallery adorning it made as remarkable an impression as his face, which seemed composed of mis-matching parts. It was as though his head had been halved like an apple, then put together a fraction off center. Something of the kind had happened; the imperfectly aligned features were the outcome of a car collision in 1950—an accident that left his long-jawed and narrow face tilted, the left side rather lower than the right, with the results that the lips were slightly aslant, the nose askew, and his eyes not only situated at uneven levels but of uneven size, the left eye being truly serpentine, with a venomous, sickly-blue squint that although it was involuntarily acquired, seemed neverthe-less to warn of bitter sediment at the bottom of his nature. But Perry had told him, "The eye doesn't matter. Because you have a wonderful smile. One of those smiles that really work." It was true that the tightening action of a smile contracted his face into its correct proportions, and made it possible to discern a less unnerving personality—an American-style "good kid" with an outgrown crew cut, sane enough but not too bright. (Actually, he was very intelligent. An I.Q. test taken in prison gave him a rating of 130; the average subject, in prison or out, scores between 90 and 110.)

Perry, too, had been maimed, and his injuries, received in a motorcycle wreck, were severer than Dick's; he had spent half a year in a State of Washington hospital and another six months on crutches, and though the accident had occurred in 1952, his chunky, dwarfish legs, broken in five places and pitifully scarred, still pained him so severely that he had become an aspirin addict. While he had fewer tattoos than his companion, they were more elaborate—not the self-inflicted work of an amateur but epics of the art contrived by Honolulu and Yokohama masters. COOKIE, the name of a nurse who had been friendly to him when he was hospitalized, was tattooed on his right biceps. Blue-furred, orange-eyed, red-fanged, a tiger snarled upon his left biceps; a spitting snake, coiled around a dagger, slithered down his arm; and elsewhere skulls gleamed, a tombstone loomed, a chrysanthemum flourished.

"O.K., beauty. Put away the comb," said Dick, dressed now and ready to go. Having discarded his work uniform, he wore gray khakis, a matching shirt, and, like Perry, ankle-high black boots. Perry, who could never find trousers to fit his truncated lower half, wore blue jeans rolled up at the bottom and a leather windbreaker. Scrubbed, combed, as tidy as two dudes setting off on a double date, they went out to the car.

Questions for Discussion

1. Is Capote writing primarily from fact or from imagination?
2. What components of fiction writing can you identify in this excerpt?
3. This book was quite controversial when it was first published in 1965. Do you find anything controversial in Capote's style or approach? What recent authors have engaged some of this same controversy?

Russell Banks
Cloudsplitter

Russell Banks was born in 1940 in Newton, Massachussetts. A native New Englander, he draws upon his own experience of small town life affected by the economic decline in the Northeast. Banks is a contributor to numerous periodicals including the New York

Times Book Review, *the* American Review, *and* Vanity Fair, *and he is the coeditor of* Lillabulero. *He received National Endowment for the Arts Fellowships in 1977 and 1983, and has been awarded the American Academy and Institute of Arts and Letters Award for works of distinction in 1986, and an O. Henry Memorial Award.*

   In Cloudsplitter, *Banks tells the story of radical abolitionist John Brown and his son Owen. The acclaim and controversy around this book represent some of the ungoing discussion among writers, critics, and readers regarding how much creative license a writer should take in the presentation of real, historical characters.*

There is yet a further reason, I suddenly realize, for my having called you back, and I must attempt to confess it, painful as it is to admit, even to myself.

   I am dying. Or I am already dead and have been dead these forty years, with nothing left of me, who once was Owen Brown, except a shadow cast on the near wall by my lamplight and these words tumbling from me like a death rattle, a last, prolonged exhalation. Absurd as it may sound to you who read these words, it is to me the literal truth. I am more the ghost of Owen Brown than I am the man himself.

   Although I was but thirty-five years old in '59 and escaped from Harpers Ferry like a rabbit through the corn and ended up safe here on my western mountaintop, my life since that day has been an after-life. In recent years, as I have grown into an old man, there have been dozens, perhaps hundreds, of mornings when I have wakened in my cold cabin with my lungs flooded and, before the sun has dried the dew off the window pane, have concluded that sometime during the night I finally died. But then hunger or some other bodily need or the animals—my dog scratching at the door, the sheep bleating, the cry of a hawk—bring me back to the sad awareness that, no, I have not died, not yet, and thus am obliged once more to grope through the gray veils that wrap me and come to full wakefulness and begin again the daily rounds of a man alive.

   Until the night that followed your arrival at my door, however, when I must indeed have gone deeper into the embrace of death than ever before. So that when in the morning I finally woke, if waking it truly was, I knew beyond all doubt that I am now he who was Owen Brown. Not he who *is* Owen Brown. Not that crotchety old man you met growling at you like a bear in its cave, but his past, his childhood and youth and his young manhood, that's who I am. It was as if your visit had sounded a final knell that drove me into a purgatory which I had been longing for all these years but had neither the courage nor the wisdom to seek on my own. As if, now that I am here, there is no going forward or back, no possible ascent to heaven or descent to hell, until I have told my story.

Thus these words, these letters, and the packets of materials which in time I will turn over to you. All my worldly effects, as it were, I bequeath to thee. Make of them, you and your professor, whatever you will. In the long, ongoing War Between the Races, this, I suppose, must be my final act, and I pray only that, before I am in error judged good, if cowardly, and my father mad, if courageous, I be given the time to complete it.

It is all very strange. Now that I have opened communications with you, I find myself unable to keep my inner voice silent. I have given off all work— my sheep and the spring lambs wander the grassy hills unaccompanied in search of water and pasturage, protected only by my faithful little dog, Flossie, who returns from the herd every few hours to the cabin door and scratches and whines outside, as if angered by my protracted absence and intent on rousing me from an inexplicable sleep.

But I am not asleep. I do now and then drift towards a dozing state, but I am driven back from it each time by the rising sound of my voice, as if it, too, has a will of its own and, like Flossie, does not want me to sleep. Whether I am seated at my table, as now, writing the words down, or in my chair in the darkness by the window with the silvery moonlight falling across my lap, or lying in my cot by the back wall staring at the low ceiling all night long and into the next day, my ears are filled always with my own voice. The words are like water in a brook that bubbles from an underground spring and spills downhill across rocks and fallen trees to where it gathers in eddies and builds a dark, still pool, moving me finally to rise from my cot and sit down at my table and begin again to write them down, my purpose being merely to break the little dam or jam and release the pressure against it and let the flow of words resume.

It is more than passing strange. And joyous, somehow. I see where I am, and yet it is as if I who was Owen Brown have flown from my mountaintop. I have today been recalling an earlier, my first, departure from this place and its similarity to this day's dying—although that was literal and this, of course, is merely figurative. Then, just as now, what a strange joy I felt! It was a full decade ago, in the spring of '89, and I had been lingering alone on this high, treeless hill for close to thirty years, waiting for the moment of my death to finish its last flash through my weary body, biding my time, helpless and silent as smoke and with all the patience of the long-dead. I was waiting, silently waiting, not so much for my actual death, which meant little to me, one way or the other, as for the pine box that contained my bones to be carried three thousand miles from the hills of California back along the railroad lines to my family's house and farm in the Adirondack mountain village of North Elba, New York. To the place that, because of the Negroes living there, we called Timbuctoo.

A letter from a distinguished woman in the East who had long honored Father's deeds had arrived at my door, just as you arrived in person last week. It informed me, not of the needs of an illustrious biographer, as you did, but of the coming re-interment of the last of the bodies of those who had fallen with Father at Harpers Ferry. The letter invited me to attend the ceremonies, which were to be held on the upcoming ninth of May, Father's birthday, at his gravesite, where my brothers' and companions' old bones, gathered from shallow graves in Virginia and elsewhere across the country, were at last to join his.

Until that cold morning, for the thirty long years since the end came at Harpers Ferry, I had hoped for no other event, for no additional particularity of circumstance, than that *my* poor bones, too, *my* remains, at last be interred there. With or without some slight ceremony, it did not matter a whit to me—so long as they were deposited in my family's yard in the plot of hard, dark, and stony ground that surrounded the huge, gray boulder in the meadow before the house. For those many years, I had been waiting for nothing but the fit and proper burial of my crumbling, shrouded old corpse in that precious dirt alongside the bodies of my father, John Brown, and my brothers Watson and Oliver, and my companions in arms who had fought beside me in the Kansas wars or were cut to pieces in the raid on Harpers Ferry or were executed on the scaffold afterwards.

All those moldering bodies! All those yellowed, long bones and grimacing skulls carted in boxes unearthed from shallow graves and buried there alongside one another! And now mine also!

But, no, not yet. I wrote back at once, saying only that I would not come, giving no excuse and explaining nothing. I was still very much alive, and silence and solitude had to remain my penance and my solace. I would not, I could not, give them up.

But then, one morning shortly after my curt note had been posted, I woke in my cot and, as I have said, believed that, finally, I, too, had died. Soon, of course, and as afterwards became usual, I saw that sadly I was not dead yet. I was still he who *is* Owen Brown, he whose dog wakes him and brings him shuffling to the door, he who releases his herd of merinos from the fold into the sloping meadow below, then returns to his cabin and washes his face in cold water and commences living another silent, solitary day.

Was it, in hopes that I was wrong, an attempt to test my reluctantly drawn conclusion that I had not died yet—as perhaps I do here now, writing these words to you ten years later? Was it an attempt to accomplish in life some new arrangement for my death? I cannot say why now and could not then, but that very day I decided to depart from this mountain for a while and return finally to our old family home in the Adirondacks, where my only proper grave lies even today. I arranged for the care of my sheep and my dog with a neighbor in the valley and departed straightway for the East.

Questions for Discussion

1. Describe the point of view in this story. How does Banks handle "narrative distance"—that is, how close the reader feels to the narrator? How would you describe the tone of the narrator's voice?
2. Does Banks attempt to imitate or recreate the subtleties and nuances of voice in the character of Owen Brown? Does it sound and feel authentic?
3. How does the author incorporate details of the historical context of this story? What historical details bring the story to life?

Anchee Min
Becoming Madame Mao

Anchee Min was born in 1957 in Shanghai, China. At seventeen, Min was sent to a Communist labor farm, where she was recruited for the lead role in Madame Mao's propaganda films. After the death of Chairman Mao and the false denunciation and ensuing execution of Madame Mao for his murder, Min served another labor sentence that lasted eight years. In 1984, she fled to the United States. Her memoir, Red Azalea, *received a New York Times* Notable Book *award in 1994 and was an international bestseller.*

In Becoming Madame Mao *Min draws Madame Mao, a largely unsympathetic character, as humanely as possible while attempting to relate accurately her complexity and cruelty.*

Prologue

What does history recognize? A dish made of a hundred sparrows—a plate of mouths.

Fourteen years since her arrest. 1991. Madame Mao Jiang Ching is seventy-seven years old. She is on the death seat. The only reason the authorities keep postponing the execution is their hope of her repentance.

Well, I won't surrender. When I was a child my mother used to tell me that I should think of myself as grass—born to be stepped on. But I think of myself as a peacock among hens. I am not being judged fairly. Side by side Mao Tse-tung and I stood, yet he is considered a god while I am a demon. Mao Tse-tung and I were married for thirty-eight years. The number is thirty-eight.

I speak to my daughter Nah. I ask her to be my biographer. She is allowed to visit me once a month. She wears a peasant woman's hairstyle—a wok-lid-cut around the ears—and she is in a man's suit. She looks unbearably silly. She does that to hurt my eyes. She was divorced and remarried and now lives in Beijing. She has a son to whom my identity has been a secret.

No, Mother. The tone is firm and stubborn.

I can't describe my disappointment. I have expectations of Nah. Too many perhaps. Maybe that's what killed her spirit. Am I different from my mother who wanted the best for me by binding my feet? Nah picks what I dislike and drops what I like. It's been that way since she saw how her father treated me. How can one not wet one's shoes when walking along the seashore all the time? Nah doesn't see the whole picture. She doesn't know how her father once worshiped me. She can't imagine that I was Mao's sunshine. I don't blame her. There was no trace of that passion left on Mao's face after he entered the Forbidden City and became a modern emperor. No trace that Mao and I were once lovers unto death.

The mother tells the daughter that both her father and she hate cowards. The words have no effect. Nah is too beaten. The mother thinks of her as a rotten piece of wood that can never be made into a beautiful piece of furniture. She is so afraid that her voice trembles when she speaks. The mother can't recognize any part of herself in the daughter.

The mother repeats the ancient story of Cima-Qinhua, the brave girl who saved her mother from a bloody riot. The model of piety. Nah listens but makes no response. Then she cries and says that she is not the mother. Can't do the things she does. And should not be requested to perform an impossible task.

Can't you lift a finger? the mother yells. It's my last wish, for heaven's sake!

Save me, Nah. Any day a bullet will be put into my head. Can you picture it? Don't you see that there has been a conspiracy against me? Do you remember the morning when Deng Xiao-ping came to your father's funeral and what he did? He just brushed fingers with me—didn't even bother to shake my hand. It was as if he questioned that I was Mao's widow. He was aware of the cameras— he purposely let the journalists catch the scene. And the other one, Marshal Ye Jian-ying. He walked past me wearing an expression as if I had murdered the Chairman myself!

Your father warned me about his comrades. But he didn't do anything to protect me. He could be heartless. His face had a vindictive glow when he made that prediction. He was jealous that I got to go on living. He would have liked to see me buried with him, like the old emperors did with their concubines. One should never have delusions about your father. It took me thirty-eight years to figure out that sly fox. He could never keep his hands away from deception. He couldn't survive a day without trickery. I had seen ghosts in his eyes stretching out their claws. A living god. The omniscient Mao. Full-of-mice-shit.

You are a historian, Nah. You should document my role in the revolution. I want you to demonstrate my sacrifices and contributions. Yes, you can do it. Forget about what your father will think about you. He is dead. I wonder what's happened to his ghost. I wonder if it rests in its grave. Watch out for his shadow.

The hands to strangle me are creeping up fast. I can feel them at my throat. That's why I am telling you this. I am not afraid of death if I know my spirit will live through the tip of your fountain pen to the lips of the people, generations to come. Tell the world the story of a heroine. If you can't print your manuscript in China, take it outside. Don't let me down. Please.

You are not a heroine, Mother! I hear my daughter fire back. You are a miserable, mad and sick woman. You can't stop spreading your disease. Like Father said, you have dug so many graves that you don't have enough bodies to lay in them!

Their dinner has turned cold. Nah stands up and kicks away her chair. Her elbow accidentally hits the table. A dish falls. Breaks. Pieces of ceramics scatter on the floor. Grease splatters on the mother's shoe. You have killed me, Nah. Madame Mao suddenly feels short of breath. Her hand grips the edge of the table to prevent herself from falling.

Pretend that you never had me, Mother.

You can't disown your mother!

Well, all my hope is gone. I am exhausted and ready to exit the stage for good. The last curtain time will be tomorrow morning at five-thirty when the guards change shift. They are usually dull at that time. The old guard will be yawning his way out while the new guard yawns his way in.

It's dark outside. A beautiful black night without stars. The prison officials have put me on a suicide watch. But they cannot beat my will. I have saved enough handkerchiefs and socks to make a rope.

The rubber walls emit a terrible smell. But all is fine with me now. Tomorrow you will read about me in the news: Madame Mao Jiang Ching committed suicide by hanging. The day to mark is May 14, 1991. Am I sad? Not really. I have lived an extraordinary life. The great moments . . . Now as I think about them for the last time, they still make my heart hammer with excitement . . .

1

She learns pain early. When she is four, her mother comes to bind her feet. The mother tells the child that she cannot afford to wait any longer. She promises that afterwards, after the pain, the girl will be beautiful. She will get to marry into a rich family where she doesn't have to walk but will be carried around in a sedan chair. The three-inch lotus feet are a symbol of prestige and class.

The girl is curious. She sits on a stool barefoot. She plays with the pile of cloth with her toes, picks up a strip, then drops it. Mother is stirring a jar of sticky rice porridge. The girl learns that the porridge will be used as glue. Good glue, strong, won't tear, Mother says. It seals out the air. The ancient mummies were preserved in the same way. The mother is in her late twenties. She is a pretty woman, long slanting almond-shaped eyes, which the girl inherited. The mother hardly smiles. She describes herself as a radish pickled in the sauce of misery. The girl is used to her mother's sadness, to her silence during family meals. And she is used to her own position—the last concubine's daughter, the most distant relative the family considers. Her father was sixty years old when she was born. He has been a stranger to her.

The mother's hair is lacquer black, wrapped in a bun and fixed with a bamboo pin. She asks the girl to sit still as she begins. She looks solemn as if she is in front of an altar. She takes the girl's right foot, washes it and wipes it dry with her blouse. She doesn't tell the girl that this is the last time she will see her feet as she knows them. The mother doesn't tell her that by the time her feet are released they will look like triangle-shaped rice cakes with toenails curled under the sole. The mother tries to concentrate on the girl's future. A future that will be better than her own.

The mother begins wrapping. The girl watches with interest. The mother applies the paste in between each layer of cloth. It is a summer noon. Outside the window are climbing little bell flowers, small and red like dripping blood. The girl sees herself, her feet being bound, in her mother's dressing mirror. Also in the frame, a delicately carved ancient vase on the table with a bunch of fresh jasmine in it. The scent is strong. The pendulum of an old clock on the wall swings with a rustic sound. The house is quiet. The other concubines are napping and the servants are sitting in the kitchen quietly peeling beans.

Sweat gathers on her mother's forehead and begins to drip like broken beads down her cheeks. The girl asks if her mother should take a break. The woman shakes her head and says that she is finishing the task. The girl looks at her feet. They are as thick as elephant legs. The girl finds it amusing. She moves her toes inside the cocoon. Is that it? she asks. When her mother moves away the jar, the girl jumps on the floor and plays.

Stay in bed from now on, her mother says, the pain will take a while.

The girl has no trouble until the third week. She is already tired with her elephant legs and now comes the pain. Her toes scream for space. Her mother is near her. She is there to prevent the girl from tearing off the strips. She guards the elephant legs as if guarding the girl's future. She keeps explaining to the crying girl why she has to endure the pain. Then it becomes too much. The girl's feet are infected. The mother's tears pour. No, no, no, don't touch them. She insists, cries, curses. Herself. Men. She asks why she didn't have a son. Again and again she tells the girl that females are like grass, born to be stepped on.

The year is 1919. Shan-dong Province, China. The town is the birthplace of Confucius. It is called Zhu. The ancient walls and gates stand high. From the girl's window the hills are like giant turtles crawling along the edge of the earth. The Yellow River runs through the town and its murky waters make their way lazily to the sea. The coast cities and provinces have been occupied by foreign forces—first the Germans and now the Japanese—since China lost the Opium War in 1858. China is collapsing and no one pays attention to the girl's cries.

The girl is never able to forget the pain, even when she becomes Madame Mao, the most powerful woman in China during the late 1960s and '70s. She recalls the pain as "evidence of the crimes of feudalism" and she expresses her outrage in a series of operas and ballets, *The Women of the Red Detachment* and *The White-Haired Girl,* among many others. She makes the billion population share her pain.

To understand the pain is to understand what the proletariat went through during the old society, she cries at a public rally. It is to understand the necessity of Communism! She believes the pain she suffered gives her the right to lead the nation. It's the kind of pain that shoots through your core, she tells the actress who plays the lead in her opera. You can't land on your toes and you can't fly either. You are trapped, chained down. There is an invisible saw. You are toeless. Your breath dies out. The whole house hears you but there is no rescue.

She remembers her fight with the pain vividly. A heroine of the real-life stage. Ripping the foot-binding cloths is her debut.

If there is no rebellion, there is no survival! she shouts at rallies during the Cultural Revolution.

My mother is shocked the moment I throw the smelly binding strips in front of her and show her my feet. They are blue and yellow, swelling and dripping with pus. A couple of flies land on the strips. The pile looks like a dead hundred-footed-octopus monster. I say to my mother, If you try to put my feet back in the wrap I shall kill myself. I mean it. I have already found a place for myself to lie. It will be in Confucius's temple. I like the couplet on its gate:

> The temple has no monk
> So the floor will be swept by the wind
> The temple has no candles
> So the light will be lit by the moon

You need to have the lotus feet, my mother cries. You are not made to labor.

Afterwards my mother quits. I wonder if she already knows that she will need me to run with her one day.

The girl's memory of her father is that he lives on liquor and is violent. Both her mother and she fear him. He hits them. There is no way to predict when his temper will rise. Each time it shocks the soul out of the girl.

He is not a poor man. Madame Mao doesn't tell the truth later when she wants to impress her fellow countrymen. She describes him as a proletarian. In fact he is a well-to-do businessman, the town carpenter and owner of a wood shop. He has four full-time workers. Two of them are blind. He uses them to sand wood. The family has food on the table and the girl goes to school.

I never understand why my father beats my mother. There never really is a reason. Nobody in the house interferes. All the wives hear the beating. All my stepbrothers and -sisters witness the act. Yet no one utters a word. If my father is not pleased with my mother, he comes to her room, takes off his shoe and starts hitting her. Concubines are bought slaves and bedmaids, but I wonder if my father's true anger is because my mother didn't produce a son for him.

This is how her father plants the seed of worthlessness in her. It is something she lives with. The moment she begins remembering how she was brought up, she experiences a rage that bursts at its own time and pace. Like the flood of the Yellow River, it comes and crashes in big waves. Its violence changes the landscape of her being. The rage gets worse as she ages. It becomes a kept beast. It breathes and grows underground while consuming her. Its constant presence makes her feel worthless. Her desire to fight it, to prove that it does not exist, lies behind her every action.

It is my nature to rebel against oppressors. When my mother tells me to learn to "eat a meatball made of your own tongue," and "hide your broken arm inside your sleeve," I fight without ever considering the consequences.

In frustration Mother hits me. She hits me with a broom. She is scared of my nature. She thinks that I will be killed like the young revolutionaries whose heads are hung on flagpoles on top of the town gate. They were slaughtered by the authorities.

Mother scolds me, calls me a *mu-yu*—a monk's chanting tool—made to be hit all the time. But I can't be set right. It is always afterwards, after she has exhausted herself from hitting me, that she breaks down and sobs. She calls herself an unfit mother and is sure that she will end up being punished in her next life. She will be made into a most unfortunate animal, a cow who when alive bears heavy burdens and when dies is eaten, its skin made into jackets and its horns into medicine.

Every time I see Mother's tear-stained face I age. I feel white hair sprouting out of my head. I am sick of seeing Mother tortured. I often wish that she were dead so she would be released from having to take care of me.

But the mother goes on living, for her, the daughter she wishes were a son. This is how misery permeates the girl's soul. Most of her life she can't be satisfied with who she is. The irony is that she truly wishes to satisfy her mother's wish. This is how she begins her acting career. Very young. In her own house. She slips into roles. When she thinks that she is not who she is, she becomes relaxed and fear free. She is in a safe place where her father's terror can no longer reach and her mother's tears can no longer wash her away.

Later on it becomes clear that Madame Mao doesn't forgive. She believes that one must collect the debts owed to one. She has little desire to understand forgiveness. Revenge, on the other hand, she understands. She understands it in the most savage way. In her life, she never hesitates to order her enemies' complete elimination. She does it naturally. It is a practice she started as a young girl.

Questions for Discussion

1. This novel frequently switches point of view. Describe the points of view represented in this excerpt. When does the author decide to switch? Why? How does this strategy affect the overall story?
2. How does Min enter into the personal, psychological world of Madame Mao? Does this approach make her more or less sympathetic as a historical figure?
3. The author often uses italics. What is the effect of this with respect to tone and structure?

Michael Cunningham
The Hours

Pulitzer Prize winner Michael Cunningham was born in Cincinnati, Ohio in 1952, grew up in Pasadena, California, and currently lives in New York City. After completing a bachelor of arts degree in English literature at Stanford University, he went on to receive his master of fine arts degree from the University of Iowa. Cunningham's literary awards include a Michener Fellowship from the University of Iowa in 1982 and a National Endowment for the Arts Fellowship in 1988. His book The Hours *won a PEN/Faulkner Award and the Pulitzer Prize and was recently made into a film. His work has appeared in* Redbook, Esquire, The Paris Review, *the* Atlantic Monthly, *and* The New Yorker.

In The Hours, *Cunningham juxtaposes the lives of two women, one contemporary, one in the 1940s, with that of Virginia Woolf, paralleling their personal and creative struggles with the demands of friends, family, and lovers.*

Prologue

She hurries from the house, wearing a coat too heavy for the weather. It is 1941. Another war has begun. She has left a note for Leonard, and another for Vanessa. She walks purposefully toward the river, certain of what she'll do, but even now she is almost distracted by the sight of the downs, the church, and a scattering of sheep, incandescent, tinged with a faint hint of sulfur, grazing under a darkening sky. She pauses, watching the sheep and the sky, then walks on. The voices murmur behind her; bombers drone in the sky, though she looks for the planes and can't see them. She walks past one of the farm workers (is his name John?), a robust, small-headed man wearing a potato-colored vest, cleaning the ditch that runs through the osier bed. He looks up at her, nods, looks down again into the brown water. As she passes him on her way to the river she thinks of how successful he is, how fortunate, to be cleaning a ditch in an osier bed. She herself has failed. She is not a writer at all, really; she is merely a gifted eccentric. Patches of sky shine in puddles left over from last night's rain. Her shoes sink slightly into the soft earth. She has failed, and now the voices are back, muttering indistinctly just beyond the range of her vision, behind her, here, no, turn and they've gone somewhere else. The voices are back and the headache is approaching as surely as rain, the headache that will crush whatever is she and replace her with itself. The headache is approaching and it seems (is she or is she not conjuring them herself?) that the bombers have appeared again in the sky. She reaches the embankment, climbs over and down again to the river. There's a fisherman upriver, far away, he won't notice her, will he? She begins searching for a stone. She works quickly but methodically, as if she were following a recipe that must be obeyed scrupulously if it's to succeed at all. She selects one roughly the size and shape of a pig's skull. Even as she lifts it and forces it into one of the pockets of her coat (the fur collar tickles her neck), she can't help noticing the stone's cold chalkiness and its color, a milky brown with spots of green. She stands close to the edge of the river, which laps against the bank, filling the small irregularities in the mud with clear water that might be a different substance altogether from the yellow-brown, dappled stuff, solid-looking as a road, that extends so steadily from bank to bank. She steps forward. She does not remove her shoes. The water is cold, but not unbearably so. She pauses, standing in cold water up to her knees. She thinks of Leonard. She thinks of his hands and his beard, the deep lines around his mouth. She thinks of Vanessa, of the children, of Vita and Ethel: So many. They have all failed, haven't they? She is suddenly, immensely sorry for them. She imagines turning around, taking the stone out of her pocket, going back to the house. She could probably return in time to destroy the notes. She could live on; she could perform that final kindness. Standing knee-deep in the moving water, she decides against it. The voices are here, the headache is coming, and if she restores herself to the care of Leonard and Vanessa they won't let her go again, will they? She decides to insist that they let her go. She wades awkwardly (the bottom is mucky) out until she is up to her waist. She glances upriver at the fisherman, who is wearing a red jacket and who does not see her. The yellow surface of the river (more yellow than brown when seen this close) murkily reflects the sky. Here, then, is the last moment of true perception, a man fishing in a red jacket and a cloudy sky reflected on opaque water. Almost involuntarily (it feels involuntary, to her) she steps or stumbles forward, and the stone pulls her in. For a moment, still, it seems like nothing; it seems like another failure; just chill water she can easily swim back out of; but then the current wraps itself around her and takes her with such sudden, muscular force it feels as if a strong man has risen from the bottom, grabbed her legs and held them to his chest. It feels personal.

More than an hour later, her husband returns from the garden. "Madame went out," the maid says, plumping a shabby pillow that releases a miniature storm of down. "She said she'd be back soon."

Leonard goes upstairs to the sitting room to listen to the news. He finds a blue envelope, addressed to him, on the table. Inside is a letter.

Dearest,
I feel certain that I am going
mad again: I feel we can't go
through another of these terrible times.
And I shant recover this time. I begin
to hear voices, and cant concentrate.
So I am doing what seems the best thing to do. You have
given me
the greatest possible happiness. You
have been in every way all that anyone
could be. I dont think two
people could have been happier till
this terrible disease came. I cant
fight it any longer, I know that I am
spoiling your life, that without me you
could work. And you will I know.
You see I cant even write this properly. I
cant read. What I want to say is that
I owe all the happiness of my life to you.
You have been entirely patient with me &
incredibly good. I want to say that—
everybody knows it. If anybody could
have saved me it would have been you.
Everything has gone from me but the
certainty of your goodness. I

cant go on spoiling your life any longer. I dont think two
people
could have been happier than we have been.

V.

Leonard races from the room, runs downstairs. He says to the maid, "I think
something has happened to Mrs. Woolf. I think she may have tried to kill
herself. Which way did she go? Did you see her leave the house?"

The maid, panicked, begins to cry. Leonard rushes out and goes to the
river, past the church and the sheep, past the osier bed. At the riverbank he
finds no one but a man in a red jacket, fishing.

She is borne quickly along by the current. She appears to be flying, a fantastic figure, arms outstretched, hair streaming, the tail of the fur coat billow-
ing behind. She floats, heavily, through shafts of brown, granular light. She
does not travel far. Her feet (the shoes are gone) strike the bottom occasionally, and when they do they summon up a sluggish cloud of muck, filled
with the black silhouettes of leaf skeletons, that stands all but stationary in
the water after she has passed along out of sight. Stripes of green-black
weed catch in her hair and the fur of her coat, and for a while her eyes are
blindfolded by a thick swatch of weed, which finally loosens itself and
floats, twisting and untwisting and twisting again.

She comes to rest, eventually, against one of the pilings of the bridge at
Southease. The current presses her, worries her, but she is firmly positioned
at the base of the squat, square column, with her back to the river and her
face against the stone. She curls there with one arm folded against her chest
and the other afloat over the rise of her hip. Some distance above her is the
bright, rippled surface. The sky reflects unsteadily there, white and heavy
with clouds, traversed by the black cutout shapes of rooks. Cars and trucks
rumble over the bridge. A small boy, no older than three, crossing the bridge
with his mother, stops at the rail, crouches, and pushes the stick he's been
carrying between the slats of the railing so it will fall into the water. His
mother urges him along but he insists on staying awhile, watching the stick
as the current takes it.

Here they are, on a day early in the Second World War: the boy and his
mother on the bridge, the stick floating over the water's surface, and Virginia's body at the river's bottom, as if she is dreaming of the surface, the
stick, the boy and his mother, the sky and the rooks. An olive-drab truck
rolls across the bridge, loaded with soldiers in uniform, who wave to the
boy who has just thrown the stick. He waves back. He demands that his
mother pick him up so he can see the soldiers better; so he will be more visible to them. All this enters the bridge, resounds through its wood and stone,
and enters Virginia's body. Her face, pressed sideways to the piling, absorbs
it all: the truck and the soldiers, the mother and the child.

Questions for Discussion

1. How does Cunningham reflect the thoughts and emotions of Virginia Woolf? Is this approach historical or purely creative?
2. How would you describe the tone and mood of this excerpt? What is Cunningham's attitude toward his subject?
3. Does this novel fit into the category of the nonfiction novel? Why or why not?

Student Writing

Real vs. Imaginary Worlds

These authors are carefully constructing fictional worlds based on real historical characters and incidents. Does this work seem different from the student work in other chapters of this book? How?

Robert F. James
Rossiya East

Robert James, profiled earlier in this textbook, is currently pursuing a master of fine arts degree in Creative Writing. His novel-in-progress, Rossiya East, *earned him a 2002–2003 John Steinbeck Fellowship of Creative Writing at San Jose State University.*

The author writes, "This excerpt is from Rossiya East, *an historical novel in progress. The book explores the Russian-American Company, Russia's fur-trading monopoly in the early 1800s, and the men who pioneered Russia's eastward expansion from Siberia, through Alyeshka (Alaska), to the northern coast of California. The majority of the characters in the book, as well as the events portrayed, are historically accurate, with fictional characters used to help tie the narrative together.*

"The greatest challenge to the historical or nonfiction novel is taking relatively static events or plot points and giving them life in a believable fashion. This excerpt, for instance, deals with the Russian's first arrival at The Presidio in Spanish California in 1806. Detailed accounts of this arrival and subsequent events do not exist. All that is known from historical documents is that on April 6, 1806, a group of scurvy-ridden Russian hunters aboard the Juno, *led by Nikolai Resanov, Court Chamberlain to Tsar Paul and the antagonist of the novel, arrived in California to strike a deal with the Spanish. At the time, the Spanish did not allow trade with foreign governments. The Russians, using General Arguello's absence in Monterey to their advantage, managed to anchor and, for six weeks, worked to win over the local population and the priesthood. General Arguello's 15-year-old daughter, Concepcion, fell in love with Resanov, and by the time the General returned to The Presidio, his hands were somewhat tied and a deal was struck with the Russians. The supplies garnered through the agreement saved the Russian settlement at New*

Archangel, Alyeshka, and provided an impetus for further eastward expansion and eventual settlement at Ft. Ross, California; what the Russians called the New Albion Coast.

"What follows, then, is my interpretation of how these events might have taken place. The Spanish officers depicted in the narrative are fictional; all other characters, in name and in spirit, are historically accurate to the best of my knowledge."

2.

April 6, 1806
The Presidio, Spanish California

Scurvy is a debilitating disease. Seamen, like those crewing the *Juno* as it neared the Spanish American coastline, were especially susceptible. In its beginning stages, as was the case with Resanov and the officers of his ship, the disease is a painful annoyance, beginning with fatigue, joint pain, bleeding gums and misshapen hairs corkscrewing from bleeding follicles. In its later stages, after continuing unchecked for a period of four to five months, scurvy claims the use of the victim's extremities: joints swell and blacken; teeth fall out from the deterioration of dentin; gums become the consistency of oozing jelly, making eating a painful and futile endeavor; chronic fatigue relegates the sailor to his hammock where, hanging his head over the side to allow the seeping blood to flow out of the mouth to prevent swallowing it, the man succumbs to the illness.

The Russian crew was beset by the beginning stages of the disease. Even Resanov was not immune. A handful of men had been placed on limited duty and moved to the forward compartments to live in what had become a makeshift sickbay. Having sailed with low rations, however, and because of Resanov's insistence on making good time, the Juno's crew entered the San Francisco Bay scurvy-ridden and largely useless.

"Do you have a plan?" Balikov had asked as the coastline came into view.

"Just sail, Captain," Resanov had said.

Balikov had given a quiet smile, himself less afflicted than the majority of the sailors because of his strict policy of eating as little of the dried seal meat as possible and making sure that he drank tea at least twice a day.

"And if the Spanish hold to their policy of firing on unexpected guests?"

"We'll deal with it when the time comes, Captain. I for one, however, don't think we'll have any trouble. If there's one thing I know, it's how to make an entrance."

Resanov devised a plan to sail into the bay under a flag of truce, the crew and officers of the ship manning the rails, singing. Balikov had laughed at the idea of singing songs as they passed under the Spanish guns, but Resanov had impressed upon him the importance of appearances.

Resanov swore that bleeding gums and corkscrew hairs would not prevent him from cutting the impressive figure he had in mind. He buttoned the brass fasteners on his royal-blue suit, affixed his sash and medals, then took up a position at the ship's bow, his hands on his hips, his lips stretched smiling over his bleeding gums. Russian voices swelled around him, the songs of the Volga swelling the crew's spirits if not their bodies.

"Well, Captain," he said. "At the very least, we'll be dramatic."

3.

"Senorita, please. It's time to turn back." Lieutenant Echeverria was, by all accounts, a simple and pleasant man. Since acquiring the task of escorting Concepcion Arguello, daughter to the Spanish commander of the Presidio, however, the lieutenant's patience had been frayed.

"My name, Lieutenant, is Dona Arguello." Concepcion had a way of both elevating her own status and belittling the lieutenant in one sentence. "I'll tell you when it's time to turn back."

"It's already past noon."

"I'm aware of the time, Lieutenant."

"Then you know that we are expected back within the hour. Already we have ridden too far to make it—"

"You worry too much."

"We are expected."

"Who is expecting us? Captain Lozano?"

"Your father."

"My father is in Monterey, and I'm of a mind to continue a bit further."

"As you wish." Echeverria reigned in his horse and turned back toward the garrison.

"My father will have you shot if you abandon me."

"It will make little difference if I abandon you or you are captured by thieves. Besides, your father is in Monterey."

Concepcion reigned in her horse as the Lieutenant made his way back through the sparse redwoods populating this particular rise above the bay. She understood the Lieutenant's tactics and, in her own way, admired him for trying to outwit her. She knew that the military had a firm grasp on the countryside and that bandits were rare. Still, she cursed the lieutenant for making her doubt.

"Fine, Lieutenant," she said. "You win."

"You shouldn't complain. You had time enough on your own last night."

"I beg your pardon?"

"I'm not a fool. You snuck down to the waterfront last night again."

"I did no such thing."

The Lieutenant only nodded his head and did his best to keep from smiling too broadly. "I suppose the dinghy at the pier just managed to sail out into the harbor on its own and tie itself back up on the opposite side this morning, is that it?"

"Sometimes, Lieutenant, I really do despise you."

Echeverria tipped his hat in mock salute. "You know I'd have it no other way."

The two rode side by side, the sloping hills disappearing beneath them through the remnants of the morning fog. As the two of them talked, the Lieutenant of his home in Barcelona and Concepcion of her dreams and desires to travel as far away from the garrison, and thus her father, as possible, the Lieutenant halted his horse and leaned forward in the saddle.

"What is it?" she asked.

The Lieutenant shushed her with his hand. "I thought I heard something."

Concepcion let a long moment pass, herself straining in her saddle as if she, even though she had no idea what she was listening for, might be of some assistance.

"It must have been my imagination," the Lieutenant said.

"What is it you thought you heard?"

"I don't know," he said. "For an instant, I thought I heard—"

"Singing," she shouted.

"What?"

"Be quiet. Do you hear it?"

The wind shifted slightly blowing up toward them from the bay just a few hundred yards away. The faint yet unmistakable sounds of a chorus of men's voices drifted up to them.

"Yes," he said. "That's what I thought I heard. A celebration?"

Concepcion laughed. "They'd have a fiesta and not invite me?"

The Lieutenant shook his head.

"Besides," she said, "it's not a Spanish song. Our soldiers only know three songs, and all of them are for drinking." She leaned forward again, now squinting toward the barely visible water rippling under the fog. "I can't hear it any more."

"Neither can I," the Lieutenant said.

"It sounded so sad," she said.

"I didn't hear it long enough to tell."

"Trust me," she said.

"It would appear I have no choice."

The two riders coaxed their horses forward, the Lieutenant paying the singing no more mind, while Concepcion could not take her eyes from the bay.

"Perhaps there are visitors?"

"We aren't expecting anyone today," the Lieutenant said.

Concepcion bit her lower lip and closed her eyes. "Foreigners?" The word was a whisper, almost a prayer.

"If there were foreigners, they'd already have been fired upon and we'd have known about it."

"Maybe," she said. "Maybe."

"There is no maybe. No foreign ships—"

"Look!" Concepcion stood in her stirrups, her elegant index finger cutting a line through the air to settle on the outline of a ship, smaller than the Spanish warships she was accustomed to, but large nonetheless, slipping through the fogbank toward the Presidio.

The Lieutenant spurred his horse into a gallop, but Concepcion had already passed him, her body straining to stay in the saddle, her hands gripping the reigns tight against the horse's lathered head. She cared nothing for the Spanish policies concerning foreigners; she only cared about the fact that someone, from some country she did not know, was here. She trembled with nervousness and excitement, scared of what the prospects of the morning might hold, and determined to not let the opportunity slip away.

The rolling hills surrounding the garrison receded. And with each stride, the horses carried them closer to the bluing waters of the bay. The Lieutenant strained to keep up with his charge, Concepcion being a more than able rider, but what troubled him most was the one word she kept repeating.

"Foreigners."

4.

"Get me my coat." Captain Lozano refused to run, regardless of the fact that he was nervous at being the superior officer in the General's absence. He did not want to belie any appearance of unease at the fact that a foreign ship had sailed directly into the bay. He walked with long, purposeful strides through the stucco hall of the garrison, his aide hurrying behind him, fitting him with the blue uniform coat he had been calling for.

"The cannons are loaded and ready, Captain."

"I know, Diego."

"Shall I give the order to fire?"

"Where is Concepcion?"

"Sir, the men are—"

"Diego, where is Lieutenant Echeverria and the Genera's daughter?"

"I've not seen them for hours."

"Go find them. He'll have all our heads if anything happens." The Captain did not break stride during the conversation, his aide running to carry out the search for Concepcion as soon as he and the Captain emerged from the barracks.

The battlements were not overly imposing, a series of 10-inch cannons lining a traditional stone and stucco wall along the garrison's bay-facing northwest side. The men were lined and ready, the cannon aimed, each crew poised to fire on the trespassing ship the moment the Captain gave the word.

"Who are they?" Lozano snatched the spy glass from one of the cannon team leaders and studied the squat ship, lined with boisterous, singing men, sailing into the harbor.

"I don't recognize the flag, but they are sailing in under a truce."

"I don't care about the truce," Lozano said. "I only want to know who these men are."

"I don't know, Sir."

"And what the devil are they singing?"

"No one knows that, either, Captain."

"Does anyone know anything about this ship? Are there more?"

"We've only seen the one, Sir."

"Diego!" The Captain eyed the *Juno* as he waited for his aide to arrive.

"Yes, Captain. I've dispatched a group of men to find—"

"Send three riders north. I want to make sure there aren't more ships coming in along with this one."

"And Concepcion?"

"Yes, Diego, you've found her?"

"No, Sir. I've dispatched a group to find her as you ordered."

Lozano nodded and repeated his order for the scouts to ride northward. He was comforted somewhat by the fact that the ship appeared to have minimal armaments. That fact, however, did not calm him completely. No arms meant merchants, and he knew that General Arguello disliked their kind more than he disliked an opposing hostile force. Merchants meant cheating and stealing, double-talk and underhanded deals. He refused to bargain with merchants, per the standing order of the Spanish government. Lozano knew what the General would expect of him in his absence.

"All the crews are ready?" he asked.

"Yes, Captain."

"Very well," he said. "We'll let the singing bastards anchor first, then we'll sink her where she sits. Wait for my orders."

Lozano turned on his heel and was gone, off to survey the other gun crews. Behind him, Lozano heard the scouts gallop northward; heard, too, the men Diego had dispatched to find the General's daughter.

The latter group, however, reined in before they even made it through the gates, Lieutenant Echeverria and Concepcion galloping into the courtyard, stopping just short of the battlement. Concepcion dismounted her lathered horse, dropped the reins to the ground for the Lieutenant to retrieve, and ran to the Captain's side.

"Isn't it grand?" she asked.

"No, girl, it is not."

Concepcion did not relinquish the smile she wore. "It is good that they've come. Who are they?"

"I don't know who they are, and it is not good that they've come. Your father would have me sink them before they have a chance to disembark."

"My father isn't here. Aren't you at least going to find out who they are?"

"No. I'm going to sink it, like I said."

"You can't be serious. You don't know who they—"

Lozano turned on her. "Why are you here?"

Concepcion swallowed hard. "I wanted to see the foreigners."

"Get inside."

"I won't."

"You will."

"I won't."

Lozano heard the choked laughter of one of the cannoneers, but the sound died before he could identify the culprit. Turning back to Concepcion, he grabbed her by the arm and led her back toward Lieutenant Echeverria.

"Lieutenant, come here." Lozano pushed Concepcion toward Echeverria. "What is your one and only duty under the General's command?"

The Lieutenant lowered his head, braced for the reprimand he knew was coming. "To look after his daughter."

"Then would you mind telling me what she is doing on the battlements next to the cannons?"

"We just rode up, Sir. I hadn't—"

"You hadn't realized that a foreign ship was in the bay?"

"Yes, Sir. I knew that—"

"Lieutenant, take her inside and see that she is out of the way. I have enough on my hands without tripping over a teenage girl."

Echeverria escorted Concepcion toward the barracks. "Are you happy, now?"

"Let go of me." Concepcion twisted her arm free of the Lieutenant's grasp. "No, I'm not happy now. He's going to sink the ship before we even know who they are."

"They don't belong here and you know it. Let's just go inside."

"I can't. I—We have to do something." Concepcion started walking back toward the battlement walls, anxious for her first earnest look at the ship. "What if it's someone important? We can't let that idiot sink them without knowing, first. He could start a war."

"Trust me," the Lieutenant said. "No one important would be on a ship like that, and there's nothing exotic about a bunch of sea-weary sailors. Come inside."

Concepcion protested, but the Lieutenant, used to her efforts at getting away from him, was able to finally pull her away from the walls and lead her back into the garrison and her room, where he closed the door and locked it, taking a seat on a chair in the hall.

For Concepcion, the problem was not getting out of the room, for she had known how to do that for years, but rather the amount of time wasted.

She knew that Lozano was serious about sinking the ship in the bay, but she was determined to see who they were first. Her window, although it was on the second floor, was not so high up if she should fall. Concepcion also knew how to cling to the wall and slide over the few feet necessary to jump down onto the flat roof of the floor below her. Because she used her route judiciously over the years, waiting until the dead of night to sneak out for a walk by the bay or a trip to the hill behind the garrison where she could look out over the water, she had not been caught, the route not discovered, even though Lieutenant Echeverria knew she slipped out sometimes at night.

Once on the ground, she ran as fast as her feet would carry her, around to the seaward facing side of the garrison and the small boats moored to the docks there. Occupied as they were with the cannons and keeping a close eye on the foreign ship, no one on the battlements noticed Concepcion and the small boat she had commandeered until it was too late. By the time one of the cannoneers pointed a finger over the battlement, Concepcion had rowed halfway out into the bay toward the ship preparing to anchor there.

Shannon Rauwerda
Talk Story: The Making of a Hawaiian Queen

Shannon Rauwerda is profiled earlier in this book. This excerpt is from a class exercise that began as a biography piece and then began to shape itself into a nonfiction novel.

The author writes, "When the professor first assigned a biography piece, I was anything but thrilled. She asked that we chose a subject from history with whom we had a personal interest. Personally, I had no interest in history. Dry, hard facts. Boring. This was going to be troublesome. But my mind began to wander, and an image popped into my head of me as a child holding a picture of my biological grandmother—a woman whom I never knew. The only information I had about my grandmother was that she was Hawaiian. When I was a child, instead of an imaginary friend I invented an imaginary life. During those confining years when I was growing up in Michigan surrounded by farmland, I stared at that picture and let my imagination go. My grandmother was actually a Hawaiian queen, and soon her people would come looking for the next matriarchal line (I had an older brother)—me! I had no idea that there really was royalty in Hawaii; it is a subject that seems to be missing from our history books.

"Years later, I moved to California and my mother returned to her birthplace of Hawaii. I visited her on the islands, and that was when I began to learn the Hawaiian part of my own family history. My grandmother's last name, Camara, is a Portuguese-Hawaiian name, similar to 'Smith' in mainland culture. Finding her family line and any remaining relatives who knew her has proven to be next to impossible. She died when my mother was four, and my mother does not even know her birthday. When my grandfather remarried, my grandmother's family and stories were buried with her.

"For my biography piece, I decided to research the last queen of Hawaii—Queen Liliuokalani. My research grew from Lili's life to the life and culture of the Hawaiian Islands. As I continued my research and the books on my shelves grew into stacks, the piece began to take on a life of its own. It became a journey of discovery. Through Lili's life and through the culture and history of Hawaii, I discovered my own heritage. As I began to experiment with voice and point-of-view, the ten- to fifteen-page biography piece exploded into a nonfiction novel.

"In order to tie together my journey and Lili's history, I decided to experiment with narrative. I tell my story in first person and Lili's in third person. When I first workshopped this piece in class, most people responded by saying that Lili's part sounded like a history report. It seemed too dry, too much like a history book. I wasn't sure how much I could push the envelope and get into her head. But she was already there! I am now revising the piece so that Lili's story, intertwined with mine, is written in a third-person narrative with what I believe to be her voice. Through this story, I will not only set history straight, but I will also discover part of my own personal and family history."

When I was in second grade, the ritual started: I stared at her for hours. Saturday afternoons were good; during the week I had school and on Sundays we had church and then Dad came for us. As my younger sister slept, drool running down her cheek and thumb stuck in her mouth, I slipped out our bedroom door. Glancing down the narrow hall, I noted that my older brother's door was shut; he was probably studying his sixth-grade readers. The clank of pans confirmed my mother's location in the kitchen, making a week's worth of goulash. (By the third day, it was soggy noodles and limp tomatoes, by the fifth our dogs had indigestion.) I slid along the walls of the hallway. My feet navigated the soft spots, avoiding those sensitive areas that creaked at just the right touch.

Outside the door of my mother's room, my head shifted slightly to the left, eyes glancing, ears listening. Time to make the move. I slipped softly into the room. A streak of sun crept in from the worn material of the cloth curtains. As if to illuminate my way, the sun's rays struck the object of my quest: the black and white photograph tucked into a small alcove in the wall. Sucking in my breath, I cradled the frame in my small hands, bringing the woman closer to my face. Blurry silhouettes of palm trees; a long white satin gown, folds of material layering the ground beneath her; and then a woman's smiling face with wreaths of tiny flowers strung around her neck, her head titled to the right as if listening to an old Hawaiian song.

I hopped up on the foot of the bed, still staring at the photograph. I recalled last week, the images of the day playing like a TV show repeated over and over in my head. Ever since Dad left, Mom's friends visited the house often. Shirley Ritzman, mom's neighbor friend, stopped by the house with her husband Harold, our mailman. Her dominating figure and booming voice commanded all attention. The poodle curls of her short Tony perm lay pressed against her pumpkin face as if shrinking from her voice. I hovered in the corner behind the soda-stained armchair while she and her husband cooed over my little sister, twirling thick ringlets of her dark hair in their fingers.

"Carol," Shirley shrieked, "She looks every tiny bit like you."

My brother, carrying drinks in non-matching glasses, played man of the house. After delivering drinks, he stood erectly in the center of the room, attending to everyone's needs: a chair pulled out for the woman, more ice for the man. His thin blond hair was cut in a crew and his arms tucked stiffly behind his back—a boy scout at attention.

"Jon, he's his father, but more respectful." Shirley whispered as if the mere mention of my father would bring tears to mother's eyes.

Who was I like, I wondered.

I didn't understand the concept of stepfamily. My family and friends came from intact families. My parents were divorced when I was five, but the introduction of stepfamilies didn't come until later in my life. My grandpa's wife was my grandmother—at least, that's what I called her.

The picture of the woman that I held in my hands was my mother's mother. She was also my grandmother, although I had never met her. This treasure in my hands was the only evidence of her existence.

My fingers traced the lines of her face. I compared the form of her fingers to mine. Same fingers. I caught my reflection in the vanity mirror. Same round cheeks that cupped when I smiled. Her wide forehead was mine, her eyes, her narrow, long nose, her high cheekbones: all mine. She was me.

I started my stories and played out scenarios in my mind. If she were alive today, we would spend our own special time together, just the two of us. People in the stores would stop their shopping and stare. Someone would exclaim, "She looks exactly like you!" Other stories began with her family. She descended from a long matriarchal line of royalty. If she had lived, she would have been queen and passed the crown from herself to my mother, who was the oldest female daughter, then down to me, the next oldest female in line. With a purple afghan from the bed draped around my shoulders, I waved to all my imaginary subjects, a golden crown of Hawaiian flowers on my head.

This was a time before I knew there was a royal family of Hawai'i; a time before schools taught the real story of the Hawaiian Islands.

During the time of Old Hawai'i, before the missionaries arrived to the islands to instill their Western ways, the Hawaiian people did not have a written language. Through their songs and chants, they recorded their traditions, customs and genealogies. One historian, Helena G. Allen (*Betrayal of Liliuokalani: Last Queen of Hawaii, 1838–1917*), writes, "Whenever a child was born into one of the families of high chiefs, it was customary to compose a chant, not only in honor of the event, but further rehearsing the genealogy of the infant, the deeds of its ancestors, and any daring acts of wonderful valor and prowess." The chiefs entrusted the "Master of the Songs" with the duty to compose the name chants glorifying the family exploits and to preserve those handed down by tradition. Memorization of the chants was vital to the preservation of the royal genealogical line through all its branches. A lost branch could mean a loss of status.

On September 2, 1838 the High Chiefess Keohokalole began labor. Her people gathered around in anticipation of their ali'i, their high chief's sacred event. Chanters began their songs, recounting the lines of Keohokalole back to the cousin of the Great Kamehameha, the leader who united all the islands of Hawai'i into one kingdom.

Before the birth of her child, Keohokalole promised the baby to High Chief Paki and High Chiefess Konia in hanai, an age-old Hawaiian custom. In hanai "among the high chiefs, a child was socially advanced to a higher position"; their parents "not only gave the child in aloha to a close relative or friend, but also . . . better[ed] the relationship among the chiefs." Hanai expressed aloha, love, and brought mana, the spirit of the gods. This act of love bound the relationships with other chiefs and brought more unity to the people and to the land.

When the infant girl emerged from Keohokalole's womb into the world, "in the ever-misty Nu'uanu Valley a rainbow spanned the dim green hillsides, dropping almost to the ground"—a sign from the gods of the birth of a great ali'i. Konia wrapped her new daughter in cloth and brought her to the highest-ranking Chiefess Kinau. Only Kinau could name the child; it was, according to custom, her right. Names were important to the Hawaiian people. They were "constant name-givers and named not only land areas but also local winds, rains and ocean currents." At the time of the child's birth, Chiefess Kinau developed an irritation in her eyes. She bequeathed the baby with the name Liliu Loloku Walania Kamahaeha—broken down in Hawaiian: smarting, tearful, a burning pain, the sore eye. Later in life the child became Liliuokalani when her brother named her heir apparent to the throne.

Her succession to the throne originated from several deaths of people close to her. First, the deaths of five of her classmates, children next in line for the throne, children who she came to regard as her own brothers and sisters, who died of a measles epidemic. Next, her own blood died. Her brother. Her sister. Then the King, Kalakaua who named her heir apparent and named her Liliuokalani.

In 1890 King Kalakaua had traveled to San Francisco in order to rally reinforcements against the group of Annexationists who had been conspiring to overthrow the monarchy and claim the Hawaiian lands. Before Kalakaua departed for the mainland, he had been in poor health. Against the wishes of his wife, Queen Kapiolani, and his sister Liliuokalani, he still undertook his mission, leaving his sister as Regent Queen. On the morning of January 29, 1891, as the people of Hawaii waited expectantly for their King's return, "a chill of horror spread through Honolulu, the Charleston was sighted rounding Diamond Head with yards of cockbill, flags at half-mast." The King was dead.

The news of the King's death traveled through word of mouth until it reached Liliuokalani, who remained at the Palace. Immediately, Liliuokalani dispatched a messenger to confirm the news. As she waited for news, others in her cabinet and ministry plotted the next step: The King was dead, but now, in his place, a Queen.

My first experience with death coincided with the start of my first period. Mom received a call from her stepmother that her half-sister, Chris, had died the day before during an operation. My brother, sister, and I didn't hear the news until the next day. I really didn't feel much. I sat on my bed and believed that tears should flow, but they never came. We really didn't spend much time with mother's family. My dad's brother and sisters took us for sleepovers and dad's ma picked us up from school when we were sick. The only thing I thought about, as I sat at the edge of my bed, was the cramping sensation in my gut. I looked down at the creeping brown stain in my sweats.

"Mom," I interrupted her on the phone. The cord stretched around the kitchen table into the dim corners of the downstairs' steps. "I think we have a situation."

Her swollen eyes stared at me. What could I possibly want at that moment? "I started my period," I said.

Her shoulders slumped; she murmured something to whomever she was speaking and called over my shoulder for my unsuspecting brother. Jon, locked in his bedroom away from all the females in the house, emerged very perturbed from his room. "Go get your sister pads or tampons for her period," my mother demanded of the unsuspecting sixteen-year-old. She handed him the car keys and a twenty. He returned from the drugstore, two bags bulging with an assortment of products, and deposited them in the bathroom where I waited scrunched over on the edge of the tub.

"You've got to be kidding me," I exclaimed. "Is this a joke?"

"Shannon, I really don't have time for this," my mother sighed as she left me alone with the abundance of choices.

I couldn't drive; I couldn't vote; I couldn't legally drink, yet I was left with a choice between pins and pads, regular absorbent, super absorbent, or something that resembled a shotgun insertion. Welcome to womanhood—this didn't have anything to do with what I learned in school about flowers and bees. Over the super absorbent pads, I pulled on a pair of gouaches and a matching vest. Mom dragged all of us to the funeral home for the showing. The showing was supposed to be in respect for the dead, but I didn't get it. The person was dead. How would they know? A blue-haired woman, face caked in orange foundation, leaned over the coffin, staring at the ashfaced body of my aunt. "She looks so peaceful," she murmured. She's dead, I thought.

I sat in the corner, bored. All the aunts looked over at me, nodding as if they knew something I didn't. Later I discovered that my mom had clued them all into my "condition."

The next morning was the funeral. "You know," I said to my mother as she busied herself with the previous night's goulash dishes, "I don't think I can go to the cemetery. My condition and all. I should stay home." She gave me the mother look: head cocked down slightly, thin eyebrows arched, brown eyes piercing. I set my half-eaten bowl of cornflakes on the floor for our drooling sheepdog, who gobbled it up in seconds. "What good is this woman's condition," I mumbled to myself as I shuffled back down the hall, "if you can't use it?"

For forty-five minutes, the procession of cars followed the body of my aunt. I sat slumped in the backseat of our Oldsmobile, the clanking of the muffler on the cement drowning out the static-filled music from the AM radio. I had no idea where we were going. There wasn't much outside of Grand Rapids except farms and apple orchards.

At a corner crossroad in the middle of a dry barren stretch of farm fields, a rusted chain-link fence enclosed the small cemetery. The cars parked along the drive next to a mound of freshly dug dirt. I hesitated, watching mourners surround the mound, and then got up the courage to emerge from the safety of the backseat.

My mom's half-sister, Bonnie, lumbered toward me, a half-smoked cigarette hanging from the corner of her mouth. She sucked in a large drag, blowing a puff in my face, the white stick still hanging from the corner. As she spoke, little puffs of smoke drifted from her mouth. "Know who that is over there?" she asked. She used the butt of her cigarette to point to a tombstone, a faded gray slab buried behind tufts of yellowing stalks of milkweed.

I shook my head.

"That's your grandma."

Bonnie turned and left, leaving me standing six feet from the grave. I approached the tombstone and knelt on the damp dirt. "I'm your granddaughter, Shannon," I whispered.

Holding my breath, I slowly brought my hand up to the stone and traced the engraved lettering. The cool stone pierced my sweaty finger. I had never known her name. "Olympia Camara," I whispered. I exhaled slowly, carrying every syllable of her name over my lips. "Tell me your story."

■ Writing Exercise ■

What stories interest you? What real or historical characters are you obsessed with? This is the place to start when you begin to cast about for a good subject for a nonfiction novel. What stories were you told as a child? Perhaps there is a local legend or infamous incident that would be fun to investigate. How has your life been impacted by particular historical events?

The memory of where you were when a specific event occurred may launch you into a story. Your own family members or ancestors may have experienced historical incidents that could be researched and developed. Scan the newspaper daily for local and national events that might provide fodder for a compelling narrative.

Once you've settled on a loose topic, research your subject with as much investigative fervor as if you were working on a literary journalism piece. Who, what, when, where—cover all the W's, especially the *why*. Research the historical context of your story through library and archival research. Conduct interviews if possible. Investigate modes of dress, fashion, food, transportation—all the details of the day-to-day life of your characters. Cast a wide net, and keep your mind open for unexpected surprises and twists of fate. Perhaps in your research, as you're looking for a date related to your main character, you uncover a series of letters between your character's mother and a long-lost brother. Suddenly the brother's story seems more interesting and relevant than your original idea—and you've found the perspective and point of view that you need.

It may seem daunting to think in terms of a novel rather than an essay. Begin with character and let scenes slowly begin to build around the desires and motivations of your characters and the people or problems he or she encounters. Write episodically—in short episodes—rather than chronologically. You don't need to begin at the beginning and write straight through to the end; in fact, that is often the least effective way to begin to construct a book-length work. Write a series of scenes, and then begin to play with how they might fit together. For your workshop, bring a short chapter to class along with a general plot summary of how you envision the work unfolding. Plot summaries are useful as *descriptive,* not prescriptive, tools—and are temporary at best. The story and the characters will likely change in unexpected ways as you forge ahead.

The Writing Workshop

The End of the Story

It's not uncommon, at the end of a writing workshop, to feel a little bereft. If you've been working on your writing alone in the confines of your basement, trying to convince your spouse or parent or roommate that writing is, indeed, a worthwhile endeavor, you'll miss being around other people who so readily share your view. Maybe this writing workshop has been your first chance to get away from the kids for an evening and take yourself seriously as a writer. Or perhaps the workshop represents a significant step in your life—to pursue the path of a writer, regardless of doubts, insecurities, and uncertainties about paying the rent.

Consider whether there are other members of the group who might wish to continue workshopping, at least for a few weeks or months, in person or via mail or email. Sometimes just setting deadlines for each other can be a valuable way to keep going and stay focused on your work.

Put your work together in a portfolio, not just as a keepsake of the class but as a way of charting your progress. Put your drafts on one side and your final, polished work on the other. Keep the comments of your peers. Often, the comments other members have made on the drafts you turned in will help guide you in your future work.

Finally, do a self-evaluation. Write your answers out in your portfolio or journal, and be as honest and thorough as possible. How has your style changed and developed? Of all the writers you read—published writers and student writers—whose work impacted you the most? Why? What assignments were the most interesting and useful? Most important, what have you learned about yourself as a writer—and as a person—in this workshop?

Revision Tips and Strategies

Balance Research and Narrative

How much historical information and detail should you include in your story? Must you tell the reader *everything*? Just as in fiction, what counts is not necessarily how much detail you include but the manner in which you present it. If you merely describe events without providing much detail or narrative development, the facts of the story will be meaningless. Choose your details carefully. Use what fiction writers call "telling" details; that is, specific details regarding character, setting, or situation that contribute something to the story and keep the narrative moving. Does it matter that your Jesse James is wearing cowboy boots with spurs? Yes, if it says something about his character, the situation he's in, or the historical context of the story.

It's easy to fall in love with research and want to include every single fascinating detail about a character or event that you've worked so hard to find. Be fair and responsible to the story: Tell it as fully and completely as you can. Be aware of your own biases, your own cultural or social lens. But don't bore your reader with endless minutiae. *You* need to know as much information as possible so that you can write clearly with confidence and authority. Readers, however,

(continued)

Revision Tips and Strategies *(continued)*

should see only the final polished result of your research and hard work.

Reconsider Point-of-View

Choosing a point of view and evaluating the amount of "narrative distance" you want from your reader is a careful balancing act. Point of view is simply deciding the best vantage point from which to tell a story. Should you use an omniscient or omnipotent point of view, or tell the story from the perspective of one of the characters? How confident do you feel assuming the voice of a real historical character? Try writing one scene from several different points of view. Which one is the most authentic, the most interesting, the most honest? Think about how "close" you want the reader to feel to the voice that is telling the story. An intimate voice can help readers feel as if they are actually experiencing the story herself, as if they really lived through the events you are describing. On the other hand, an objective, omniscient voice and point of view may help you paint a bigger picture and present a broader, more sweeping version of events.

Keep Your Skis on the Slope

Writing a novel—nonfiction or otherwise—can be quite unlike the more immediate gratification of writing essays or short stories. The investment of time and energy is more substantial, particularly if you have done a significant amount of research. Consequently, the risk may feel more daunting. What happens if you discover—after writing 100 pages or so—that you've written it from the "wrong" point of view? Or what if the primary thread of your plot or narrative arc suddenly seems like a worthless digression—and, heaven forbid, you have to start over?

The pleasure of writing a longer work is that you have room to stretch out, to develop ideas, subplots, subtle themes, and complexities between characters. The challenge is to stay with the process all the way through to the end—especially when you don't necessarily know where you're going to end up.

I like to compare this to skiing during a blizzard. It can be terrifying to suddenly encounter a whiteout. The air fills with driving wind and snow; suddenly you can't see your companions, the surrounding trees, or even the ground beneath your feet. How do you reach the bottom of the mountain? You begin to move because you have no choice. And you quickly learn to trust your feet, to trust your sense of intuition. You feel the ground beneath your boots; you carefully turn and slide over bumps and moguls; you keep your body facing downhill. And it's not long before you see the shadowy outline of the lodge.

It's important to acknowledge feelings of doubt and vulnerability as you write. You may feel deeply invested in what you've written at a certain point, but as you write you must remain open to the process and open to change. The story will begin to take on a life of its own, even if you're keeping very close to historical fact. You have to be willing to throw things away, rewrite a scene or chapter, start over again and again. Keep your skis on the slope.

Or, to reiterate: The most important writing advice is to keep your butt in the chair.

For Further Reading

Bausch, Richard. *Hello to the Cannibals*

Berendt, John. *Midnight in the Garden of Good and Evil*

Duras, Marguerite. *The Lover*

Gloss, Molly. *Wild Life*

Mailer, Norman. *Executioner's Song*

Oates, Joyce Carol. *Black Water*

Ondaatje, Michael. *Running in the Family, Billy the Kid*

Thernstrom, Melanie. *The Dead Girl*

Wolfe, Tom. *The Right Stuff*

Chapter 7

The Writerly Life

Introduction

What does it take to be a writer? And how do you measure success?

Trying to make a living as a writer can seem nearly impossible. Very few people make a living from their writing. On the other hand, it's not impossible. Working as a journalist, copywriter, or even proofreader can immeasurably improve your writing style, help you meet other writers and editors, and teach you a great deal about the publishing field.

Must you work as a writer in order to develop your creative writing? Certainly not. Many writers support themselves by teaching, driving cabs, waiting tables, or painting houses. Some work as office managers, lawyers, or engineers. There is no hard and fast rule. For some writers, however, working as a reporter on a local newspaper is where they began to learn style—and how to meet deadlines. Proofreading magazine copy is where they learned grammar and punctuation. Writing ad copy is where they learned rhythm and brevity.

Do you need a degree in writing in order to be a writer? Yes. No. Maybe. It depends upon what you want to do. Studying creative writing at a community college or university will allow you to study with working writers, develop a breadth and depth of knowledge in literature, and help you get to know other writers. Many people, however, pursue these same goals on their own. Some writers prefer structure; others do not. Some thrive in groups; others work better alone.

There is no single or best way to become a writer.

So how do you know what's right for you? How do you begin? The first step is to take yourself seriously as a writer. Stop thinking of it as a dream, fantasy, or hobby. This is who you are and what you do. Don't feel apologetic about it. Think of it as a process, an ongoing action, a lifestyle, and not a means to an end. Will you ever write a bestseller? Who knows. And it shouldn't matter. You write because you love writing and you want to improve.

Consider your tools. Do you work best on a computer, or must you write everything by hand? If you write by hand, do you prefer lined or unlined paper? Blue or black ink? Take a trip to the office supply store. What makes you feel like writing? What gets you in the mood?

Time is the next obstacle. This is a huge block for most people. Probably just about everyone you know has said at one time or another, "Gosh, I'd like to write a novel someday, but I just don't have the time." Time is very tricky. It's not going to stop and give you weeks or months or years to write your book. It doesn't matter if you're a student, a parent, a grandparent, an office worker, a teacher, or a plumber. There is and never will be enough time to write. And there are always interruptions and distractions. A deadline at work. The children's music lessons. Dinner to prepare and work projects to finish.

So what do you do? You have to trick time. Get up fifteen minutes earlier than usual and write before the kids get out of bed. Give yourself another fifteen minutes at night when the house is quiet. Carry a notepad to work and write on your lunch hour. Take a tape recorder or dictaphone in the car on long drives or on your commute to work and talk out your ideas and stories. Carry small notebooks in your purse, in your briefcase, in the back pocket of your jeans. Make notes in restaurants and on subways and while you're waiting at the airport. Put a notebook and pen next to your bed at night and write down your dreams and thoughts as soon as you wake up in the morning. Ideas are everywhere. Don't let them escape.

Do you have the talent to be a writer? This is an impossible and almost irrelevant question. Some writers discover their writing ability very young, when they are children or young students. Other writers don't find their voice and style until much, much later in life. Talent has been defined as one percent inspiration and ninety-nine percent perspiration. All that truly matters is that ninety-nine percent.

Like any artist or craftsperson, you must diligently work on craft. Become an expert on technique. Are diction, grammar, and punctuation important? Absolutely. Just like musical notes to a composer or tubes of paint to a painter, words and punctuation are your creative tools. The more you know about them the better! Read grammar and usage books. Buy a good dictionary and thesaurus. Check the *Oxford English Dictionary* for word origins and distinctions in meaning. Become a word expert.

Read, read, read. Read everything you can get your hands on. Think about what writers you love, what writers you hate, and why. When you find an author you admire, copy a page or two of the language. Type it out on your computer or copy it by hand. Get inside the rhythm and feel of the sentences and paragraphs. What practical and creative choices has this author made and why?

Dedicate yourself to revision. Commit yourself to the process of writing and not just the end result.

Get involved in a writing community. Seek out the best bookstores in your town and join a reading or writing group. Get a schedule of visiting writers coming to local universities or bookstores and attend their readings.

Join a neighborhood book group. Go to a writers' conference. Find other writers who want to meet and exchange work.

Essentially, being a writer means thinking about writing all the time. It means reading and rereading your own work and the work of others; daydreaming, night dreaming, and constantly thinking about words. Being a writer means observing the world and taking the risk of revealing how you feel about it.

Should you send your creative work out to contests and publishers? Again, the answer is yes and no. If you have worked hard on your manuscript and feel that you have a handle on structure and style, then by all means send it out. But the work must have three things: voice, identity, and heart. If you are trying to write for a particular market or publication, or strictly conform to someone else's expectations, you might find more success as a commercial rather than a literary writer. Allow yourself the time and focus to develop your own voice and style. When you feel ready, begin to send your work out. Read writers' magazines and periodicals so you know what publications are seeking work. Be consistent and don't give up. Expect rejections but enjoy your successes, because if you stick with it, you will have them.

There are lots of people in the world who will tell you why you shouldn't be a writer. It doesn't pay. It's hard to get published. No one values creativity anymore. But you decide whom to listen to. You decide how to live your life. Few things in life are more satisfying than expressing yourself creatively and knowing that your words have made a difference, big or small, in the world.

It's been said that it takes ten years from the day you begin taking yourself seriously as a writer to actually publish a book. Can you give yourself ten years? That sounds daunting. Begin with one day. Begin with ten minutes. Ten minutes a day, starting today.

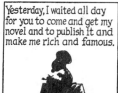

PEANUTS © United Feature Syndicate, Inc.

Richard Bausch
So Long Ago, So Near

Richard Bausch, born in 1945 in Fort Benning, Georgia, has worked as a singer-songwriter and comedian, a United States Air Force survival instructor, and a professor of English and creative writing. He currently teaches at George Mason University in Fairfax, Virginia. About his novels and short stories, Bausch contends, "My only criterion is that fiction make feeling, that it deepen feeling." Bausch has received several awards and fellowships, including PEN/Faulkner Award nominations in 1982 for Take Me Back *and in 1988 for* Spirits and Other Stories, *and an American Academy of Arts and Letters Academy Award in Literature in 1993. His most recent novel is* Hello to the Cannibals.*

In this essay, Bausch reminisces about his life and addresses the complex issue of how memory becomes story, and how we create meaning in our lives. How does this essay reveal how a writer observes and reflects upon the world?

Indulge me, a moment.

I have often said glibly that the thing that separates the young from the old is the knowledge of what Time really is; not just how fast, but how illusive and arbitrary and mutable it is. When you are twenty, the idea of twenty years is only barely conceivable, and since that amount of time makes up your whole life, it seems an enormous thing—a vast, roomy expanse, going on into indefiniteness. You arrive at forty with a sense of the error in this way of seeing, and maturity, um, can be said to have set in.

And the truest element of this aspect of real time, of course, is the sense of the nearness of time past.

I have a memory of being bathed by my father on my seventh birthday. Morning, rainy light at a window. The swish and wash of lukewarm water. My own body, soft-feeling & small under the solid strong hands, lathered with soap. I said, "Well, I guess I'm a big boy now."

He said, "No, not quite."

I remember feeling a bit surprised, perhaps even downcast, that he didn't simply agree with me, as most of the adults in our large family usually did. He ran the towel over me, ruffled my hair with it, drying me off. I went across the hall into my room, and dressed for the April day. Baseball season was starting.

Let me go back there for a little while, to that bath, my seventh birthday. At the time, I wasn't old enough to understand the difference between the humoring of children, which is a large part of any talk with them, and truth-telling, which is what my father did. I loved his rough hands on me,

---

and the smell of him—aftershave, and cigarettes, and sometimes the redolence of my mother's perfume.

He hated lies, and lying. He was a storyteller, and he must have learned early how to exaggerate and heighten things, to make the telling go better, to entertain and enthrall. He was so good at it. He could spin it out and do all the voices and set the scene and take you to the laughs, and there simply *had* to have been elements that he fabricated. And yet he hated lies. Any trouble you ever got into in our house always had to do with that: you learned very early that even if you *had* done something wrong, something for which you wanted some kind of an excuse, or explanation, it had better not involve telling a lie.

I was often in some kind of mischief at school—my twin, Robert, and I had a talent for making other kids laugh, and for imitating our teachers' gestures and voice mannerisms. Well, we were the sons of a storyteller. Neither of us liked school very much; and the teachers, the nuns of Saint Bernadette's, knew it. They kept tabs on us. They were at some pains to discipline us. And whenever we got into a scrape at school, we lived in dread that our father would ask us, that evening, how things had gone at school. I remember sitting at the dinner table as he and my mother told stories, or commented happily on the various people—friends and family—who inhabited our lives then. Bobbie and I would sit there in awful anticipation of the question: "How was school today?" You couldn't gloss over anything—you couldn't use a coverall word like "fine." You had to be specific, and you had to tell it all, the truth. You were *compelled* to do so by what you knew of the value he set upon the truth. And never mind philosophical truth, or the truth of experience, really; he wanted to know what happened in the day, what was said and done, and how it went—*that* kind of truth.

I have no memory—not even a glimmer—of how and when we learned that this was what he expected from us, and that the surest way to earn his displeasure was by lying to him. I don't have much of a memory of him telling us this; I recall him talking about how it was a thing *his* father expected, but by then I was in my teens, and I understood it then as an echo of a kind, a source.

All right.

I remember being surprised that in my father's truthful opinion I was not a big boy yet. I remember that we had two boys our age living next door to us, and that this took place on Kenross Avenue in Montgomery County, Maryland. I know intellectually that the year was 1952, and that Truman was still president. I could not have said who Truman was then, and I recall that a few months later, in the summer, when the Republican Convention was on our little General Electric Black and White television, I saw all those people in the arena, with Eisenhower standing there on the podium, and I guessed the number to be everyone in the world. "No," my father said, "It's not even a small fraction of the number." I didn't know the word *fraction* and yet I understood what he meant.

Sometime around then I saw film of the war that had just ended, and I was told by my mother that another war was going on, in Korea. A summer evening—we were driving past an army post, and I had seen the anti-aircraft guns, the olive drab barrels aimed at the sky. I wondered aloud why we couldn't hear the guns.

"It's on the other side of the world, honey. Thousands of miles away."

In 1952, my mother was thirty-four years old. Now, I'm almost twenty years older than that, and this is the math I'm always doing—have been doing, like a kind of mental nerve-tic, since I was twenty-seven years old, and a father for the first time myself.

When my son Wes was fourteen months old, we moved to Iowa, where I attended the Writer's Workshop. I spent a lot of time with him that year, and as he grew slightly older I decided to conduct a sort of experiment: I'd see if I could manage to keep in his memory the times we had at Iowa—the swing set and sandbox outside the Hawkeye Court apartments, the little amusement park by the river in Iowa City, with its Ferris Wheel and its kiddie train. I'd ask him about it, almost daily: "Do you remember the swing set? The Sandbox? Do you remember how I used to push you on the swings, and you didn't want to go in the house? Remember the summer nights when it would be getting dark, and we'd go to that park and ride in the kiddie train?" Yes, he remembered. He was three, and then four, and then five, and he remembered. He offered elements of that time, so he wasn't merely remembering *my* memory: yes, the swing set and the sandbox—but did I remember the red wagon that got stuck there, and then buried there by the other children? I did. Yes, the Kiddie train, but remember the Buffalo? Yes, there had been a small enclosure with Bison standing in it; the big Ferris Wheel, yes, but did I remember riding it and being stopped at the very top?

Oh, yes.

I had begun to think I might be able to help my son carry that part of his life with him into his own adulthood—earliest memories that have chronological shape. It became important that he have it all to keep. And then one winter evening, as we were riding in the car on the way to a movie, I asked him about Iowa again, and he recalled nothing—it was all simply gone. I asked him about the swing set, the sandbox, the park, the train, the Ferris Wheel, even the Buffalo. To each one he said, "No." Innocently, simply, without the slightest trace of perplexity or anything of what I was feeling, which was sorrow. You could see him striving to get something of it back, but it was like a game, and there was nothing. No, he had no recollection of any of it. I don't think it had been more than a week or two since we had gone through this little litany of memory, and even so it had all disappeared from his mind, and my description of it was only a story, now.

When I was fifteen, my Great Grandmother, Minnie Roddy, died. Minnie had for the most part raised my mother, because Minnie's daughter had had to go to work for the government when my mother was still a baby. They all lived with my Aunt Daisy, Minnie's sister, in a big sprawling Victorian house with a wide porch that had blue-gray painted boards and white trim. When Minnie began to fail, my mother went over there, and we later learned, through the talk of the adults in the rooms of the two houses, that she was holding the old woman in her arms in the last moments. Minnie used to tell me stories, sitting in the breakfast nook, by the windows where younger children ran. Summer evenings, the cousins and aunts and uncles out on the lawn, throwing horseshoes. The bell-like clang of the metal on metal when someone hit one of the posts, or scored a ringer or a leaner. Fire-flies rising in the shallow pools of shade in the spaces between the houses, in the cloud-shaped willow tree—you couldn't see its trunk for the droop-ing filamental mass of its branches—at the edge of the property. Minnie talking, telling me about coming from Ireland on a ship; about her hus-band—who had come to America after killing a man in a fight one after-noon in a pub in Dublin. Her voice would trail off, and the louder voices out the window would distract me. I'd nod and pretend to listen. I was always reading books, as Bobbie was, but it showed more on me, and I was the one, after all, who believed that I had a vocation. I was planning for the priest-hood. Minnie Roddy would say, "You'll grow up and tell these stories. You'll grow up and be a writer."

And she would go on talking, unscrolling her memory of earlier days, of my mother as a young girl; of Ireland, and a childhood spent, for the most part, in the latter part of the Nineteenth Century. I didn't hear most of it. I nodded and pretended to listen, while this woman—this tiny slip of a lady with her wire framed glasses and her clear large blue eyes—tried to give me treasure, something to store up, for the arrival of a season I was not and am not ready for.

When she died, it was decided that Bobbie and I were old enough to attend the funeral. I felt a strange detached curiosity about the whole thing: I was actually going to see a dead person. I told one of the other boys in my class, speaking it out with a sort of quiet, fake-brave shrug. "I'm going to see a dead person today."

"Who?"

"My great grandmother."

"Jesus, no kidding?"

I was, I suppose, even a little proud of the fact. Minnie had lived to great age, and her going seemed natural enough, and so far away from my own life and world that I could only think of it in a sort of abstract haze. I was still young enough and egocentric enough to be unable quite to imag-ine my own demise.

The day of the funeral was bright and chilly. I don't recall whether it was Spring or Fall. It wasn't summer, because I was in school. I think it was fall. We rode with our parents to the funeral home, and I was like a secret traveler in the back seat, planning my exploration of this curiosity, death, this unreal element of the life I was in so permanently. I was wildly curious; I understood, according to the tenets of the faith I had been raised in that Minnie Roddy would not be there, but only her body, the empty vessel she had vacated. She was in that blue elsewhere that I associated with the sky, and we could now pray to her.

Blue is the important color, here.

Standing over the box where she lay, looking like a bad likeness of herself, I saw the forking, colorless veins in her bony hands, the fingers of which were wound with a black rosary; and I saw the blue place at her ear lobe, where blue did not belong. I marked it, and knew that I would never forget it.

This sounds as though I were marking things with the flaccid, nervous sensitivity of one of those pretentious people who like to think of themselves as a romantic central figure in their own drama: the incipient artist, observing everything with an eye to later recording it. I do not mean it this way at all, and it was not like that at all. I was a child, still. I knew next to nothing about anything, especially about myself. And I don't know that I have learned much since then, either.

I suppose I have to admit that it might just be impossible to have it both ways: to claim that I was not that hypersensitive romantic figure, the artist-as-a-young man, and still report the impressions of a moment like that one, standing over the body of a woman who had lived a life so separate from mine, and nothing like mine, and whose reality could not have anticipated that she would be a figure in my speech, a character in a story I would tell, even as she told me about all the living she had seen and done, and I pretended to listen. In any case, I do not mean this the way it will sound. I mean to express the quality of a memory, in order to say something about this life we live, so much of which is fugitive, so much of which is lost in the living of it.

The room we were in was banked with flowers, and there were chairs in rows, as though someone might give a lecture, or a homily. Minnie's coffin looked to have been where it was long enough for this prodigious wall of flowers to grow up on three sides of it. There was a dim light, a candle burning at one end. The light was brightest where she lay, with her eyes shut in a way that made you understand they would not open again. The skin looked oddly transparent, like the synthetic skin of a doll. And there was the blue place at the ear, the place, I knew, where the cosmetics of the mortician hadn't quite taken. I stood there and looked with a kind of detached, though respectful silence at this, aware of it not as death, quite, but death's signature. I was conscious of the difference. I spent my minute there, head bowed, and then walked back to my seat at the rear of the room, with the other young people, all in their early teens, like me. I saw my mother and my Aunt Florence come from where I had just been, and my mother had a handkerchief that she held to her nose. She sobbed, once. Earlier, when we had arrived, Florence had come up to my mother and said, "You scared the be-Jesus out of me." I don't know—or I don't remember—what this was about; I think it had something to do with what had gone on last night, at the viewing. Perhaps my mother had gotten woozy, or swooned. It was the first time I had ever heard the phrase *be-Jesus.*

Florence and my mother sat down, and a priest led us in the rosary. If he said anything about the woman who lay behind him in the long box, I don't recall it. We were in the room for a time, and then people began to file out. I remained in my seat, and I have no idea why. Others crossed in front of me, and maybe I was saying my own prayers—it seems to me now that I must've felt some pang of guilt for my oddly remote observation of everything, and was trying to say the words of a prayer, repeating them inwardly in an attempt to say them not out of automatic memory but actually to enter into the meaning of them:

> Hail Mary, full of grace, the Lord is with thee. Blessed art thou among women and blessed is the fruit of thy womb, Jesus. Holy Mary, Mother of God, pray for us sinners, now and at the hour of our death, Amen.

The others were all filing quietly out of the long room, and I saw the mortician step to the side of the casket, where we had each stood only moments before. With a practical sureness, the nearly offhand familiarity of experience, he reached into the white satin that ringed Minnie Roddy's head, and pushed downward on it, a tucking motion, and Minnie slipped from her sleeping pose. Her head dropped down into that box like a stone.

Something must have shown in my face; and the mortician's wife— let us call them the Hallorans, because I no longer recall the name—saw the change in my features. Later, as I was getting into the back of my father's car, Aunt Florence leaned in and said "Honey, Mrs. Halloran wanted me to tell you that Mr. Halloran was only making it so Minnie could rest better."

I nodded. I don't believe I said anything. It was almost as if I had stumbled upon someone in a privy act; I felt the same kind of embarrassment. But there was something else in it, too, a kind of species-thrill: this was the human end, a reality I was not expecting. I am trying to express this as exactly as I can, and of course it is finally inexpressible. I know that all my fascination was gone, and I sat there in the back of the car, looking out at the sunny streets of Washington, and felt numb, far down.

That memory is as present to me as the moment, almost a decade earlier, when I said to my father that I was a big boy, and he told me the truth, that I was not a big boy. Not yet. Those memories are as near as the memory of asking, in the first line of this story, for your indulgence.

Of course, this is not an original perception; yet one arrives at it in life—doesn't one?—with the sense of having had a revelation: one's personal past is a *place,* and everything that resides there does so in contemporaneous time. What then, of the collective past? The collective memory? That is where chronology really is. We come from the chaos of ourselves to the world, and we yearn to know what happened to all the others who came before us. So we impose Time on the flow of events, and call it history. For me, Memory is always *story*. True memory is nothing like the organized surface of a story, yet that is all we have to tell it, and know it, and experience it again: but if we are doomed to put our remembered life into stories, we are blessed by it, too.

I never spoke to my mother and father, or even to my brothers and sisters, about what I had seen at the funeral home. I don't know why, now. I can't recall why. Perhaps it was too private, finally; and perhaps I did not want to have it in memory, didn't want to fix it there in the telling. But it has never left me. It is with all the others, large and small, important and meaningless, all waiting in the same timeless dark, to drift toward the surface when I write, or daydream, or sleep.

Annie Dillard
The Writing Life

Annie Dillard won the Pulitzer Prize in 1975 for Pilgrim at Tinker Creek, *her first significant publication. A writer, editor, and scholar, Dillard has turned her talent to poetry, fiction, literary criticism, history, essays, and memoir, and her notable books include* An American Childhood. *She is writer-in-residence at Wesleyan University, Middletown, Connecticut, and serves on the National Committee for U.S.-China relations and the Catholic Commission on Intellectual and Cultural Affairs.*

In the Writing Life *(1989), Dillard addresses the process of writing not as a manual or guide, but as an artistic study.*

1

When you write, you lay out a line of words. The line of words is a miner's pick, a woodcarver's gouge, a surgeon's probe. You wield it, and it digs a path you follow. Soon you find yourself deep in new territory. Is it a dead end, or have you located the real subject? You will know tomorrow, or this time next year.

You make the path boldly and follow it fearfully. You go where the path leads. At the end of the path, you find a box canyon. You hammer out reports, dispatch bulletins.

The writing has changed, in your hands, and in a twinkling, from an expression of your notions to an epistemological tool. The new place interests you because it is not clear. You attend. In your humility, you lay down the words carefully, watching all the angles. Now the earlier writing looks soft and careless. Process is nothing; erase your tracks. The path is not the work. I hope your tracks have grown over; I hope birds ate the crumbs; I hope you will toss it all and not look back.

The line of words is a hammer. You hammer against the walls of your house. You tap the walls, lightly, everywhere. After giving many years' attention to these things, you know what to listen for. Some of the walls are bearing walls; they have to stay, or everything will fall down. Other walls can go with impunity; you can hear the difference. Unfortunately, it is often a bearing wall that has to go. It cannot be helped. There is only one solution, which appalls you, but there it is. Knock it out. Duck.

Courage utterly opposes the bold hope that this is such fine stuff the work needs it, or the world. Courage, exhausted, stands on bare reality; this writing weakens the work. You must demolish the work and start over. You can save some of the sentences, like bricks. It will be a miracle if you can save some of the paragraphs, no matter how excellent in themselves or hard-won. You can waste a year worrying about it, or you can get it over with now. (Are you a woman, or a mouse?)

The part you must jettison is not only the best-written part; it is also, oddly, that part which was to have been the very point. It is the original key passage, the passage on which the rest was to hang, and from which you yourself drew the courage to begin. Henry James knew it well, and said it best. In his preface to *The Spoils of Poynton*, he pities the writer, in a comical pair of sentences that rises to a howl: "Which is the work in which he hasn't surrendered, under dire difficulty, the best thing he meant to have kept? In which indeed, before the dreadful *done*, doesn't he ask himself what has become of the thing all for the sweet sake of which it was to proceed to that extremity?"

So it is that a writer writes many books. In each book, he intended several urgent and vivid points, many of which he sacrificed as the book's form hardened. "The youth gets together his materials to build a bridge to the moon," Thoreau noted mournfully, "or perchance a palace or temple on the earth, and at length the middle-aged man concludes to build a wood-shed with them." The writer returns to these materials, these passionate subjects, as to unfinished business, for they are his life's work.

2

It is the beginning of a work that the writer throws away.

A painting covers its tracks. Painters work from the ground up. The latest version of a painting overlays earlier versions, and obliterates them. Writers, on the other hand, work from left to right. The discardable chapters are on the left. The latest version of a literary work begins somewhere in the work's middle, and hardens toward the end. The earlier version remains lumpishly on the left; the work's beginning greets the reader with the wrong hand. In those early pages and chapters anyone may find bold leaps to nowhere, read the brave beginnings of dropped themes, hear a tone since abandoned, discover blind alleys, track red herrings, and laboriously learn a setting now false.

Several delusions weaken the writer's resolve to throw away work. If he has read his pages too often, those pages will have a necessary quality, the ring of the inevitable, like poetry known by heart; they will perfectly answer their own familiar rhythms. He will retain them. He may retain those pages if they possess some virtues, such as power in themselves, though they lack the cardinal virtue, which is pertinence to, and unity with, the book's thrust. Sometimes the writer leaves his early chapters in place from gratitude; he cannot contemplate them or read them without feeling again the blessed relief that exalted him when the words first appeared—relief that he was writing anything at all. That beginning served to get him where he was going, after all; surely the reader needs it, too, as groundwork. But no.

Every year the aspiring photographer brought a stack of his best prints to an old, honored photographer, seeking his judgment. Every year the old man studied the prints and painstakingly ordered them into two piles, bad and good. Every year the old man moved a certain landscape print into the bad stack. At length he turned to the young man: "You submit this same landscape every year, and every year I put it on the bad stack. Why do you like it so much?" The young photographer said, "Because I had to climb a mountain to get it."

A cabdriver sang his songs to me, in New York. Some we sang together. He had turned the meter off; he drove around midtown, singing. One long song he sang twice; it was the only dull one. I said, You already sang that one; let's sing something else. And he said, "You don't know how long it took me to get that one together."

How many books do we read from which the writer lacked courage to tie off the umbilical cord? How many gifts do we open from which the writer neglected to remove the price tag? Is it pertinent, is it courteous, for us to learn what it cost the writer personally?

3

The written word is weak. Many people prefer life to it. Life gets your blood going, and it smells good. Writing's mere writing, literature is mere. It appeals only to the subtlest senses—the imagination's vision, and the imagination's hearing—and the moral sense, and the intellect. This writing that you do, that so thrills you, that so rocks and exhilarates you, as if you were dancing next to the band, is barely audible to anyone else. The reader's ear must adjust down from loud life to the subtle, imaginary sounds of the written word. An ordinary reader picking up a book can't yet hear a thing; it will take half an hour to pick up the writing's modulations, its ups and downs and louds and softs.

An intriguing entomological experiment shows that a male butterfly will ignore a living female butterfly of his own species in favor of a painted cardboard one, if the cardboard one is big. If the cardboard one is bigger than he is, bigger than any female butterfly ever could be, he jumps the piece of cardboard. Over and over again, he jumps the piece of cardboard. Nearby, the real, living female butterfly opens and closes her wings in vain.

Films and television stimulate the body's senses too, in big ways. A nine-foot handsome face, and its three-foot-wide smile, are irresistible. Look at the long legs on that man, as high as a wall, and coming straight toward you. The music builds. The moving, lighted screen fills your brain. You do not like filmed car chases? See if you can turn away. Try not to watch. Even knowing you are manipulated, you are still as helpless as the male butterfly drawn to painted cardboard.

That is the movies. That is their ground. The printed word cannot compete with the movies on their ground, and should not. You can describe beautiful faces, car chases, or valleys full of Indians on horseback until you run out of words, and you will not approach the movies' spectacle. Novels written with film contracts in mind have a faint but unmistakable, and ruinous, odor. I cannot name what, in the text, alerts the reader to suspect the writer of mixed motives; I cannot specify which sentences, in several books, have caused me to read on with increasing dismay, and finally close the books because I smelled a rat. Such books seem uneasy being books; they seem eager to fling off their disguises and jump onto screens.

Why would anyone read a book instead of watching big people move on a screen? Because a book can be literature. It is a subtle thing—a poor thing, but our own. In my view, the more literary the book—the more purely verbal, crafted sentence by sentence, the more imaginative, reasoned, and deep—the more likely people are to read it. The people who read are the people who like literature, after all, whatever that might be. They like, or require, what books alone have. If they want to see films that evening, they will find films. If they do not like to read, they will not. People who read are not too lazy to flip on the television; they prefer books. I cannot imagine a sorrier pursuit than struggling for years to write a book that attempts to appeal to people who do not read in the first place.

4

On the Fourth of July, my husband and our friends drove into the city, Roanoke, to see the fireworks. I begged off; I wanted to keep working. I was working hard, although of course it did not seem hard enough at the time— a finished chapter every few weeks. I castigated myself daily for writing too slowly. Even when passages seemed to come easily, as though I were copying from a folio held open by smiling angels, the manuscript revealed the usual signs of struggle—bloodstains, teethmarks, gashes, and burns.

This night, as on most nights, I entered the library at dusk. The building was locked and dark. I had a key. Every night I let myself in, climbed the stairs, found my way between the tall stacks in the dark, located and unlocked my study's door, and turned on the light. I remembered how many stacks I had to hit with my hand in the dark before I turned down the row to my study. Even if I left only to get a drink of water, I felt and counted the stacks with my hand again to find my room. Once, in daylight, I glanced at a book on a stack's corner, a book I presumably touched every night with my hand. The book was *The World I Live In*, by Helen Keller. I read it at once: it surprised me by its strong and original prose.

When I flicked on my carrel light, there it all was: the bare room with yellow cinder-block walls; the big, flattened venetian blind and my drawing taped to it; two or three quotations taped up on index cards; and on a far table some ever-changing books, the fielder's mitt, and a yellow bag of chocolate-covered peanuts. There was the long, blond desk and its chair, and on the desk a dozen different-colored pens, some big index cards in careful, splayed piles, and my messy yellow legal pads. As soon as I saw that desktop, I remembered the task: the chapter, its problems, its phrases, its points.

This night I was concentrating on the chapter. The horizon of my consciousness was the contracted circle of yellow light inside my study—the lone lamp in the enormous, dark library. I leaned over the desk. I worked by hand. I doodled deliriously in the legal-pad margins. I fiddled with the index cards. I reread a sentence maybe a hundred times, and if I kept it I changed it seven or eight times, often substantially.

Now a June bug was knocking at my window. I was wrestling inside a sentence. I must have heard it a dozen times before it registered—before I noticed that I had been hearing a bug knock for half an hour. It made a hollow, bonking sound. Some people call the same fumbling, heavy insects "May beetles." It must have been attracted to my light—what little came between the slats of the blind. I dislike June bugs. Back to work. Knock again, knock again, and finally, to learn what monster of a fat, brown June bug could fly up to a second story and thump so insistently at my window as though it wanted admittance—at last, unthinkingly, I parted the venetian blind slats with my fingers, to look out.

And there were the fireworks, far away. It was the Fourth of July. I had forgotten. They were red and yellow, blue and green and white; they blossomed high in the black sky many miles away. The fireworks seemed as distant as the stars, but I could hear the late banging their bursting made. The sound, those bangs so muffled and out of sync, accompanied at random the silent, far sprays of color widening and raining down. It was the Fourth of July, and I had forgotten all of wide space and all of historical time. I opened the blinds a crack like eyelids, and it all came exploding in on me at once— oh yes, the world.

5

Here is a fairly sober version of what happens in the small room between the writer and the work itself. It is similar to what happens between a painter and the canvas.

First you shape the vision of what the projected work of art will be. The vision, I stress, is no marvelous thing: it is the work's intellectual structure and aesthetic surface. It is a chip of mind, a pleasing intellectual object. It is a vision of the work, not of the world. It is a glowing thing, a blurred thing of beauty. Its structure is at once luminous and translucent; you can see the world through it. After you receive the initial charge of this imaginary object, you add to it at once several aspects, and incubate it most gingerly as it grows into itself.

Many aspects of the work are still uncertain, of course; you know that. You know that if you proceed you will change things and learn things, that the form will grow under your hands and develop new and richer lights. But that change will not alter the vision or its deep structures; it will only enrich it. You know that, and you are right.

But you are wrong if you think that in the actual writing, or in the actual painting, you are filling in the vision. You cannot fill in the vision. You cannot even bring the vision to light. You are wrong if you think that you can in any way take the vision and tame it to the page. The page is jealous and tyrannical; the page is made of time and matter; the page always wins. The vision is not so much destroyed, exactly, as it is, by the time you have finished, forgotten. It has been replaced by this changeling, this bastard, this opaque lightless chunky ruinous work.

Here is how it happens. The vision is, *sub specie aeternitatis,* a set of mental relationships, a coherent series of formal possibilities. In the actual rooms of time, however, it is a page or two of legal paper filled with words and questions; it is a terrible diagram, a few books' names in a margin, an ambiguous doodle, a corner folded down in a library book. These are memos from the thinking brain to witless hope.

Nevertheless, ignoring the provisional and pathetic nature of these scraps, and bearing the vision itself in mind—having it before your sights like the very Grail—you begin to scratch out the first faint marks on the canvas, on the page. You begin the work proper. Now you have gone and done it. Now the thing is no longer a vision: it is paper.

Words lead to other words and down the garden path. You adjust the paints' values and hues not to the world, not to the vision, but to the rest of the paint. The materials are stubborn and rigid; push is always coming to shove. You can fly—you can fly higher than you thought possible—but you can never get off the page. After every passage another passage follows, more sentences, more everything on drearily down. Time and materials hound the work; the vision recedes ever farther into the dim realms.

And so you continue the work, and finish it. Probably by now you have been forced to toss the most essential part of the vision. But this is a concern for mere nostalgia now: for before your eyes, and stealing your heart, is this fighting and frail finished product, entirely opaque. You can see nothing through it. It is only itself, a series of well-known passages, some colored paint. Its relationship to the vision that impelled it is the relationship between any energy and any work, anything unchanging to anything temporal.

The work is not the vision itself, certainly. It is not the vision filled in, as if it had been a coloring book. It is not the vision reproduced in time; that were impossible. It is rather a simulacrum and a replacement. It is a golem. You try—-you try every time—to reproduce the vision, to let your light so shine before men. But you can only come along with your bushel and hide it.

6

Who will teach me to write? a reader wanted to know.

The page, the page, that eternal blankness, the blankness of eternity which you cover slowly, affirming time's scrawl as a right and your daring as necessity; the page, which you cover woodenly, ruining it, but asserting your freedom and power to act, acknowledging that you ruin everything you touch but touching it nevertheless, because acting is better than being here in mere opacity; the page, which you cover slowly with the crabbed thread of your gut; the page in the purity of its possibilities; the page of your death, against which you pit such flawed excellences as you can muster with all your life's strength: that page will teach you to write.

There is another way of saying this. Aim for the chopping block. If you aim for the wood, you will have nothing. Aim past the wood, aim through the wood; aim for the chopping block.

May Sarton
Journal of a Solitude

May Sarton, born in Wondelgem, Belgium in 1912, moved to America in 1916 and became a naturalized citizen in 1924. An eclectic writer, Sarton wrote novels, short stories, plays, screenplays, poetry, autobiography/memoir, nonfiction, and children's books. Over the course of her long career, Sarton garnered over thirty awards, fellowships, and honorary doctorate degrees, including the Reynolds Lyric Award, Poetry Society of America (1952), a Human Rights Award (1985), and a Northeast Author Award (1990). She died of breast cancer in 1995 after a remarkably prolific career.

Sarton's many published journals provide an honest portrayal of the creative, intellectual, and emotional life of a writer. Her honesty and keen eye for detail in nature—and human nature—are a wonderful source of insight and inspiration.

January 5th

And now it is time that I laid aside, at least for a few hours a day, the world that pours in here from the outside, and resumed my own life in this nunnery where one woman meditates alone. But there is no way of "laying aside" a knock at the door. Yesterday afternoon, after hours of answering letters in quiet desperation, I decided to wash the bathroom floor and had just finished, dirty and triumphant, when the doorbell jangled and there outside in the sleeting snow was a woman from Ohio, on her way to Concord, who had simply decided to knock as she passed through Nelson. She had written me a week or so ago a long, good letter about *Kinds of Love,* one I had not yet answered, but luckily I did remember it. What people never realize is that I cannot remember every letter that falls in here, because there are so many from strangers, and I have to read them and then literally put them away from me to be able to breathe. She stayed half an hour and by doing so broke the slow rhythm of late afternoon, when I wander about doing odd jobs, answering a few cards, whatever comes easily and naturally, but do not ask myself to summon real psychic energy or deep response.

After that interruption the furnace suddenly went off; so I built a big fire in the cozy room to keep Punch, the parrot, warm, then called for help. The men were here in an hour. I shall never get used to this joy of living in the country—when help is needed, it is there.

At nine I forced myself to look at and listen to Nixon's nonconversation with four TV pundits. His answer that one cannot be asked to project a vibrant dream when in the middle of a nightmare summed it all up—his total lack of vision in the humane sense. For it is surely just in the nightmare time that vibrant dreams are born and can be communicated effectively . . . Churchill in 1940, Roosevelt in the Depression years. What a cramped little soul comes through from Nixon! What was fascinating was the conjunction of this strangely dead hour with what followed immediately—an interview by Brinkley with six editors of high-school magazines, two blacks, a Chinese, four middle-class whites. These kids were articulate, caring, thoughtful, and realistic. But what has Nixon said to give them hope? Still, their talk warmed the cold air and I went to bed feeling happy about the future and in the thought of what the eighteen-year-old vote may do to change the crass defeatist atmosphere.

And now . . . and now . . . toward the inner world. Yesterday from D, who is carrying a fearful load at the moment as he is both getting an M.A. in education and teaching full time in a public high school: "Just an excruciatingly short note, May, to wish for you the absolute calm and unfathomed strength needed to face a gruelling year, a single day.

We see little of each other, but we fight together, and we do not fail."
Among the best memories of 1970 are those two long conversations I had
with D about our private lives, about love. We recognized each other
as the same breed, those who must find a balance between going naked
(in the Yeatsian sense, "There's more enterprise in walking naked")
and being tough enough to survive such intensity of caring and such
openness, between a driving need to share experience and the need
for time to experience, and that means solitude, a balance between the
need to become oneself and to give of oneself . . . and of course they
are closely related. D is very aware of the problems of women, sensitive
to the needs of a woman lover for her own independence, her own
growth; he has suffered because he is generous. But he has also had the
guts to cut off what did not and could not work. It was especially illuminating to me as I ponder the problems of women to see it, in this
instance, from the other side. D has been expected to accept unfaith-
fulness without demur ("I have to have my independence"), an absolute
demand not to be pinned down in any way, and what looks from where
I sit like plain cruelty. He is younger than his girl by seven years or so,
but very much older in wisdom. I have the greatest respect for this
man. Would he be what he is in his early twenties if he had not gone
through suicidal depression at thirteen or fourteen, followed by years
of psychiatry? He has very great strength now, strength also to carry a
big load of work. I think of him and of those much younger kids on
TV last night with such a surge of hope and faith, and with humility. At
his age I was a good lover only in the romantic sense of the word—I had
not even begun to think of the "other" as he does, and I was ambitious
in a rather cheap way.

It is hope-giving to consider the young, and it is also hope-giving to
consider growth as a constant. Here I am at fifty-eight and in this past year I
have only begun to understand what loving is . . . forced to my knees again
and again like a gardener planting bulbs or weeding, so that I may once
more bring a relationship to flower, keep it truly alive.

I am reading the letters of Carrington, the young woman painter
who attached herself so fervently and selflessly to Lytton Strachey and
committed suicide shortly after his death. The book is disturbing. There is
something in me that resents so much talk about feeling and so many personal interchanges. Yet the strength of Bloomsbury may have been just
this—their fantastic honesty about personal life. They accepted that in a
given lifetime there are going to be many and complex relationships that
nourish, and many kinds of love. They accepted that nearly everyone concerned with the arts is going to have to come to terms with sexual ambiva-
lence, and to cope with being bisexual, and that passionate friendships
may include sex. (How sane this appears after the revolting male exhibi-
tionism and role-playing of Miller, Mailer, and Hemingway!) They
achieved not only an amazing richness of production of works of art (in

painting, poetry, the novel) that were seminal, works of economics that were also seminal, but led extraordinary lives without becoming messy or self-indulgent. If they were neurotics, and perhaps they were, they were civilized and civilizing neurotics. They are resented especially by Americans because within our puritanical ethos it doesn't seem quite "right." We can accept far more readily the confessed neurotic, drug-taking or whatever, who edifies by his horrible example! They were simply a little too good to be true. How hard they worked, and what fun they had! Maybe the gossip, incessant, witty, and sometimes malicious, occasionally offends our sense of decorum—with reason. But decorum seemed to them, no doubt, altogether a matter of *how* things are done, not *what* things are said or done.

Presumably Willa Cather lived a private life of some intensity, but she was exceedingly careful to keep it out of the public eye, even to the extent of forbidding the publication of any letter after her death. How very different this attitude to Virginia Woolf's open admission that *Orlando* was based on her friendship with Vita Sackville-West. Is it, here in America, parents who stand in the way? The fear of hurting a parent if one is honest?

My own belief is that one regards oneself, if one is a serious writer, as an instrument for experiencing. Life—all of it—flows through this instrument and is distilled through it into works of art. How one lives as a private person is intimately bound into the work. And at some point I believe one has to stop holding back for fear of alienating some imaginary reader or real relative or friend, and come out with personal truth. If we are to understand the human condition, and if we are to accept ourselves in all the complexity, self-doubt, extravagance of feeling, guilt, joy, the slow freeing of the self to its full capacity for action and creation, both as human being and as artist, we have to know all we can about each other, and we have to be willing to go naked.

Joan Didion
On Keeping a Notebook

Joan Didion was born in Sacramento, California in 1934. After receiving a bachelor of arts degree from the University of California, Berkeley, she worked as a promotional copywriter for Vogue *magazine in New York City and later became associate feature editor. An elegant stylist and gifted journalist, Didion writes both fiction and nonfiction—novels, short stories, social commentary, screenplays, and essays. Her numerous awards include first prize in* Vogue's *Prix de Paris (1956), a National Book Critics Circle Prize nomination in nonfiction (1980), and an American Book Award nomination in nonfiction (1981), both for* The White Album.

The following essay is useful to aspiring and experienced writers as it allows us to see how a writer's mind works out concepts and ideas in a writing journal.

"'That woman Estelle,'" the note reads, "'is partly the reason why George Sharp and I are separated today.' *Dirty crepe-de-Chine wrapper, hotel bar, Wilmington RR, 9:45 a.m. August Monday morning.*"

Since the note is in my notebook, it presumably has some meaning to me. I study it for a long while. At first I have only the most general notion of what I was doing on an August Monday morning in the bar of the hotel across from the Pennsylvania Railroad station in Wilmington, Delaware (waiting for a train? missing one? 1960? 1961? why Wilmington?), but I do remember being there. The woman in the dirty crepe-de-Chine wrapper had come down from her room for a beer, and the bartender had heard before the reason why George Sharp and she were separated today. "Sure," he said, and went on mopping the floor. "You told me." At the other end of the bar is a girl. She is talking, pointedly, not to the man beside her but to a cat lying in the triangle of sunlight cast through the open door. She is wearing a plaid silk dress from Peck & Peck, and the hem is coming down.

Here is what it is: the girl has been on the Eastern Shore, and now she is going back to the city, leaving the man beside her, and all she can see ahead are the viscous summer sidewalks and the 3 a.m. long-distance calls that will make her lie awake and then sleep drugged through all the steaming mornings left in August (1960? 1961?). Because she must go directly from the train to lunch in New York, she wishes that she had a safety pin for the hem of the plaid silk dress, and she also wishes that she could forget about the hem and the lunch and stay in the cool bar that smells of disinfectant and malt and make friends with the woman in the crepe-de-Chine wrapper. She is afflicted by a little self-pity, and she wants to compare Estelles. That is what that was all about.

Why did I write it down? In order to remember, of course, but exactly what was it I wanted to remember? How much of it actually happened? Did any of it? Why do I keep a notebook at all? It is easy to deceive oneself on all those scores. The impulse to write things down is a peculiarly compulsive one, inexplicable to those who do not share it, useful only accidentally, only secondarily, in the way that any compulsion tries to justify itself. I suppose that it begins or does not begin in the cradle. Although I have felt compelled to write things down since I was five years old, I doubt that my daughter ever will, for she is a singularly blessed and accepting child, delighted with life exactly as life presents itself to her, unafraid to go to sleep and unafraid to wake up. Keepers of private notebooks are a different breed altogether, lonely and resistant rearrangers of things, anxious malcontents, children afflicted apparently at birth with some presentiment of loss.

My first notebook was a Big Five tablet, given to me by my mother with the sensible suggestion that I stop whining and learn to amuse myself by writing down my thoughts. She returned the tablet to me a few years ago; the first entry is an account of a woman who believed herself to be freezing to death in the Arctic night, only to find, when day broke, that she had stumbled onto the Sahara Desert, where she would die of the heat before lunch. I have no idea what turn of a five-year-old's mind could have prompted to insistently "ironic" and exotic a story, but it does reveal a certain predilection for the extreme which has dogged me into adult life; perhaps if I were analytically inclined I would find it a truer story than any I might have told about Donald Johnson's birthday party or the day my cousin Brenda put Kitty Litter in the aquarium.

So the point of my keeping a notebook has never been, nor is it now, to have an accurate factual record of what I have been doing or thinking. That would be a different impulse entirely, an instinct for reality which I sometimes envy but do not possess. At no point have I ever been able successfully to keep a diary; my approach to daily life ranges from the grossly negligent to the merely absent, and on those few occasions when I have tried dutifully to record a day's events, boredom has so overcome me that the results are mysterious at best. What is this business about "shopping, typing piece, dinner with E, depressed"? Shopping for what? Typing what piece? Who is E? Was this "E" depressed, or was I depressed? Who cares?

In fact I have abandoned altogether that kind of pointless entry; instead I tell what some would call lies. "That's simply not true," the members of my family frequently tell me when they come up against my memory of a shared event. "The party was *not* for you, the spider was *not* a black widow, *it wasn't that way at all*." Very likely they are right, for not only have I always had trouble distinguishing between what happened and what merely might have happened, but I remain unconvinced that the distinction, for my purposes, matters. The cracked crab that I recall having for lunch the day my father came home from Detroit in 1945 must certainly be embroidery, worked into the day's pattern to lend verisimilitude; I was ten years old and would not now remember the cracked crab. The day's events did not turn on cracked crab. And yet it is precisely that fictitious crab that makes me see the afternoon all over again, a home movie run all too often, the father bearing gifts, the child weeping, an exercise in family love and guilt. Or that is what it was to me. Similarly, perhaps it never did snow that August in Vermont; perhaps there never were flurries in the night wind, and maybe no one else felt the ground hardening and summer already dead even as we pretended to bask in it, but that was how it felt to me, and it might as well have snowed, could have snowed, did snow.

How it felt to me: that is getting closer to the truth about a notebook. I sometimes delude myself about why I keep a notebook, imagine that some thrifty virtue derives from preserving everything observed. See enough and write it down, I tell myself, and then some morning when the world seems drained of wonder, some day when I am only going through the motions of doing what I am supposed to do, which is write—on that bankrupt morning

I will simply open my notebook and there it will all be, a forgotten account with accumulated interest, paid passage back to the world out there: dialogue overheard in hotels and elevators and at the hat-check counter in Pavillon (one middle-aged man shows his hat check to another and says, "That's my old football number"); impressions of Bettina Aptheker and Benjamin Sonnenberg and Teddy ("Mr. Acapulco") Stauffer; careful *aperçus* about tennis bums and failed fashion models and Greek shipping heiresses, one of whom taught me a significant lesson (a lesson I could have learned from F. Scott Fitzgerald, but perhaps we all must meet the very rich for ourselves) by asking, when I arrived to interview her in her orchid-filled sitting room on the second day of a paralyzing New York blizzard, whether it was snowing outside.

I imagine, in other words, that the notebook is about other people. But of course it is not. I have no real business with what one stranger said to another at the hat-check counter in Pavillon; in fact I suspect that the line "That's my old football number" touched not my own imagination at all, but merely some memory of something once read, probably "The Eighty-Yard Run." Nor is my concern with a woman in a dirty crepe-de-Chine wrapper in a Wilmington bar. My stake is always, of course, in the unmentioned girl in the plaid silk dress. *Remember what it was to be me:* that is always the point.

It is a difficult point to admit. We are brought up in the ethic that others, any others, all others, are by definition more interesting than ourselves; taught to be diffident, just this side of self-effacing. ("You're the least important person in the room and don't forget it," Jessica Mitford's governess would hiss in her ear on the advent of any social occasion; I copied that into my notebook because it is only recently that I have been able to enter a room without hearing some such phrase in my inner ear.) Only the very young and the very old may recount their dreams at breakfast, dwell upon self, interrupt with memories of beach picnics and favorite Liberty lawn dresses and the rainbow trout in a creek near Colorado Springs. The rest of us are expected, rightly, to affect absorption in other people's favorite dresses, other people's trout.

And so we do. But our notebooks give us away, for however dutifully we record what we see around us, the common denominator of all we see is always, transparently, shamelessly, the implacable "I." We are not talking here about the kind of notebook that is patently for public consumption, a structural conceit for binding together a series of graceful *pensées;* we are talking about something private, about bits of the mind's string too short to use, an indiscriminate and erratic assemblage with meaning only for its maker.

And sometimes even the maker has difficulty with the meaning. There does not seem to be, for example, any point in my knowing for the rest of my life that, during 1964, 720 tons of soot fell on every square mile of New

York City, yet there it is in my notebook, labeled "FACT." Nor do I really need to remember that Ambrose Bierce liked to spell Leland Stanford's name "£eland $tanford" or that "smart women almost always wear black in Cuba," a fashion hint without much potential for practical application. And does not the relevance of these notes seem marginal at best?:

> In the basement museum of the Inyo County Courthouse in Independence, California, sign pinned to a mandarin coat: "This MANDARIN COAT was often worn by Mrs. Minnie S. Brooks when giving lectures on her TEAPOT COLLECTION."

> Redhead getting out of car in front of Beverly Wilshire Hotel, chinchilla stole, Vuitton bags with tags reading:
>
>
>
> MRS LOU FOX
>
> HOTEL SAHARA
>
> VEGAS
>
>

Well, perhaps not entirely marginal. As a matter of fact, Mrs. Minnie S. Brooks and her MANDARIN COAT pull me back into my own childhood, for although I never knew Mrs. Brooks and did not visit Inyo County until I was thirty, I grew up in just such a world, in houses cluttered with Indian relics and bits of gold ore and ambergris and the souvenirs my Aunt Mercy Farnsworth brought back from the Orient. It is a long way from that world to Mrs. Lou Fox's world, where we all live now, and is it not just as well to remember that? Might not Mrs. Minnie S. Brooks help me to remember what I am? Might not Mrs. Lou Fox help me to remember what I am not?

But sometimes the point is harder to discern. What exactly did I have in mind when I noted down that it cost the father of someone I know $650 a month to light the place on the Hudson in which he lived before the Crash? What use was I planning to make of this line by Jimmy Hoffa: "I may have my faults, but being wrong ain't one of them"? And although I think it interesting to know where the girls who travel with the Syndicate have their hair done when they find themselves on the West Coast, will I ever make suitable use of it? Might I not be better off just passing it on to John O'Hara? What is a recipe for sauerkraut doing in my notebook? What kind of magpie keeps this notebook? *"He was born the night the Titanic went down."* That seems a nice enough line, and I even recall who said it, but is it not really a better line in life than it could ever be in fiction?

But of course that is exactly it: not that I should ever use the line, but that I should remember the woman who said it and the afternoon I heard it. We were on her terrace by the sea, and we were finishing the wine left from lunch, trying to get what sun there was, a California winter sun. The woman whose husband was born the night the *Titanic* went down wanted to rent her house, wanted to go back to her children in Paris. I remember wishing that I could afford the house, which cost $1,000 a month. "Someday you will," she said lazily. "Someday it all comes." There in the sun on her terrace it seemed easy to believe in someday, but later I had a low-grade afternoon hangover and ran over a black snake on the way to the supermarket and was flooded with inexplicable fear when I heard the checkout clerk explaining to the man ahead of me why she was finally divorcing her husband. "He left me no choice," she said over and over as she punched the register. "He has a little seven-month-old baby by her, he left me no choice." I would like to believe that my dread then was for the human condition, but of course it was for me, because I wanted a baby and did not then have one and because I wanted to own the house that cost $1,000 a month to rent and because I had a hangover.

It all comes back. Perhaps it is difficult to see the value in having one's self back in that kind of mood, but I do see it; I think we are well advised to keep on nodding terms with the people we used to be, whether we find them attractive company or not. Otherwise they turn up unannounced and surprise us, come hammering on the mind's door at 4 a.m. of a bad night and demand to know who deserted them, who betrayed them, who is going to make amends. We forget all too soon the things we thought we could never forget. We forget the loves and the betrayals alike, forget what we whispered and what we screamed, forget who we were. I have already lost touch with a couple of people I used to be; one of them, a seventeen-year-old, presents little threat, although it would be of some interest to me to know again what it feels like to sit on a river levee drinking vodka-and-orange-juice and listening to Les Paul and Mary Ford and their echoes sing "How High the Moon" on the car radio. (You see I still have the scenes, but I no longer perceive myself among those present, no longer could even improvise the dialogue.) The other one, a twenty-three-year-old, bothers me more. She was always a good deal of trouble, and I suspect she will reappear when I least want to see her, skirts too long, shy to the point of aggravation, always the injured party, full of recriminations and little hurts and stories I do not want to hear again, at once saddening me and angering me with her vulnerability and ignorance, an apparition all the more insistent for being so long banished.

It is a good idea, then, to keep in touch, and I suppose that keeping in touch is what notebooks are all about. And we are all on our own when it comes to keeping those lines open to ourselves: your notebook will never help me, nor mine you. *"So what's new in the whiskey business?"* What could that possibly mean to you? To me it means a blonde in a Pucci bathing suit sitting with a couple of fat men by the pool at the Beverly Hills Hotel. Another man approaches, and they all regard one another in silence for a while. "So what's new in the whiskey business?" one of the fat men finally says by way of welcome, and the blonde stands up, arches one foot and dips it in the pool, looking all the while at the cabaña where Baby Pignatari is talking on the telephone. That is all there is to that, except that several years later I saw the blonde coming out of Saks Fifth Avenue in New York with her California complexion and a voluminous mink coat. In the harsh wind that day she looked old and irrevocably tired to me, and even the skins in the mink coat were not worked the way they were doing them that year, not the way she would have wanted them done, and there is the point of the story. For a while after that I did not like to look in the mirror, and my eyes would skim the newspapers and pick out only the deaths, the cancer victims, the premature coronaries, the suicides, and I stopped riding the Lexington Avenue IRT because I noticed for the first time that all the strangers I had seen for years—the man with the seeing-eye dog, the spinster who read the classified pages every day, the fat girl who always got off with me at Grand Central—looked older than they once had.

It all comes back. Even that recipe for sauerkraut: even that brings it back. I was on Fire Island when I first made that sauerkraut, and it was raining, and we drank a lot of bourbon and ate the sauerkraut and went to bed at ten, and I listened to the rain and the Atlantic and felt safe. I made the sauerkraut again last night and it did not make me feel any safer, but that is, as they say, another story.

Appendix

Useful Publications for Creative Nonfiction Writers

The following publications can help you identify potential markets, editors, agents, writers conferences, and writing programs in creative nonfiction, as well as help you learn how to prepare book proposals and manuscripts for submission to contests and publishers.

Poets & Writers Magazine
The AWP (Associated Writing Programs) *Writers Chronicle*
The Directory of Literary Magazines
The International Directory of Literary Magazines
Literary Marketplace (an enormous publication; in the library and on the Web)
Writer's Digest
The MLA (Modern Language Association) Stylebook
The Chicago Manual of Style

Magazines and Journals That Publish Creative Nonfiction

Be sure to check each publication for current editorial policy.

ACM (Another Chicago Magazine)
Agni
American Scholar
Antaeus
Atlantic Monthly
Audubon
Bay Nature

Boulevard
Chicago Reader
Conjunctions
Creative Nonfiction
Earth, The Science of Our Planet
Epoch
Esquire

The Fourth Genre
Georgia Review
Gettysburg Review
Granta
Harper's
High Country News
High Plains Literary Review
Hudson Review
Hungry Mind Review
Iowa Review
Iowa Woman
Kenyon Review
Massachusetts Review
Michigan Quarterly
Missouri Review
New England Review
The New Yorker

North American Review
Northwest Review
Orion
Partisan Review
Petroglyph
Puerto del Sol
Salmagundi
Sewanee Review
Southern Humanities Review
Southwest Review
The Sun
Tikkun
Threepenny Review
Vanity Fair
Virginia Quarterly
Whole Earth Review
Yale Review

Courses and Programs in Creative Nonfiction

This list is partial at best as programs constantly change and develop. Also, many community colleges offer courses in creative nonfiction.

Antioch University, Los Angeles
Colorado State University
Columbia University School of
   the Arts
Emerson College
Florida International University
George Mason University
Goddard College
Goucher College
Humboldt State University
Indiana University
Johns Hopkins University
Louisiana State University
Massachusetts Institute of
   Technology (MIT)

New College of California
New School University
Northwestern University
Ohio University
St. Mary's College of California
San Jose State University
Southern Illinois University
   Carbondale
Southwest Texas State
   University
University of Alabama
University of Alaska,
   Anchorage
University of Arizona
University of Arkansas

University of California, Davis
University of California, Irvine
University of Florida
University of Idaho
University of Iowa
University of Maine at
Farmington
University of Memphis
University of Minnesota
University of Montana
University of Nebraska
at Lincoln
University of New Orleans

University of Nevada
at Las Vegas
University of North Carolina
at Wilmington
University of Oregon
University of Pittsburgh
University of San Francisco
University of Southern
California
University of Vermont
Vermont College
West Virginia University

Index